The Arab-Israeli Conflict its History in Maps

Second edition

Martin Gilbert

Weidenfeld and Nicolson London

First published August 1974
Second impression April 1975
Second edition 1976

Weidenfeld and Nicolson
11 St John's Hill London SW11

ISBN 0 297 77240 6 cased
ISBN 0 297 77241 4 paperback

Printed in Great Britain by
Redwood Burn Limited, Trowbridge & Esher

Preface

In this atlas I have traced the history of Arab-Jewish conflict from the turn of the century to the present day. I have tried to show something of the increasing intensity and bitterness of the conflict, of the types of incidents which it provoked, and of the views of those involved in it.

The majority of the maps in this atlas depict wars, conflict and violence, which have brought terrible suffering to all those caught up in them – Jew and Arab, soldier and civilian, adult and child. But there are also maps which show the various attempts to bring the conflict to an end, through proposals for agreed boundaries, through the signing of cease-fire agreements, and through negotiations. No map can show how peace will come, but they do show how much it is needed.

I am extremely grateful to Mr T.A. Bicknell, the cartographer, whose expertise has been invaluable, and who has dealt patiently with my many demands and amendments. I am also grateful to the many people who have provided me with factual material, who have scrutinized my drafts while they were being prepared, and who have given me the benefit of their professional knowledge and guidance. I should of course be grateful for readers' suggestions for further maps, for extra material, and for corrections.

I should like to thank all those who have provided me with extra material for the new maps which I have specially prepared for this second edition.

Merton College
Oxford

MARTIN GILBERT

12 April 1976

Maps

PART SIX: THE YOM KIPPUR WAR

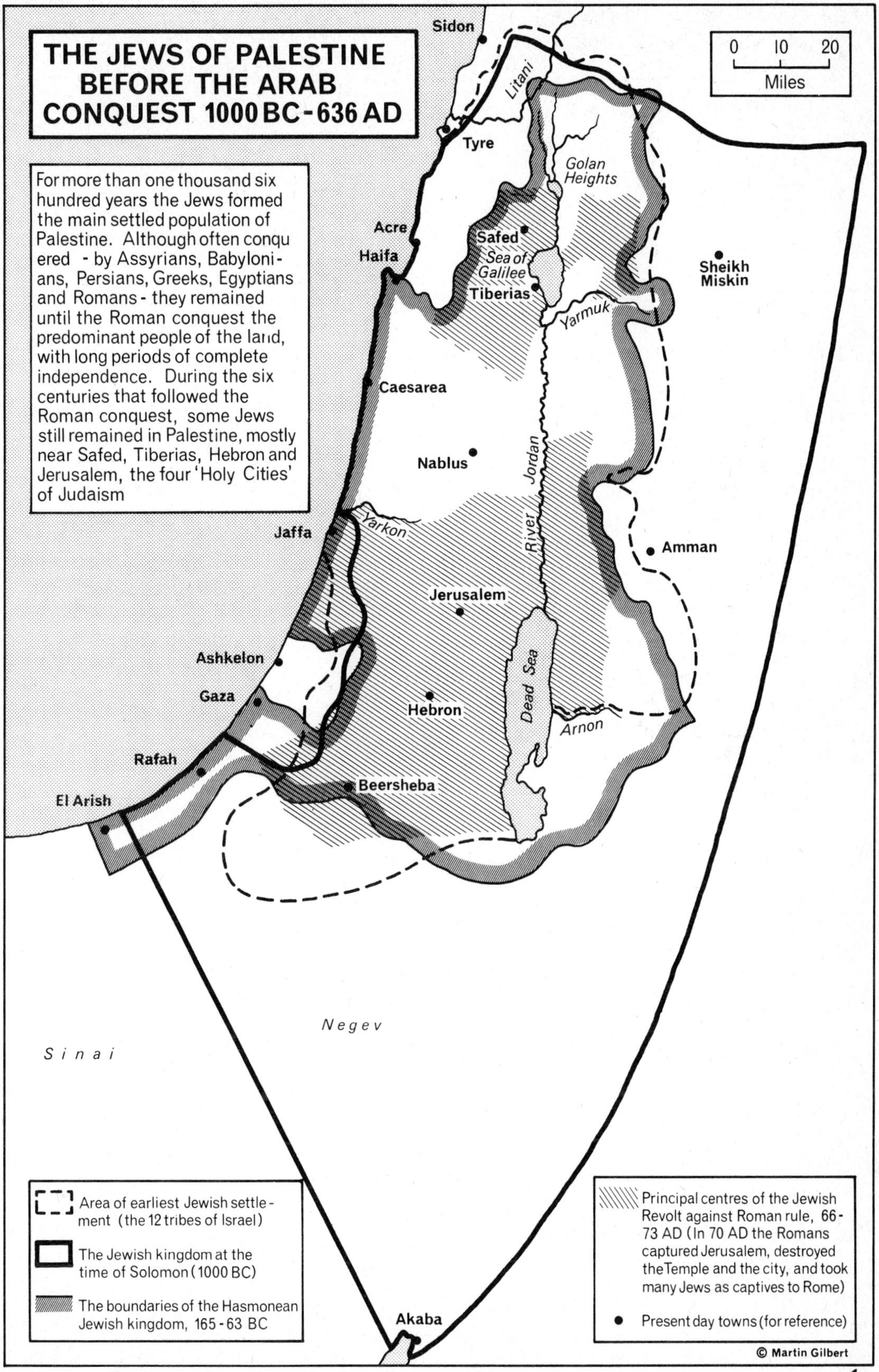
THE JEWS OF PALESTINE BEFORE THE ARAB CONQUEST 1000 BC-636 AD
For more than one thousand six hundred years the Jews formed the main settled population of Palestine. Although often conquered - by Assyrians, Babylonians, Persians, Greeks, Egyptians and Romans - they remained until the Roman conquest the predominant people of the land, with long periods of complete independence. During the six centuries that followed the Roman conquest, some Jews still remained in Palestine, mostly near Safed, Tiberias, Hebron and Jerusalem, the four 'Holy Cities' of Judaism
0 10 20
Miles
Sidon
Litani
Tyre
Golan Heights
Acre
Haifa
Safed
Sea of Galilee
Tiberias
Sheikh Miskin
Yarmuk
Caesarea
Nablus
Jordan
River
Yarkon
Jaffa
Amman
Jerusalem
Ashkelon
Gaza
Hebron
Dead Sea
Arnon
Rafah
Beersheba
El Arish
Negev
Sinai
Akaba
Area of earliest Jewish settlement (the 12 tribes of Israel)
The Jewish kingdom at the time of Solomon (1000 BC)
The boundaries of the Hasmonean Jewish kingdom, 165-63 BC
Principal centres of the Jewish Revolt against Roman rule, 66-73 AD (In 70 AD the Romans captured Jerusalem, destroyed the Temple and the city, and took many Jews as captives to Rome)
Present day towns (for reference)
© Martin Gilbert

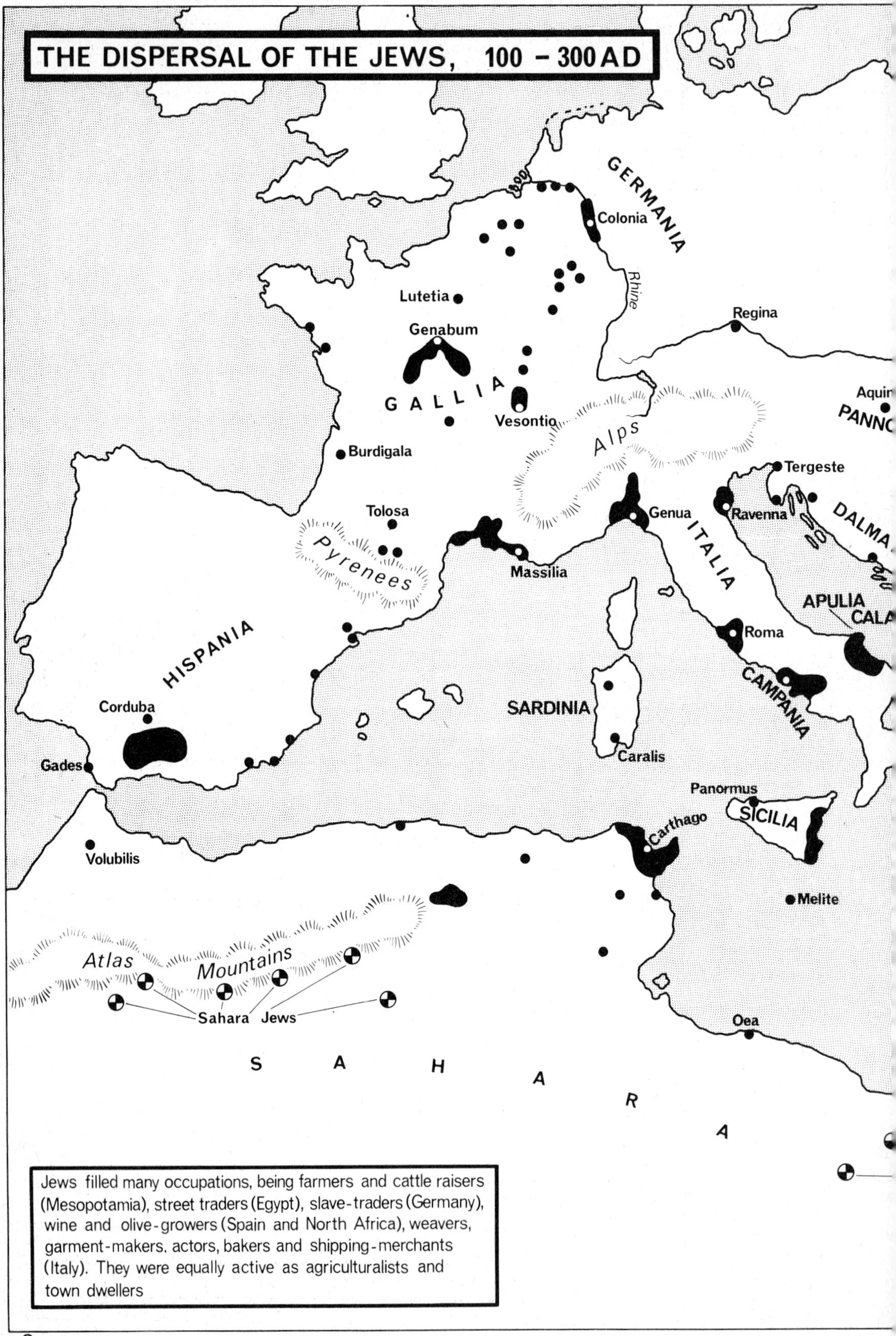
THE DISPERSAL OF THE JEWS, 100 – 300 AD
GERMANIA
Colonia
Rhine
Lutetia
Regina
Genabum
GALLIA
Vesontio
Alps
Aquir
PANNO
Burdigala
Tergeste
Tolosa
Genua
Ravenna
DALMA
Pyrenees
Massilia
ITALIA
APULIA
CALA
HISPANIA
Roma
CAMPANIA
SARDINIA
Corduba
Gades
Caralis
Panormus
SICILIA
Carthago
Volubilis
Melite
Atlas Mountains
Sahara Jews
Oea
SAHARA
Jews filled many occupations, being farmers and cattle raisers (Mesopotamia), street traders (Egypt), slave-traders (Germany), wine and olive-growers (Spain and North Africa), weavers, garment-makers, actors, bakers and shipping-merchants (Italy). They were equally active as agriculturalists and town dwellers

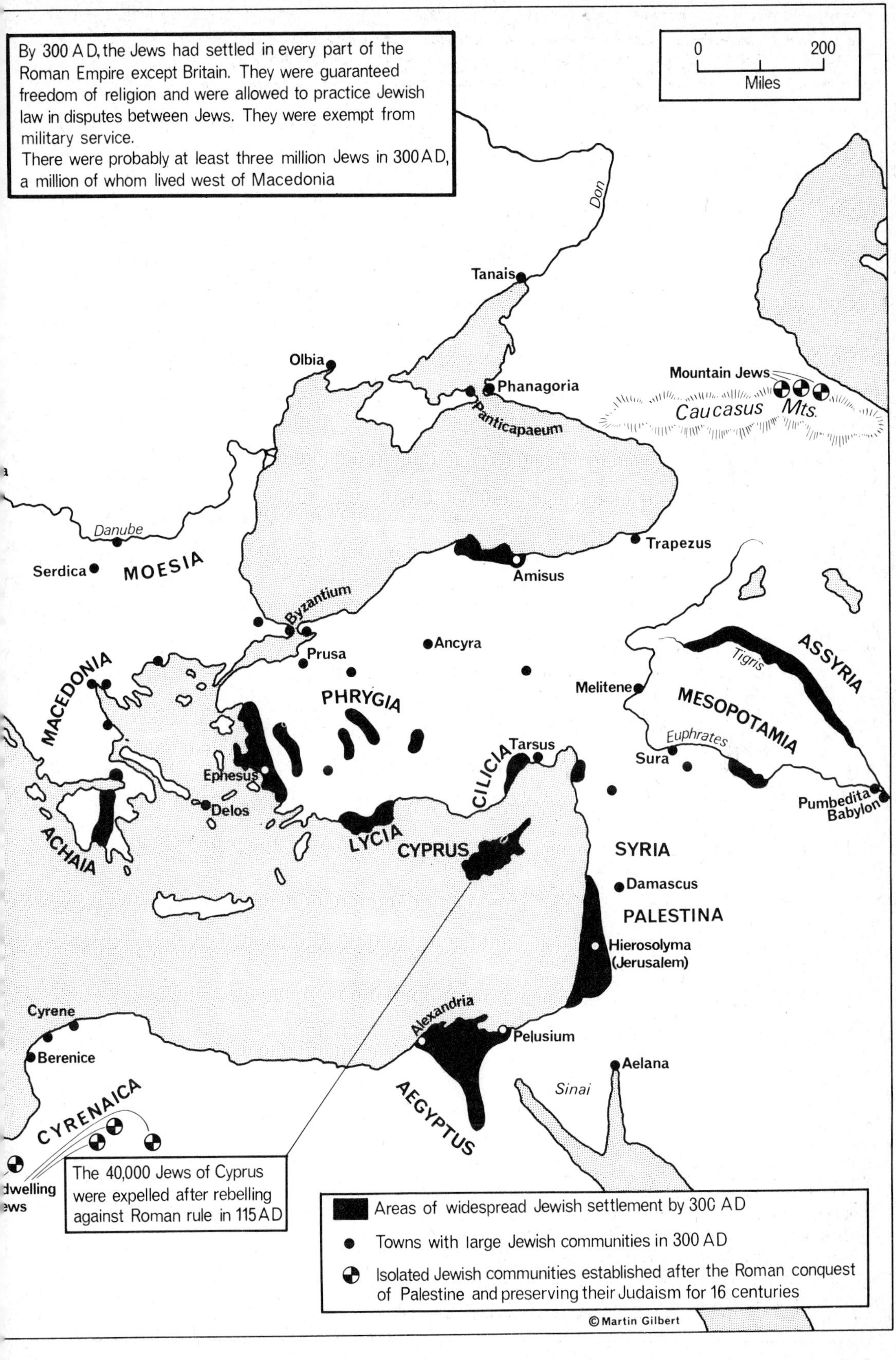

By 300 A D, the Jews had settled in every part of the Roman Empire except Britain. They were guaranteed freedom of religion and were allowed to practice Jewish law in disputes between Jews. They were exempt from military service.
There were probably at least three million Jews in 300 A D, a million of whom lived west of Macedonia
0
200
Miles
Don
Tanais
Olbia
Phanagoria
Panticapaeum
Mountain Jews
Caucasus Mts.
Danube
Serdica
MOESIA
Trapezus
Amisus
Byzantium
Prusa
Ancyra
MACEDONIA
PHRYGIA
Melitene
ASSYRIA
Tigris
MESOPOTAMIA
Euphrates
Sura
Tarsus
CILICIA
Ephesus
Delos
LYCIA
CYPRUS
ACHAIA
Pumbedita
Babylon
SYRIA
Damascus
PALESTINA
Hierosolyma (Jerusalem)
Cyrene
Berenice
Alexandria
Pelusium
Aelana
Sinai
CYRENAICA
AEGYPTUS
dwelling
ews
The 40,000 Jews of Cyprus were expelled after rebelling against Roman rule in 115 A D
Areas of widespread Jewish settlement by 300 AD
Towns with large Jewish communities in 300 AD
Isolated Jewish communities established after the Roman conquest of Palestine and preserving their Judaism for 16 centuries
© Martin Gilbert

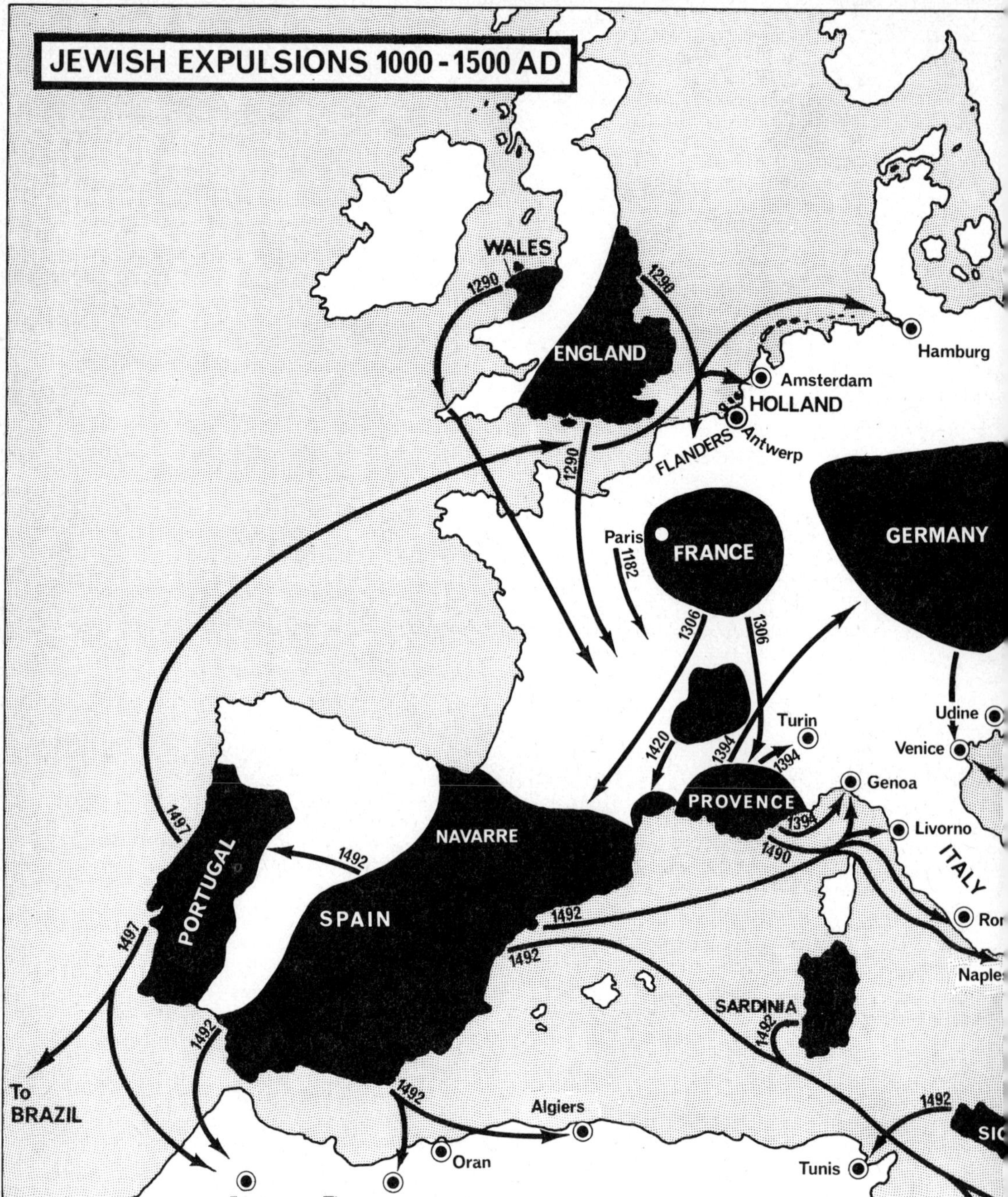
JEWISH EXPULSIONS 1000 - 1500 AD
WALES
1290
ENGLAND
1290
1290
Hamburg
Amsterdam
HOLLAND
Antwerp
FLANDERS
Paris
FRANCE
1182
GERMANY
1306
1306
Udine
Venice
Turin
1420
1394
1394
Genoa
PROVENCE
1394
Livorno
1490
ITALY
NAVARRE
1492
1497
PORTUGAL
SPAIN
1492
1492
1497
SARDINIA
1492
1492
1492
To
BRAZIL
1492
Algiers
Oran
Fez
Tlemcen
Tunis
1492
Tripoli
M A G H R E B

■	Jewish communities with date of expulsion
➔	Direction of the flight and dispersal of expelled Jews, mostly to Poland, Italy and the Ottoman Empire
◉	Principal places of resettlement including Palestine

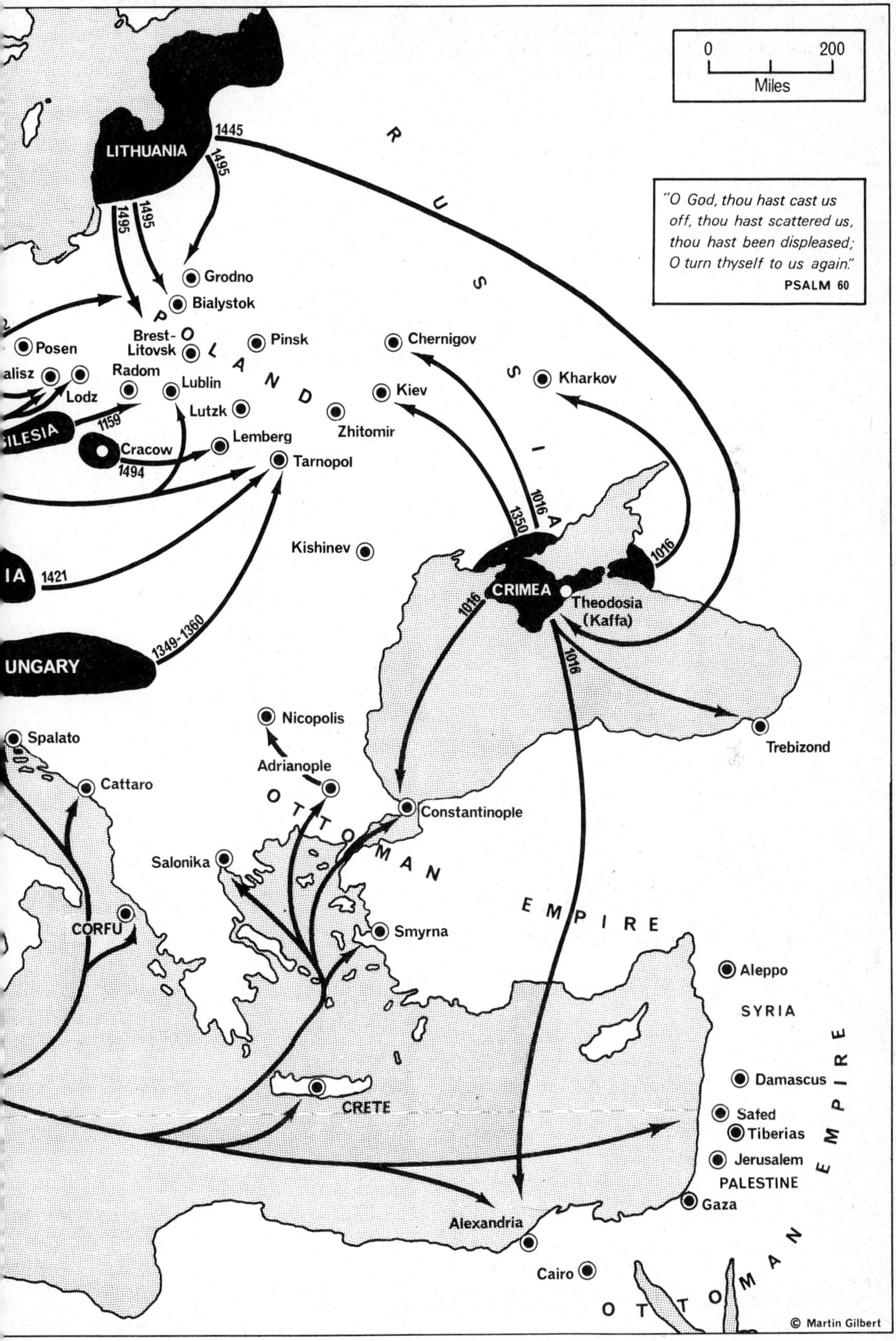

0
200
Miles
"O God, thou hast cast us off, thou hast scattered us, thou hast been displeased; O turn thyself to us again."
PSALM 60
LITHUANIA
1445
1495
1495
1495
1495
R U S S I A
POLAND
Grodno
Bialystok
Brest-Litovsk
Posen
alisz
Lodz
Radom
Lublin
Pinsk
Lutzk
Lemberg
Tarnopol
Zhitomir
Kiev
Chernigov
Kharkov
ILESIA
1159
Cracow
1494
IA
1421
UNGARY
1349-1360
Kishinev
1016
1350
1016
1016
1016
CRIMEA
Theodosia (Kaffa)
Trebizond
Nicopolis
Adrianople
Spalato
Cattaro
Constantinople
Salonika
OTTOMAN EMPIRE
CORFU
Smyrna
Aleppo
SYRIA
Damascus
Safed
Tiberias
Jerusalem
PALESTINE
Gaza
CRETE
Alexandria
Cairo
OTTOMAN EMPIRE
© Martin Gilbert

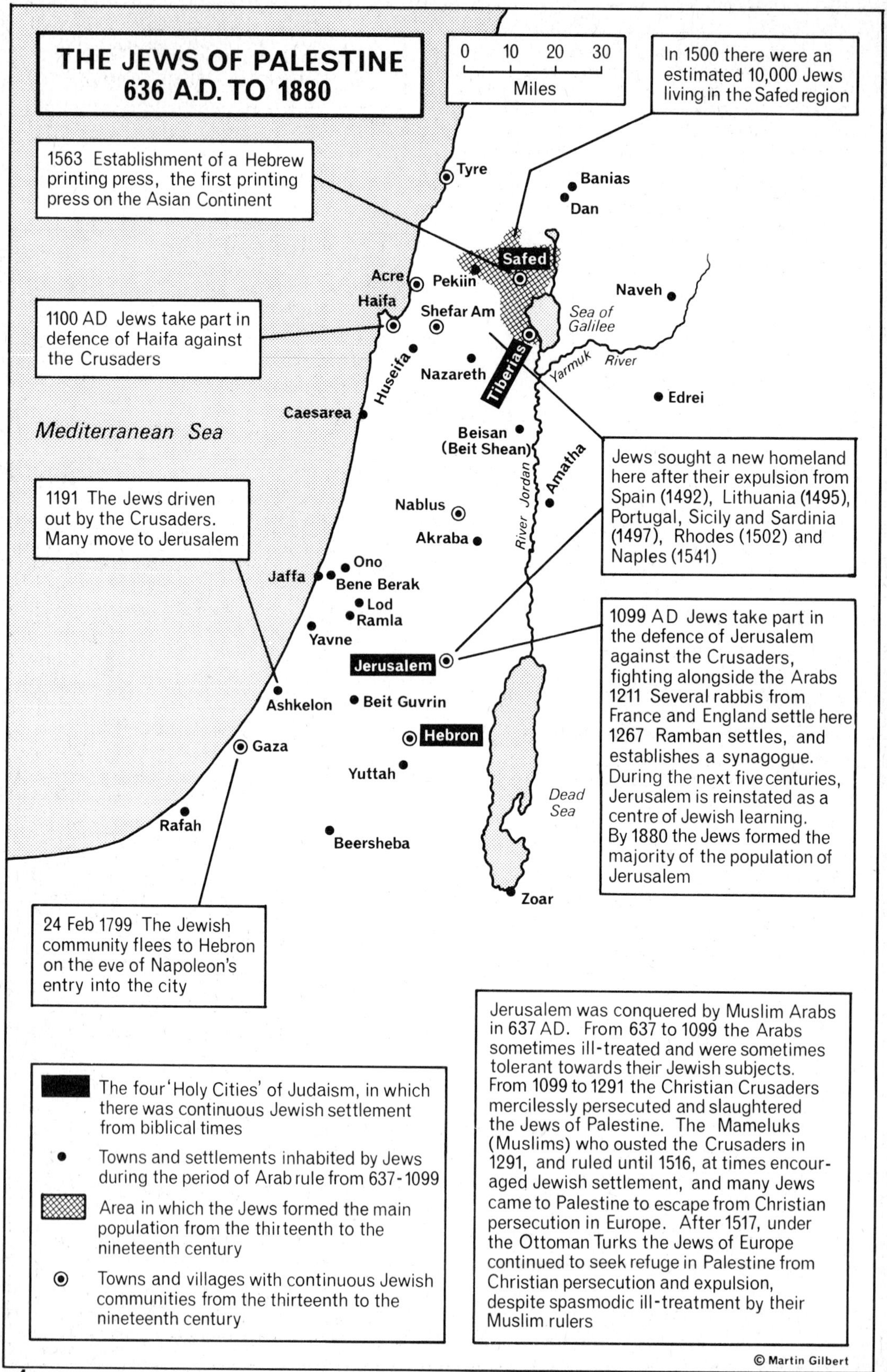
THE JEWS OF PALESTINE
636 A.D. TO 1880
0 10 20 30
Miles
In 1500 there were an estimated 10,000 Jews living in the Safed region
1563 Establishment of a Hebrew printing press, the first printing press on the Asian Continent
Tyre
Banias
Dan
Safed
Acre
Pekiin
Haifa
Naveh
Shefar Am
Sea of Galilee
1100 AD Jews take part in defence of Haifa against the Crusaders
Tiberias
Huseifa
Nazareth
Yarmuk River
Edrei
Caesarea
Mediterranean Sea
Beisan (Beit Shean)
Amatha
River Jordan
Jews sought a new homeland here after their expulsion from Spain (1492), Lithuania (1495), Portugal, Sicily and Sardinia (1497), Rhodes (1502) and Naples (1541)
1191 The Jews driven out by the Crusaders. Many move to Jerusalem
Nablus
Akraba
Ono
Jaffa
Bene Berak
Lod
Ramla
Yavne
1099 AD Jews take part in the defence of Jerusalem against the Crusaders, fighting alongside the Arabs
1211 Several rabbis from France and England settle here
1267 Ramban settles, and establishes a synagogue.
During the next five centuries, Jerusalem is reinstated as a centre of Jewish learning.
By 1880 the Jews formed the majority of the population of Jerusalem
Jerusalem
Ashkelon
Beit Guvrin
Hebron
Gaza
Yuttah
Dead Sea
Rafah
Beersheba
Zoar
24 Feb 1799 The Jewish community flees to Hebron on the eve of Napoleon's entry into the city
The four 'Holy Cities' of Judaism, in which there was continuous Jewish settlement from biblical times
Towns and settlements inhabited by Jews during the period of Arab rule from 637-1099
Area in which the Jews formed the main population from the thirteenth to the nineteenth century
Towns and villages with continuous Jewish communities from the thirteenth to the nineteenth century
Jerusalem was conquered by Muslim Arabs in 637 AD. From 637 to 1099 the Arabs sometimes ill-treated and were sometimes tolerant towards their Jewish subjects. From 1099 to 1291 the Christian Crusaders mercilessly persecuted and slaughtered the Jews of Palestine. The Mameluks (Muslims) who ousted the Crusaders in 1291, and ruled until 1516, at times encouraged Jewish settlement, and many Jews came to Palestine to escape from Christian persecution in Europe. After 1517, under the Ottoman Turks the Jews of Europe continued to seek refuge in Palestine from Christian persecution and expulsion, despite spasmodic ill-treatment by their Muslim rulers
© Martin Gilbert

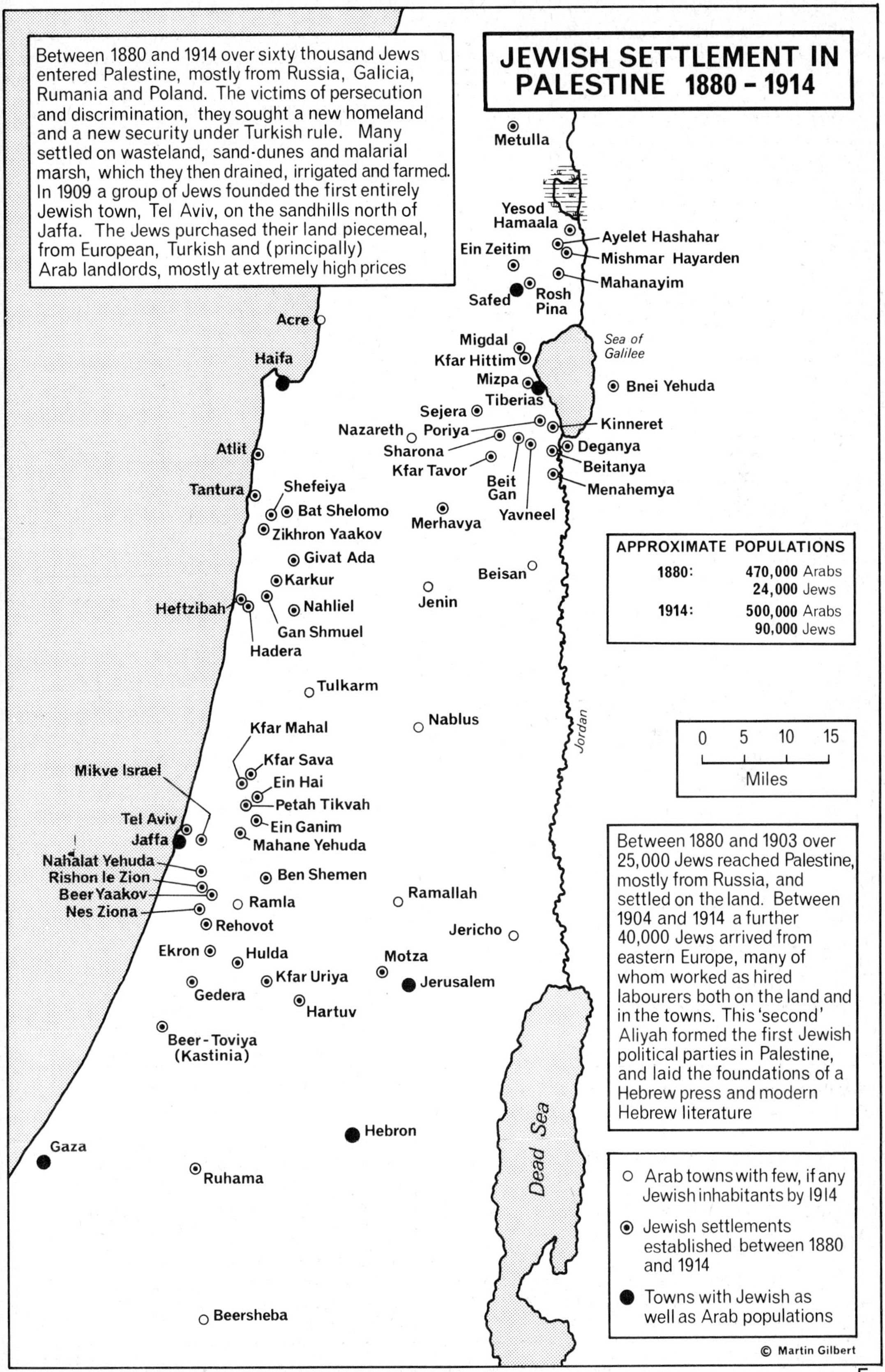

JEWISH SETTLEMENT IN PALESTINE 1880 – 1914

Between 1880 and 1914 over sixty thousand Jews entered Palestine, mostly from Russia, Galicia, Rumania and Poland. The victims of persecution and discrimination, they sought a new homeland and a new security under Turkish rule. Many settled on wasteland, sand-dunes and malarial marsh, which they then drained, irrigated and farmed. In 1909 a group of Jews founded the first entirely Jewish town, Tel Aviv, on the sandhills north of Jaffa. The Jews purchased their land piecemeal, from European, Turkish and (principally) Arab landlords, mostly at extremely high prices

Metulla

Yesod Hamaala

Ein Zeitim

Ayelet Hashahar

Mishmar Hayarden

Mahanayim

Safed

Rosh Pina

Acre

Haifa

Migdal

Kfar Hittim

Mizpa

Tiberias

Sea of Galilee

Bnei Yehuda

Sejera

Nazareth

Poriya

Kinneret

Sharona

Deganya

Atlit

Kfar Tavor

Beitanya

Tantura

Beit Gan

Menahemya

Shefeiya

Bat Shelomo

Merhavya

Yavneel

Zikhron Yaakov

Givat Ada

Beisan

Karkur

Jenin

Heftzibah

Nahliel

Gan Shmuel

Hadera

Tulkarm

Kfar Mahal

Nablus

Kfar Sava

Ein Hai

Mikve Israel

Petah Tikvah

Tel Aviv

Ein Ganim

Jaffa

Mahane Yehuda

Nahalat Yehuda

Ben Shemen

Rishon le Zion

Ramallah

Beer Yaakov

Ramla

Nes Ziona

Jericho

Rehovot

Ekron

Hulda

Motza

Gedera

Kfar Uriya

Jerusalem

Hartuv

Beer-Toviya (Kastinia)

Jordan

Gaza

Hebron

Ruhama

Dead Sea

Beersheba

APPROXIMATE POPULATIONS

1880:	470,000 Arabs
	24,000 Jews
1914:	500,000 Arabs
	90,000 Jews

0 5 10 15
Miles

Between 1880 and 1903 over 25,000 Jews reached Palestine, mostly from Russia, and settled on the land. Between 1904 and 1914 a further 40,000 Jews arrived from eastern Europe, many of whom worked as hired labourers both on the land and in the towns. This 'second' Aliyah formed the first Jewish political parties in Palestine, and laid the foundations of a Hebrew press and modern Hebrew literature

○ Arab towns with few, if any Jewish inhabitants by 1914

◉ Jewish settlements established between 1880 and 1914

● Towns with Jewish as well as Arab populations

© Martin Gilbert

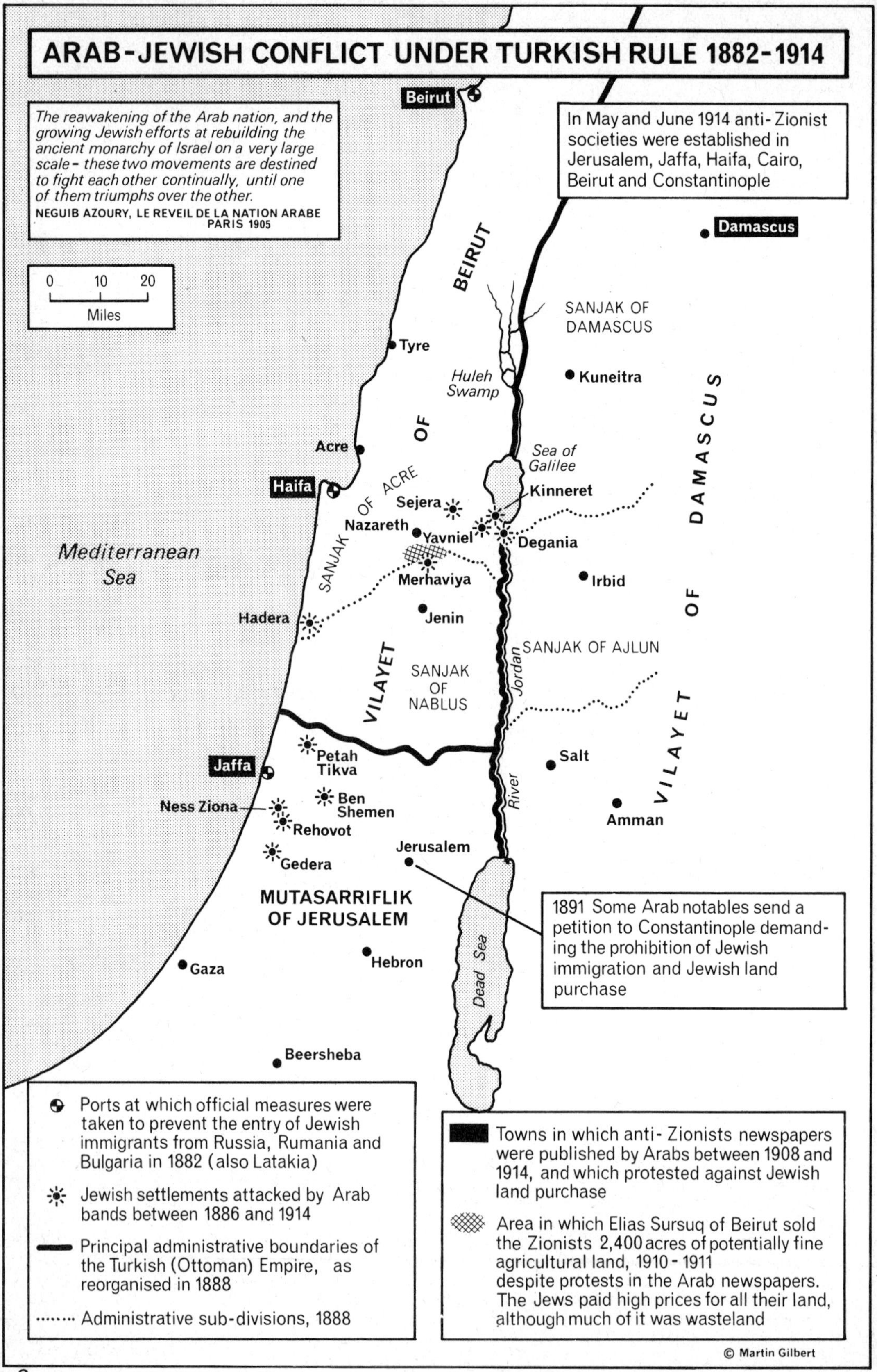
ARAB-JEWISH CONFLICT UNDER TURKISH RULE 1882-1914
The reawakening of the Arab nation, and the growing Jewish efforts at rebuilding the ancient monarchy of Israel on a very large scale - these two movements are destined to fight each other continually, until one of them triumphs over the other.
NEGUIB AZOURY, LE REVEIL DE LA NATION ARABE PARIS 1905
In May and June 1914 anti-Zionist societies were established in Jerusalem, Jaffa, Haifa, Cairo, Beirut and Constantinople
0 10 20
Miles
Beirut
Damascus
BEIRUT
SANJAK OF DAMASCUS
Tyre
Huleh Swamp
Kuneitra
DAMASCUS
OF
Acre
Sea of Galilee
Haifa
SANJAK OF ACRE
Kinneret
Sejera
Nazareth
Yavniel
Degania
Mediterranean Sea
Merhaviya
Irbid
Hadera
Jenin
SANJAK OF AJLUN
VILAYET
SANJAK OF NABLUS
Jordan
VILAYET
Petah Tikva
Jaffa
Salt
Ben Shemen
Ness Ziona
River
Rehovot
Amman
Jerusalem
Gedera
MUTASARRIFLIK OF JERUSALEM
1891 Some Arab notables send a petition to Constantinople demanding the prohibition of Jewish immigration and Jewish land purchase
Dead Sea
Gaza
Hebron
Beersheba
Ports at which official measures were taken to prevent the entry of Jewish immigrants from Russia, Rumania and Bulgaria in 1882 (also Latakia)
Jewish settlements attacked by Arab bands between 1886 and 1914
Principal administrative boundaries of the Turkish (Ottoman) Empire, as reorganised in 1888
Administrative sub-divisions, 1888
Towns in which anti-Zionists newspapers were published by Arabs between 1908 and 1914, and which protested against Jewish land purchase
Area in which Elias Sursuq of Beirut sold the Zionists 2,400 acres of potentially fine agricultural land, 1910-1911 despite protests in the Arab newspapers. The Jews paid high prices for all their land, although much of it was wasteland
© Martin Gilbert

BRITAIN'S PROMISE TO THE ARABS: 1915

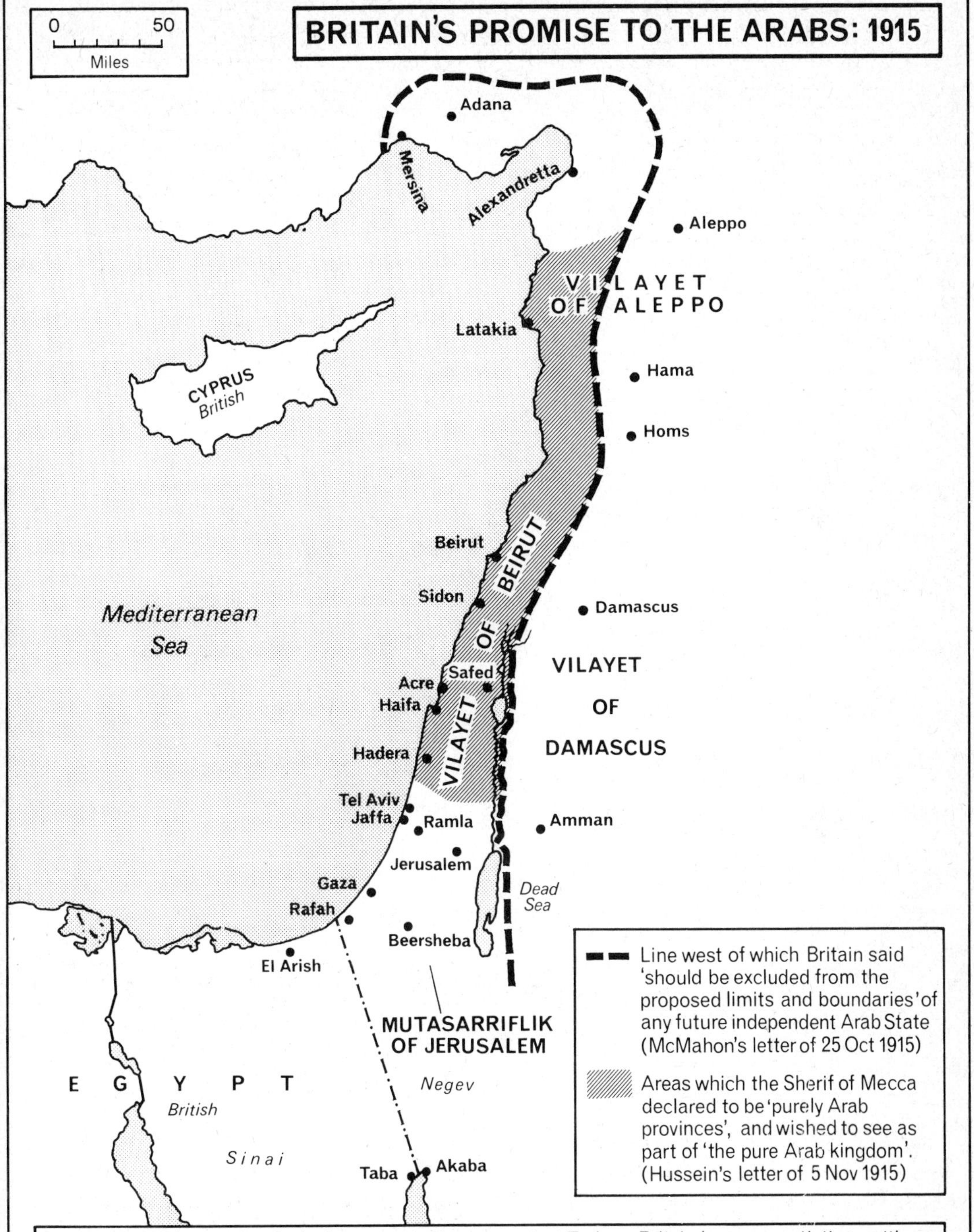

0 50
Miles
Adana
Mersina
Alexandretta
Aleppo
VILAYET OF ALEPPO
Latakia
Hama
Homs
CYPRUS
British
Beirut
Sidon
VILAYET OF BEIRUT
Damascus
Mediterranean Sea
VILAYET OF DAMASCUS
Safed
Acre
Haifa
Hadera
Tel Aviv
Jaffa
Ramla
Amman
Jerusalem
Gaza
Rafah
Dead Sea
Beersheba
El Arish
MUTASARRIFLIK OF JERUSALEM
EGYPT
British
Negev
Sinai
Taba
Akaba
Line west of which Britain said 'should be excluded from the proposed limits and boundaries' of any future independent Arab State (McMahon's letter of 25 Oct 1915)
Areas which the Sherif of Mecca declared to be 'purely Arab provinces', and wished to see as part of 'the pure Arab kingdom'. (Hussein's letter of 5 Nov 1915)

In 1915, in an attempt to win Arab support in the war against Turkey, Britain began negotiations with Hussein, Sherif of Mecca. On 25 Oct 1915 the British High Commissioner in Cairo, Sir H. McMahon, informed Hussein that Britain was 'prepared to recognize and support the independence of the Arabs....' But, he added, the Eastern Mediterranean littoral would have to be entirely excluded from any future Arab State. In his reply on 5 Nov 1915, Hussein insisted on the inclusion of the Vilayet of Beirut, but made no mention of the Mutasarriflik of Jerusalem. But on 14 Dec 1915 McMahon replied that any such inclusion 'will require careful consideration'. On 1 Jan 1916 Hussein warned McMahon: 'the people of Beirut will decidedly never accept such isolations'. At no point in the correspondence was any mention made of southern Palestine, Jerusalem or the Jews

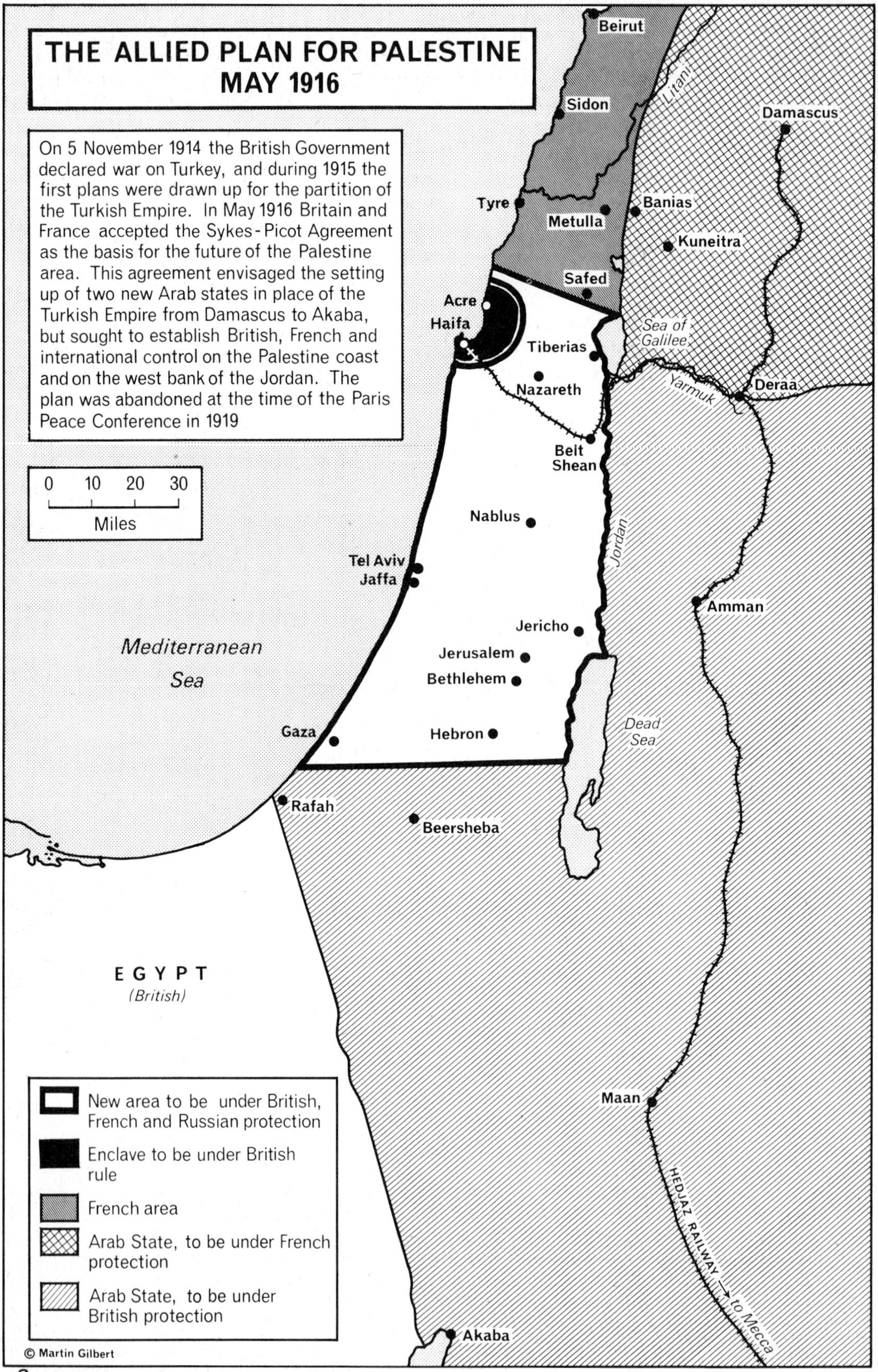
THE ALLIED PLAN FOR PALESTINE
MAY 1916
On 5 November 1914 the British Government declared war on Turkey, and during 1915 the first plans were drawn up for the partition of the Turkish Empire. In May 1916 Britain and France accepted the Sykes-Picot Agreement as the basis for the future of the Palestine area. This agreement envisaged the setting up of two new Arab states in place of the Turkish Empire from Damascus to Akaba, but sought to establish British, French and international control on the Palestine coast and on the west bank of the Jordan. The plan was abandoned at the time of the Paris Peace Conference in 1919
0 10 20 30
Miles
Beirut
Sidon
Litani
Damascus
Tyre
Metulla
Banias
Kuneitra
Safed
Acre
Haifa
Tiberias
Sea of Galilee
Nazareth
Yarmuk
Deraa
Beit Shean
Nablus
Jordan
Tel Aviv
Jaffa
Amman
Jericho
Jerusalem
Bethlehem
Mediterranean Sea
Gaza
Hebron
Dead Sea
Rafah
Beersheba
EGYPT
(British)
Maan
HEDJAZ RAILWAY → to Mecca
Akaba
New area to be under British, French and Russian protection
Enclave to be under British rule
French area
Arab State, to be under French protection
Arab State, to be under British protection
© Martin Gilbert

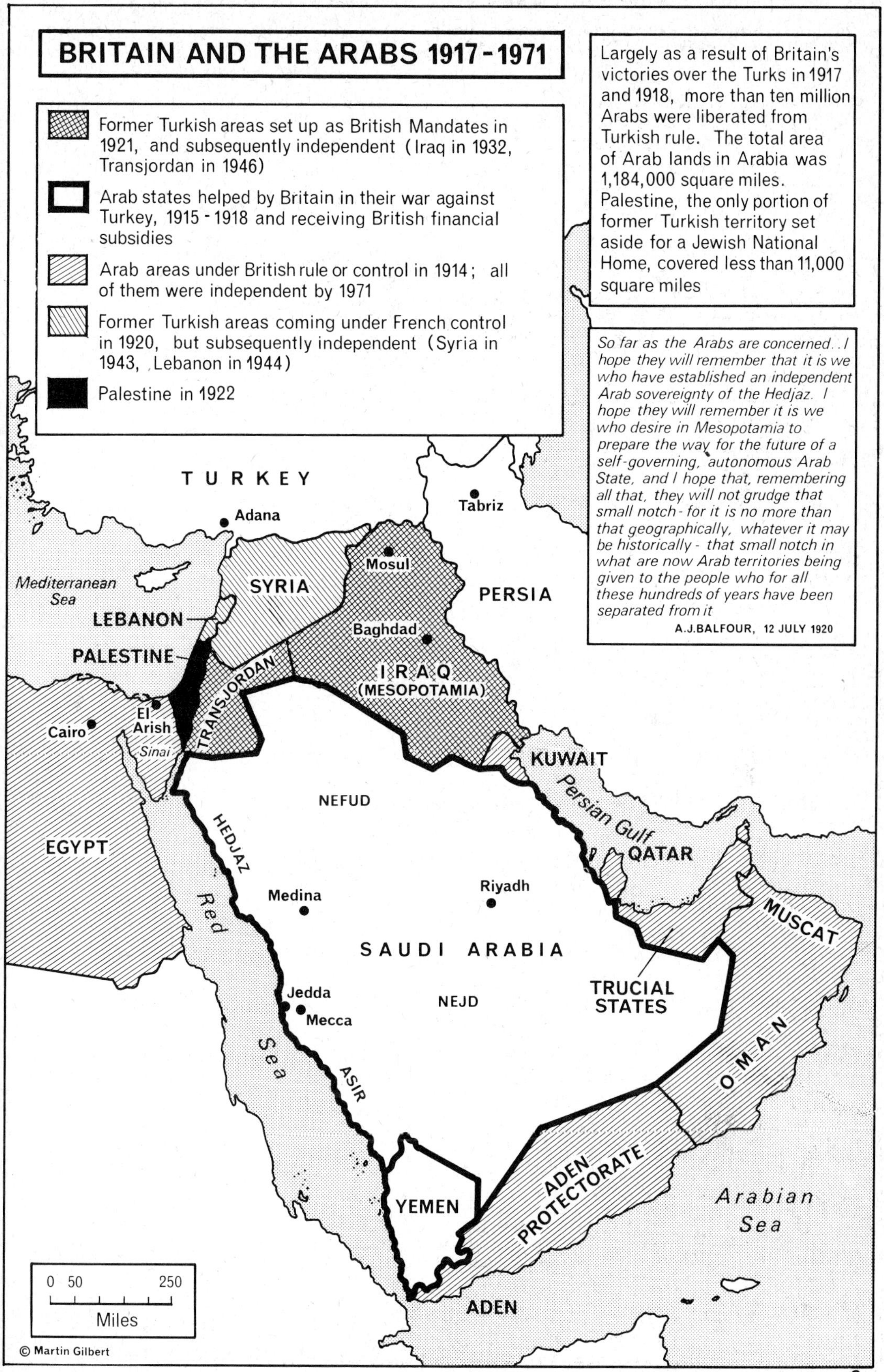
BRITAIN AND THE ARABS 1917-1971
Former Turkish areas set up as British Mandates in 1921, and subsequently independent (Iraq in 1932, Transjordan in 1946)
Arab states helped by Britain in their war against Turkey, 1915-1918 and receiving British financial subsidies
Arab areas under British rule or control in 1914; all of them were independent by 1971
Former Turkish areas coming under French control in 1920, but subsequently independent (Syria in 1943, Lebanon in 1944)
Palestine in 1922
Largely as a result of Britain's victories over the Turks in 1917 and 1918, more than ten million Arabs were liberated from Turkish rule. The total area of Arab lands in Arabia was 1,184,000 square miles. Palestine, the only portion of former Turkish territory set aside for a Jewish National Home, covered less than 11,000 square miles
So far as the Arabs are concerned..I hope they will remember that it is we who have established an independent Arab sovereignty of the Hedjaz. I hope they will remember it is we who desire in Mesopotamia to prepare the way for the future of a self-governing, autonomous Arab State, and I hope that, remembering all that, they will not grudge that small notch - for it is no more than that geographically, whatever it may be historically - that small notch in what are now Arab territories being given to the people who for all these hundreds of years have been separated from it
A.J.BALFOUR, 12 JULY 1920
TURKEY
Adana
Tabriz
Mosul
Mediterranean Sea
SYRIA
PERSIA
LEBANON
Baghdad
PALESTINE
TRANSJORDAN
IRAQ (MESOPOTAMIA)
El Arish
Cairo
Sinai
KUWAIT
Persian Gulf
NEFUD
HEDJAZ
EGYPT
QATAR
Red Sea
Medina
Riyadh
MUSCAT
SAUDI ARABIA
Jedda
Mecca
NEJD
TRUCIAL STATES
OMAN
ASIR
ADEN PROTECTORATE
YEMEN
Arabian Sea
ADEN
0 50 250
Miles
© Martin Gilbert

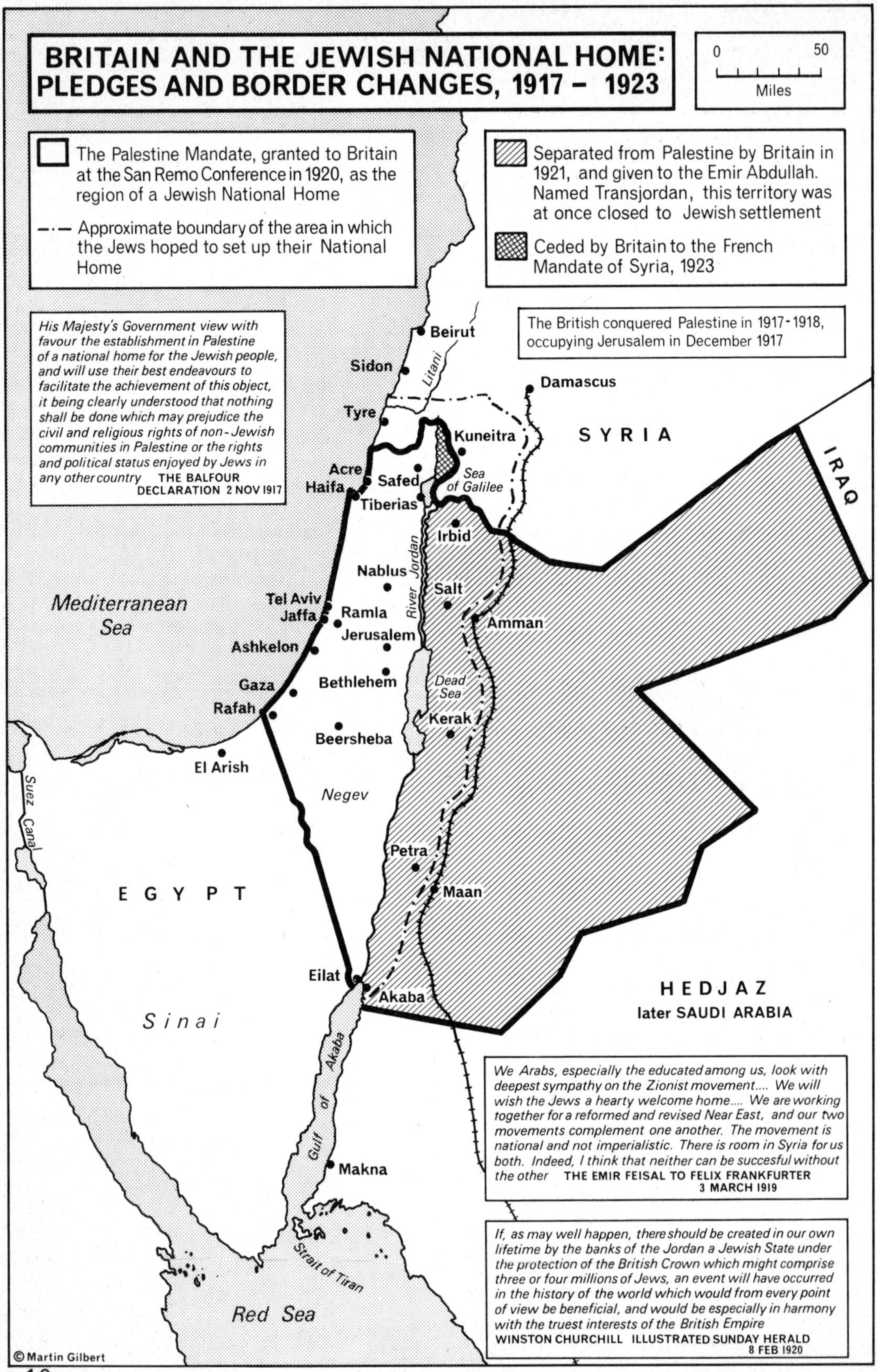
BRITAIN AND THE JEWISH NATIONAL HOME: PLEDGES AND BORDER CHANGES, 1917 - 1923
0
50
Miles
The Palestine Mandate, granted to Britain at the San Remo Conference in 1920, as the region of a Jewish National Home
Approximate boundary of the area in which the Jews hoped to set up their National Home
Separated from Palestine by Britain in 1921, and given to the Emir Abdullah. Named Transjordan, this territory was at once closed to Jewish settlement
Ceded by Britain to the French Mandate of Syria, 1923
His Majesty's Government view with favour the establishment in Palestine of a national home for the Jewish people, and will use their best endeavours to facilitate the achievement of this object, it being clearly understood that nothing shall be done which may prejudice the civil and religious rights of non-Jewish communities in Palestine or the rights and political status enjoyed by Jews in any other country THE BALFOUR DECLARATION 2 NOV 1917
The British conquered Palestine in 1917-1918, occupying Jerusalem in December 1917
Beirut
Sidon
Litani
Damascus
Tyre
SYRIA
Kuneitra
Acre
Haifa
Safed
Sea of Galilee
Tiberias
IRAQ
Irbid
River Jordan
Nablus
Salt
Mediterranean Sea
Tel Aviv
Jaffa
Ramla
Amman
Jerusalem
Ashkelon
Gaza
Bethlehem
Dead Sea
Rafah
Kerak
Beersheba
El Arish
Suez Canal
Negev
Petra
EGYPT
Maan
Eilat
Akaba
HEDJAZ
later SAUDI ARABIA
Sinai
Gulf of Akaba
We Arabs, especially the educated among us, look with deepest sympathy on the Zionist movement.... We will wish the Jews a hearty welcome home.... We are working together for a reformed and revised Near East, and our two movements complement one another. The movement is national and not imperialistic. There is room in Syria for us both. Indeed, I think that neither can be succesful without the other THE EMIR FEISAL TO FELIX FRANKFURTER 3 MARCH 1919
Makna
Strait of Tiran
Red Sea
If, as may well happen, there should be created in our own lifetime by the banks of the Jordan a Jewish State under the protection of the British Crown which might comprise three or four millions of Jews, an event will have occurred in the history of the world which would from every point of view be beneficial, and would be especially in harmony with the truest interests of the British Empire WINSTON CHURCHILL ILLUSTRATED SUNDAY HERALD 8 FEB 1920
© Martin Gilbert

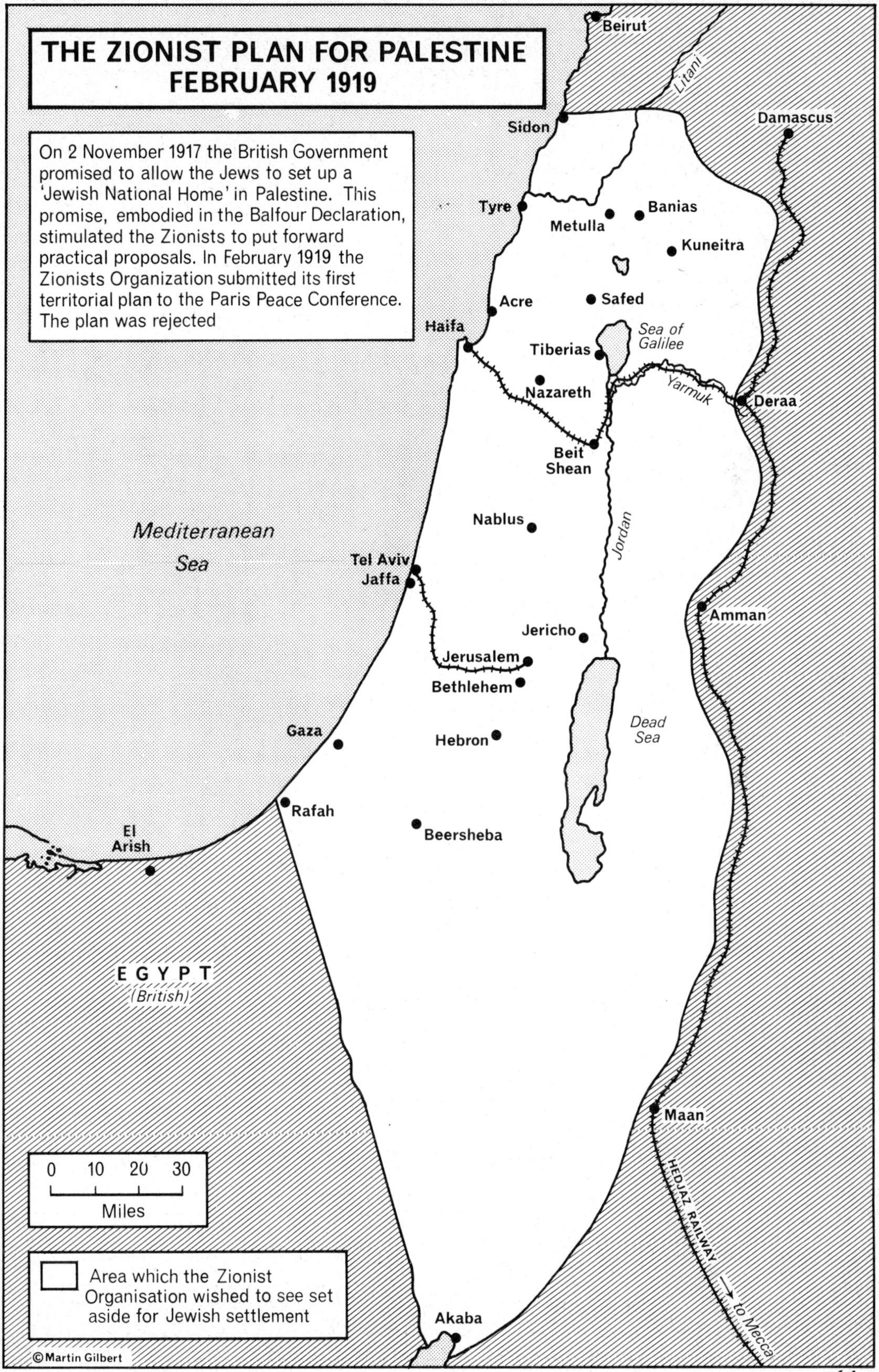
THE ZIONIST PLAN FOR PALESTINE
FEBRUARY 1919
On 2 November 1917 the British Government promised to allow the Jews to set up a 'Jewish National Home' in Palestine. This promise, embodied in the Balfour Declaration, stimulated the Zionists to put forward practical proposals. In February 1919 the Zionists Organization submitted its first territorial plan to the Paris Peace Conference. The plan was rejected
Beirut
Litani
Damascus
Sidon
Tyre
Metulla
Banias
Kuneitra
Acre
Safed
Haifa
Sea of Galilee
Tiberias
Nazareth
Yarmuk
Deraa
Beit Shean
Nablus
Jordan
Mediterranean Sea
Tel Aviv
Jaffa
Amman
Jericho
Jerusalem
Bethlehem
Dead Sea
Gaza
Hebron
Rafah
Beersheba
El Arish
EGYPT
(British)
Maan
HEDJAZ RAILWAY
to Mecca
0 10 20 30
Miles
Area which the Zionist Organisation wished to see set aside for Jewish settlement
Akaba
©Martin Gilbert

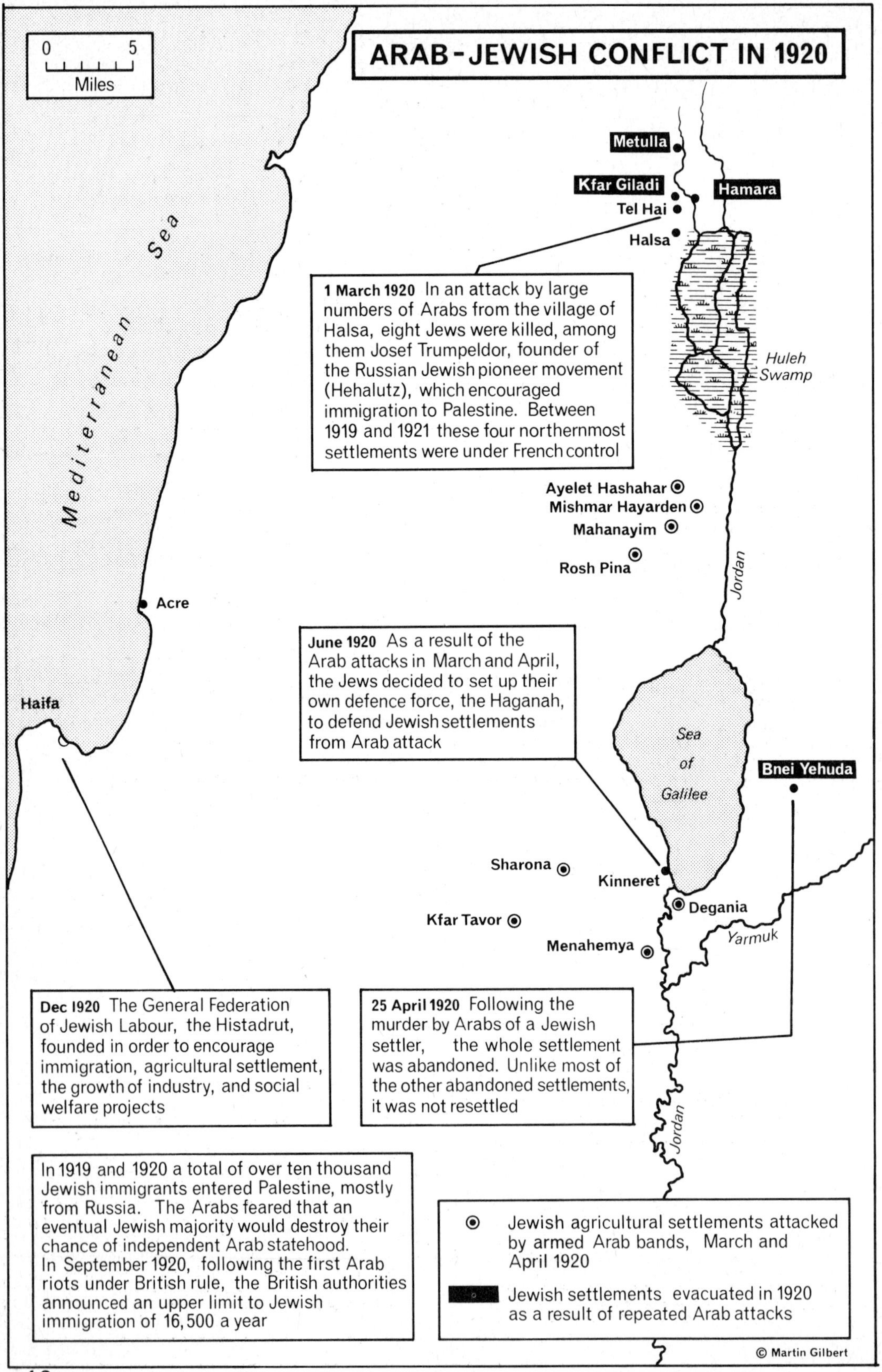
ARAB-JEWISH CONFLICT IN 1920
0 5
Miles
Mediterranean Sea
Metulla
Kfar Giladi
Hamara
Tel Hai
Halsa
Huleh Swamp
1 March 1920 In an attack by large numbers of Arabs from the village of Halsa, eight Jews were killed, among them Josef Trumpeldor, founder of the Russian Jewish pioneer movement (Hehalutz), which encouraged immigration to Palestine. Between 1919 and 1921 these four northernmost settlements were under French control
Ayelet Hashahar
Mishmar Hayarden
Mahanayim
Rosh Pina
Jordan
Acre
June 1920 As a result of the Arab attacks in March and April, the Jews decided to set up their own defence force, the Haganah, to defend Jewish settlements from Arab attack
Haifa
Sea of Galilee
Bnei Yehuda
Sharona
Kinneret
Degania
Kfar Tavor
Menahemya
Yarmuk
Dec 1920 The General Federation of Jewish Labour, the Histadrut, founded in order to encourage immigration, agricultural settlement, the growth of industry, and social welfare projects
25 April 1920 Following the murder by Arabs of a Jewish settler, the whole settlement was abandoned. Unlike most of the other abandoned settlements, it was not resettled
Jordan
In 1919 and 1920 a total of over ten thousand Jewish immigrants entered Palestine, mostly from Russia. The Arabs feared that an eventual Jewish majority would destroy their chance of independent Arab statehood.
In September 1920, following the first Arab riots under British rule, the British authorities announced an upper limit to Jewish immigration of 16,500 a year
Jewish agricultural settlements attacked by armed Arab bands, March and April 1920
Jewish settlements evacuated in 1920 as a result of repeated Arab attacks
© Martin Gilbert

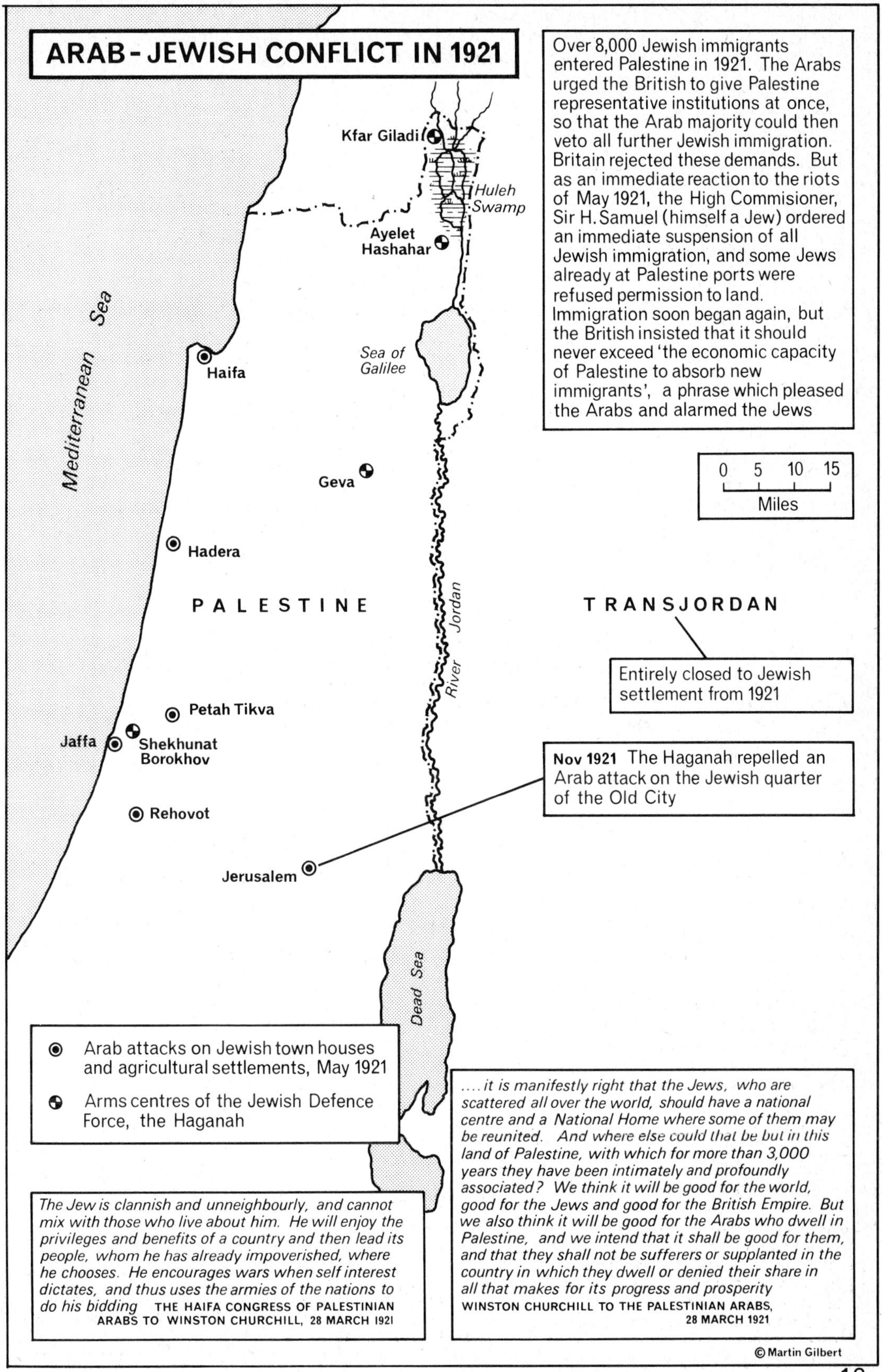
ARAB - JEWISH CONFLICT IN 1921
Over 8,000 Jewish immigrants entered Palestine in 1921. The Arabs urged the British to give Palestine representative institutions at once, so that the Arab majority could then veto all further Jewish immigration. Britain rejected these demands. But as an immediate reaction to the riots of May 1921, the High Commisioner, Sir H. Samuel (himself a Jew) ordered an immediate suspension of all Jewish immigration, and some Jews already at Palestine ports were refused permission to land. Immigration soon began again, but the British insisted that it should never exceed 'the economic capacity of Palestine to absorb new immigrants', a phrase which pleased the Arabs and alarmed the Jews
Kfar Giladi
Huleh Swamp
Ayelet Hashahar
Mediterranean Sea
Haifa
Sea of Galilee
Geva
0 5 10 15
Miles
Hadera
PALESTINE
River Jordan
TRANSJORDAN
Entirely closed to Jewish settlement from 1921
Petah Tikva
Jaffa
Shekhunat Borokhov
Nov 1921 The Haganah repelled an Arab attack on the Jewish quarter of the Old City
Rehovot
Jerusalem
Dead Sea
Arab attacks on Jewish town houses and agricultural settlements, May 1921
Arms centres of the Jewish Defence Force, the Haganah
....it is manifestly right that the Jews, who are scattered all over the world, should have a national centre and a National Home where some of them may be reunited. And where else could that be but in this land of Palestine, with which for more than 3,000 years they have been intimately and profoundly associated? We think it will be good for the world, good for the Jews and good for the British Empire. But we also think it will be good for the Arabs who dwell in Palestine, and we intend that it shall be good for them, and that they shall not be sufferers or supplanted in the country in which they dwell or denied their share in all that makes for its progress and prosperity
WINSTON CHURCHILL TO THE PALESTINIAN ARABS, 28 MARCH 1921
The Jew is clannish and unneighbourly, and cannot mix with those who live about him. He will enjoy the privileges and benefits of a country and then lead its people, whom he has already impoverished, where he chooses. He encourages wars when self interest dictates, and thus uses the armies of the nations to do his bidding
THE HAIFA CONGRESS OF PALESTINIAN ARABS TO WINSTON CHURCHILL, 28 MARCH 1921
© Martin Gilbert

THE JEWISH SETTLEMENTS IN THE VALLEY OF JEZREEL 1921–1925

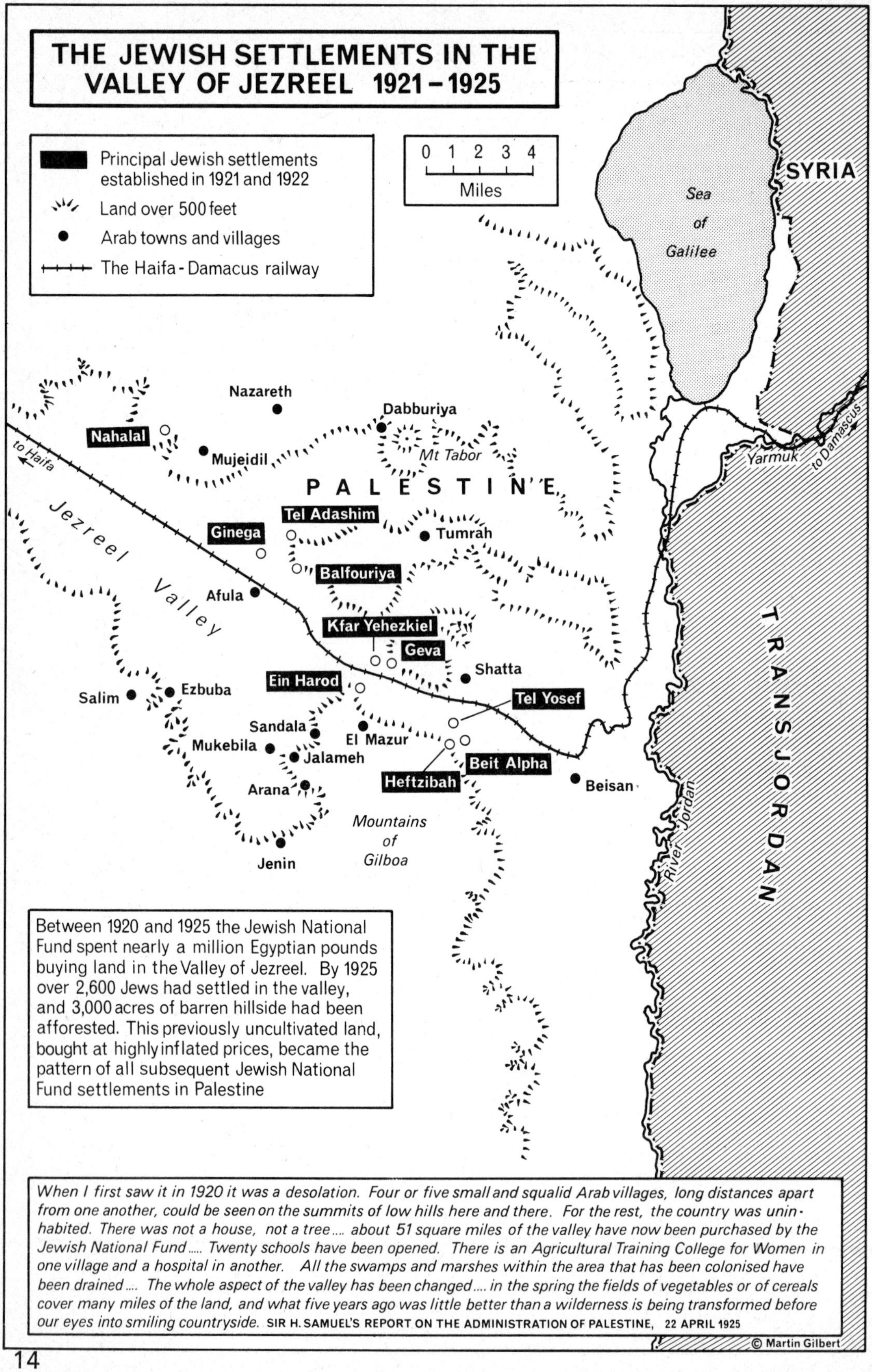

Principal Jewish settlements established in 1921 and 1922
Land over 500 feet
Arab towns and villages
The Haifa - Damacus railway
0 1 2 3 4
Miles
SYRIA
Sea of Galilee
Nazareth
Dabburiya
Nahalal
Mujeidil
Mt Tabor
to Haifa
PALESTINE
Jezreel Valley
Tel Adashim
Ginega
Tumrah
Balfouriya
Afula
Kfar Yehezkiel
Geva
Shatta
Ein Harod
Tel Yosef
Salim
Ezbuba
Sandala
El Mazur
Mukebila
Jalameh
Beit Alpha
Heftzibah
Beisan
Arana
Mountains of Gilboa
Jenin
Yarmuk
to Damascus
River Jordan
TRANSJORDAN

Between 1920 and 1925 the Jewish National Fund spent nearly a million Egyptian pounds buying land in the Valley of Jezreel. By 1925 over 2,600 Jews had settled in the valley, and 3,000 acres of barren hillside had been afforested. This previously uncultivated land, bought at highly inflated prices, became the pattern of all subsequent Jewish National Fund settlements in Palestine

When I first saw it in 1920 it was a desolation. Four or five small and squalid Arab villages, long distances apart from one another, could be seen on the summits of low hills here and there. For the rest, the country was uninhabited. There was not a house, not a tree.... about 51 square miles of the valley have now been purchased by the Jewish National Fund..... Twenty schools have been opened. There is an Agricultural Training College for Women in one village and a hospital in another. All the swamps and marshes within the area that has been colonised have been drained.... The whole aspect of the valley has been changed.... in the spring the fields of vegetables or of cereals cover many miles of the land, and what five years ago was little better than a wilderness is being transformed before our eyes into smiling countryside. SIR H. SAMUEL'S REPORT ON THE ADMINISTRATION OF PALESTINE, 22 APRIL 1925

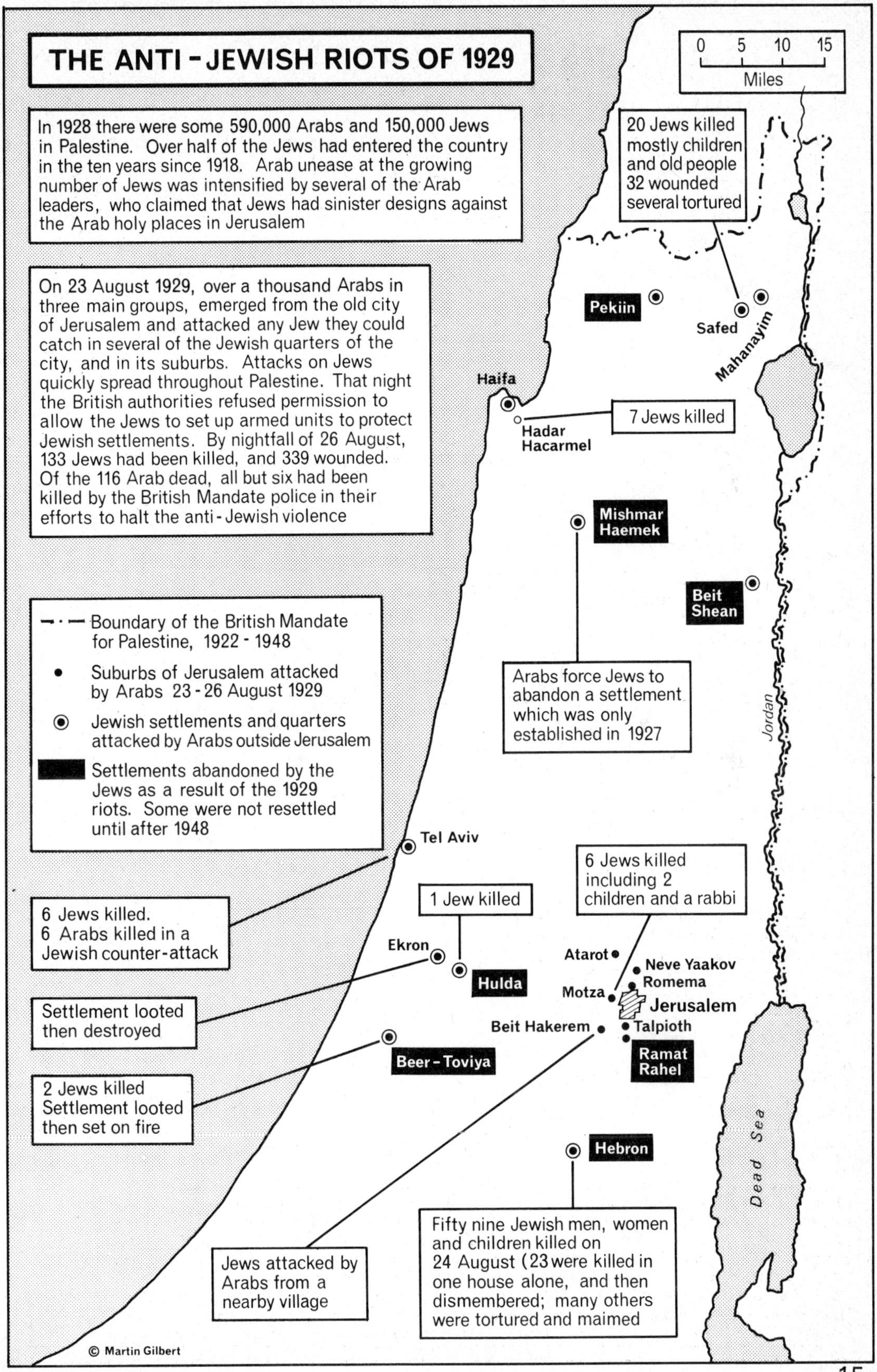
THE ANTI-JEWISH RIOTS OF 1929
In 1928 there were some 590,000 Arabs and 150,000 Jews in Palestine. Over half of the Jews had entered the country in the ten years since 1918. Arab unease at the growing number of Jews was intensified by several of the Arab leaders, who claimed that Jews had sinister designs against the Arab holy places in Jerusalem
On 23 August 1929, over a thousand Arabs in three main groups, emerged from the old city of Jerusalem and attacked any Jew they could catch in several of the Jewish quarters of the city, and in its suburbs. Attacks on Jews quickly spread throughout Palestine. That night the British authorities refused permission to allow the Jews to set up armed units to protect Jewish settlements. By nightfall of 26 August, 133 Jews had been killed, and 339 wounded. Of the 116 Arab dead, all but six had been killed by the British Mandate police in their efforts to halt the anti-Jewish violence
Boundary of the British Mandate for Palestine, 1922 - 1948
Suburbs of Jerusalem attacked by Arabs 23 - 26 August 1929
Jewish settlements and quarters attacked by Arabs outside Jerusalem
Settlements abandoned by the Jews as a result of the 1929 riots. Some were not resettled until after 1948
0 5 10 15
Miles
20 Jews killed mostly children and old people 32 wounded several tortured
Pekiin
Safed
Mahanayim
Haifa
Hadar Hacarmel
7 Jews killed
Mishmar Haemek
Beit Shean
Arabs force Jews to abandon a settlement which was only established in 1927
Jordan
Tel Aviv
6 Jews killed. 6 Arabs killed in a Jewish counter-attack
1 Jew killed
6 Jews killed including 2 children and a rabbi
Ekron
Hulda
Settlement looted then destroyed
Atarot
Neve Yaakov
Romema
Motza
Jerusalem
Beit Hakerem
Talpioth
Ramat Rahel
Beer - Toviya
2 Jews killed Settlement looted then set on fire
Hebron
Dead Sea
Jews attacked by Arabs from a nearby village
Fifty nine Jewish men, women and children killed on 24 August (23 were killed in one house alone, and then dismembered; many others were tortured and maimed
© Martin Gilbert

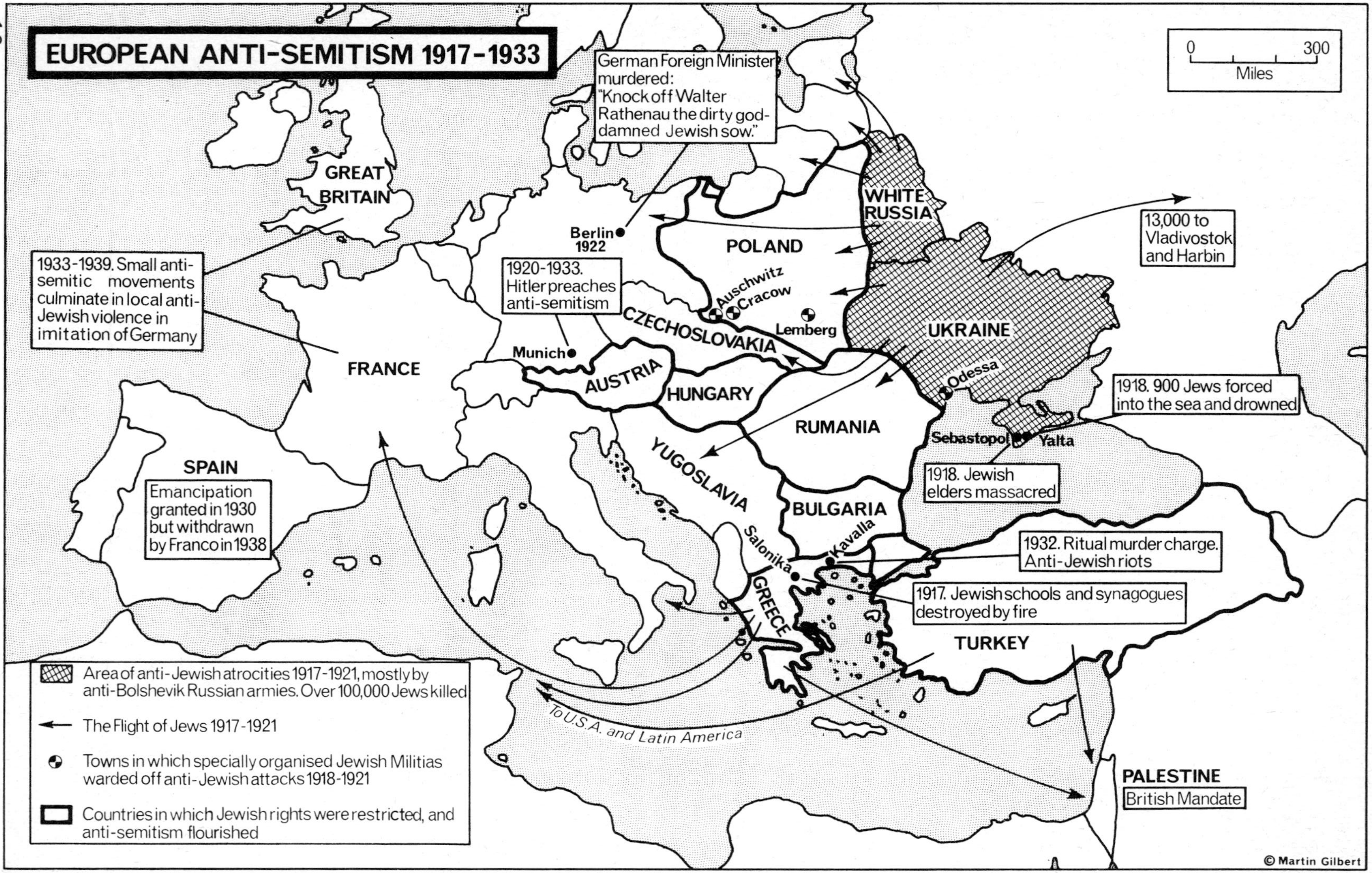
EUROPEAN ANTI-SEMITISM 1917-1933
0 300
Miles
German Foreign Minister murdered: "Knock off Walter Rathenau the dirty god-damned Jewish sow."
GREAT BRITAIN
Berlin 1922
POLAND
WHITE RUSSIA
13,000 to Vladivostok and Harbin
1933-1939. Small anti-semitic movements culminate in local anti-Jewish violence in imitation of Germany
1920-1933. Hitler preaches anti-semitism
Auschwitz
Cracow
Lemberg
UKRAINE
CZECHOSLOVAKIA
Munich
FRANCE
AUSTRIA
HUNGARY
Odessa
1918. 900 Jews forced into the sea and drowned
RUMANIA
Sebastopol
Yalta
YUGOSLAVIA
SPAIN
1918. Jewish elders massacred
Emancipation granted in 1930 but withdrawn by Franco in 1938
BULGARIA
Kavalla
Salonika
1932. Ritual murder charge. Anti-Jewish riots
GREECE
1917. Jewish schools and synagogues destroyed by fire
TURKEY
Area of anti-Jewish atrocities 1917-1921, mostly by anti-Bolshevik Russian armies. Over 100,000 Jews killed
The Flight of Jews 1917-1921
Towns in which specially organised Jewish Militias warded off anti-Jewish attacks 1918-1921
Countries in which Jewish rights were restricted, and anti-semitism flourished
To U.S.A. and Latin America
PALESTINE
British Mandate
© Martin Gilbert

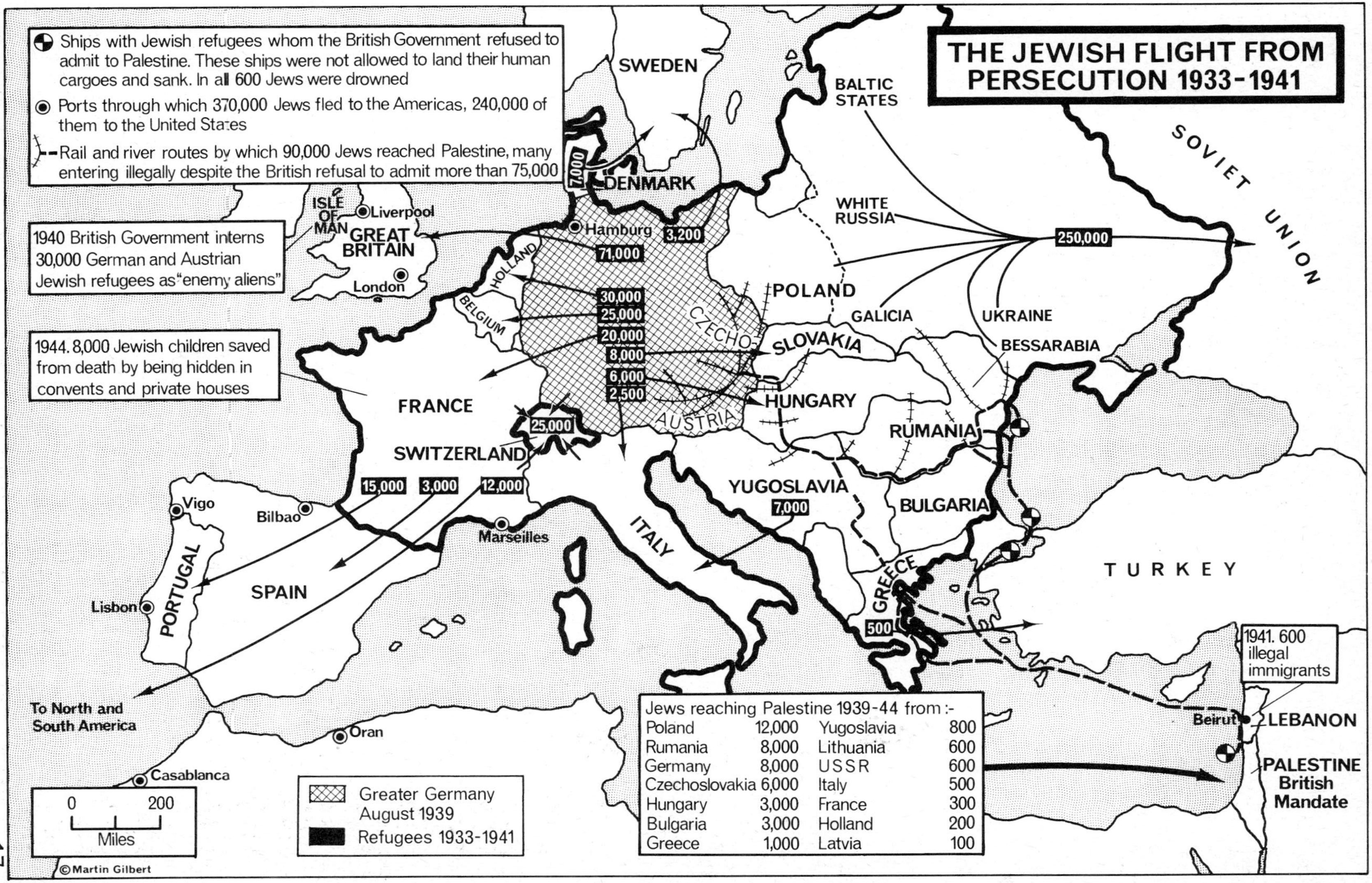
THE JEWISH FLIGHT FROM PERSECUTION 1933-1941
Ships with Jewish refugees whom the British Government refused to admit to Palestine. These ships were not allowed to land their human cargoes and sank. In all 600 Jews were drowned
Ports through which 370,000 Jews fled to the Americas, 240,000 of them to the United States
Rail and river routes by which 90,000 Jews reached Palestine, many entering illegally despite the British refusal to admit more than 75,000
1940 British Government interns 30,000 German and Austrian Jewish refugees as "enemy aliens"
1944. 8,000 Jewish children saved from death by being hidden in convents and private houses
1941. 600 illegal immigrants
Jews reaching Palestine 1939-44 from:-
Poland 12,000
Rumania 8,000
Germany 8,000
Czechoslovakia 6,000
Hungary 3,000
Bulgaria 3,000
Greece 1,000
Yugoslavia 800
Lithuania 600
USSR 600
Italy 500
France 300
Holland 200
Latvia 100
Greater Germany August 1939
Refugees 1933-1941
SWEDEN
DENMARK
BALTIC STATES
WHITE RUSSIA
SOVIET UNION
POLAND
GALICIA
UKRAINE
BESSARABIA
CZECHO-SLOVAKIA
HUNGARY
RUMANIA
AUSTRIA
YUGOSLAVIA
BULGARIA
GREECE
TURKEY
LEBANON
Beirut
PALESTINE British Mandate
ISLE OF MAN
Liverpool
GREAT BRITAIN
London
Hamburg
HOLLAND
BELGIUM
FRANCE
SWITZERLAND
ITALY
SPAIN
PORTUGAL
Vigo
Bilbao
Lisbon
Marseilles
Oran
Casablanca
To North and South America
7,000
3,200
71,000
30,000
25,000
20,000
8,000
6,000
2,500
25,000
250,000
15,000
3,000
12,000
7,000
500
0
200
Miles
©Martin Gilbert

ARAB FEARS OF A JEWISH MAJORITY IN PALESTINE
1920 - 1939

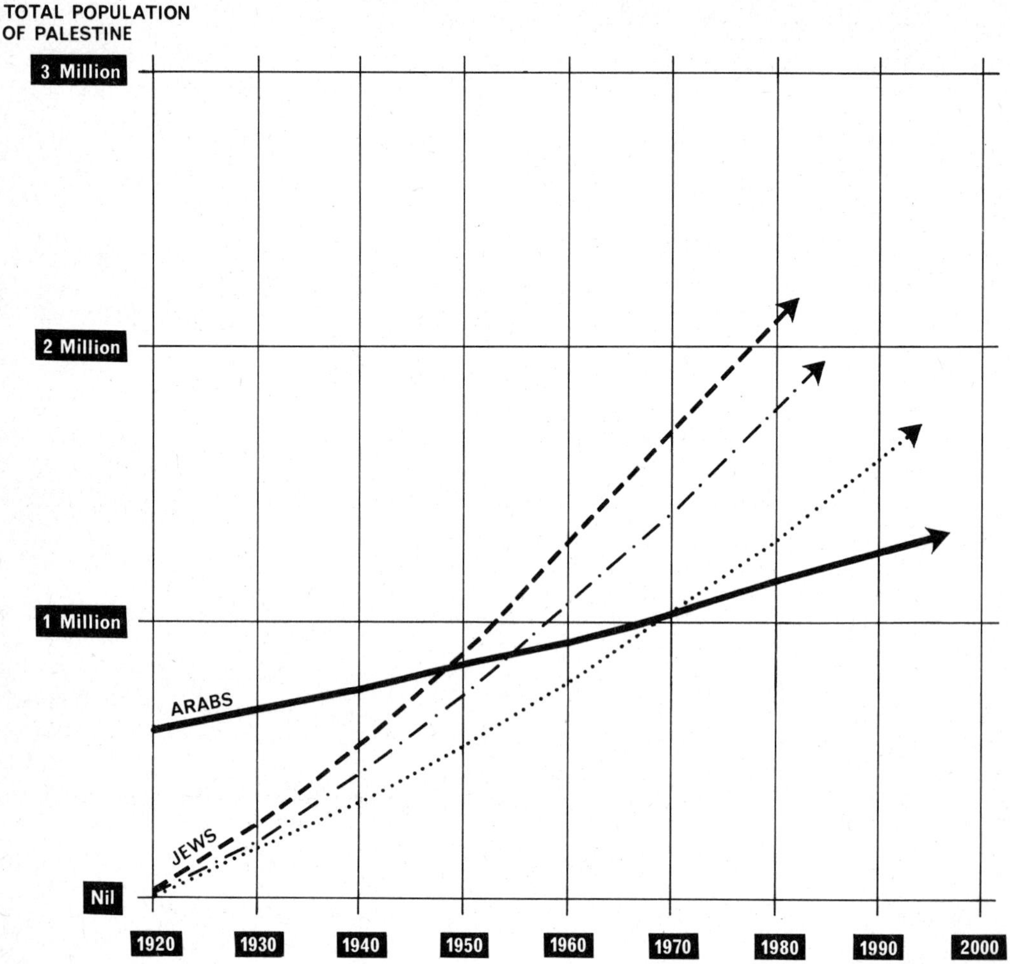

TOTAL POPULATION
OF PALESTINE
3 Million
2 Million
1 Million
Nil
ARABS
JEWS
1920
1930
1940
1950
1960
1970
1980
1990
2000

——— Estimated growth of the Arab population of Palestine, 1920 - 2000

- - - - Estimated Jewish population, allowing for an annual immigration of 25,000 from 1930 (Jews would then equal Arabs by 1948)

— · — Estimated Jewish population, allowing for an annual immigration restricted to 15,000 (Jews would then equal Arabs by 1956)

· · · · · · · · Estimated Jewish population, allowing for an annual immigration restricted to 10,000 (Jews would then equal Arabs by 1969)

These estimates were prepared by the British Government in 1929

As well as 360 000 Jewish immigrants between 1919 and 1939, over 50,000 Arabs also immigrated to Palestine (from nearby Arab States) attracted by the improving agricultural conditions and growing job opportunities, most of them created by the Jews

On the 17 May 1939, following a decade of Arab protest, the British Government issued a White Paper restricting Jewish immigration to 15,000 a year for five years, after which no immigration whatsoever would be allowed without Arab permission. The White Paper made it possible for the Arabs to prevent the Jews ever becoming a majority in Palestine

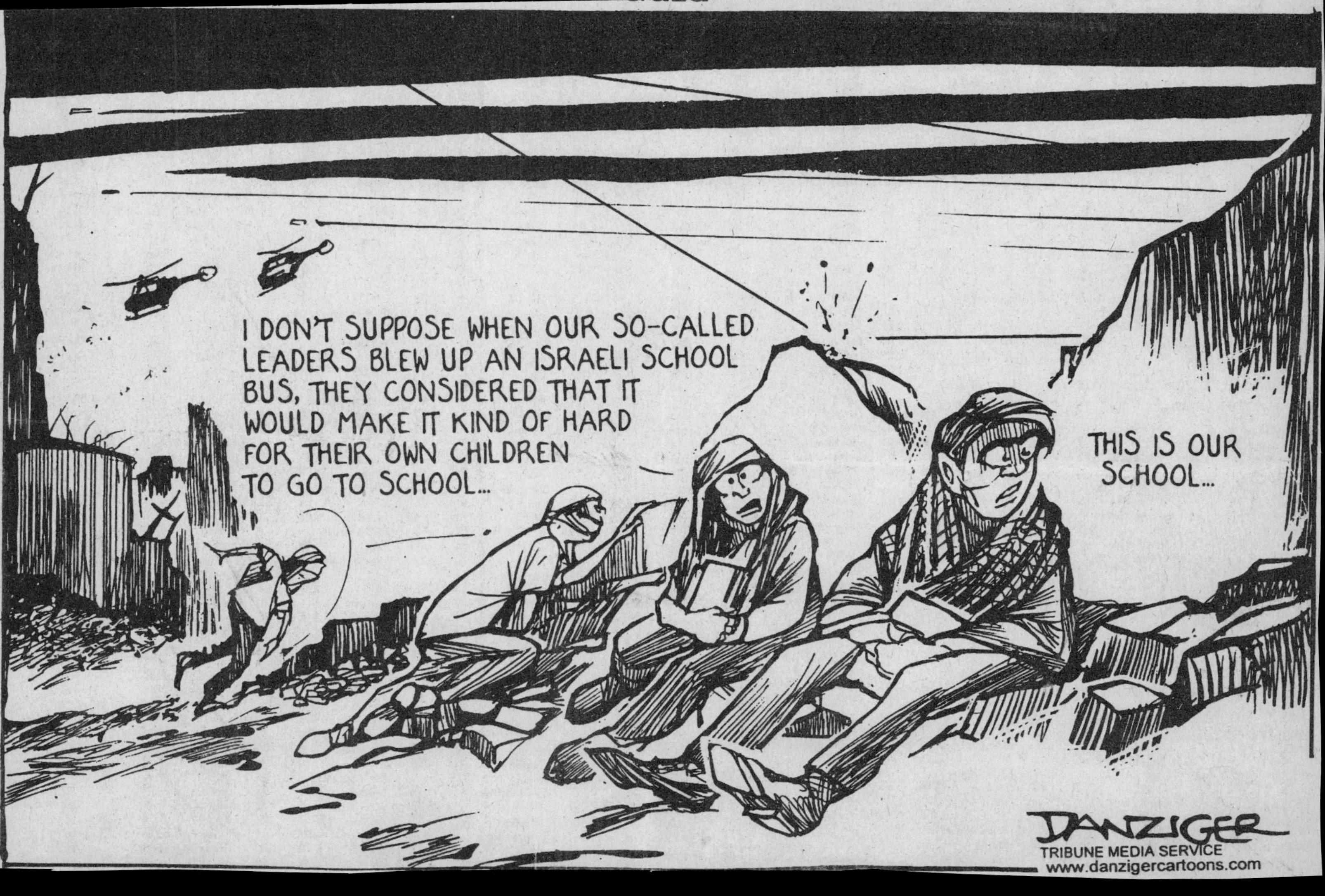
I DON'T SUPPOSE WHEN OUR SO-CALLED LEADERS BLEW UP AN ISRAELI SCHOOL BUS, THEY CONSIDERED THAT IT WOULD MAKE IT KIND OF HARD FOR THEIR OWN CHILDREN TO GO TO SCHOOL...
THIS IS OUR SCHOOL...
DANZIGER
TRIBUNE MEDIA SERVICE
www.danzigercartoons.com

aIA p	30.40	-.42
ChipA p	16.00	-.21
apDev p	20.00	-.49
hartA p	15.85	-.36
onst p	36.34	-1.20
ntTrA p	12.82	-.53
loAgG p	22.89	-.76
lGrA p	21.77	-.73
YdA p	5.58	-.04
ntEqA p	20.26	-.24
elGrth p	25.85	-.91
mCGA p	31.16	-1.55
umitl	19.15	-.71
alu p	13.79	-.17
eingA p	23.79	-.74
M Funds B:		
alB t	30.28	-.42
ChipB t	15.60	-.20
apDvB t	19.41	-.48
hartB t	15.53	-.36
onstB t	35.30	-1.16
ntTrB t	12.70	-.52
lAgGB t	22.10	-.73
lGrB t	21.01	-.71
lTlcmB t	21.04	-1.52
YldB t	5.59	-.04
tlEqB t	19.51	-.23
GrthB t	24.05	-.84
aluB t	13.24	-.16
eingB t	22.65	-.70
M Funds C:		
ChpC t	15.59	-.21
alue t	13.24	-.17
M Global Theme:		
lbTlcA p	22.09	-1.60
AF Funds:		
djMtg	9.86	...
ger Funds B:		
apApr t	11.27	-.34
gCpGB t	12.45	-.23
mCap t	6.95	-.38
eghany Funds:		
TGr&Inc	29.52	-.37
&CGroN	30.67	+.06
iance Advisor Cl:		
GrAdv	30.56	-.77
iance Cap A:		
lian p	5.98	-.17
rIncA p	3.86	-.01
thF p	46.27	-1.15
AGvA p	7.50	...
GthA p	30.07	-.77
echA p	99.99	-5.17
liance Cap B:		
wthB t	34.83	-.87
rIncB p	3.80	-.02
AGB t	7.52	...
GthB p	28.28	-.72
echB t	93.98	-4.86
VldPrB t	9.32	-.08
liance Cap C:		

[illegible]	14.84	...
IncoA p	15.72	...
IntBdA p	13.21	+.02
ICAA p	31.86	-.19
NEcoA p	25.00	-.44
N PerA p	26.79	-.26
NwWrldA	22.33	-.25
SmCpA p	32.84	-.89
TxExA p	11.73	-.01
WshA p	30.06	+.11
American Funds B:		
GrwthB t	30.80	-.61
Amer Skandia B:		
JanCapB	17.84	-.56
Armada Cl I:		
EqGroI p	28.49	-.18
EqInI p	16.02	+.04
IntlEqI p	12.45	-.05
Artisan Funds:		
Intl	20.86	-.10
MidCap	25.42	-.68
Barclays Glob Inv:		
S&P 500	24.17	-.23
Baron Funds:		
Asset	52.08	-1.84
SmCap	13.62	-.30
Bear Stearns Fds:		
S&PStrA	32.28	-.55
S&PStrB t	31.66	-.53
S&PStrC	31.65	-.53
Berger Group:		
GrInc p	17.29	-.46
Growth p	15.25	-.68
NewGn p	22.95	-1.63
SCVInv	25.32	-.38
SmCoG p	5.69	-.19
Berkshire Funds:		
Focus	34.54	-2.78
Bernstein Fds:		
IntDur	12.42	+.01
DivMu	13.54	...
NYMu	13.42	...
TxMgIntV	20.01	-.05
IntVal2	20.07	-.04
EmMkts	15.15	-.18
Brandywine Fds:		
Brndywn	29.00	-.64
Burnhm p	44.46	-.77
CGM Funds:		
Mutl	22.31	+.06
Calvert Group:		
Inco p	16.26	-.01
SocialA p	31.26	-.21
TxF VT	15.30	...
Chase Vista A:		
GroInc p	38.73	+.07
Citizens Funds:		
CitCGSt	27.74	-.70
CitEGrSt	27.73	-.79
Clipper	82.20	+.38
Cohen & Steers:		

Eaton Vance Cl B:		
HiIncB t	5.76	-.02
NatlMB tf	9.53	...
TxMGB t	22.34	-.23
Eaton Vance Cl C:		
TxMGC p	21.46	-.22
Enterprise Cl A:		
GwthA p	20.93	+.04
Enterprise Cl B:		
GwthB p	20.21	+.03
Evergreen A:		
BalanA	8.84	-.05
FoundA	18.59	-.06
LgCoGA t	8.24	-.17
MunBdA	6.93	...
OmegA	29.12	-.94
SmCoGA	5.08	-.24
Evergreen B:		
FoundB	18.46	-.05
GroIncB	25.09	-.50
OmegB t	26.71	-.86
Evergreen Y:		
EqIncY	21.53	-.01
EvrgrnY	15.60	-.09
FoundY	18.60	-.06
IntlGrY	7.82	-.03
StkSelY	15.76	-.18
Excelsior Funds:		
BlendEq	44.63	-.52
ValRestr	31.48	-.82
Federated A:		
AmLdrA	24.16	-.15
CapApA	24.92	-.46
EqInA p	18.79	-.38
GrStratA	32.31	-1.02
HiInBdA	8.59	-.02
IntlEqA	22.38	-.21
IntSmCA	25.75	-.17
US GvtA	7.69	+.01
UtilFdA	10.34	-.09
Federated B:		
ALdrB t	24.01	-.15
EqIncB	18.79	-.38
HiInBB t	8.58	-.02
StrIncB	8.16	-.02
Federated F:		
GISI F	8.59	+.02
Federated Instl:		
GnmaIS	11.04	+.01
Hi Yld	6.76	-.03
IncTrS	10.08	+.01
MxCapI	27.21	-.27
MaxCpS	27.14	-.27
StockTr	32.48	-.18
Fidelity Adv Foc B:		
TechB p	24.11	-1.75
Fidelity Adv Foc T:		
TechT	24.54	-1.78
Fidelity Advisor A:		
EqGrA t	63.81	-1.36
Fidelity Advisor B:		

Biotch r	84.06	-4.83
Brokr r	54.69	-.84
Comp r	79.66	-4.92
DvCm r	46.36	-3.13
Electr r	73.53	-5.12
EngSv r	32.47	-.44
FinSv r	106.89	+.68
Health r	161.23	-.57
Softwr r	77.23	-5.29
Tech r	107.90	-7.38
Telcm r	53.30	-1.50
UtilGr r	58.32	-.69
Fidelity Spartan:		
EqIdx	47.45	-.45
500In r	92.38	-.89
GovIn	10.28	+.02
IntmMu	9.60	...
InvGrBd	10.06	+.02
MuniInc	12.35	...
StIntMu	10.02	...
TotMktIn	33.75	-.54
Fifth Third Inst:		
QualGr	21.35	-.18
First Amer Fds Y:		
EqIdxI p	25.01	-.24
FxdInc p	10.70	+.01
Intl	12.56	...
LgCapGr p	15.92	-.43
LgCpVal p	18.56	-.03
First Eagle:		
SoGenGlb	25.73	-.04
First Investors A		
BlChpA p	25.26	-.24
TxExA p	10.01	...
Firstar Fds Inst:		
EqIdx	87.58	-.84
Firsthand Funds:		
Tech Lead	35.68	-2.09
Tech Val	82.06	-5.97
Flag Investors A:		
CommA p	30.94	-.94
ValBldA p	22.96	-.14
Fortis Funds:		
CapitlA p	17.71	-.23
GrwthA p	27.31	-1.12
Frank/Temp Frnk A:		
AGE A p	2.10	-.01
BalInv p	34.87	-.09
BioDisA p	72.30	-3.57
CalGroA p	43.37	-2.08
CalInsA p	12.01	+.01
DNTCA p	25.57	-.60
FedTFA p	11.64	+.01
GwthIncA	14.94	-.41
GrwthA p	36.90	-.39
HYTFA p	10.44	...
IncomA p	2.28	...
InsTFA p	11.65	+.01
SCapGA p	38.32	-2.03
USGovA p	6.67	+.01

ICAP Funds:		
Equity	43.74	+.08
IDEX Funds A:		
JCCGlbA p	36.89	-.55
JCCGrA p	36.94	-1.52
JCCGrT	37.77	-1.55
IDEX Funds B:		
JCCGlB t	35.73	-.54
JCCGrB t	35.42	-1.47
Invesco Funds:		
BalI p	17.26	-.19
BlChGrI p	6.71	-.40
DynmI p	23.49	-1.09
EqIncI p	15.31	-.10
EuropI r	18.90	-.38
FinSvcI p	30.21	+.24
HlthScI p	66.19	-1.86
HiYldI r	5.20	-.01
LeisurI p	42.34	-.48
SelIncI p	5.85	...
SmCoGI p	15.96	-.75
Tech	65.78	-4.40
TlecmI p	39.37	-2.06
TotRtnI p	26.62	...
Invesco Funds Inst:		
Tech	66.34	-4.43
Ivy Funds:		
IntlA p	34.19	-.14
JP Morgan Funds:		
SmCoOp	14.48	-.81
Janus :		
Balncd	22.10	-.12
Enterpr	53.81	-3.43
EqInc	22.87	-.22
FlxInc	8.98	+.01
Fund	38.76	-1.04
Gl LifeSci	20.59	-.58
GlTech	21.96	-1.18
GrInc	37.30	-.61
Mercury	34.95	-1.32
Olympus	42.96	-1.63
Orion	7.25	-.44
Ovrseas	30.77	-.40
ShTmBd	2.86	...
SplSitu	19.37	-.43
StratVal	10.67	-.10
Twen	61.39	-2.34
Ventur	66.47	-3.35
WrldW	65.09	-.93
Janus Aspen Instl:		
AggGr	36.63	-2.30
Balanced	24.10	-.14
CapAppr	26.67	-.78
Growth	27.31	-.72
IntlGr	31.46	-.41
WrldwGr	37.82	-.51
JapanFd	11.73	+.07
John Hancock A:		
BondA p	14.35	+.02
[illegible]	18.75	+.14

SvInvB p	22.59	+.08
StrIncB	6.66	...
TechB p	8.55	-.57
Kaufm p	4.24	-.08
Kemper Funds A:		
BluChA	20.20	-.13
DrHiRA	33.85	+.18
GrthA	15.36	-.44
HiYldA	5.80	-.01
MuniA	9.67	...
Retire6	11.56	-.03
SmCpA	6.41	-.38
TechA	23.20	-1.47
TotRtA	10.86	-.03
USGovA	8.39	+.02
USMtgA	6.75	+.02
Kemper Funds B:		
DrmHiR	33.69	+.18
HiYldB t	5.80	...
TechB t	21.02	-1.33
TotRtB t	10.85	-.03
Kinetics Funds:		
Internet	25.81	-1.03
Kopp EGA	18.67	-1.10
Legg Mason:		
OpporTr t	10.10	-.35
SplInv p	33.76	-.70
ValTr p	62.93	-1.05
Liberty Class A:		
FedSA	10.14	+.02
FundA	9.84	-.06
StrtInA	5.89	-.01
TxEA p	12.72	+.01
Liberty Class B:		
FundB t	9.81	-.06
GrStkB	17.29	-.38
StrtInB t	5.89	-.01
US G&IB t	22.06	+.02
UtilB t	25.56	+.23
Liberty Class IT&Z:		
AcornFZ	16.02	-.25
IntlZ	23.79	-.34
Liberty-Stein Roe:		
GrthStk	49.28	-1.07
YngInv	31.13	-.58
Longleaf Partners:		
Partners	21.71	+.11
Realty	14.04	-.01
SmCap	20.85	-.21
Lord Abbett A:		
AffilA p	14.71	+.02
BdDebA p	8.17	-.02
DevGtA p	15.49	-.57
GvScA p	2.50	...
Lord Abbett B:		
AffildB p	14.74	+.02
BdDbB p	8.17	-.03
Lutheran Bro A:		
BroHi	6.25	-.02
Fund	26.45	-.31

NewDA t	20.38	-.69
RschA p	27.83	-.60
StGrA p	31.06	-1.32
TotRA p	15.37	...
UtilA p	12.77	-.06
MFS Funds B:		
MA ITB	20.22	-.16
CapOpB	18.48	-.55
EmGB t	48.38	-1.55
MIGB	17.86	-.47
MCapB	16.03	-.87
RschB	26.64	-.57
StGrB p	30.42	-1.30
TotRB t	15.36	-.01
UtilB	12.73	-.06
MFS Funds C:		
CapOpC t	18.42	-.54
MITC t	20.13	-.16
MIGC	17.80	-.47
EmGrC t	48.12	-1.54
RschC t	26.66	-.57
MPAM Funds:		
BondFd	12.63	+.02
IncmStk	11.88	-.03
LgCpStk	11.35	-.12
MdCpStk	11.03	-.26
PAIntMu	12.55	+.01
MainStay Funds A:		
CapApA	51.47	-.84
EqIdx	43.20	-.42
MainStay Funds B:		
CapApB t	49.36	-.80
ConvB t	14.62	-.21
HYldBB t	6.36	-.03
TotRtB t	25.76	-.23
ValueB t	19.22	+.05
Mairs & Power:		
Growth	107.95	+.22
Managers Funds:		
SpEq	84.32	-3.16
IntlEq	51.39	-.09
Marshall Funds:		
IntBdY	9.19	+.01
Marsico Funds:		
Focus p	18.53	-.26
Gr&Inc p	17.66	-.26
Mass Mutual Inst:		
CoreBdS	10.99	+.02
CoreEqS	16.06	-.05
IntlEqS	14.74	-.31
Mercury Funds I:		
HWIntlVal	25.38	-.06
MergerFd	17.30	+.03
Merrill Lynch A:		
BalCapA	31.45	-.06
BaVlA	34.46	-.21
FundlGA	24.30	-.25
GlAlA t	14.26	-.02
GlbTchA	16.41	-1.00
Growth	22.97	-.65

GlbValB t	15.91	-.28
GrowthB t	20.78	-.59
Merrill Lynch C:		
Fcus20C p	6.51	-.50
FdGrC t	22.85	-.23
Merrill Lynch D:		
BalCapD p	31.36	-.06
BaVlD p	34.33	-.21
FdGrD p	24.00	-.24
GlAlD p	14.23	-.02
GrowthD p	22.80	-.64
S&P500 p	16.44	-.16
USGvMtg p	9.57	+.02
Montgomery Fds:		
GrowthR	19.35	-.32
Morg St Dean Wit B:		
AgrEqB p	14.52	+.01
AmOppB	37.96	+.06
CEdBsB	11.22	-.09
DevGrB	31.10	-1.23
DivGtB	53.95	+.25
DivInB	6.78	-.02
EuroB	19.10	-.20
GlbDivB	11.29	-.03
GlobUtB	18.48	+.01
GrwthB	16.61	-.37
HlthScB	21.35	-.45
HiYldB	3.42	-.06
InfoB	22.37	-1.28
IntlB p	10.00	-.03
MktLdT	17.68	-.32
MCEquB	27.17	-1.99
SP500B	14.02	-.14
SCGroB	29.31	-2.19
StratB	20.33	-.12
ToRtnB	21.01	-.53
USGvtB	8.81	+.02
UtilB	19.94	-.05
ValAdB	36.50	-.14
Morg St Dean Wit C:		
HlthScC t	21.35	-.45
Munder Funds:		
FtTchA p	9.94	-.70
NetNetA p	38.78	-2.64
Munder Funds B:		
FtTchB p	9.87	-.69
NetNetB	38.08	-2.60
Munder Funds C/II:		
NetNetC	38.10	-2.60
Mutual Series:		
BeacnZ	14.16	-.07
DiscZ	21.58	-.05
EuropZ	17.72	...
QualfdZ	17.03	-.08
SharesZ	20.36	-.08
Nations Funds Inv A:		
NBlChA r	31.16	-.30
FocEqA t	18.00	-.23
Nations Funds Inv B:		
FocEqB t	17.68	-.23

Nch II	34.2
Northeast Investo	
Trust	8.2
Northern Funds:	
FixIn	9.8
GrEq	22.1
IntTxEx	10.0
IntGrEq	12.4
MidCpGr	17.3
SelEq	30.4
SmCpGr	13.9
Technly	34.9
Nuveen Cl A:	
GlStkA p	25.7
Nuveen Cl R:	
InMun R	10.5
IntDMBd	9.
Nvest Funds A:	
GwthA p	9.
StarA p	18.
Nvest Funds B:	
StarB t	17.
Oak Assoc Fds:	
PinOkAg	51.
RedOakT	23.
WhiteOkG	66.
Oakmark Funds I:	
IntlI	14.
OakmrkI	27.
SelectI	20.
One Group A:	
EqIndx p	30.
LgCpGA p	21.
One Group B:	
EqIndx t	30.
LgGr t	20.
One Group I:	
Bond I	10.
DvrsEqI	14.
DvrIntlI	14.
DvMdCpI	18.
EqIndxI	30.
GvBdI p	9.
IncBdI	7.
IntBondI	10.
IntTFI	10.
IntlEqI	18.
LgCpVlI	15.
LgGrI	20.
MidCpVlI	14.
MidGrI	23.
MuniIncI	9.
STBdI	10
TxFrBdI	12
Oppenheimer A:	
CpIncA p	12
CapApA p	52
ChIncA p	10
Disc p	47

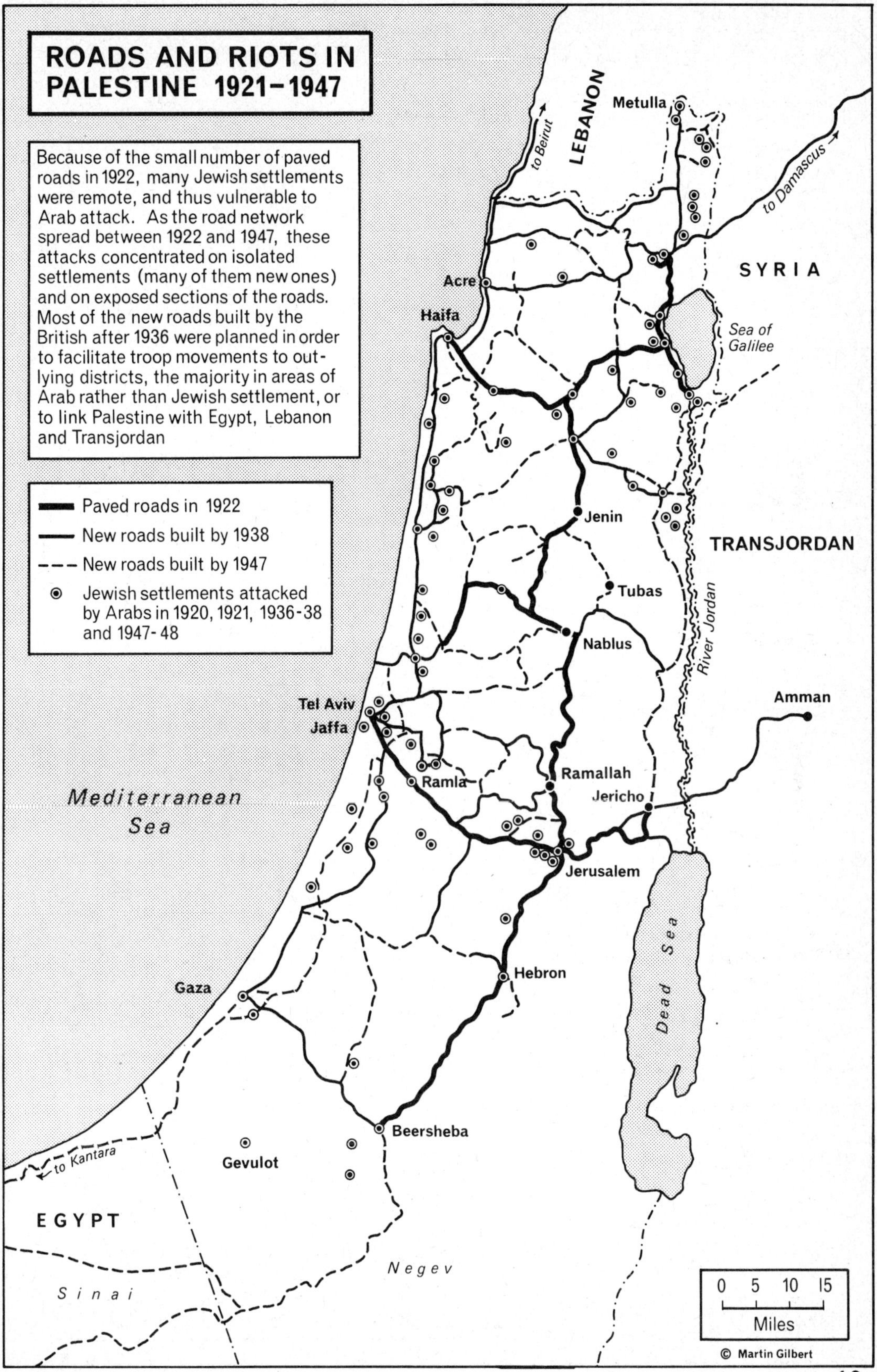

ROADS AND RIOTS IN PALESTINE 1921–1947
Because of the small number of paved roads in 1922, many Jewish settlements were remote, and thus vulnerable to Arab attack. As the road network spread between 1922 and 1947, these attacks concentrated on isolated settlements (many of them new ones) and on exposed sections of the roads. Most of the new roads built by the British after 1936 were planned in order to facilitate troop movements to outlying districts, the majority in areas of Arab rather than Jewish settlement, or to link Palestine with Egypt, Lebanon and Transjordan
Paved roads in 1922
New roads built by 1938
New roads built by 1947
Jewish settlements attacked by Arabs in 1920, 1921, 1936-38 and 1947-48
LEBANON
to Beirut
Metulla
to Damascus
SYRIA
Acre
Haifa
Sea of Galilee
Jenin
TRANSJORDAN
Tubas
Nablus
River Jordan
Tel Aviv
Jaffa
Amman
Ramla
Ramallah
Jericho
Mediterranean Sea
Jerusalem
Dead Sea
Hebron
Gaza
Beersheba
Gevulot
to Kantara
EGYPT
Negev
Sinai
0 5 10 15
Miles
© Martin Gilbert

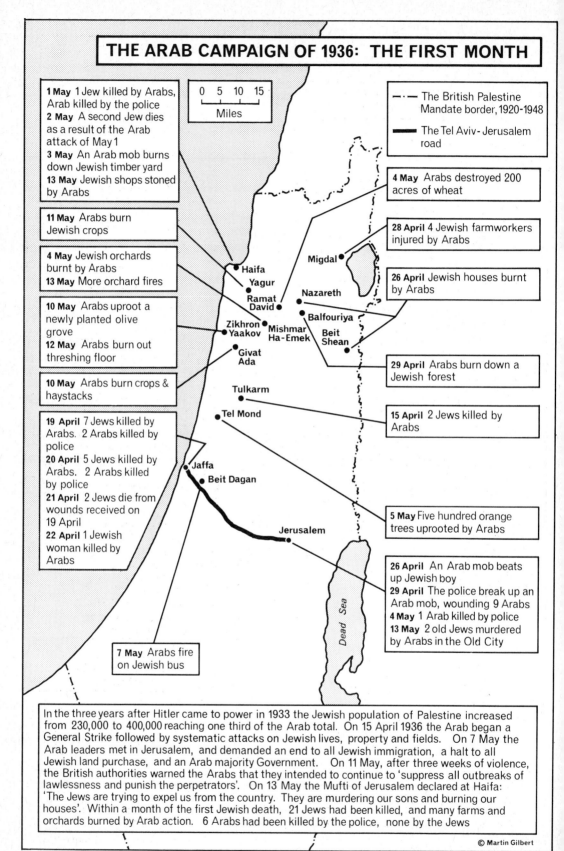

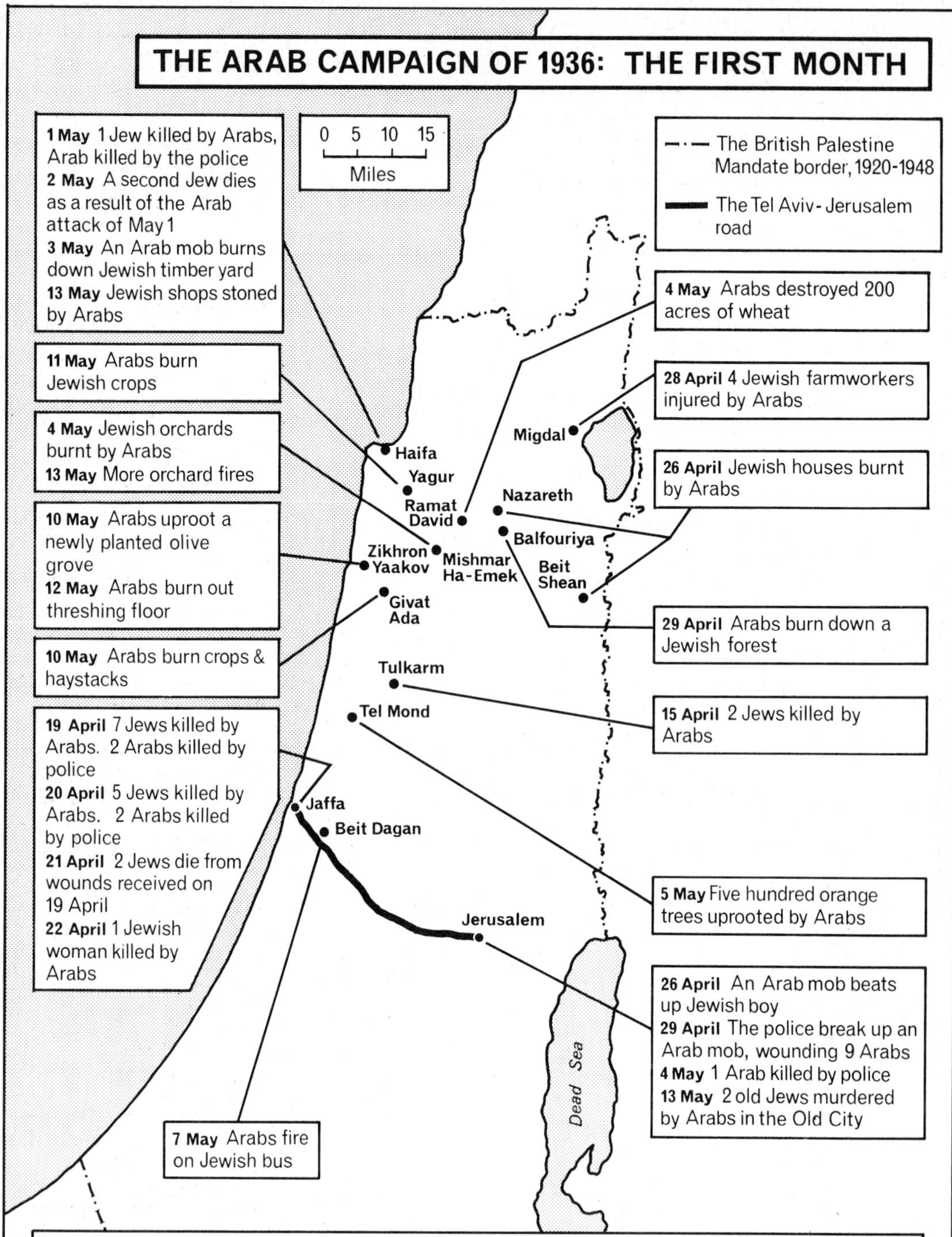
THE ARAB CAMPAIGN OF 1936: THE FIRST MONTH
0 5 10 15
Miles
The British Palestine Mandate border, 1920-1948
The Tel Aviv - Jerusalem road
1 May 1 Jew killed by Arabs, Arab killed by the police
2 May A second Jew dies as a result of the Arab attack of May 1
3 May An Arab mob burns down Jewish timber yard
13 May Jewish shops stoned by Arabs
11 May Arabs burn Jewish crops
4 May Jewish orchards burnt by Arabs
13 May More orchard fires
10 May Arabs uproot a newly planted olive grove
12 May Arabs burn out threshing floor
10 May Arabs burn crops & haystacks
19 April 7 Jews killed by Arabs. 2 Arabs killed by police
20 April 5 Jews killed by Arabs. 2 Arabs killed by police
21 April 2 Jews die from wounds received on 19 April
22 April 1 Jewish woman killed by Arabs
7 May Arabs fire on Jewish bus
4 May Arabs destroyed 200 acres of wheat
28 April 4 Jewish farmworkers injured by Arabs
26 April Jewish houses burnt by Arabs
29 April Arabs burn down a Jewish forest
15 April 2 Jews killed by Arabs
5 May Five hundred orange trees uprooted by Arabs
26 April An Arab mob beats up Jewish boy
29 April The police break up an Arab mob, wounding 9 Arabs
4 May 1 Arab killed by police
13 May 2 old Jews murdered by Arabs in the Old City
Haifa
Yagur
Ramat David
Migdal
Nazareth
Balfouriya
Zikhron Yaakov
Mishmar Ha-Emek
Beit Shean
Givat Ada
Tulkarm
Tel Mond
Jaffa
Beit Dagan
Jerusalem
Dead Sea

In the three years after Hitler came to power in 1933 the Jewish population of Palestine increased from 230,000 to 400,000 reaching one third of the Arab total. On 15 April 1936 the Arab began a General Strike followed by systematic attacks on Jewish lives, property and fields. On 7 May the Arab leaders met in Jerusalem, and demanded an end to all Jewish immigration, a halt to all Jewish land purchase, and an Arab majority Government. On 11 May, after three weeks of violence, the British authorities warned the Arabs that they intended to continue to 'suppress all outbreaks of lawlessness and punish the perpetrators'. On 13 May the Mufti of Jerusalem declared at Haifa: 'The Jews are trying to expel us from the country. They are murdering our sons and burning our houses'. Within a month of the first Jewish death, 21 Jews had been killed, and many farms and orchards burned by Arab action. 6 Arabs had been killed by the police, none by the Jews

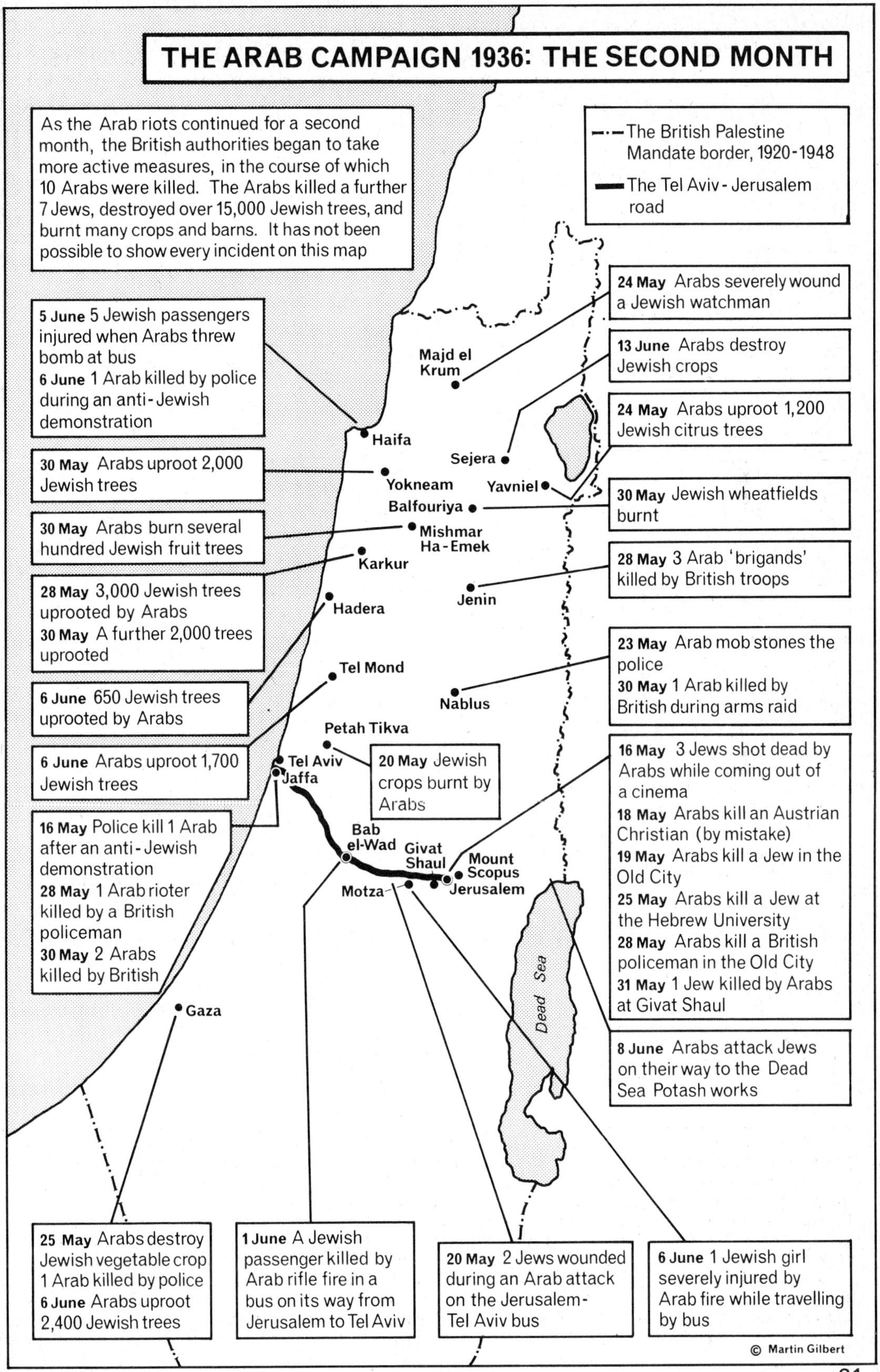
THE ARAB CAMPAIGN 1936: THE SECOND MONTH
As the Arab riots continued for a second month, the British authorities began to take more active measures, in the course of which 10 Arabs were killed. The Arabs killed a further 7 Jews, destroyed over 15,000 Jewish trees, and burnt many crops and barns. It has not been possible to show every incident on this map
The British Palestine Mandate border, 1920-1948
The Tel Aviv - Jerusalem road
24 May Arabs severely wound a Jewish watchman
13 June Arabs destroy Jewish crops
24 May Arabs uproot 1,200 Jewish citrus trees
30 May Jewish wheatfields burnt
28 May 3 Arab 'brigands' killed by British troops
23 May Arab mob stones the police
30 May 1 Arab killed by British during arms raid
16 May 3 Jews shot dead by Arabs while coming out of a cinema
18 May Arabs kill an Austrian Christian (by mistake)
19 May Arabs kill a Jew in the Old City
25 May Arabs kill a Jew at the Hebrew University
28 May Arabs kill a British policeman in the Old City
31 May 1 Jew killed by Arabs at Givat Shaul
8 June Arabs attack Jews on their way to the Dead Sea Potash works
5 June 5 Jewish passengers injured when Arabs threw bomb at bus
6 June 1 Arab killed by police during an anti-Jewish demonstration
30 May Arabs uproot 2,000 Jewish trees
30 May Arabs burn several hundred Jewish fruit trees
28 May 3,000 Jewish trees uprooted by Arabs
30 May A further 2,000 trees uprooted
6 June 650 Jewish trees uprooted by Arabs
6 June Arabs uproot 1,700 Jewish trees
16 May Police kill 1 Arab after an anti-Jewish demonstration
28 May 1 Arab rioter killed by a British policeman
30 May 2 Arabs killed by British
20 May Jewish crops burnt by Arabs
Majd el Krum
Haifa
Sejera
Yokneam
Yavniel
Balfouriya
Mishmar Ha-Emek
Karkur
Jenin
Hadera
Tel Mond
Nablus
Petah Tikva
Tel Aviv
Jaffa
Bab el-Wad
Givat Shaul
Mount Scopus
Motza
Jerusalem
Dead Sea
Gaza
25 May Arabs destroy Jewish vegetable crop
1 Arab killed by police
6 June Arabs uproot 2,400 Jewish trees
1 June A Jewish passenger killed by Arab rifle fire in a bus on its way from Jerusalem to Tel Aviv
20 May 2 Jews wounded during an Arab attack on the Jerusalem-Tel Aviv bus
6 June 1 Jewish girl severely injured by Arab fire while travelling by bus
© Martin Gilbert

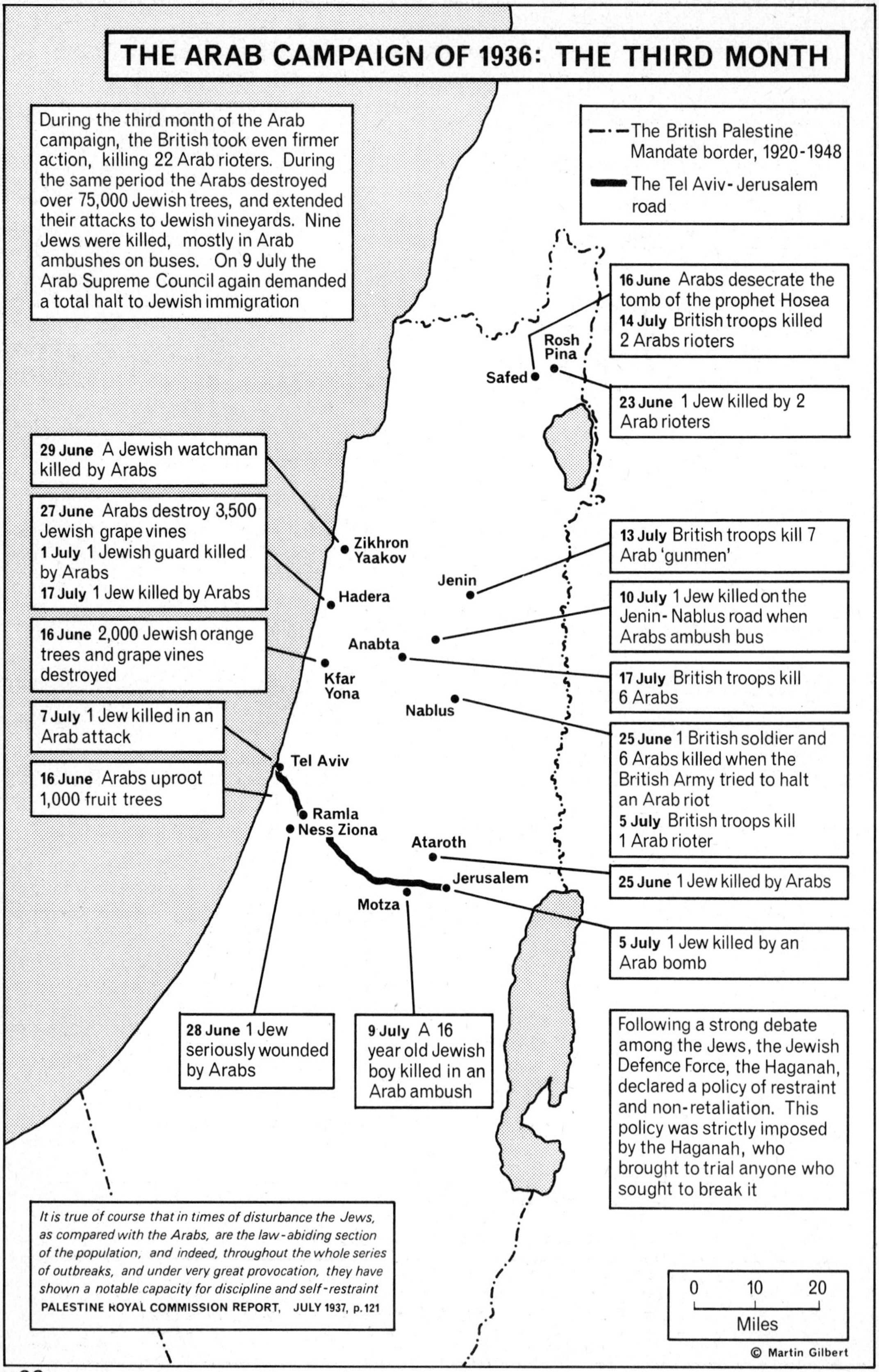
THE ARAB CAMPAIGN OF 1936: THE THIRD MONTH
During the third month of the Arab campaign, the British took even firmer action, killing 22 Arab rioters. During the same period the Arabs destroyed over 75,000 Jewish trees, and extended their attacks to Jewish vineyards. Nine Jews were killed, mostly in Arab ambushes on buses. On 9 July the Arab Supreme Council again demanded a total halt to Jewish immigration
The British Palestine Mandate border, 1920-1948
The Tel Aviv-Jerusalem road
16 June Arabs desecrate the tomb of the prophet Hosea
14 July British troops killed 2 Arabs rioters
Rosh Pina
Safed
23 June 1 Jew killed by 2 Arab rioters
29 June A Jewish watchman killed by Arabs
27 June Arabs destroy 3,500 Jewish grape vines
1 July 1 Jewish guard killed by Arabs
17 July 1 Jew killed by Arabs
Zikhron Yaakov
Hadera
Jenin
13 July British troops kill 7 Arab 'gunmen'
10 July 1 Jew killed on the Jenin-Nablus road when Arabs ambush bus
16 June 2,000 Jewish orange trees and grape vines destroyed
Anabta
Kfar Yona
Nablus
17 July British troops kill 6 Arabs
7 July 1 Jew killed in an Arab attack
Tel Aviv
16 June Arabs uproot 1,000 fruit trees
25 June 1 British soldier and 6 Arabs killed when the British Army tried to halt an Arab riot
5 July British troops kill 1 Arab rioter
Ramla
Ness Ziona
Ataroth
Jerusalem
Motza
25 June 1 Jew killed by Arabs
5 July 1 Jew killed by an Arab bomb
28 June 1 Jew seriously wounded by Arabs
9 July A 16 year old Jewish boy killed in an Arab ambush
Following a strong debate among the Jews, the Jewish Defence Force, the Haganah, declared a policy of restraint and non-retaliation. This policy was strictly imposed by the Haganah, who brought to trial anyone who sought to break it
It is true of course that in times of disturbance the Jews, as compared with the Arabs, are the law-abiding section of the population, and indeed, throughout the whole series of outbreaks, and under very great provocation, they have shown a notable capacity for discipline and self-restraint
PALESTINE ROYAL COMMISSION REPORT, JULY 1937, p.121
0 10 20
Miles
© Martin Gilbert

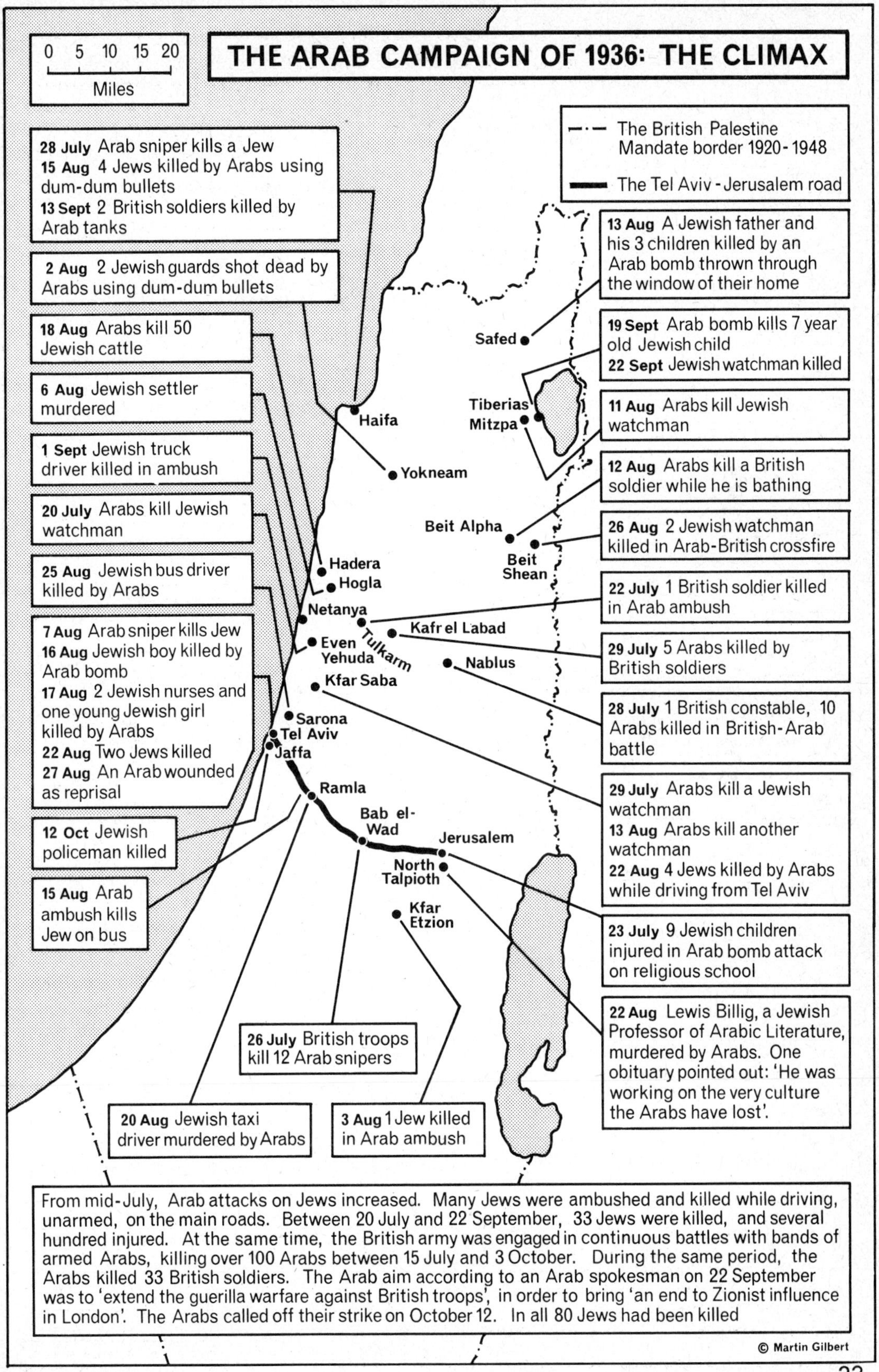
THE ARAB CAMPAIGN OF 1936: THE CLIMAX
0 5 10 15 20
Miles
The British Palestine Mandate border 1920-1948
The Tel Aviv - Jerusalem road
28 July Arab sniper kills a Jew
15 Aug 4 Jews killed by Arabs using dum-dum bullets
13 Sept 2 British soldiers killed by Arab tanks
2 Aug 2 Jewish guards shot dead by Arabs using dum-dum bullets
18 Aug Arabs kill 50 Jewish cattle
6 Aug Jewish settler murdered
1 Sept Jewish truck driver killed in ambush
20 July Arabs kill Jewish watchman
25 Aug Jewish bus driver killed by Arabs
7 Aug Arab sniper kills Jew
16 Aug Jewish boy killed by Arab bomb
17 Aug 2 Jewish nurses and one young Jewish girl killed by Arabs
22 Aug Two Jews killed
27 Aug An Arab wounded as reprisal
12 Oct Jewish policeman killed
15 Aug Arab ambush kills Jew on bus
13 Aug A Jewish father and his 3 children killed by an Arab bomb thrown through the window of their home
19 Sept Arab bomb kills 7 year old Jewish child
22 Sept Jewish watchman killed
11 Aug Arabs kill Jewish watchman
12 Aug Arabs kill a British soldier while he is bathing
26 Aug 2 Jewish watchman killed in Arab-British crossfire
22 July 1 British soldier killed in Arab ambush
29 July 5 Arabs killed by British soldiers
28 July 1 British constable, 10 Arabs killed in British-Arab battle
29 July Arabs kill a Jewish watchman
13 Aug Arabs kill another watchman
22 Aug 4 Jews killed by Arabs while driving from Tel Aviv
23 July 9 Jewish children injured in Arab bomb attack on religious school
22 Aug Lewis Billig, a Jewish Professor of Arabic Literature, murdered by Arabs. One obituary pointed out: 'He was working on the very culture the Arabs have lost'.
26 July British troops kill 12 Arab snipers
20 Aug Jewish taxi driver murdered by Arabs
3 Aug 1 Jew killed in Arab ambush
Safed
Tiberias
Mitzpa
Haifa
Yokneam
Beit Alpha
Beit Shean
Hadera
Hogla
Netanya
Kafr el Labad
Even Yehuda
Tulkarm
Nablus
Kfar Saba
Sarona
Tel Aviv
Jaffa
Ramla
Bab el-Wad
Jerusalem
North Talpioth
Kfar Etzion
From mid-July, Arab attacks on Jews increased. Many Jews were ambushed and killed while driving, unarmed, on the main roads. Between 20 July and 22 September, 33 Jews were killed, and several hundred injured. At the same time, the British army was engaged in continuous battles with bands of armed Arabs, killing over 100 Arabs between 15 July and 3 October. During the same period, the Arabs killed 33 British soldiers. The Arab aim according to an Arab spokesman on 22 September was to 'extend the guerilla warfare against British troops', in order to bring 'an end to Zionist influence in London'. The Arabs called off their strike on October 12. In all 80 Jews had been killed
© Martin Gilbert

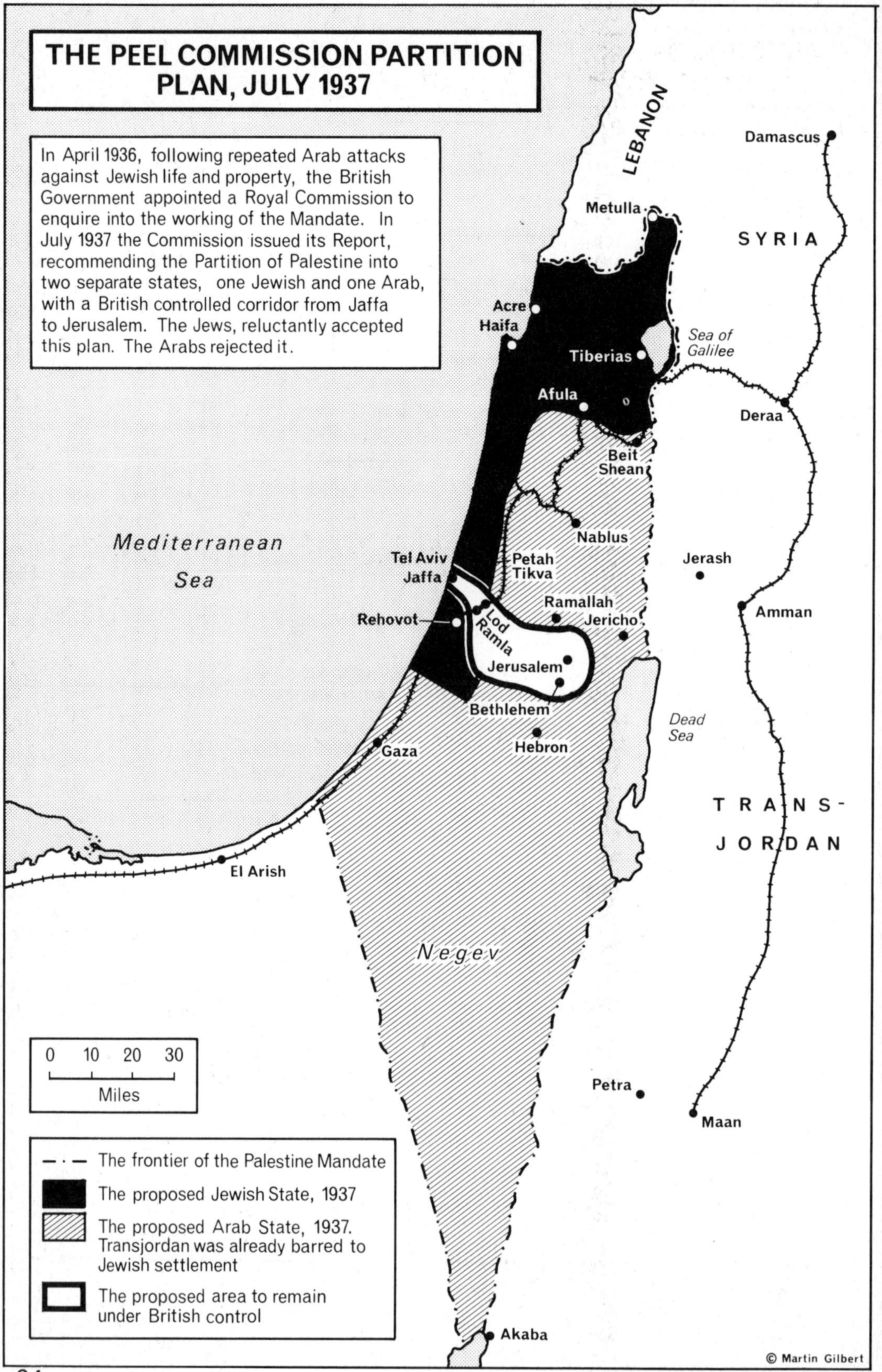
THE PEEL COMMISSION PARTITION PLAN, JULY 1937
In April 1936, following repeated Arab attacks against Jewish life and property, the British Government appointed a Royal Commission to enquire into the working of the Mandate. In July 1937 the Commission issued its Report, recommending the Partition of Palestine into two separate states, one Jewish and one Arab, with a British controlled corridor from Jaffa to Jerusalem. The Jews, reluctantly accepted this plan. The Arabs rejected it.
LEBANON
Damascus
Metulla
SYRIA
Acre
Haifa
Tiberias
Sea of Galilee
Afula
Deraa
Beit Shean
Nablus
Mediterranean Sea
Tel Aviv
Jaffa
Petah Tikva
Jerash
Amman
Ramallah
Jericho
Rehovot
Lod
Ramla
Jerusalem
Bethlehem
Dead Sea
Gaza
Hebron
TRANS-JORDAN
El Arish
Negev
0 10 20 30
Miles
Petra
Maan
The frontier of the Palestine Mandate
The proposed Jewish State, 1937
The proposed Arab State, 1937. Transjordan was already barred to Jewish settlement
The proposed area to remain under British control
Akaba
© Martin Gilbert

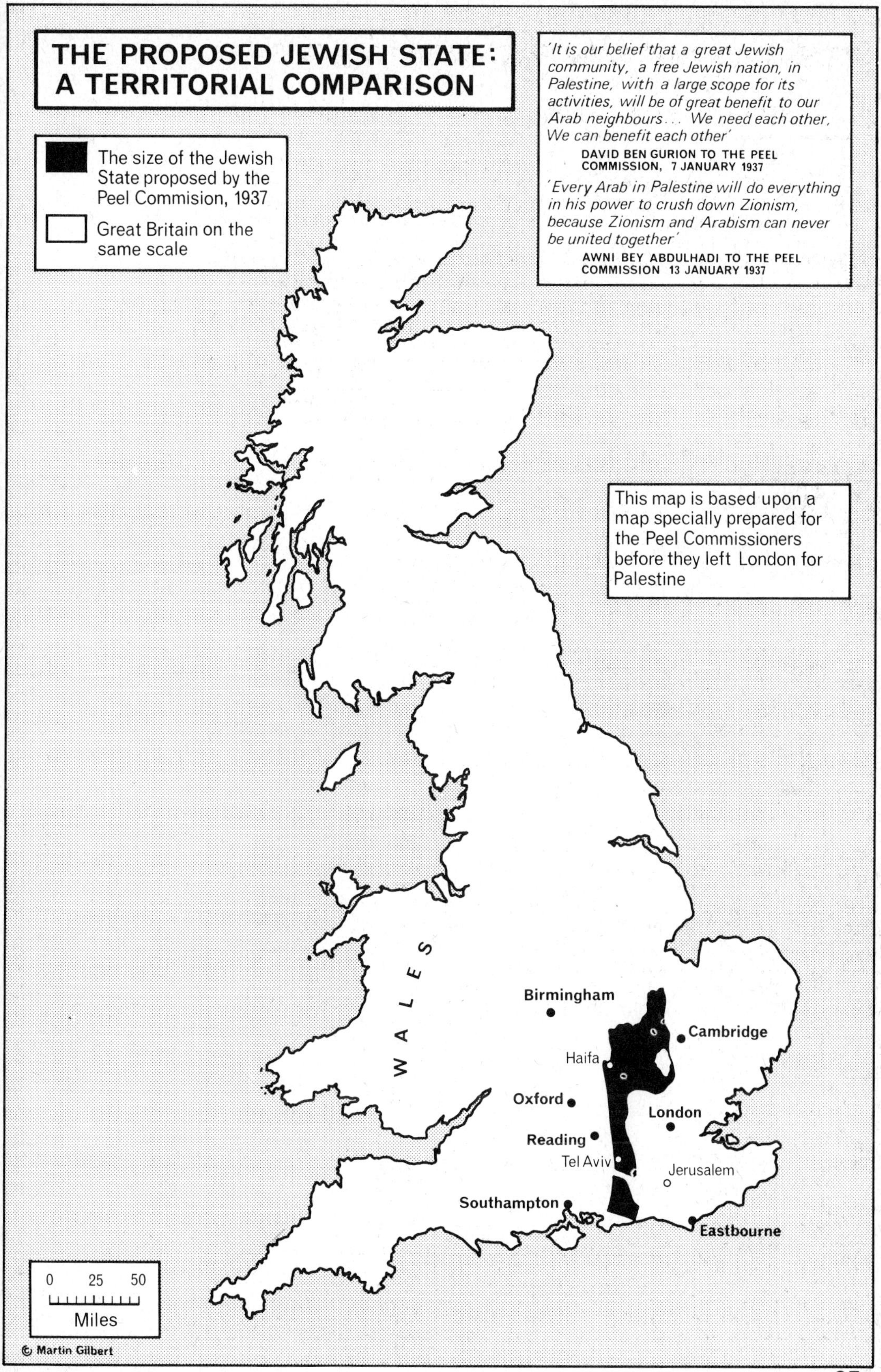
THE PROPOSED JEWISH STATE: A TERRITORIAL COMPARISON
The size of the Jewish State proposed by the Peel Commision, 1937
Great Britain on the same scale
'It is our belief that a great Jewish community, a free Jewish nation, in Palestine, with a large scope for its activities, will be of great benefit to our Arab neighbours... We need each other, We can benefit each other'
DAVID BEN GURION TO THE PEEL COMMISSION, 7 JANUARY 1937
'Every Arab in Palestine will do everything in his power to crush down Zionism, because Zionism and Arabism can never be united together'
AWNI BEY ABDULHADI TO THE PEEL COMMISSION 13 JANUARY 1937
This map is based upon a map specially prepared for the Peel Commissioners before they left London for Palestine
WALES
Birmingham
Cambridge
Haifa
Oxford
London
Reading
Tel Aviv
Jerusalem
Southampton
Eastbourne
0 25 50
Miles
© Martin Gilbert

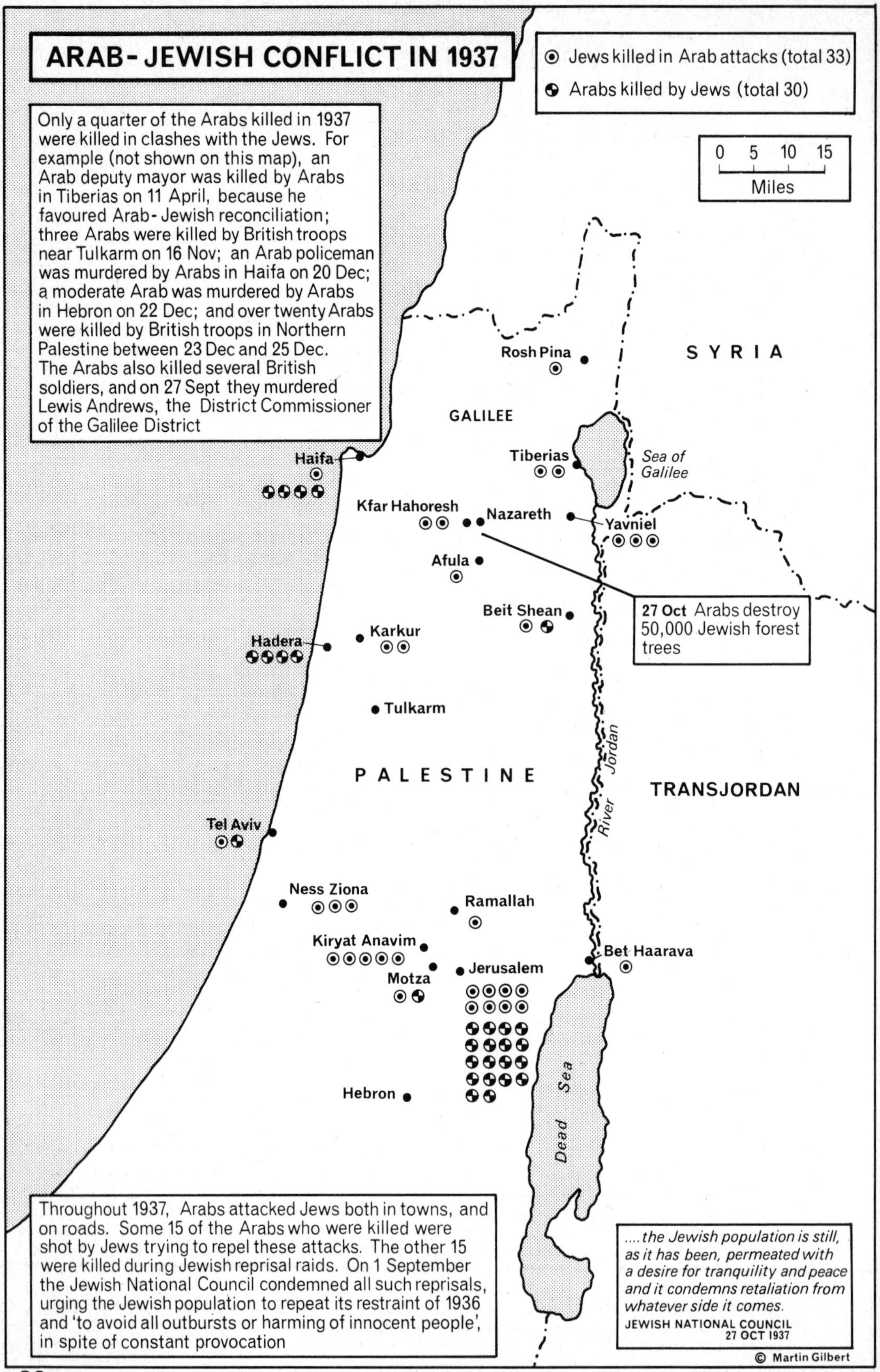

ARAB-JEWISH CONFLICT IN 1937
Jews killed in Arab attacks (total 33)
Arabs killed by Jews (total 30)
0 5 10 15
Miles
Only a quarter of the Arabs killed in 1937 were killed in clashes with the Jews. For example (not shown on this map), an Arab deputy mayor was killed by Arabs in Tiberias on 11 April, because he favoured Arab-Jewish reconciliation; three Arabs were killed by British troops near Tulkarm on 16 Nov; an Arab policeman was murdered by Arabs in Haifa on 20 Dec; a moderate Arab was murdered by Arabs in Hebron on 22 Dec; and over twenty Arabs were killed by British troops in Northern Palestine between 23 Dec and 25 Dec. The Arabs also killed several British soldiers, and on 27 Sept they murdered Lewis Andrews, the District Commissioner of the Galilee District
Rosh Pina
SYRIA
GALILEE
Haifa
Tiberias
Sea of Galilee
Kfar Hahoresh
Nazareth
Yavniel
Afula
27 Oct Arabs destroy 50,000 Jewish forest trees
Beit Shean
Karkur
Hadera
Tulkarm
PALESTINE
River Jordan
TRANSJORDAN
Tel Aviv
Ness Ziona
Ramallah
Kiryat Anavim
Bet Haarava
Motza
Jerusalem
Hebron
Dead Sea
Throughout 1937, Arabs attacked Jews both in towns, and on roads. Some 15 of the Arabs who were killed were shot by Jews trying to repel these attacks. The other 15 were killed during Jewish reprisal raids. On 1 September the Jewish National Council condemned all such reprisals, urging the Jewish population to repeat its restraint of 1936 and 'to avoid all outbursts or harming of innocent people', in spite of constant provocation
....the Jewish population is still, as it has been, permeated with a desire for tranquility and peace and it condemns retaliation from whatever side it comes.
JEWISH NATIONAL COUNCIL 27 OCT 1937
© Martin Gilbert

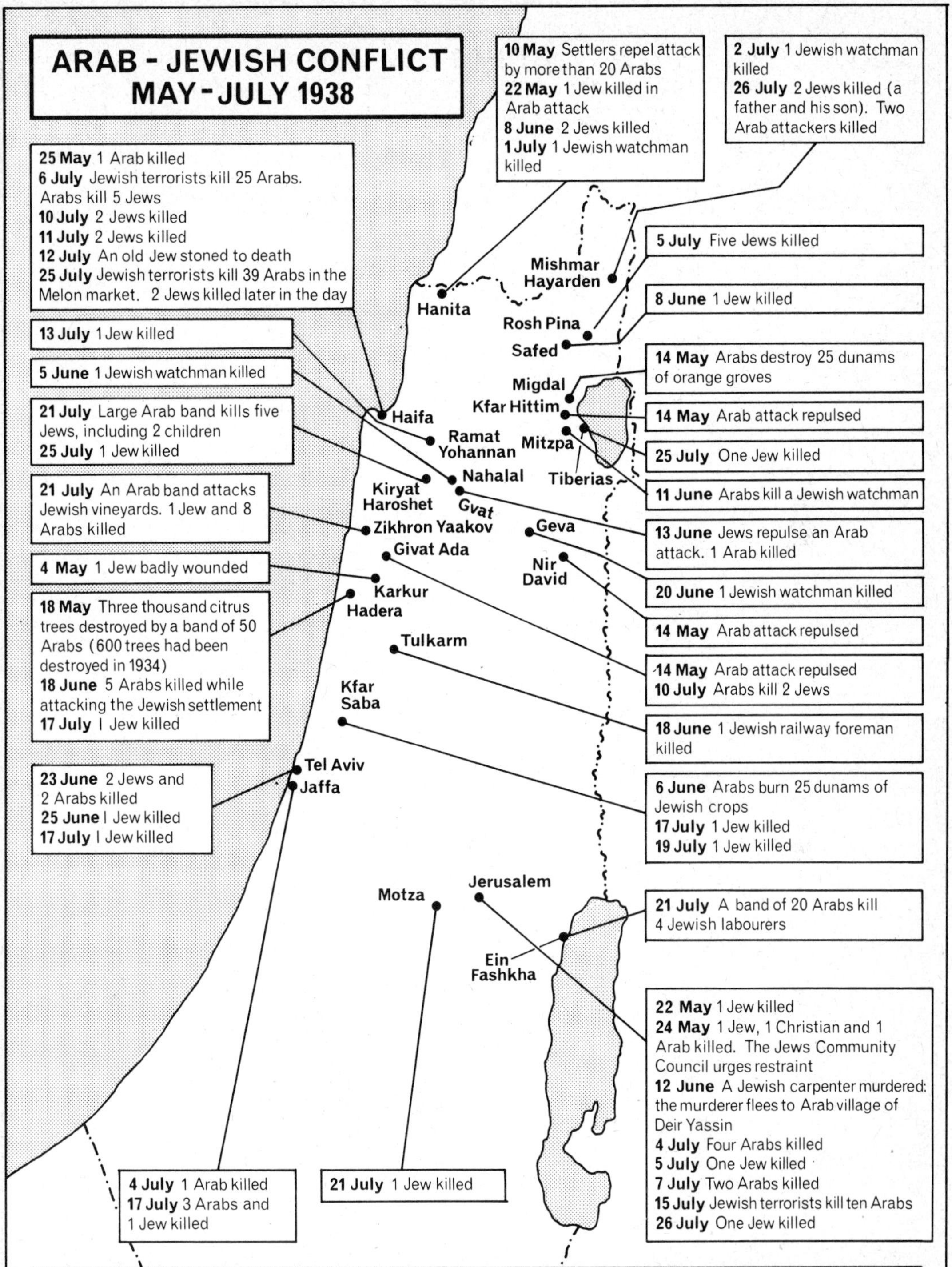
ARAB - JEWISH CONFLICT
MAY - JULY 1938
10 May Settlers repel attack by more than 20 Arabs
22 May 1 Jew killed in Arab attack
8 June 2 Jews killed
1 July 1 Jewish watchman killed
2 July 1 Jewish watchman killed
26 July 2 Jews killed (a father and his son). Two Arab attackers killed
25 May 1 Arab killed
6 July Jewish terrorists kill 25 Arabs. Arabs kill 5 Jews
10 July 2 Jews killed
11 July 2 Jews killed
12 July An old Jew stoned to death
25 July Jewish terrorists kill 39 Arabs in the Melon market. 2 Jews killed later in the day
5 July Five Jews killed
8 June 1 Jew killed
13 July 1 Jew killed
5 June 1 Jewish watchman killed
14 May Arabs destroy 25 dunams of orange groves
21 July Large Arab band kills five Jews, including 2 children
25 July 1 Jew killed
14 May Arab attack repulsed
25 July One Jew killed
21 July An Arab band attacks Jewish vineyards. 1 Jew and 8 Arabs killed
11 June Arabs kill a Jewish watchman
13 June Jews repulse an Arab attack. 1 Arab killed
4 May 1 Jew badly wounded
20 June 1 Jewish watchman killed
18 May Three thousand citrus trees destroyed by a band of 50 Arabs (600 trees had been destroyed in 1934)
18 June 5 Arabs killed while attacking the Jewish settlement
17 July 1 Jew killed
14 May Arab attack repulsed
14 May Arab attack repulsed
10 July Arabs kill 2 Jews
18 June 1 Jewish railway foreman killed
23 June 2 Jews and 2 Arabs killed
25 June 1 Jew killed
17 July 1 Jew killed
6 June Arabs burn 25 dunams of Jewish crops
17 July 1 Jew killed
19 July 1 Jew killed
21 July A band of 20 Arabs kill 4 Jewish labourers
22 May 1 Jew killed
24 May 1 Jew, 1 Christian and 1 Arab killed. The Jews Community Council urges restraint
12 June A Jewish carpenter murdered: the murderer flees to Arab village of Deir Yassin
4 July Four Arabs killed
5 July One Jew killed
7 July Two Arabs killed
15 July Jewish terrorists kill ten Arabs
26 July One Jew killed
4 July 1 Arab killed
17 July 3 Arabs and 1 Jew killed
21 July 1 Jew killed
Mishmar Hayarden
Hanita
Rosh Pina
Safed
Migdal
Kfar Hittim
Haifa
Ramat Yohannan
Mitzpa
Tiberias
Nahalal
Kiryat Haroshet
Gvat
Zikhron Yaakov
Geva
Givat Ada
Nir David
Karkur
Hadera
Tulkarm
Kfar Saba
Tel Aviv
Jaffa
Motza
Jerusalem
Ein Fashkha

The Arab campaign continued throughout 1938 and 1939. Partly intended as a protest against Britain for allowing Jewish immigration, its main efforts were aimed against Jewish settlements, and Jewish road traffic. At this time a small group of Jewish extremists began to commit regular terrorist acts. This map shows the principal Arab-Jewish incidents in the three months between May and July 1938, when 59 Jews were killed by Arabs, and 102 Arabs by Jews. Most of the Arabs were killed in three bomb attacks by Jewish terrorists. Most of the Jews were killed singly, during Arab attacks on scattered and isolated settlements. The frequent clashes between Arab bands and British troops are not shown; nor are the many occasions on which Arabs were killed by Arabs

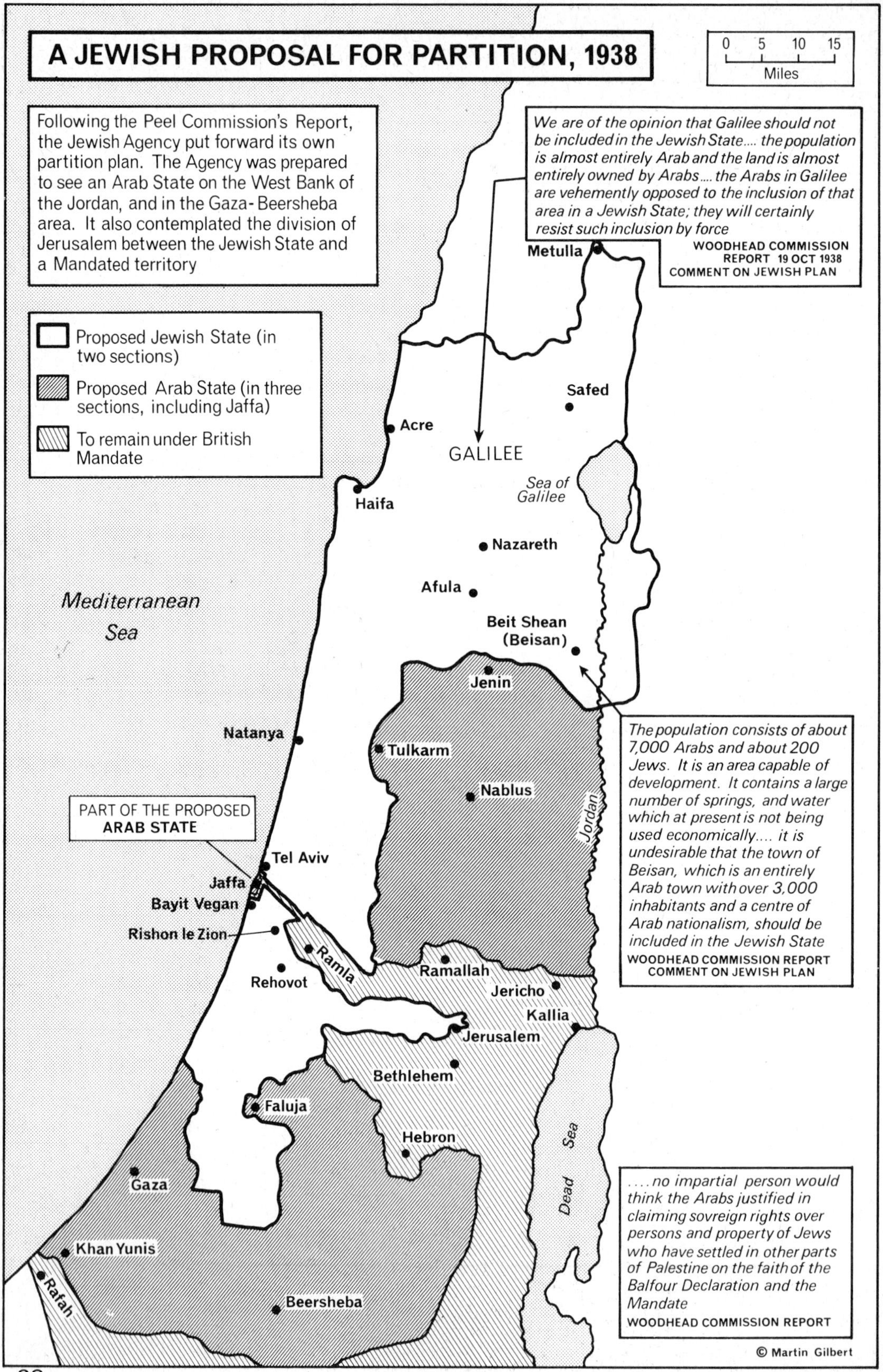
A JEWISH PROPOSAL FOR PARTITION, 1938
0 5 10 15
Miles
Following the Peel Commission's Report, the Jewish Agency put forward its own partition plan. The Agency was prepared to see an Arab State on the West Bank of the Jordan, and in the Gaza-Beersheba area. It also contemplated the division of Jerusalem between the Jewish State and a Mandated territory
We are of the opinion that Galilee should not be included in the Jewish State.... the population is almost entirely Arab and the land is almost entirely owned by Arabs.... the Arabs in Galilee are vehemently opposed to the inclusion of that area in a Jewish State; they will certainly resist such inclusion by force
WOODHEAD COMMISSION REPORT 19 OCT 1938 COMMENT ON JEWISH PLAN
Proposed Jewish State (in two sections)
Proposed Arab State (in three sections, including Jaffa)
To remain under British Mandate
Metulla
Safed
Acre
GALILEE
Sea of Galilee
Haifa
Nazareth
Afula
Mediterranean Sea
Beit Shean (Beisan)
Jenin
Natanya
Tulkarm
Nablus
Jordan
PART OF THE PROPOSED ARAB STATE
Tel Aviv
Jaffa
Bayit Vegan
Rishon le Zion
Ramla
Rehovot
Ramallah
Jericho
Kallia
Jerusalem
Bethlehem
Faluja
Hebron
Dead Sea
Gaza
Khan Yunis
Rafah
Beersheba
The population consists of about 7,000 Arabs and about 200 Jews. It is an area capable of development. It contains a large number of springs, and water which at present is not being used economically.... it is undesirable that the town of Beisan, which is an entirely Arab town with over 3,000 inhabitants and a centre of Arab nationalism, should be included in the Jewish State
WOODHEAD COMMISSION REPORT COMMENT ON JEWISH PLAN
....no impartial person would think the Arabs justified in claiming sovreign rights over persons and property of Jews who have settled in other parts of Palestine on the faith of the Balfour Declaration and the Mandate
WOODHEAD COMMISSION REPORT
© Martin Gilbert

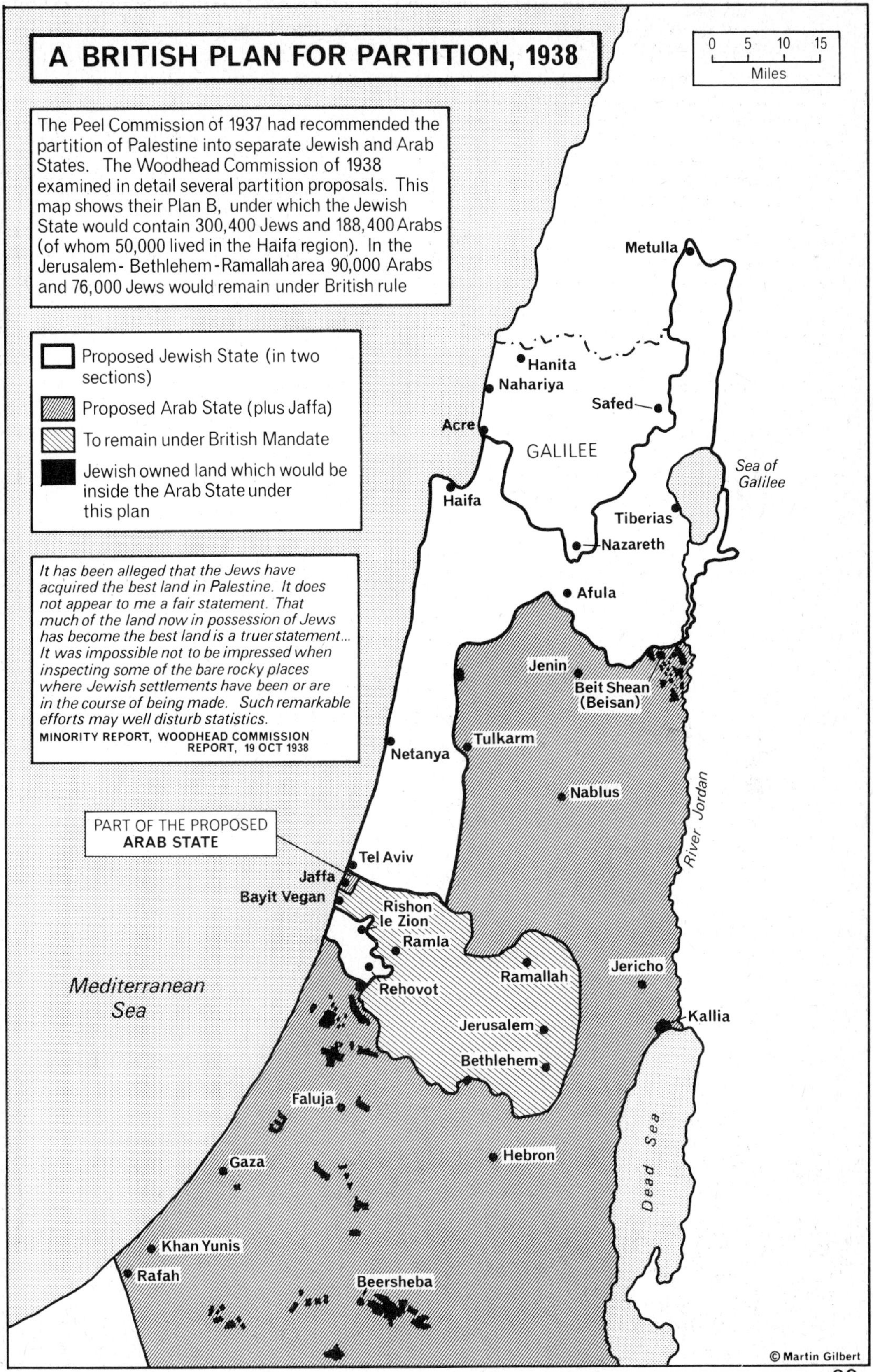
A BRITISH PLAN FOR PARTITION, 1938
0 5 10 15
Miles
The Peel Commission of 1937 had recommended the partition of Palestine into separate Jewish and Arab States. The Woodhead Commission of 1938 examined in detail several partition proposals. This map shows their Plan B, under which the Jewish State would contain 300,400 Jews and 188,400 Arabs (of whom 50,000 lived in the Haifa region). In the Jerusalem - Bethlehem - Ramallah area 90,000 Arabs and 76,000 Jews would remain under British rule
Proposed Jewish State (in two sections)
Proposed Arab State (plus Jaffa)
To remain under British Mandate
Jewish owned land which would be inside the Arab State under this plan
It has been alleged that the Jews have acquired the best land in Palestine. It does not appear to me a fair statement. That much of the land now in possession of Jews has become the best land is a truer statement... It was impossible not to be impressed when inspecting some of the bare rocky places where Jewish settlements have been or are in the course of being made. Such remarkable efforts may well disturb statistics.
MINORITY REPORT, WOODHEAD COMMISSION REPORT, 19 OCT 1938
PART OF THE PROPOSED ARAB STATE
Metulla
Hanita
Nahariya
Safed
Acre
GALILEE
Sea of Galilee
Haifa
Tiberias
Nazareth
Afula
Jenin
Beit Shean (Beisan)
Tulkarm
Netanya
Nablus
River Jordan
Tel Aviv
Jaffa
Bayit Vegan
Rishon le Zion
Ramla
Ramallah
Jericho
Rehovot
Mediterranean Sea
Kallia
Jerusalem
Bethlehem
Faluja
Gaza
Hebron
Dead Sea
Khan Yunis
Rafah
Beersheba
© Martin Gilbert

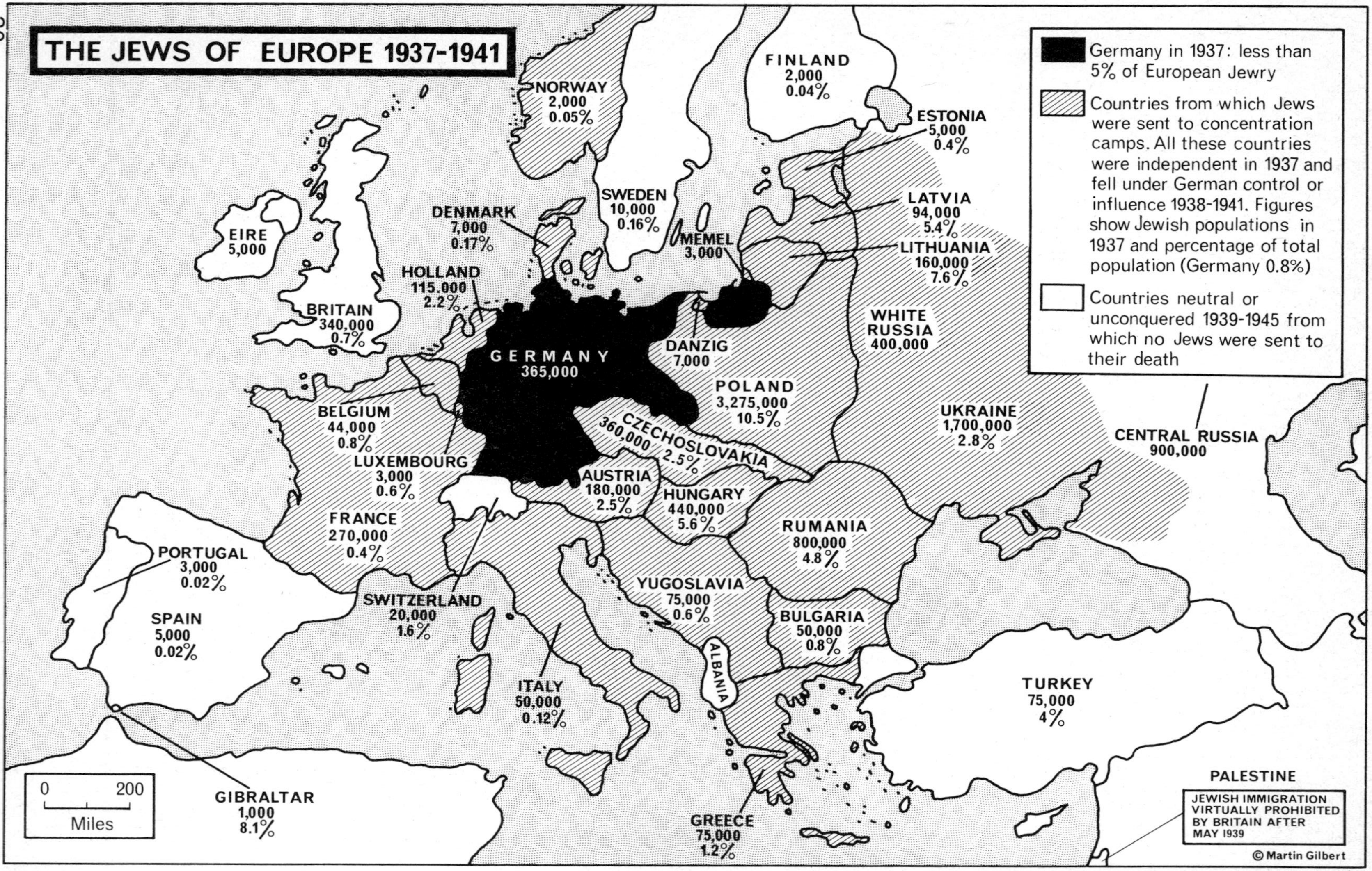
THE JEWS OF EUROPE 1937-1941
Germany in 1937: less than 5% of European Jewry
Countries from which Jews were sent to concentration camps. All these countries were independent in 1937 and fell under German control or influence 1938-1941. Figures show Jewish populations in 1937 and percentage of total population (Germany 0.8%)
Countries neutral or unconquered 1939-1945 from which no Jews were sent to their death
NORWAY 2,000 0.05%
FINLAND 2,000 0.04%
SWEDEN 10,000 0.16%
ESTONIA 5,000 0.4%
LATVIA 94,000 5.4%
LITHUANIA 160,000 7.6%
MEMEL 3,000
DENMARK 7,000 0.17%
EIRE 5,000
HOLLAND 115,000 2.2%
BRITAIN 340,000 0.7%
GERMANY 365,000
DANZIG 7,000
WHITE RUSSIA 400,000
POLAND 3,275,000 10.5%
BELGIUM 44,000 0.8%
CZECHOSLOVAKIA 360,000 2.5%
UKRAINE 1,700,000 2.8%
CENTRAL RUSSIA 900,000
LUXEMBOURG 3,000 0.6%
AUSTRIA 180,000 2.5%
HUNGARY 440,000 5.6%
FRANCE 270,000 0.4%
RUMANIA 800,000 4.8%
PORTUGAL 3,000 0.02%
YUGOSLAVIA 75,000 0.6%
SWITZERLAND 20,000 1.6%
BULGARIA 50,000 0.8%
SPAIN 5,000 0.02%
ALBANIA
TURKEY 75,000 4%
ITALY 50,000 0.12%
GIBRALTAR 1,000 8.1%
GREECE 75,000 1.2%
PALESTINE
JEWISH IMMIGRATION VIRTUALLY PROHIBITED BY BRITAIN AFTER MAY 1939
0 200 Miles
© Martin Gilbert

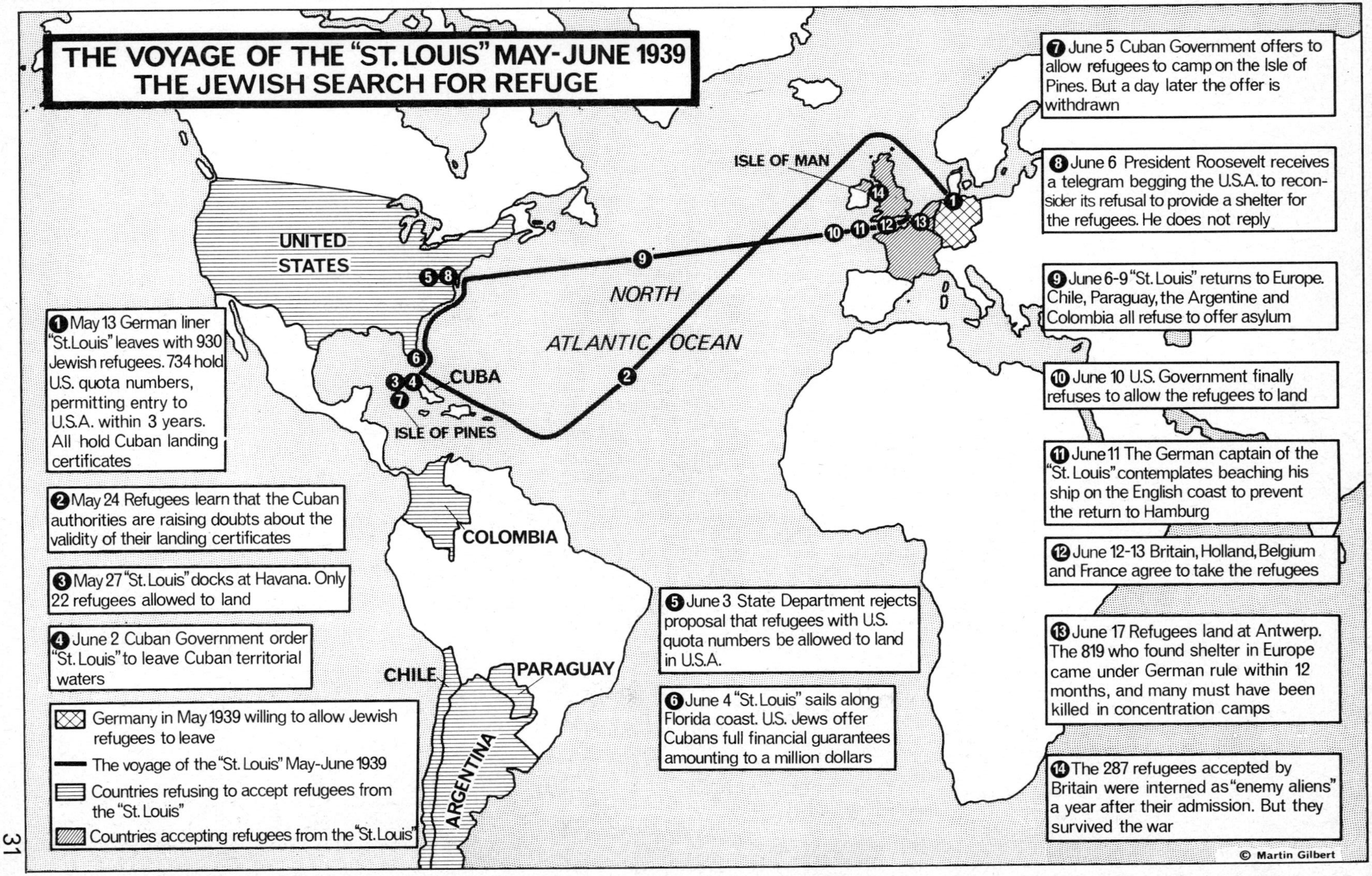
THE VOYAGE OF THE "ST. LOUIS" MAY-JUNE 1939
THE JEWISH SEARCH FOR REFUGE
UNITED STATES
CUBA
ISLE OF PINES
NORTH ATLANTIC OCEAN
ISLE OF MAN
COLOMBIA
CHILE
PARAGUAY
ARGENTINA
1 May 13 German liner "St.Louis" leaves with 930 Jewish refugees. 734 hold U.S. quota numbers, permitting entry to U.S.A. within 3 years. All hold Cuban landing certificates
2 May 24 Refugees learn that the Cuban authorities are raising doubts about the validity of their landing certificates
3 May 27 "St. Louis" docks at Havana. Only 22 refugees allowed to land
4 June 2 Cuban Government order "St. Louis" to leave Cuban territorial waters
5 June 3 State Department rejects proposal that refugees with U.S. quota numbers be allowed to land in U.S.A.
6 June 4 "St. Louis" sails along Florida coast. U.S. Jews offer Cubans full financial guarantees amounting to a million dollars
7 June 5 Cuban Government offers to allow refugees to camp on the Isle of Pines. But a day later the offer is withdrawn
8 June 6 President Roosevelt receives a telegram begging the U.S.A. to reconsider its refusal to provide a shelter for the refugees. He does not reply
9 June 6-9 "St. Louis" returns to Europe. Chile, Paraguay, the Argentine and Colombia all refuse to offer asylum
10 June 10 U.S. Government finally refuses to allow the refugees to land
11 June 11 The German captain of the "St. Louis" contemplates beaching his ship on the English coast to prevent the return to Hamburg
12 June 12-13 Britain, Holland, Belgium and France agree to take the refugees
13 June 17 Refugees land at Antwerp. The 819 who found shelter in Europe came under German rule within 12 months, and many must have been killed in concentration camps
14 The 287 refugees accepted by Britain were interned as "enemy aliens" a year after their admission. But they survived the war
Germany in May 1939 willing to allow Jewish refugees to leave
The voyage of the "St. Louis" May-June 1939
Countries refusing to accept refugees from the "St. Louis"
Countries accepting refugees from the "St. Louis"
© Martin Gilbert

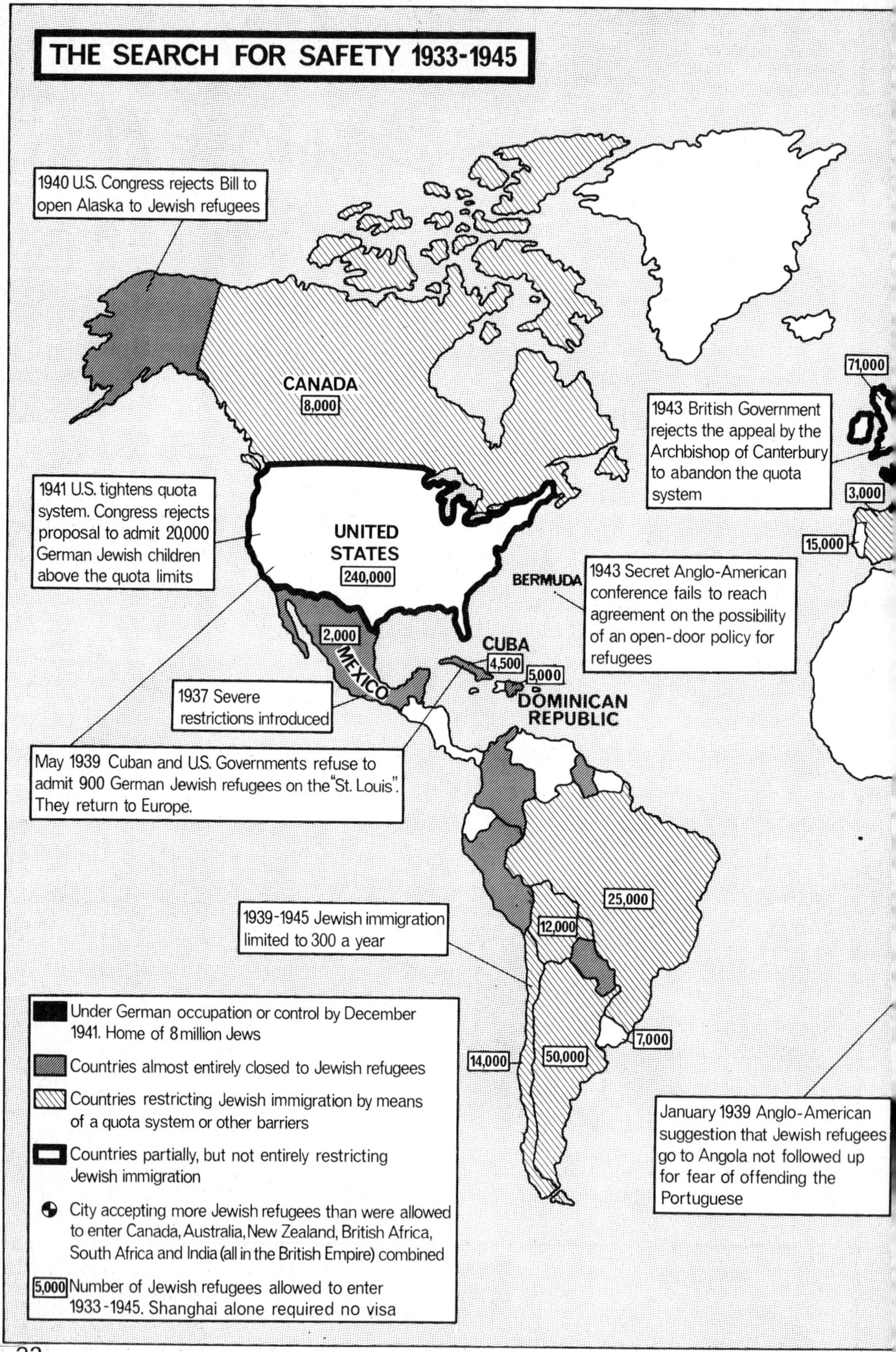
THE SEARCH FOR SAFETY 1933-1945
1940 U.S. Congress rejects Bill to open Alaska to Jewish refugees
CANADA
8,000
1943 British Government rejects the appeal by the Archbishop of Canterbury to abandon the quota system
71,000
3,000
15,000
1941 U.S. tightens quota system. Congress rejects proposal to admit 20,000 German Jewish children above the quota limits
UNITED STATES
240,000
BERMUDA
1943 Secret Anglo-American conference fails to reach agreement on the possibility of an open-door policy for refugees
2,000
MEXICO
CUBA
4,500
5,000
DOMINICAN REPUBLIC
1937 Severe restrictions introduced
May 1939 Cuban and U.S. Governments refuse to admit 900 German Jewish refugees on the "St. Louis". They return to Europe.
25,000
12,000
1939-1945 Jewish immigration limited to 300 a year
7,000
14,000
50,000
January 1939 Anglo-American suggestion that Jewish refugees go to Angola not followed up for fear of offending the Portuguese
Under German occupation or control by December 1941. Home of 8 million Jews
Countries almost entirely closed to Jewish refugees
Countries restricting Jewish immigration by means of a quota system or other barriers
Countries partially, but not entirely restricting Jewish immigration
City accepting more Jewish refugees than were allowed to enter Canada, Australia, New Zealand, British Africa, South Africa and India (all in the British Empire) combined
5,000 Number of Jewish refugees allowed to enter 1933-1945. Shanghai alone required no visa

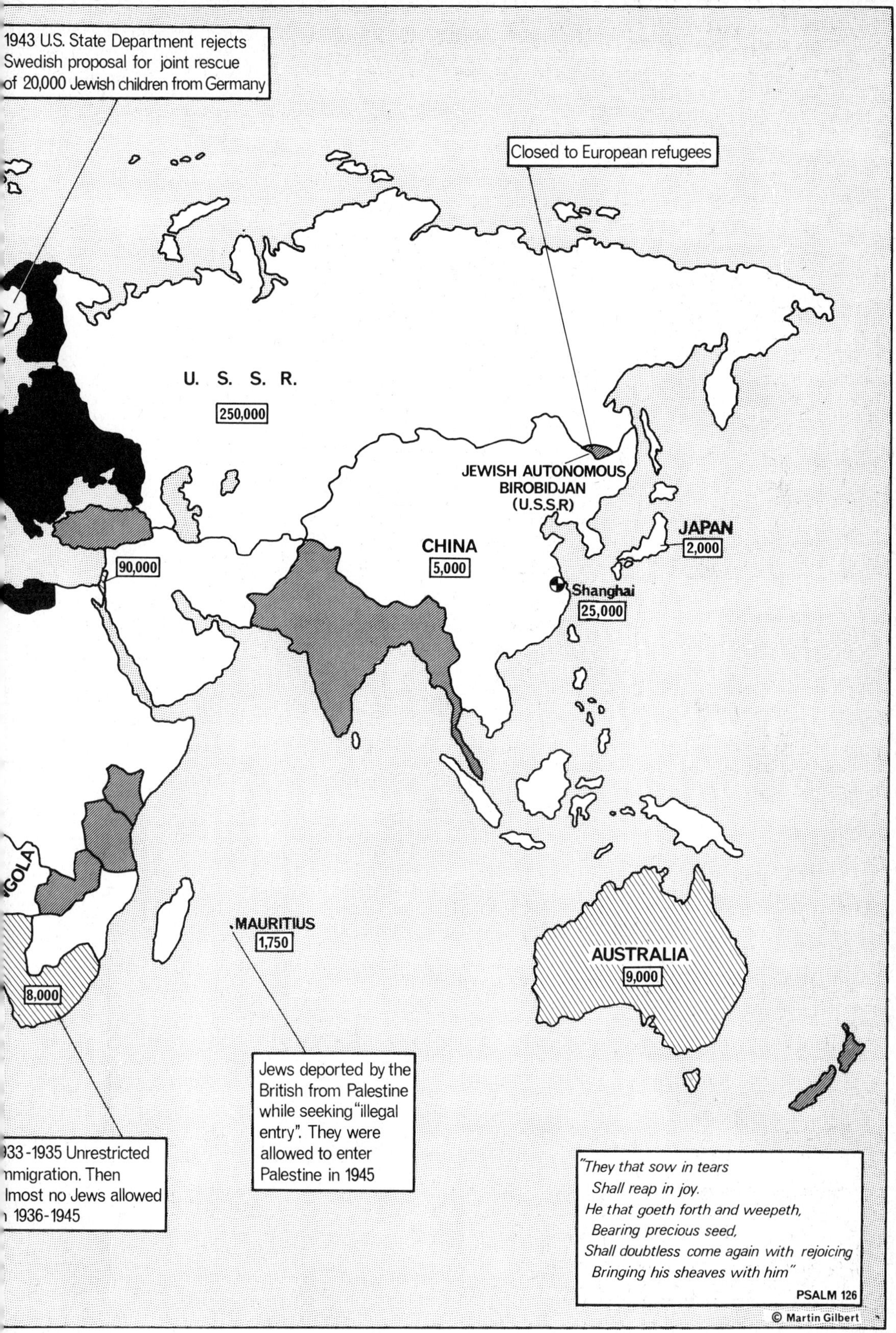

1943 U.S. State Department rejects Swedish proposal for joint rescue of 20,000 Jewish children from Germany
Closed to European refugees
U. S. S. R.
250,000
JEWISH AUTONOMOUS BIROBIDJAN (U.S.S.R)
JAPAN
2,000
CHINA
5,000
Shanghai
25,000
90,000
GOLA
MAURITIUS
1,750
AUSTRALIA
9,000
8,000
Jews deported by the British from Palestine while seeking "illegal entry". They were allowed to enter Palestine in 1945
33-1935 Unrestricted mmigration. Then lmost no Jews allowed 1936-1945
"They that sow in tears
Shall reap in joy.
He that goeth forth and weepeth,
Bearing precious seed,
Shall doubtless come again with rejoicing
Bringing his sheaves with him"
PSALM 126
© Martin Gilbert

JEWISH SETTLEMENTS AND IMMIGRATION, 1931 – 1942

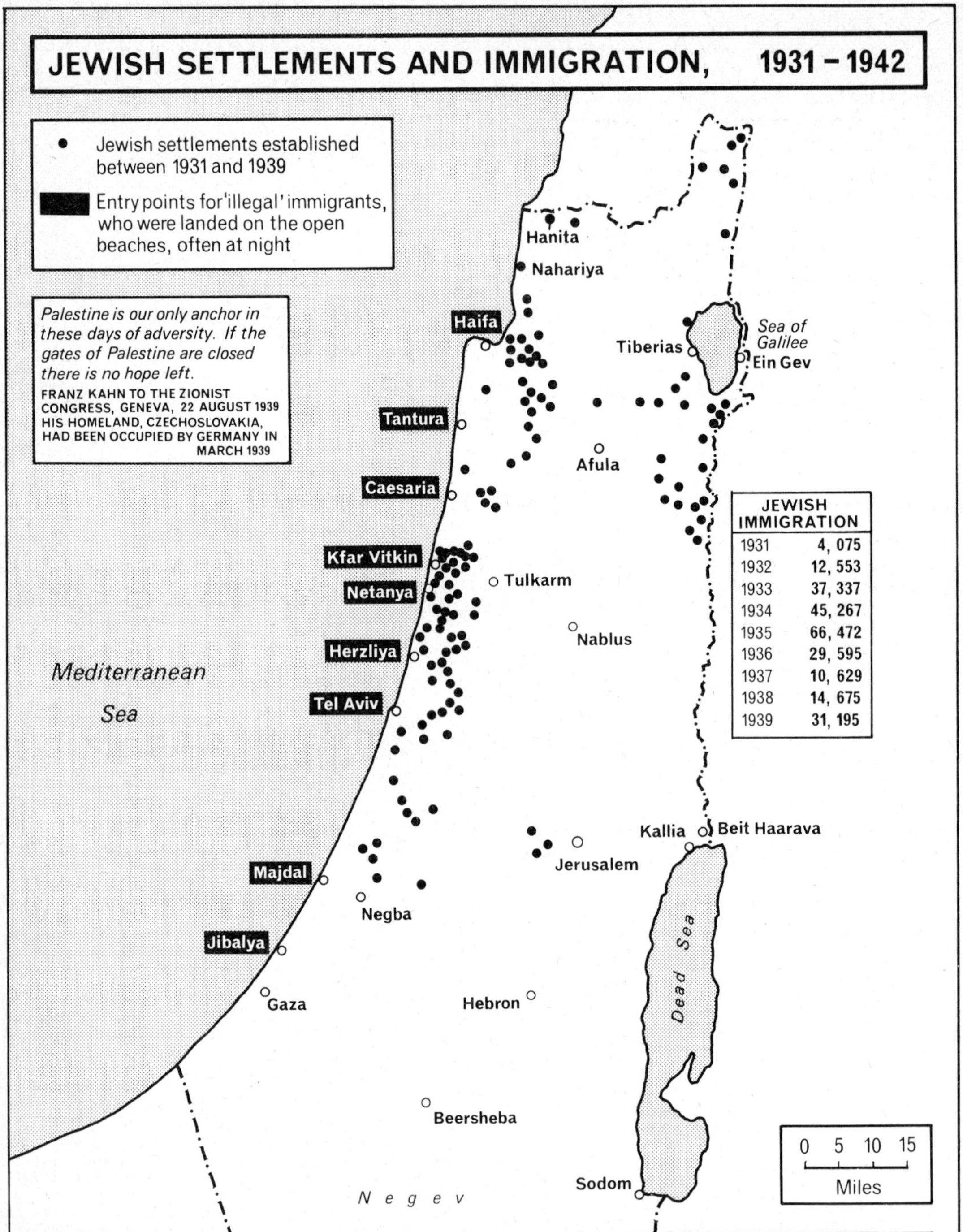

Jewish settlements established between 1931 and 1939
Entry points for 'illegal' immigrants, who were landed on the open beaches, often at night
Hanita
Nahariya
Haifa
Tiberias
Sea of Galilee
Ein Gev
Tantura
Afula
Caesaria
Kfar Vitkin
Netanya
Tulkarm
Nablus
Herzliya
Mediterranean Sea
Tel Aviv
Kallia
Beit Haarava
Jerusalem
Majdal
Negba
Jibalya
Dead Sea
Gaza
Hebron
Beersheba
Sodom
Negev
0 5 10 15
Miles

Palestine is our only anchor in these days of adversity. If the gates of Palestine are closed there is no hope left.

FRANZ KAHN TO THE ZIONIST CONGRESS, GENEVA, 22 AUGUST 1939 HIS HOMELAND, CZECHOSLOVAKIA, HAD BEEN OCCUPIED BY GERMANY IN MARCH 1939

JEWISH IMMIGRATION	
1931	**4, 075**
1932	**12, 553**
1933	**37, 337**
1934	**45, 267**
1935	**66, 472**
1936	**29, 595**
1937	**10, 629**
1938	**14, 675**
1939	**31, 195**

Despite the Arab riots of 1929, Jewish immigration continued to grow, and Jewish settlements were founded throughout Palestine. The Arab leaders protested against this new influx of immigrants and refugees, and following a new Arab campaign in 1936, the British authorities introduced a strict limit to Jewish immigration (a maximum of 8,000 between August 1937 and March 1938). As a result of still more Arab pressure, the British published their Palestine White Paper on 17 May 1939. Only 10,643 Jews were allowed to enter in 1940, 4,592 in 1941 and 4,206 in 1942, at a time when the fierce German persecution of Jews in Europe made the need for a place of refuge a desperate one. Between July 1934 and September 1939 the Zionists disembarked 15,000 'illegal' immigrants on the Palestine coast, from a total of 43 ships. On 4 September 1939 two 'illegal' immigrants were killed when their ship was fired on by a British cutter. Later 'illegals' were deported to Cyprus and Mauritius

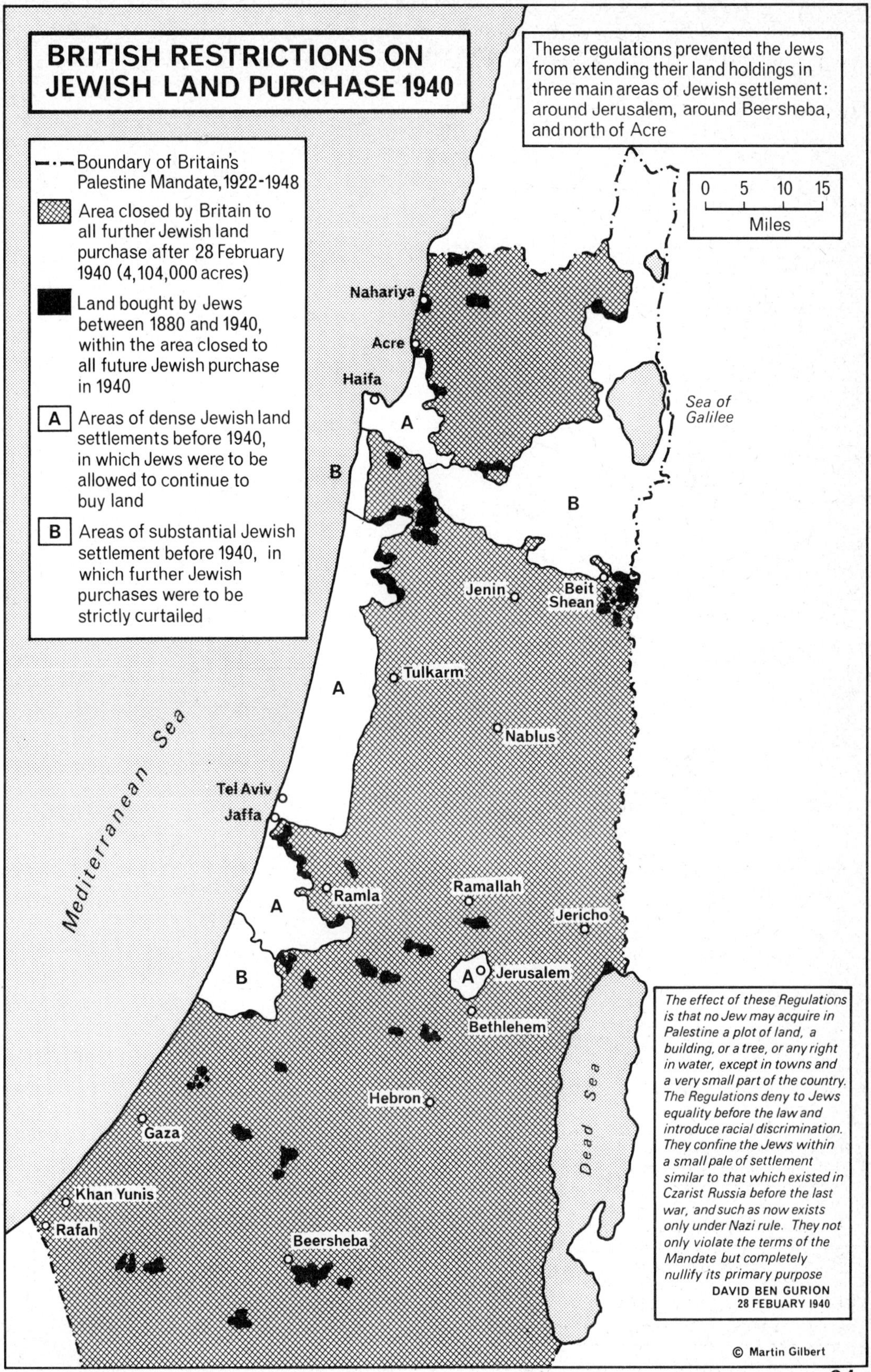
BRITISH RESTRICTIONS ON JEWISH LAND PURCHASE 1940
Boundary of Britain's Palestine Mandate, 1922-1948
Area closed by Britain to all further Jewish land purchase after 28 February 1940 (4,104,000 acres)
Land bought by Jews between 1880 and 1940, within the area closed to all future Jewish purchase in 1940
A Areas of dense Jewish land settlements before 1940, in which Jews were to be allowed to continue to buy land
B Areas of substantial Jewish settlement before 1940, in which further Jewish purchases were to be strictly curtailed
These regulations prevented the Jews from extending their land holdings in three main areas of Jewish settlement: around Jerusalem, around Beersheba, and north of Acre
0 5 10 15
Miles
Nahariya
Acre
Haifa
A
B
Sea of Galilee
B
Jenin
Beit Shean
Tulkarm
A
Nablus
Mediterranean Sea
Tel Aviv
Jaffa
Ramla
A
Ramallah
Jericho
B
A
Jerusalem
Bethlehem
Hebron
Gaza
Dead Sea
Khan Yunis
Rafah
Beersheba
The effect of these Regulations is that no Jew may acquire in Palestine a plot of land, a building, or a tree, or any right in water, except in towns and a very small part of the country. The Regulations deny to Jews equality before the law and introduce racial discrimination. They confine the Jews within a small pale of settlement similar to that which existed in Czarist Russia before the last war, and such as now exists only under Nazi rule. They not only violate the terms of the Mandate but completely nullify its primary purpose
DAVID BEN GURION
28 FEBUARY 1940
© Martin Gilbert

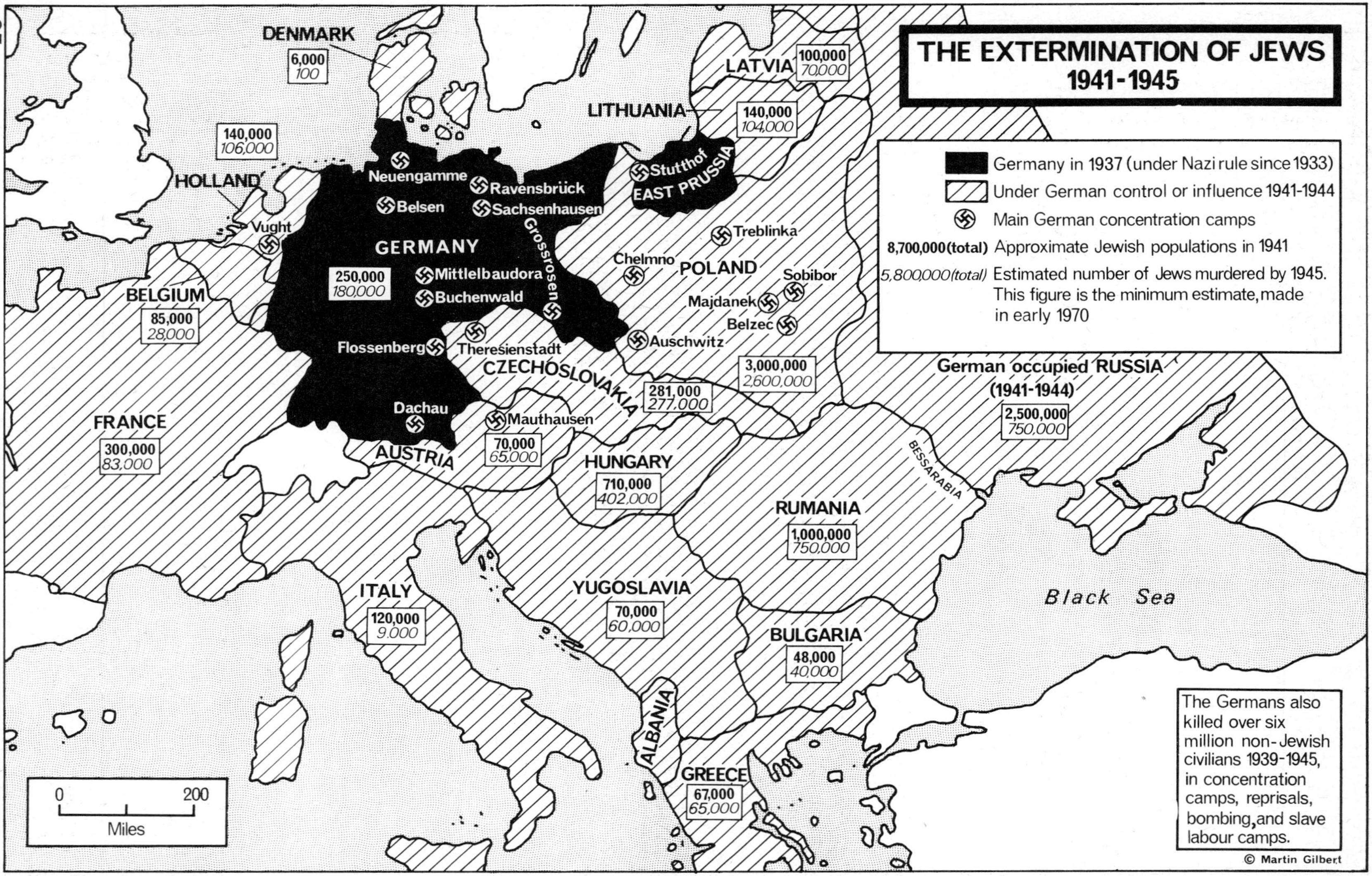
THE EXTERMINATION OF JEWS
1941-1945
Germany in 1937 (under Nazi rule since 1933)
Under German control or influence 1941-1944
Main German concentration camps
8,700,000 (total) Approximate Jewish populations in 1941
5,800,000 (total) Estimated number of Jews murdered by 1945. This figure is the minimum estimate, made in early 1970
DENMARK
6,000
100
HOLLAND
140,000
106,000
BELGIUM
85,000
28,000
FRANCE
300,000
83,000
GERMANY
250,000
180,000
Neuengamme
Belsen
Ravensbrück
Sachsenhausen
Grossrosen
Mittlelbaudora
Buchenwald
Flossenberg
Theresienstadt
Dachau
Vught
AUSTRIA
Mauthausen
70,000
65,000
CZECHOSLOVAKIA
281,000
277,000
LATVIA
100,000
70,000
LITHUANIA
140,000
104,000
Stutthof
EAST PRUSSIA
POLAND
Treblinka
Chelmno
Sobibor
Majdanek
Belzec
Auschwitz
3,000,000
2,600,000
German occupied RUSSIA
(1941-1944)
2,500,000
750,000
BESSARABIA
HUNGARY
710,000
402,000
RUMANIA
1,000,000
750,000
YUGOSLAVIA
70,000
60,000
ITALY
120,000
9,000
BULGARIA
48,000
40,000
ALBANIA
GREECE
67,000
65,000
Black Sea
0
200
Miles
The Germans also killed over six million non-Jewish civilians 1939-1945, in concentration camps, reprisals, bombing, and slave labour camps.
© Martin Gilbert

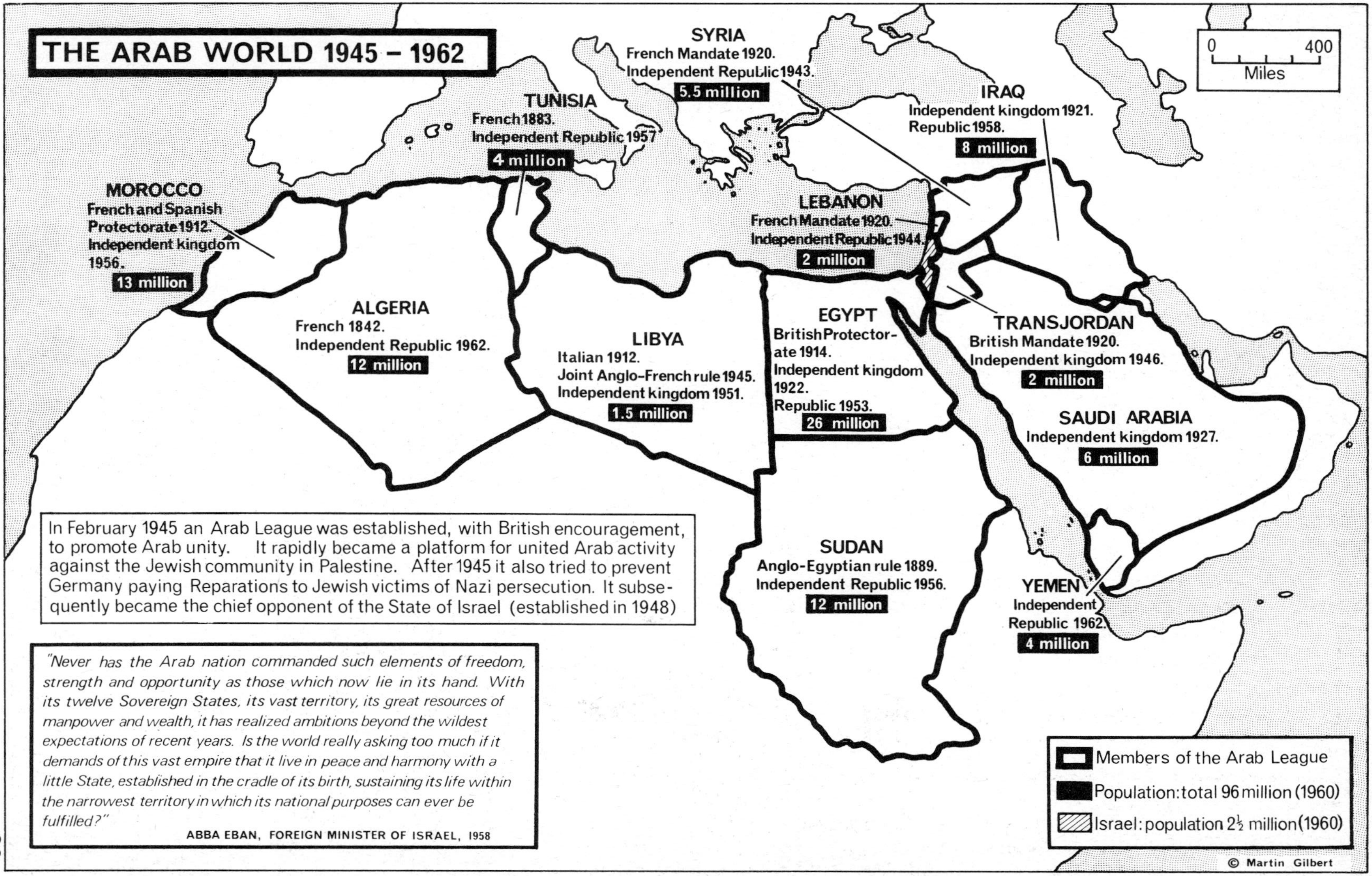
THE ARAB WORLD 1945 – 1962
MOROCCO
French and Spanish Protectorate 1912.
Independent kingdom 1956.
13 million
ALGERIA
French 1842.
Independent Republic 1962.
12 million
TUNISIA
French 1883.
Independent Republic 1957
4 million
LIBYA
Italian 1912.
Joint Anglo-French rule 1945.
Independent kingdom 1951.
1.5 million
EGYPT
British Protectorate 1914.
Independent kingdom 1922.
Republic 1953.
26 million
SUDAN
Anglo-Egyptian rule 1889.
Independent Republic 1956.
12 million
SYRIA
French Mandate 1920.
Independent Republic 1943.
5.5 million
LEBANON
French Mandate 1920.
Independent Republic 1944.
2 million
IRAQ
Independent kingdom 1921.
Republic 1958.
8 million
TRANSJORDAN
British Mandate 1920.
Independent kingdom 1946.
2 million
SAUDI ARABIA
Independent kingdom 1927.
6 million
YEMEN
Independent Republic 1962.
4 million
0
400
Miles
Members of the Arab League
Population: total 96 million (1960)
Israel: population 2½ million (1960)
© Martin Gilbert

In February 1945 an Arab League was established, with British encouragement, to promote Arab unity. It rapidly became a platform for united Arab activity against the Jewish community in Palestine. After 1945 it also tried to prevent Germany paying Reparations to Jewish victims of Nazi persecution. It subsequently became the chief opponent of the State of Israel (established in 1948)

"Never has the Arab nation commanded such elements of freedom, strength and opportunity as those which now lie in its hand. With its twelve Sovereign States, its vast territory, its great resources of manpower and wealth, it has realized ambitions beyond the wildest expectations of recent years. Is the world really asking too much if it demands of this vast empire that it live in peace and harmony with a little State, established in the cradle of its birth, sustaining its life within the narrowest territory in which its national purposes can ever be fulfilled?"

ABBA EBAN, FOREIGN MINISTER OF ISRAEL, 1958

THE JEWISH AGENCY'S PARTITION PLAN, AUGUST 1946

In 1946 the Jewish Agency put forward a new partition plan. As well as an Arab and a Jewish State, this plan envisaged that the Arabs would retain Jaffa as a coastal enclave, and Jerusalem would be put under international control. The Jewish Agency wanted both the Negev and the western shore of the Dead Sea to be within a Jewish State.

From December 1945 to April 1946 an Anglo-American Committee of Inquiry had examined the problem of Jewish immigration, and the position of those Jews who had survived Nazi persecution. The Committee had rejected the idea of the Partition of Palestine into an Arab and a Jewish State, and had recommended 'bi-nationalism': a single State under continuing British control, with the immediate grant of 100,000 immigration certificates to Jews, and an end to the land purchase restrictions of 1940

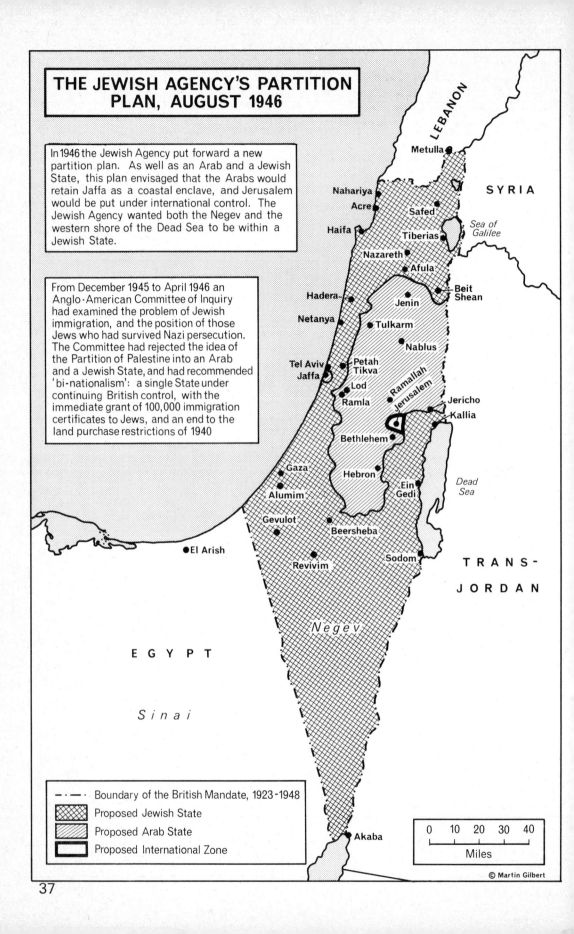

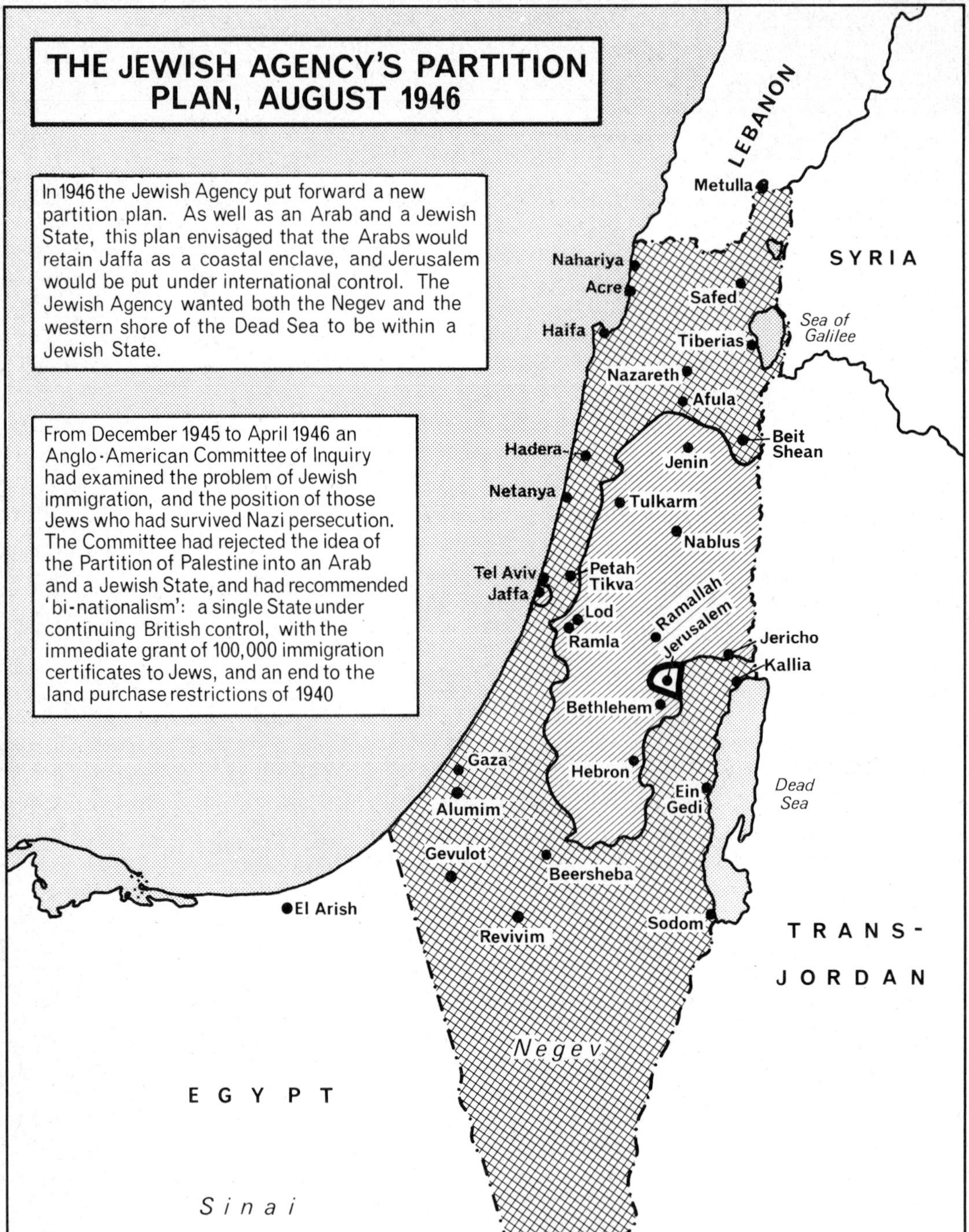
LEBANON
Metulla
SYRIA
Nahariya
Acre
Safed
Haifa
Tiberias
Sea of Galilee
Nazareth
Afula
Beit Shean
Hadera
Jenin
Netanya
Tulkarm
Nablus
Tel Aviv
Jaffa
Petah Tikva
Ramallah
Lod
Jerusalem
Ramla
Jericho
Kallia
Bethlehem
Gaza
Hebron
Alumim
Ein Gedi
Dead Sea
Gevulot
Beersheba
El Arish
Revivim
Sodom
TRANS-JORDAN
Negev
EGYPT
Sinai
Boundary of the British Mandate, 1923-1948
Proposed Jewish State
Proposed Arab State
Proposed International Zone
Akaba
0 10 20 30 40
Miles
© Martin Gilbert

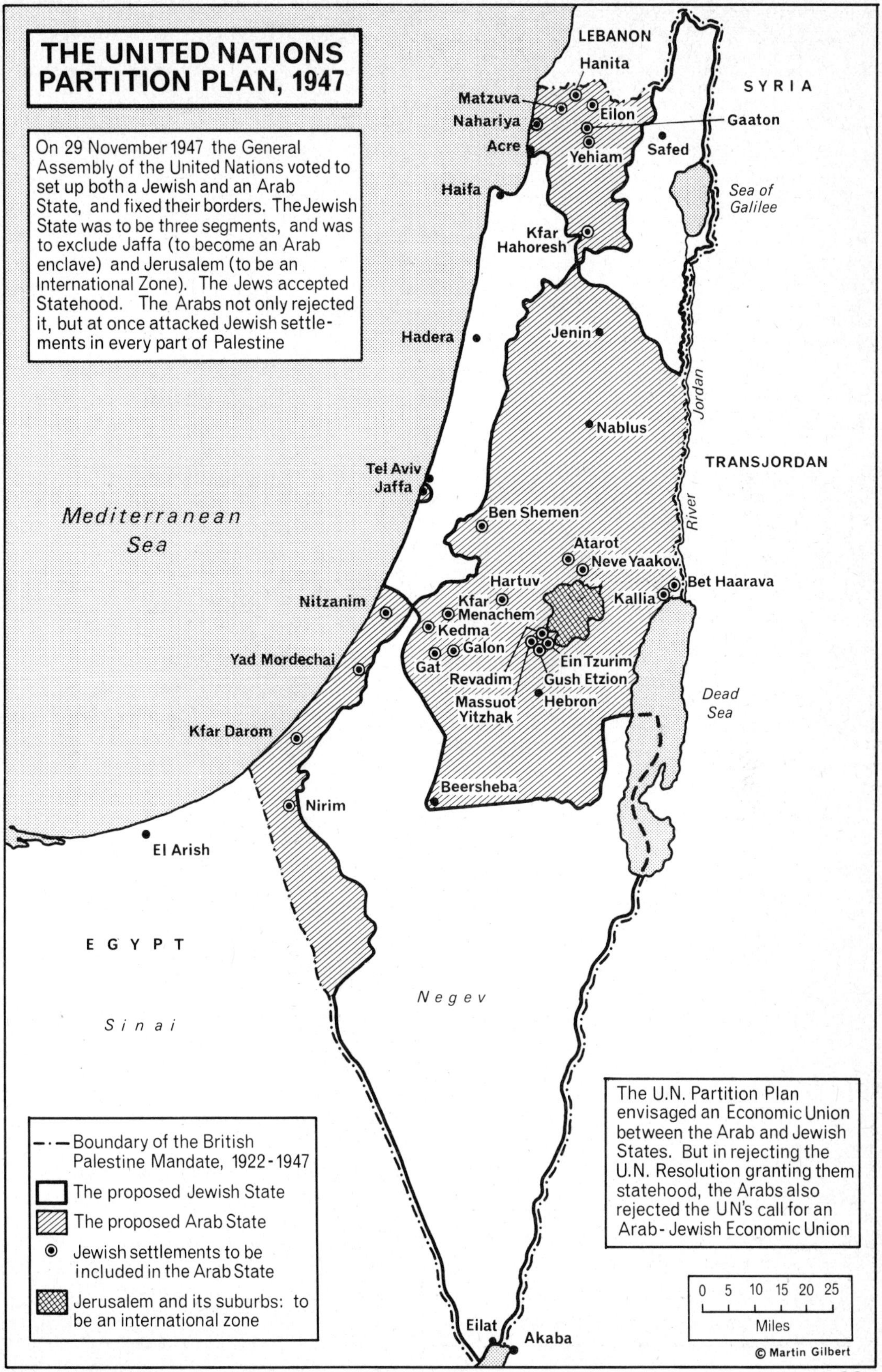
THE UNITED NATIONS PARTITION PLAN, 1947
On 29 November 1947 the General Assembly of the United Nations voted to set up both a Jewish and an Arab State, and fixed their borders. The Jewish State was to be three segments, and was to exclude Jaffa (to become an Arab enclave) and Jerusalem (to be an International Zone). The Jews accepted Statehood. The Arabs not only rejected it, but at once attacked Jewish settlements in every part of Palestine
LEBANON
Hanita
SYRIA
Matzuva
Nahariya
Eilon
Gaaton
Acre
Yehiam
Safed
Haifa
Sea of Galilee
Kfar Hahoresh
Hadera
Jenin
Jordan
Nablus
TRANSJORDAN
Tel Aviv
Jaffa
Mediterranean Sea
Ben Shemen
River
Atarot
Neve Yaakov
Hartuv
Bet Haarava
Nitzanim
Kfar Menachem
Kallia
Kedma
Galon
Gat
Yad Mordechai
Ein Tzurim
Revadim
Gush Etzion
Massuot Yitzhak
Hebron
Dead Sea
Kfar Darom
Beersheba
Nirim
El Arish
EGYPT
Negev
Sinai
Boundary of the British Palestine Mandate, 1922-1947
The proposed Jewish State
The proposed Arab State
Jewish settlements to be included in the Arab State
Jerusalem and its suburbs: to be an international zone
The U.N. Partition Plan envisaged an Economic Union between the Arab and Jewish States. But in rejecting the U.N. Resolution granting them statehood, the Arabs also rejected the UN's call for an Arab-Jewish Economic Union
0 5 10 15 20 25
Miles
Eilat
Akaba
© Martin Gilbert

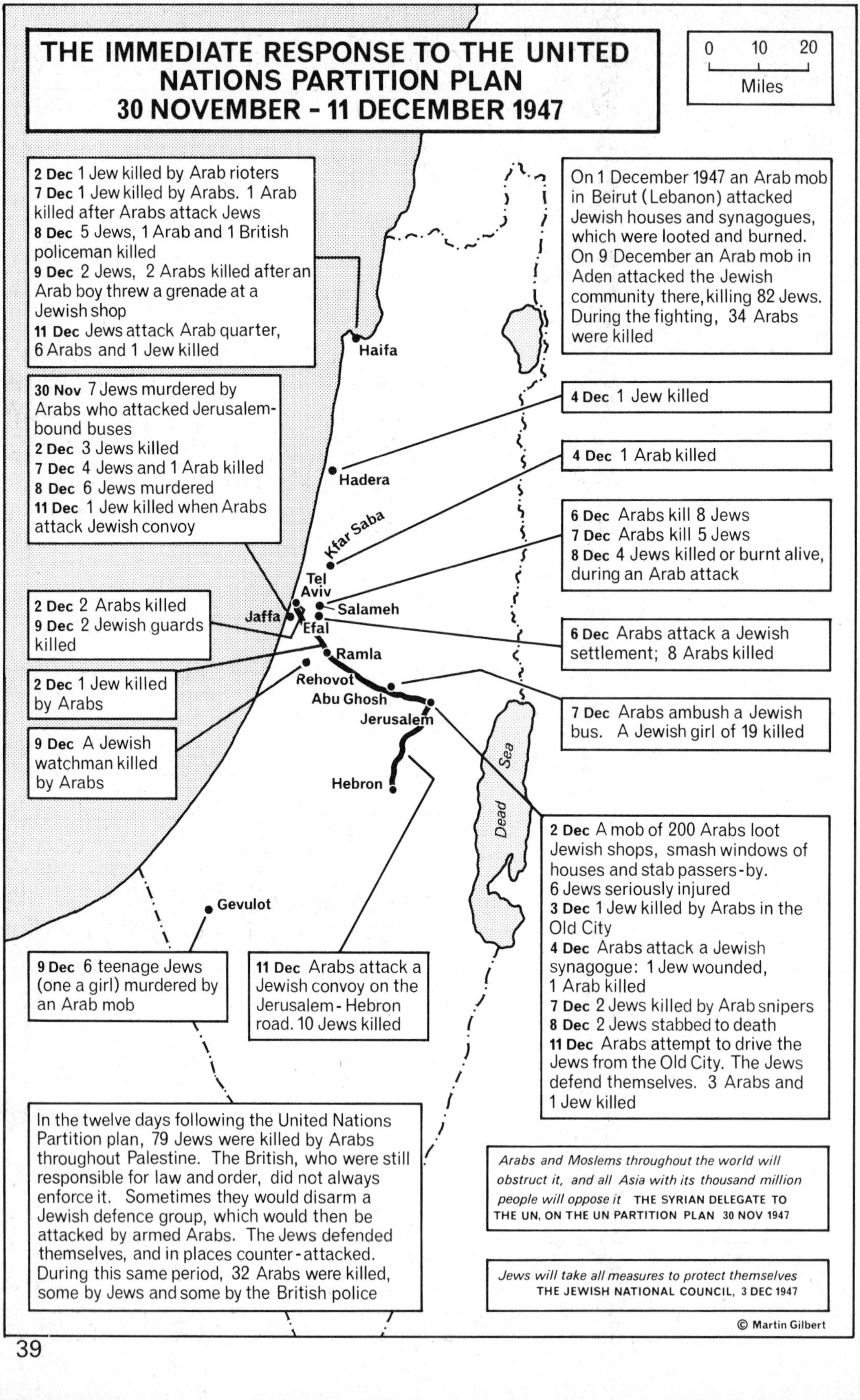

THE IMMEDIATE RESPONSE TO THE UNITED NATIONS PARTITION PLAN 30 NOVEMBER - 11 DECEMBER 1947
0 10 20
Miles
2 Dec 1 Jew killed by Arab rioters
7 Dec 1 Jew killed by Arabs. 1 Arab killed after Arabs attack Jews
8 Dec 5 Jews, 1 Arab and 1 British policeman killed
9 Dec 2 Jews, 2 Arabs killed after an Arab boy threw a grenade at a Jewish shop
11 Dec Jews attack Arab quarter, 6 Arabs and 1 Jew killed
On 1 December 1947 an Arab mob in Beirut (Lebanon) attacked Jewish houses and synagogues, which were looted and burned. On 9 December an Arab mob in Aden attacked the Jewish community there, killing 82 Jews. During the fighting, 34 Arabs were killed
Haifa
30 Nov 7 Jews murdered by Arabs who attacked Jerusalem-bound buses
2 Dec 3 Jews killed
7 Dec 4 Jews and 1 Arab killed
8 Dec 6 Jews murdered
11 Dec 1 Jew killed when Arabs attack Jewish convoy
4 Dec 1 Jew killed
4 Dec 1 Arab killed
Hadera
Kfar Saba
6 Dec Arabs kill 8 Jews
7 Dec Arabs kill 5 Jews
8 Dec 4 Jews killed or burnt alive, during an Arab attack
Tel Aviv
Salameh
Jaffa
Efal
2 Dec 2 Arabs killed
9 Dec 2 Jewish guards killed
6 Dec Arabs attack a Jewish settlement; 8 Arabs killed
Ramla
2 Dec 1 Jew killed by Arabs
Rehovot
Abu Ghosh
Jerusalem
7 Dec Arabs ambush a Jewish bus. A Jewish girl of 19 killed
9 Dec A Jewish watchman killed by Arabs
Hebron
Dead Sea
2 Dec A mob of 200 Arabs loot Jewish shops, smash windows of houses and stab passers-by. 6 Jews seriously injured
3 Dec 1 Jew killed by Arabs in the Old City
4 Dec Arabs attack a Jewish synagogue: 1 Jew wounded, 1 Arab killed
7 Dec 2 Jews killed by Arab snipers
8 Dec 2 Jews stabbed to death
11 Dec Arabs attempt to drive the Jews from the Old City. The Jews defend themselves. 3 Arabs and 1 Jew killed
Gevulot
9 Dec 6 teenage Jews (one a girl) murdered by an Arab mob
11 Dec Arabs attack a Jewish convoy on the Jerusalem - Hebron road. 10 Jews killed
In the twelve days following the United Nations Partition plan, 79 Jews were killed by Arabs throughout Palestine. The British, who were still responsible for law and order, did not always enforce it. Sometimes they would disarm a Jewish defence group, which would then be attacked by armed Arabs. The Jews defended themselves, and in places counter-attacked. During this same period, 32 Arabs were killed, some by Jews and some by the British police
Arabs and Moslems throughout the world will obstruct it, and all Asia with its thousand million people will oppose it THE SYRIAN DELEGATE TO THE UN, ON THE UN PARTITION PLAN 30 NOV 1947
Jews will take all measures to protect themselves THE JEWISH NATIONAL COUNCIL, 3 DEC 1947
© Martin Gilbert

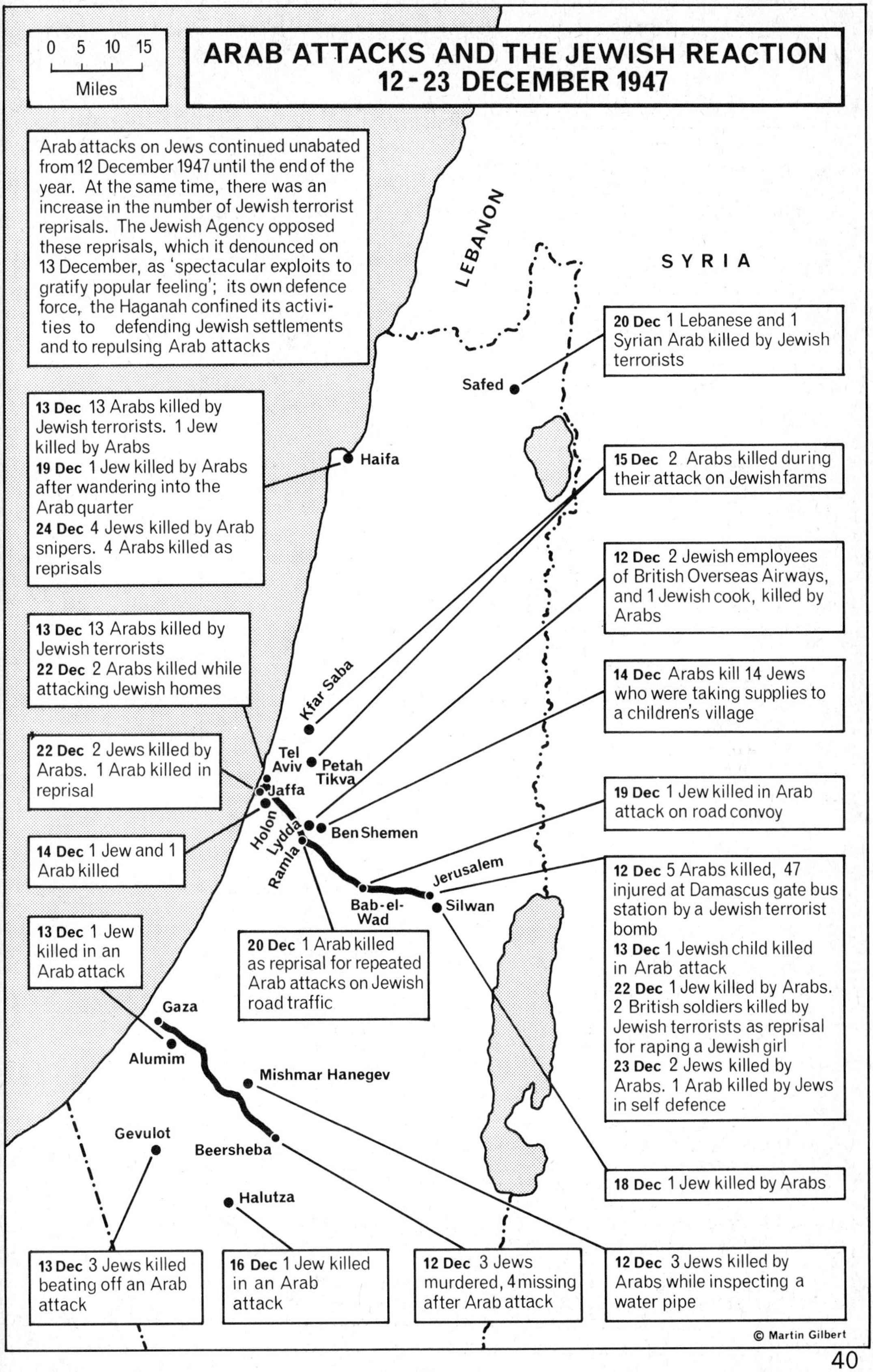

0 5 10 15
Miles
ARAB ATTACKS AND THE JEWISH REACTION
12 - 23 DECEMBER 1947
Arab attacks on Jews continued unabated from 12 December 1947 until the end of the year. At the same time, there was an increase in the number of Jewish terrorist reprisals. The Jewish Agency opposed these reprisals, which it denounced on 13 December, as 'spectacular exploits to gratify popular feeling'; its own defence force, the Haganah confined its activities to defending Jewish settlements and to repulsing Arab attacks
LEBANON
SYRIA
20 Dec 1 Lebanese and 1 Syrian Arab killed by Jewish terrorists
Safed
13 Dec 13 Arabs killed by Jewish terrorists. 1 Jew killed by Arabs
19 Dec 1 Jew killed by Arabs after wandering into the Arab quarter
24 Dec 4 Jews killed by Arab snipers. 4 Arabs killed as reprisals
Haifa
15 Dec 2 Arabs killed during their attack on Jewish farms
12 Dec 2 Jewish employees of British Overseas Airways, and 1 Jewish cook, killed by Arabs
13 Dec 13 Arabs killed by Jewish terrorists
22 Dec 2 Arabs killed while attacking Jewish homes
Kfar Saba
14 Dec Arabs kill 14 Jews who were taking supplies to a children's village
22 Dec 2 Jews killed by Arabs. 1 Arab killed in reprisal
Tel Aviv
Petah Tikva
Jaffa
19 Dec 1 Jew killed in Arab attack on road convoy
Holon
Lydda
Ramla
Ben Shemen
14 Dec 1 Jew and 1 Arab killed
Jerusalem
12 Dec 5 Arabs killed, 47 injured at Damascus gate bus station by a Jewish terrorist bomb
13 Dec 1 Jewish child killed in Arab attack
22 Dec 1 Jew killed by Arabs. 2 British soldiers killed by Jewish terrorists as reprisal for raping a Jewish girl
23 Dec 2 Jews killed by Arabs. 1 Arab killed by Jews in self defence
Bab-el-Wad
Silwan
13 Dec 1 Jew killed in an Arab attack
20 Dec 1 Arab killed as reprisal for repeated Arab attacks on Jewish road traffic
Gaza
Alumim
Mishmar Hanegev
Gevulot
Beersheba
18 Dec 1 Jew killed by Arabs
Halutza
13 Dec 3 Jews killed beating off an Arab attack
16 Dec 1 Jew killed in an Arab attack
12 Dec 3 Jews murdered, 4 missing after Arab attack
12 Dec 3 Jews killed by Arabs while inspecting a water pipe
© Martin Gilbert

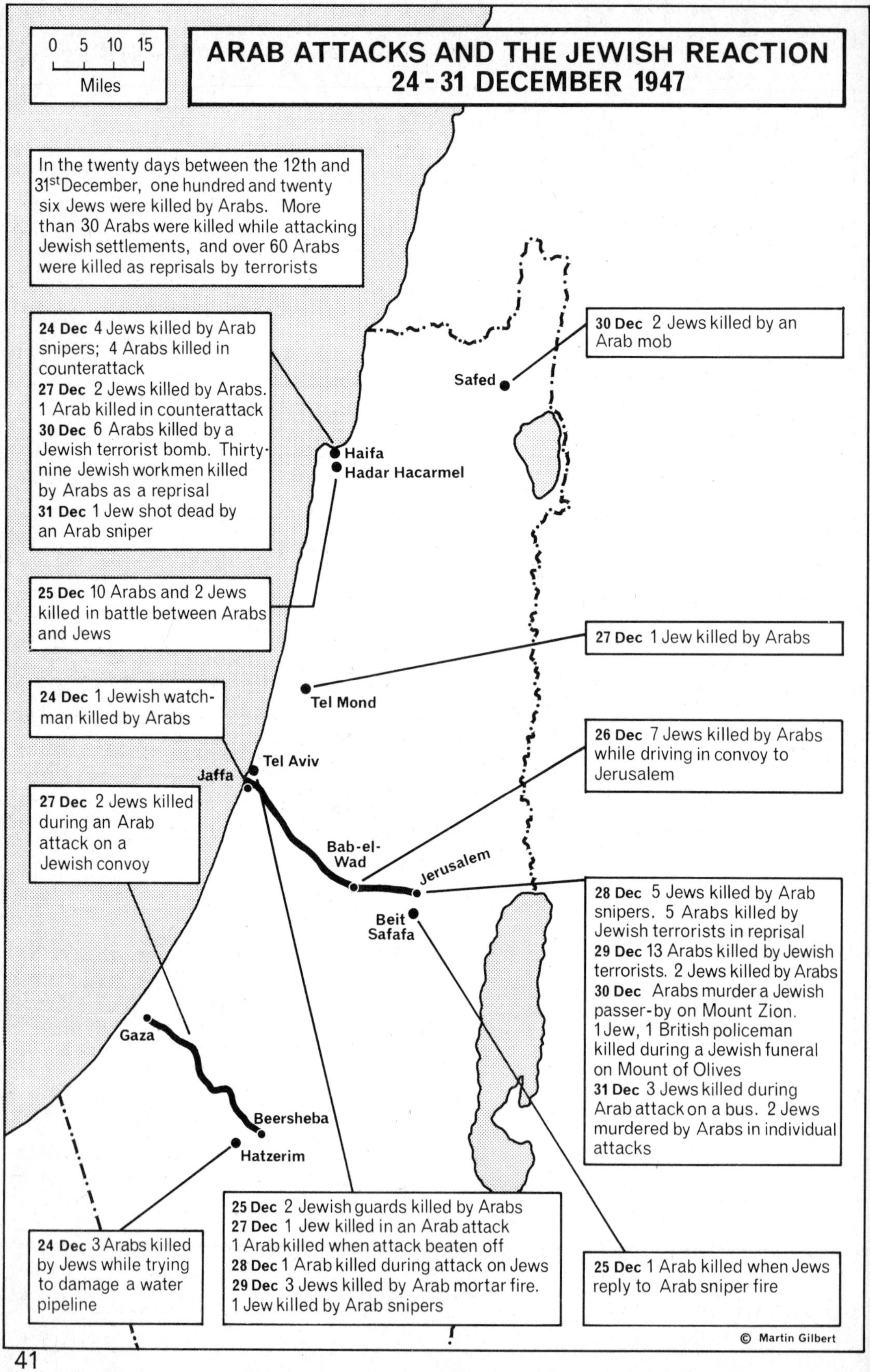

0 5 10 15
Miles
ARAB ATTACKS AND THE JEWISH REACTION
24 - 31 DECEMBER 1947
In the twenty days between the 12th and 31st December, one hundred and twenty six Jews were killed by Arabs. More than 30 Arabs were killed while attacking Jewish settlements, and over 60 Arabs were killed as reprisals by terrorists
24 Dec 4 Jews killed by Arab snipers; 4 Arabs killed in counterattack
27 Dec 2 Jews killed by Arabs. 1 Arab killed in counterattack
30 Dec 6 Arabs killed by a Jewish terrorist bomb. Thirty-nine Jewish workmen killed by Arabs as a reprisal
31 Dec 1 Jew shot dead by an Arab sniper
25 Dec 10 Arabs and 2 Jews killed in battle between Arabs and Jews
24 Dec 1 Jewish watchman killed by Arabs
27 Dec 2 Jews killed during an Arab attack on a Jewish convoy
30 Dec 2 Jews killed by an Arab mob
Safed
Haifa
Hadar Hacarmel
27 Dec 1 Jew killed by Arabs
Tel Mond
26 Dec 7 Jews killed by Arabs while driving in convoy to Jerusalem
Tel Aviv
Jaffa
Bab-el-Wad
Jerusalem
Beit Safafa
28 Dec 5 Jews killed by Arab snipers. 5 Arabs killed by Jewish terrorists in reprisal
29 Dec 13 Arabs killed by Jewish terrorists. 2 Jews killed by Arabs
30 Dec Arabs murder a Jewish passer-by on Mount Zion. 1 Jew, 1 British policeman killed during a Jewish funeral on Mount of Olives
31 Dec 3 Jews killed during Arab attack on a bus. 2 Jews murdered by Arabs in individual attacks
Gaza
Beersheba
Hatzerim
24 Dec 3 Arabs killed by Jews while trying to damage a water pipeline
25 Dec 2 Jewish guards killed by Arabs
27 Dec 1 Jew killed in an Arab attack
1 Arab killed when attack beaten off
28 Dec 1 Arab killed during attack on Jews
29 Dec 3 Jews killed by Arab mortar fire.
1 Jew killed by Arab snipers
25 Dec 1 Arab killed when Jews reply to Arab sniper fire
© Martin Gilbert

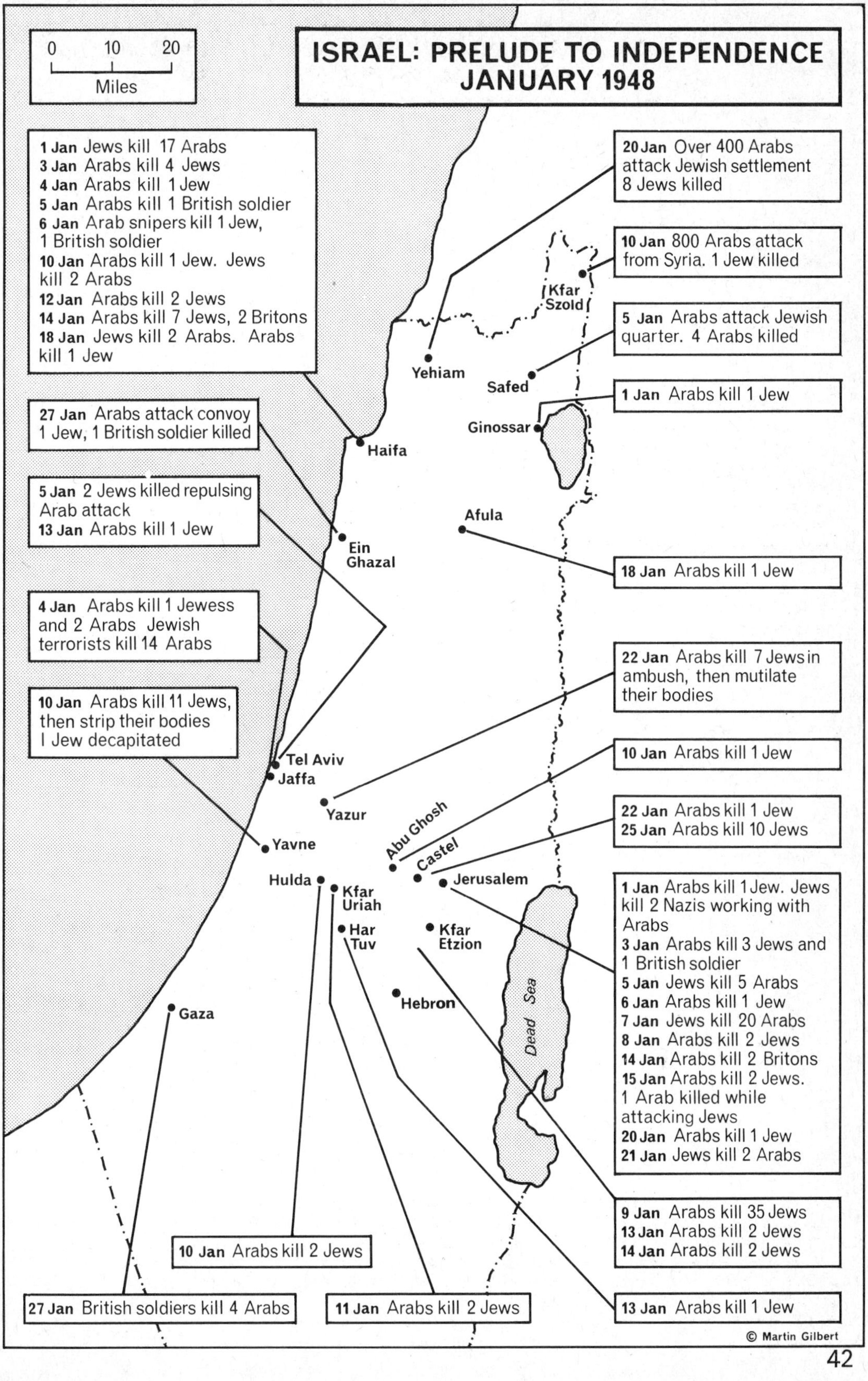
0 10 20
Miles
ISRAEL: PRELUDE TO INDEPENDENCE
JANUARY 1948
1 Jan Jews kill 17 Arabs
3 Jan Arabs kill 4 Jews
4 Jan Arabs kill 1 Jew
5 Jan Arabs kill 1 British soldier
6 Jan Arab snipers kill 1 Jew, 1 British soldier
10 Jan Arabs kill 1 Jew. Jews kill 2 Arabs
12 Jan Arabs kill 2 Jews
14 Jan Arabs kill 7 Jews, 2 Britons
18 Jan Jews kill 2 Arabs. Arabs kill 1 Jew
20 Jan Over 400 Arabs attack Jewish settlement 8 Jews killed
10 Jan 800 Arabs attack from Syria. 1 Jew killed
5 Jan Arabs attack Jewish quarter. 4 Arabs killed
1 Jan Arabs kill 1 Jew
27 Jan Arabs attack convoy 1 Jew, 1 British soldier killed
5 Jan 2 Jews killed repulsing Arab attack
13 Jan Arabs kill 1 Jew
18 Jan Arabs kill 1 Jew
4 Jan Arabs kill 1 Jewess and 2 Arabs Jewish terrorists kill 14 Arabs
22 Jan Arabs kill 7 Jews in ambush, then mutilate their bodies
10 Jan Arabs kill 11 Jews, then strip their bodies I Jew decapitated
10 Jan Arabs kill 1 Jew
22 Jan Arabs kill 1 Jew
25 Jan Arabs kill 10 Jews
1 Jan Arabs kill 1 Jew. Jews kill 2 Nazis working with Arabs
3 Jan Arabs kill 3 Jews and 1 British soldier
5 Jan Jews kill 5 Arabs
6 Jan Arabs kill 1 Jew
7 Jan Jews kill 20 Arabs
8 Jan Arabs kill 2 Jews
14 Jan Arabs kill 2 Britons
15 Jan Arabs kill 2 Jews. 1 Arab killed while attacking Jews
20 Jan Arabs kill 1 Jew
21 Jan Jews kill 2 Arabs
9 Jan Arabs kill 35 Jews
13 Jan Arabs kill 2 Jews
14 Jan Arabs kill 2 Jews
10 Jan Arabs kill 2 Jews
27 Jan British soldiers kill 4 Arabs
11 Jan Arabs kill 2 Jews
13 Jan Arabs kill 1 Jew
Kfar Szold
Yehiam
Safed
Ginossar
Haifa
Afula
Ein Ghazal
Tel Aviv
Jaffa
Yazur
Abu Ghosh
Castel
Yavne
Hulda
Kfar Uriah
Jerusalem
Har Tuv
Kfar Etzion
Hebron
Gaza
Dead Sea
© Martin Gilbert

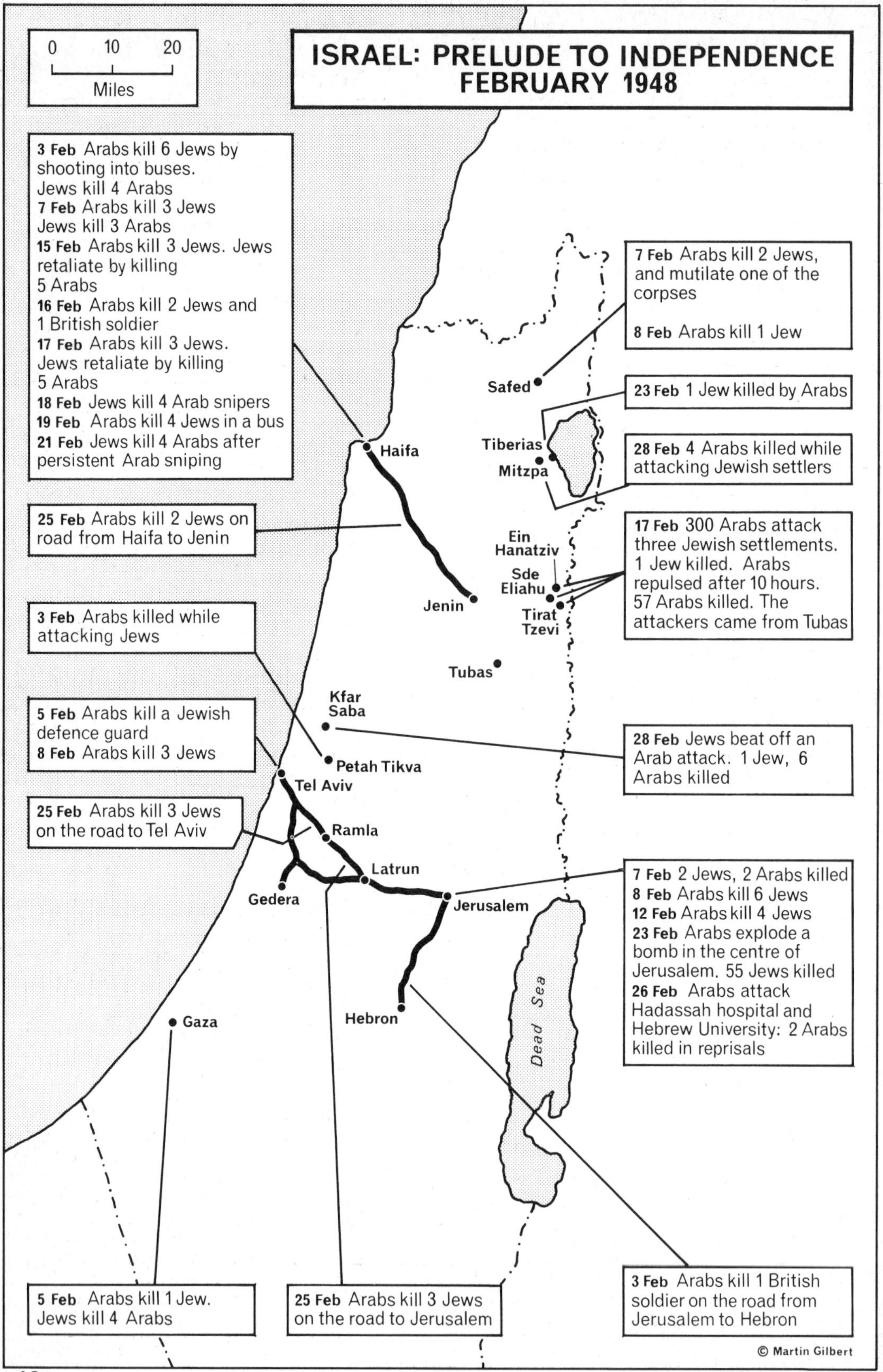
ISRAEL: PRELUDE TO INDEPENDENCE FEBRUARY 1948
0 10 20
Miles
3 Feb Arabs kill 6 Jews by shooting into buses. Jews kill 4 Arabs
7 Feb Arabs kill 3 Jews Jews kill 3 Arabs
15 Feb Arabs kill 3 Jews. Jews retaliate by killing 5 Arabs
16 Feb Arabs kill 2 Jews and 1 British soldier
17 Feb Arabs kill 3 Jews. Jews retaliate by killing 5 Arabs
18 Feb Jews kill 4 Arab snipers
19 Feb Arabs kill 4 Jews in a bus
21 Feb Jews kill 4 Arabs after persistent Arab sniping
25 Feb Arabs kill 2 Jews on road from Haifa to Jenin
3 Feb Arabs killed while attacking Jews
5 Feb Arabs kill a Jewish defence guard
8 Feb Arabs kill 3 Jews
25 Feb Arabs kill 3 Jews on the road to Tel Aviv
5 Feb Arabs kill 1 Jew. Jews kill 4 Arabs
25 Feb Arabs kill 3 Jews on the road to Jerusalem
7 Feb Arabs kill 2 Jews, and mutilate one of the corpses
8 Feb Arabs kill 1 Jew
23 Feb 1 Jew killed by Arabs
28 Feb 4 Arabs killed while attacking Jewish settlers
17 Feb 300 Arabs attack three Jewish settlements. 1 Jew killed. Arabs repulsed after 10 hours. 57 Arabs killed. The attackers came from Tubas
28 Feb Jews beat off an Arab attack. 1 Jew, 6 Arabs killed
7 Feb 2 Jews, 2 Arabs killed
8 Feb Arabs kill 6 Jews
12 Feb Arabs kill 4 Jews
23 Feb Arabs explode a bomb in the centre of Jerusalem. 55 Jews killed
26 Feb Arabs attack Hadassah hospital and Hebrew University: 2 Arabs killed in reprisals
3 Feb Arabs kill 1 British soldier on the road from Jerusalem to Hebron
Safed
Tiberias
Mitzpa
Haifa
Ein Hanatziv
Sde Eliahu
Tirat Tzevi
Jenin
Tubas
Kfar Saba
Petah Tikva
Tel Aviv
Ramla
Latrun
Gedera
Jerusalem
Hebron
Gaza
Dead Sea
© Martin Gilbert

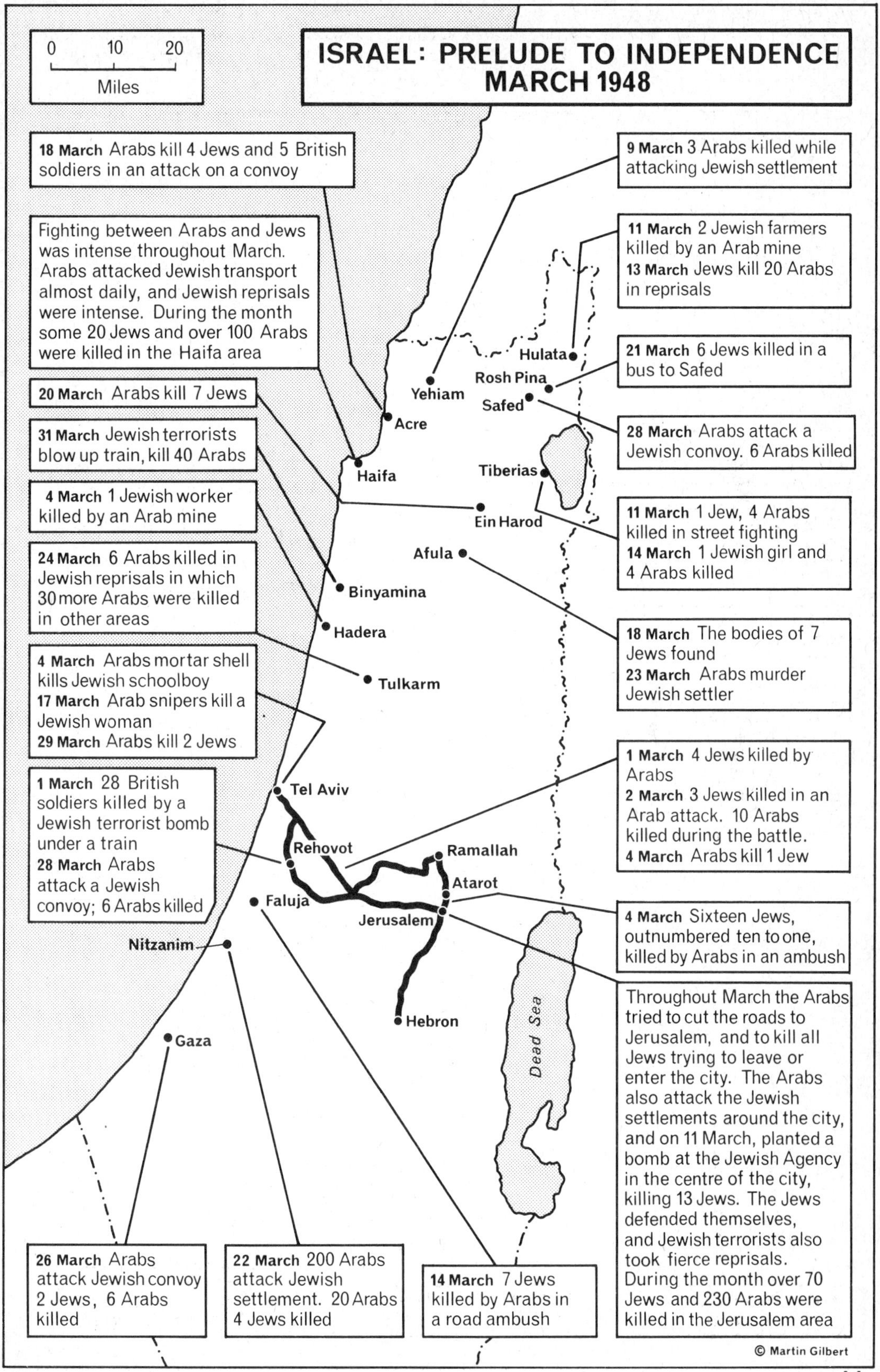

ISRAEL: PRELUDE TO INDEPENDENCE
MARCH 1948
0 10 20
Miles
18 March Arabs kill 4 Jews and 5 British soldiers in an attack on a convoy
Fighting between Arabs and Jews was intense throughout March. Arabs attacked Jewish transport almost daily, and Jewish reprisals were intense. During the month some 20 Jews and over 100 Arabs were killed in the Haifa area
20 March Arabs kill 7 Jews
31 March Jewish terrorists blow up train, kill 40 Arabs
4 March 1 Jewish worker killed by an Arab mine
24 March 6 Arabs killed in Jewish reprisals in which 30 more Arabs were killed in other areas
4 March Arabs mortar shell kills Jewish schoolboy
17 March Arab snipers kill a Jewish woman
29 March Arabs kill 2 Jews
1 March 28 British soldiers killed by a Jewish terrorist bomb under a train
28 March Arabs attack a Jewish convoy; 6 Arabs killed
9 March 3 Arabs killed while attacking Jewish settlement
11 March 2 Jewish farmers killed by an Arab mine
13 March Jews kill 20 Arabs in reprisals
21 March 6 Jews killed in a bus to Safed
28 March Arabs attack a Jewish convoy. 6 Arabs killed
11 March 1 Jew, 4 Arabs killed in street fighting
14 March 1 Jewish girl and 4 Arabs killed
18 March The bodies of 7 Jews found
23 March Arabs murder Jewish settler
1 March 4 Jews killed by Arabs
2 March 3 Jews killed in an Arab attack. 10 Arabs killed during the battle.
4 March Arabs kill 1 Jew
4 March Sixteen Jews, outnumbered ten to one, killed by Arabs in an ambush
Throughout March the Arabs tried to cut the roads to Jerusalem, and to kill all Jews trying to leave or enter the city. The Arabs also attack the Jewish settlements around the city, and on 11 March, planted a bomb at the Jewish Agency in the centre of the city, killing 13 Jews. The Jews defended themselves, and Jewish terrorists also took fierce reprisals. During the month over 70 Jews and 230 Arabs were killed in the Jerusalem area
26 March Arabs attack Jewish convoy 2 Jews, 6 Arabs killed
22 March 200 Arabs attack Jewish settlement. 20 Arabs 4 Jews killed
14 March 7 Jews killed by Arabs in a road ambush
Hulata
Rosh Pina
Yehiam
Safed
Acre
Haifa
Tiberias
Ein Harod
Afula
Binyamina
Hadera
Tulkarm
Tel Aviv
Rehovot
Ramallah
Atarot
Faluja
Jerusalem
Nitzanim
Hebron
Gaza
Dead Sea
© Martin Gilbert

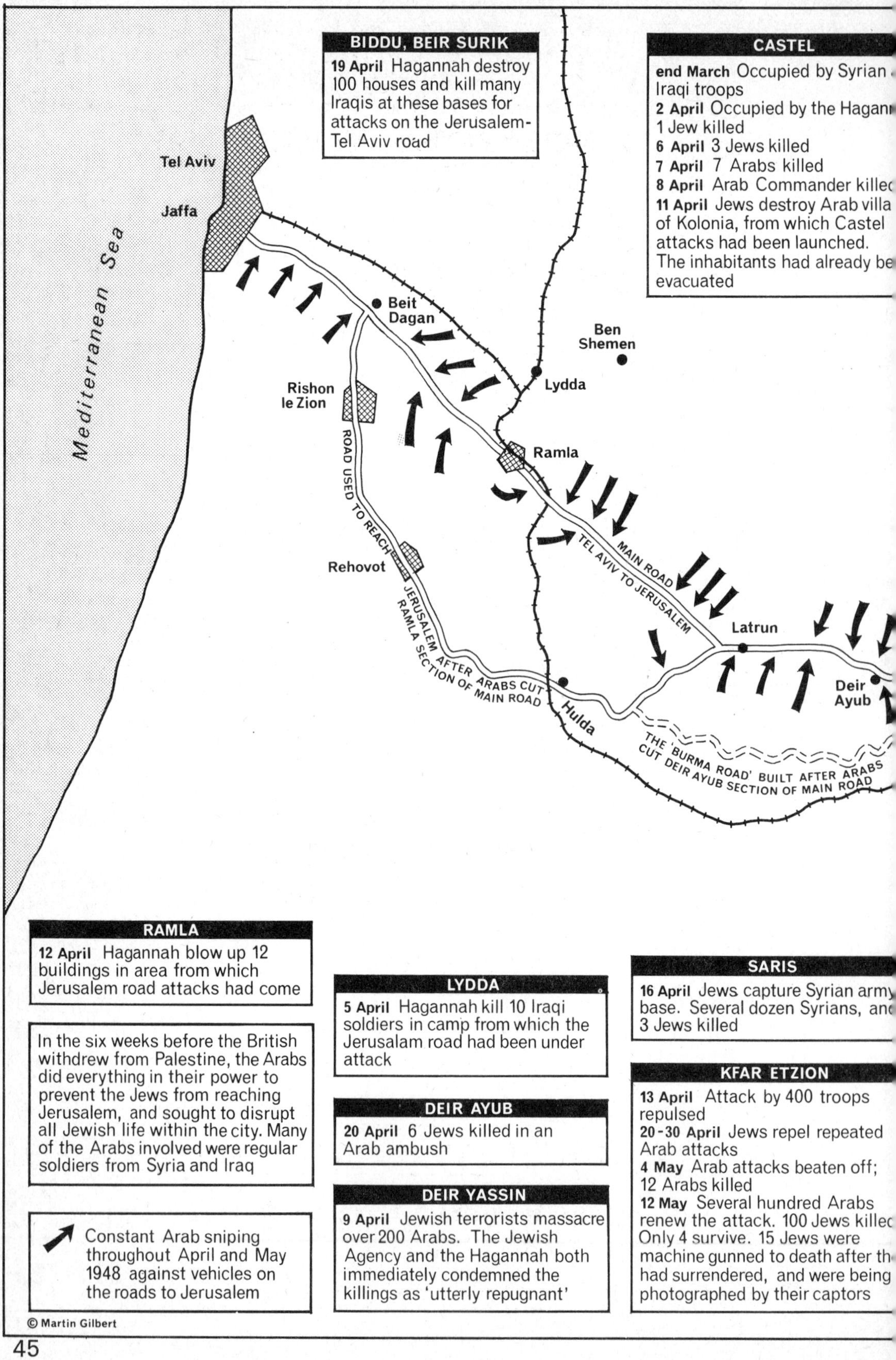

BIDDU, BEIR SURIK
19 April Hagannah destroy 100 houses and kill many Iraqis at these bases for attacks on the Jerusalem-Tel Aviv road
CASTEL
end March Occupied by Syrian
Iraqi troops
2 April Occupied by the Hagan
1 Jew killed
6 April 3 Jews killed
7 April 7 Arabs killed
8 April Arab Commander kille
11 April Jews destroy Arab villa
of Kolonia, from which Castel
attacks had been launched.
The inhabitants had already be
evacuated
Tel Aviv
Jaffa
Mediterranean Sea
Beit Dagan
Ben Shemen
Lydda
Rishon le Zion
Ramla
ROAD USED TO REACH JERUSALEM AFTER ARABS CUT RAMLA SECTION OF MAIN ROAD
TEL AVIV TO JERUSALEM MAIN ROAD
Rehovot
Latrun
Deir Ayub
Hulda
THE 'BURMA ROAD' BUILT AFTER ARABS CUT DEIR AYUB SECTION OF MAIN ROAD
RAMLA
12 April Hagannah blow up 12 buildings in area from which Jerusalem road attacks had come
In the six weeks before the British withdrew from Palestine, the Arabs did everything in their power to prevent the Jews from reaching Jerusalem, and sought to disrupt all Jewish life within the city. Many of the Arabs involved were regular soldiers from Syria and Iraq
Constant Arab sniping throughout April and May 1948 against vehicles on the roads to Jerusalem
LYDDA
5 April Hagannah kill 10 Iraqi soldiers in camp from which the Jerusalam road had been under attack
DEIR AYUB
20 April 6 Jews killed in an Arab ambush
DEIR YASSIN
9 April Jewish terrorists massacre over 200 Arabs. The Jewish Agency and the Hagannah both immediately condemned the killings as 'utterly repugnant'
SARIS
16 April Jews capture Syrian arm
base. Several dozen Syrians, an
3 Jews killed
KFAR ETZION
13 April Attack by 400 troops
repulsed
20-30 April Jews repel repeated
Arab attacks
4 May Arab attacks beaten off;
12 Arabs killed
12 May Several hundred Arabs
renew the attack. 100 Jews kille
Only 4 survive. 15 Jews were
machine gunned to death after th
had surrendered, and were being
photographed by their captors
© Martin Gilbert

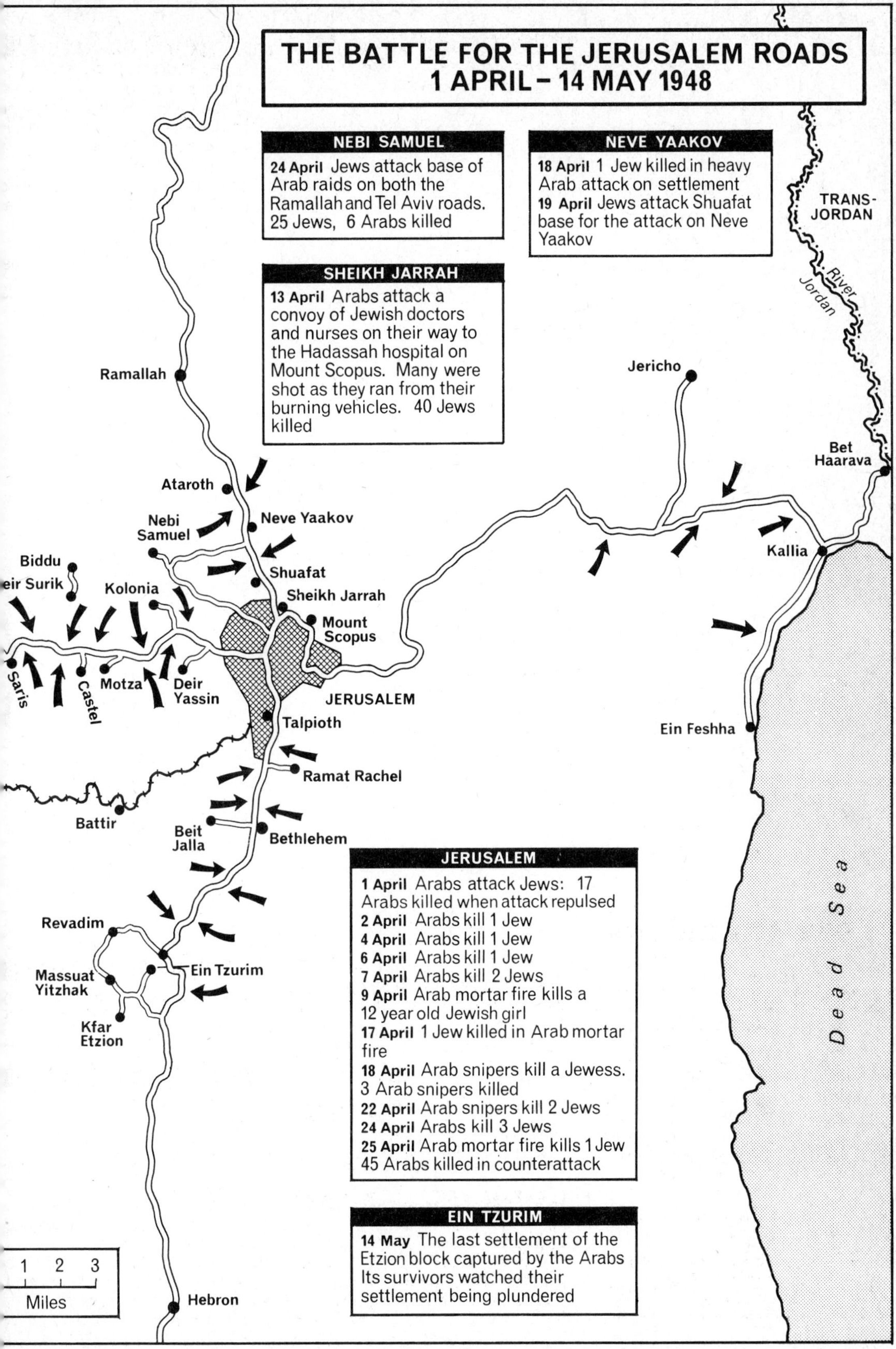
THE BATTLE FOR THE JERUSALEM ROADS
1 APRIL – 14 MAY 1948
NEBI SAMUEL
24 April Jews attack base of Arab raids on both the Ramallah and Tel Aviv roads. 25 Jews, 6 Arabs killed
NEVE YAAKOV
18 April 1 Jew killed in heavy Arab attack on settlement
19 April Jews attack Shuafat base for the attack on Neve Yaakov
SHEIKH JARRAH
13 April Arabs attack a convoy of Jewish doctors and nurses on their way to the Hadassah hospital on Mount Scopus. Many were shot as they ran from their burning vehicles. 40 Jews killed
TRANS-JORDAN
River Jordan
Ramallah
Jericho
Bet Haarava
Ataroth
Neve Yaakov
Nebi Samuel
Shuafat
Kallia
Biddu
eir Surik
Kolonia
Sheikh Jarrah
Mount Scopus
Saris
Castel
Motza
Deir Yassin
JERUSALEM
Talpioth
Ein Feshha
Ramat Rachel
Battir
Beit Jalla
Bethlehem
Dead Sea
JERUSALEM
1 April Arabs attack Jews: 17 Arabs killed when attack repulsed
2 April Arabs kill 1 Jew
4 April Arabs kill 1 Jew
6 April Arabs kill 1 Jew
7 April Arabs kill 2 Jews
9 April Arab mortar fire kills a 12 year old Jewish girl
17 April 1 Jew killed in Arab mortar fire
18 April Arab snipers kill a Jewess. 3 Arab snipers killed
22 April Arab snipers kill 2 Jews
24 April Arabs kill 3 Jews
25 April Arab mortar fire kills 1 Jew 45 Arabs killed in counterattack
Revadim
Massuat Yitzhak
Ein Tzurim
Kfar Etzion
EIN TZURIM
14 May The last settlement of the Etzion block captured by the Arabs Its survivors watched their settlement being plundered
1 2 3
Miles
Hebron

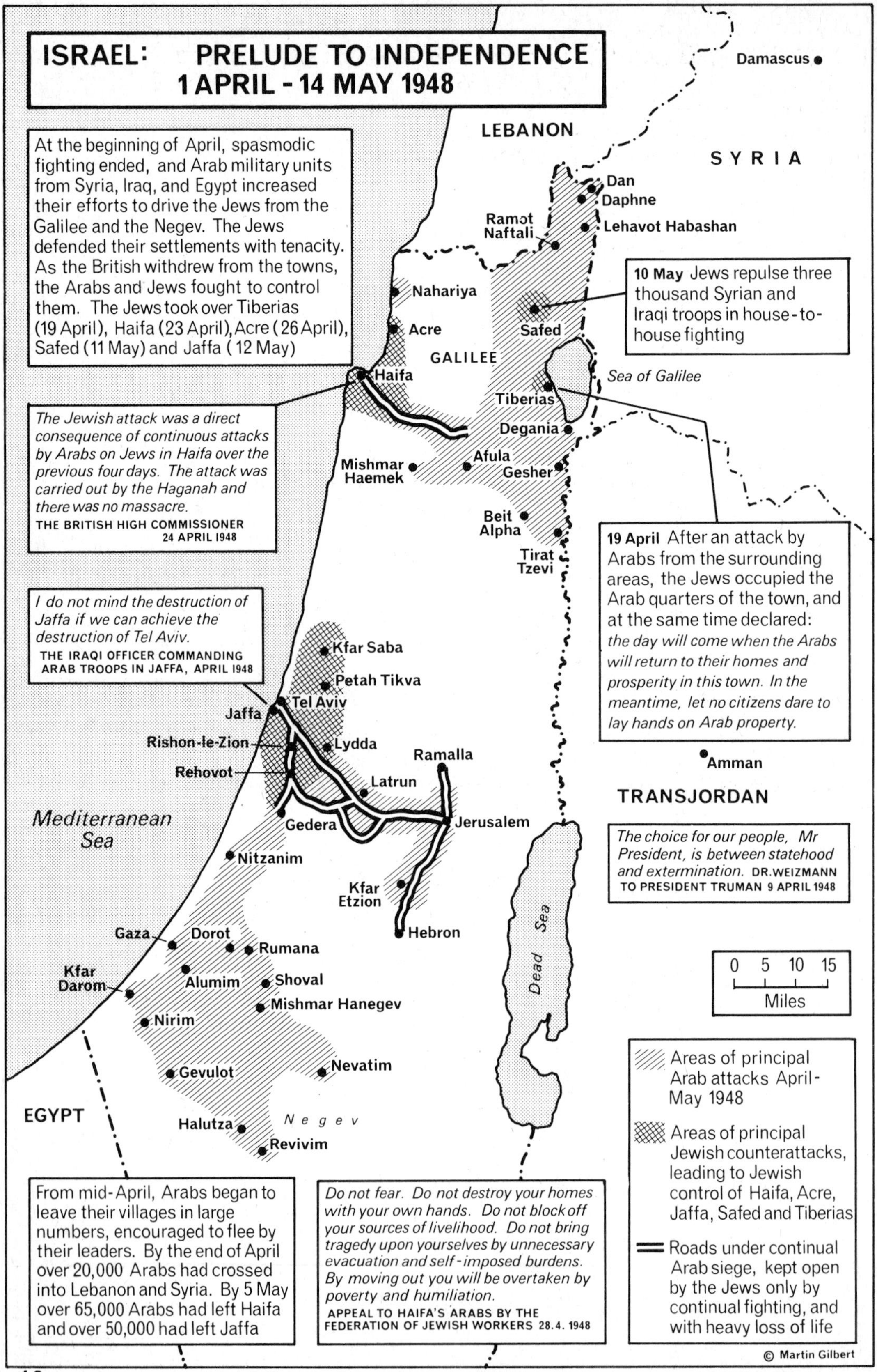
ISRAEL: PRELUDE TO INDEPENDENCE
1 APRIL - 14 MAY 1948
At the beginning of April, spasmodic fighting ended, and Arab military units from Syria, Iraq, and Egypt increased their efforts to drive the Jews from the Galilee and the Negev. The Jews defended their settlements with tenacity. As the British withdrew from the towns, the Arabs and Jews fought to control them. The Jews took over Tiberias (19 April), Haifa (23 April), Acre (26 April), Safed (11 May) and Jaffa (12 May)
The Jewish attack was a direct consequence of continuous attacks by Arabs on Jews in Haifa over the previous four days. The attack was carried out by the Haganah and there was no massacre.
THE BRITISH HIGH COMMISSIONER 24 APRIL 1948
I do not mind the destruction of Jaffa if we can achieve the destruction of Tel Aviv.
THE IRAQI OFFICER COMMANDING ARAB TROOPS IN JAFFA, APRIL 1948
10 May Jews repulse three thousand Syrian and Iraqi troops in house-to-house fighting
19 April After an attack by Arabs from the surrounding areas, the Jews occupied the Arab quarters of the town, and at the same time declared: the day will come when the Arabs will return to their homes and prosperity in this town. In the meantime, let no citizens dare to lay hands on Arab property.
The choice for our people, Mr President, is between statehood and extermination. DR. WEIZMANN TO PRESIDENT TRUMAN 9 APRIL 1948
From mid-April, Arabs began to leave their villages in large numbers, encouraged to flee by their leaders. By the end of April over 20,000 Arabs had crossed into Lebanon and Syria. By 5 May over 65,000 Arabs had left Haifa and over 50,000 had left Jaffa
Do not fear. Do not destroy your homes with your own hands. Do not block off your sources of livelihood. Do not bring tragedy upon yourselves by unnecessary evacuation and self-imposed burdens. By moving out you will be overtaken by poverty and humiliation.
APPEAL TO HAIFA'S ARABS BY THE FEDERATION OF JEWISH WORKERS 28.4.1948
Areas of principal Arab attacks April-May 1948
Areas of principal Jewish counterattacks, leading to Jewish control of Haifa, Acre, Jaffa, Safed and Tiberias
Roads under continual Arab siege, kept open by the Jews only by continual fighting, and with heavy loss of life
0 5 10 15
Miles
Damascus
LEBANON
SYRIA
Dan
Daphne
Ramot Naftali
Lehavot Habashan
Nahariya
Acre
Safed
GALILEE
Haifa
Sea of Galilee
Tiberias
Degania
Afula
Mishmar Haemek
Gesher
Beit Alpha
Tirat Tzevi
Kfar Saba
Petah Tikva
Tel Aviv
Jaffa
Rishon-le-Zion
Lydda
Ramalla
Rehovot
Latrun
Amman
TRANSJORDAN
Mediterranean Sea
Gedera
Jerusalem
Nitzanim
Kfar Etzion
Hebron
Dead Sea
Gaza
Dorot
Rumana
Kfar Darom
Alumim
Shoval
Mishmar Hanegev
Nirim
Nevatim
Gevulot
EGYPT
Halutza
Negev
Revivim
© Martin Gilbert

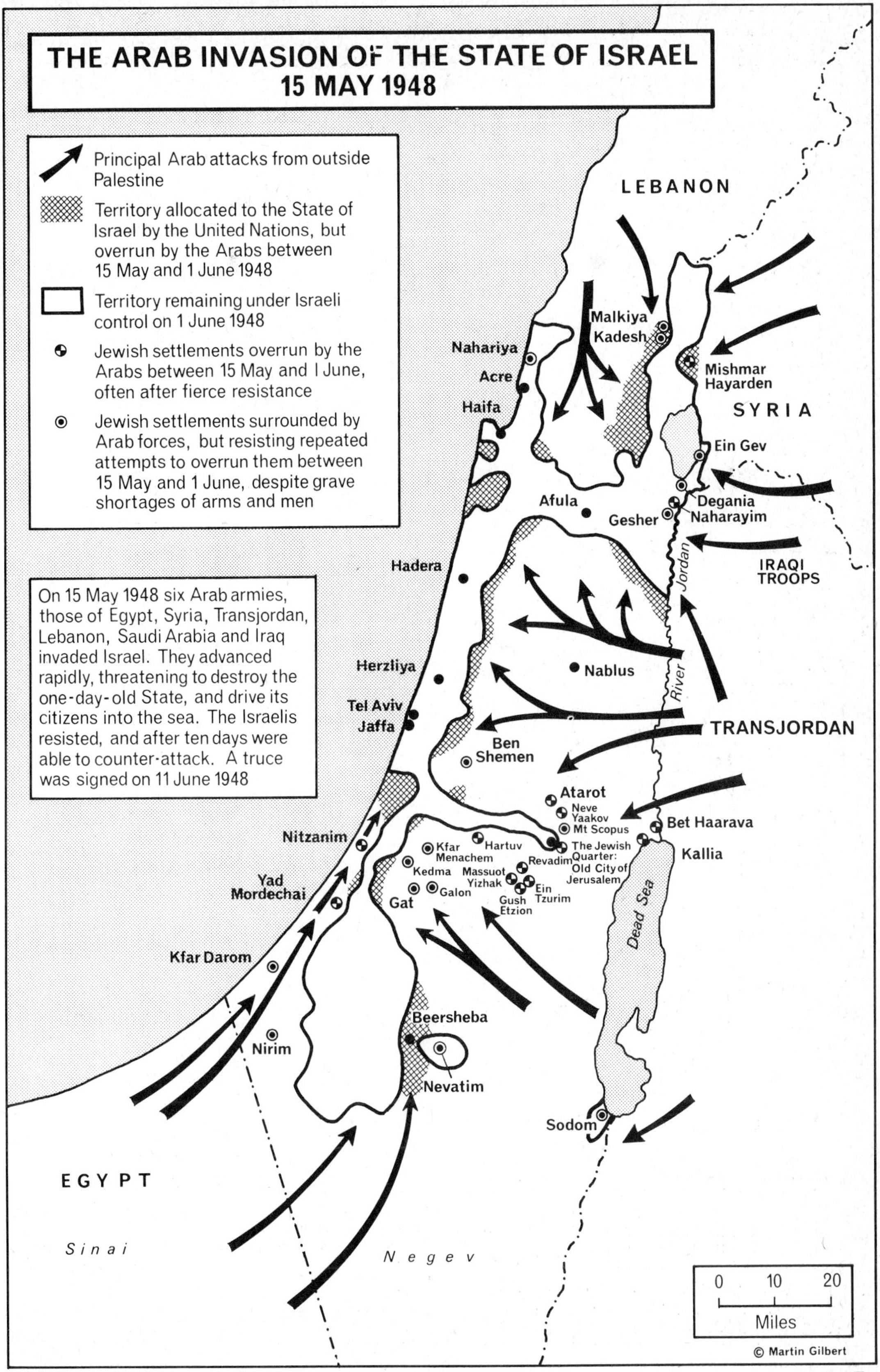

THE ARAB INVASION OF THE STATE OF ISRAEL
15 MAY 1948
Principal Arab attacks from outside Palestine
Territory allocated to the State of Israel by the United Nations, but overrun by the Arabs between 15 May and 1 June 1948
Territory remaining under Israeli control on 1 June 1948
Jewish settlements overrun by the Arabs between 15 May and I June, often after fierce resistance
Jewish settlements surrounded by Arab forces, but resisting repeated attempts to overrun them between 15 May and 1 June, despite grave shortages of arms and men
On 15 May 1948 six Arab armies, those of Egypt, Syria, Transjordan, Lebanon, Saudi Arabia and Iraq invaded Israel. They advanced rapidly, threatening to destroy the one-day-old State, and drive its citizens into the sea. The Israelis resisted, and after ten days were able to counter-attack. A truce was signed on 11 June 1948
LEBANON
Malkiya
Kadesh
Nahariya
Acre
Haifa
Mishmar Hayarden
SYRIA
Ein Gev
Afula
Gesher
Degania
Naharayim
Jordan
IRAQI TROOPS
Hadera
Nablus
Herzliya
River
Tel Aviv
Jaffa
TRANSJORDAN
Ben Shemen
Atarot
Neve Yaakov
Mt Scopus
Bet Haarava
Kallia
Nitzanim
Kfar Menachem
Hartuv
The Jewish Quarter: Old City of Jerusalem
Revadim
Kedma
Massuot Yizhak
Yad Mordechai
Galon
Ein Tzurim
Gat
Gush Etzion
Dead Sea
Kfar Darom
Beersheba
Nirim
Nevatim
Sodom
EGYPT
Sinai
Negev
0
10
20
Miles
© Martin Gilbert

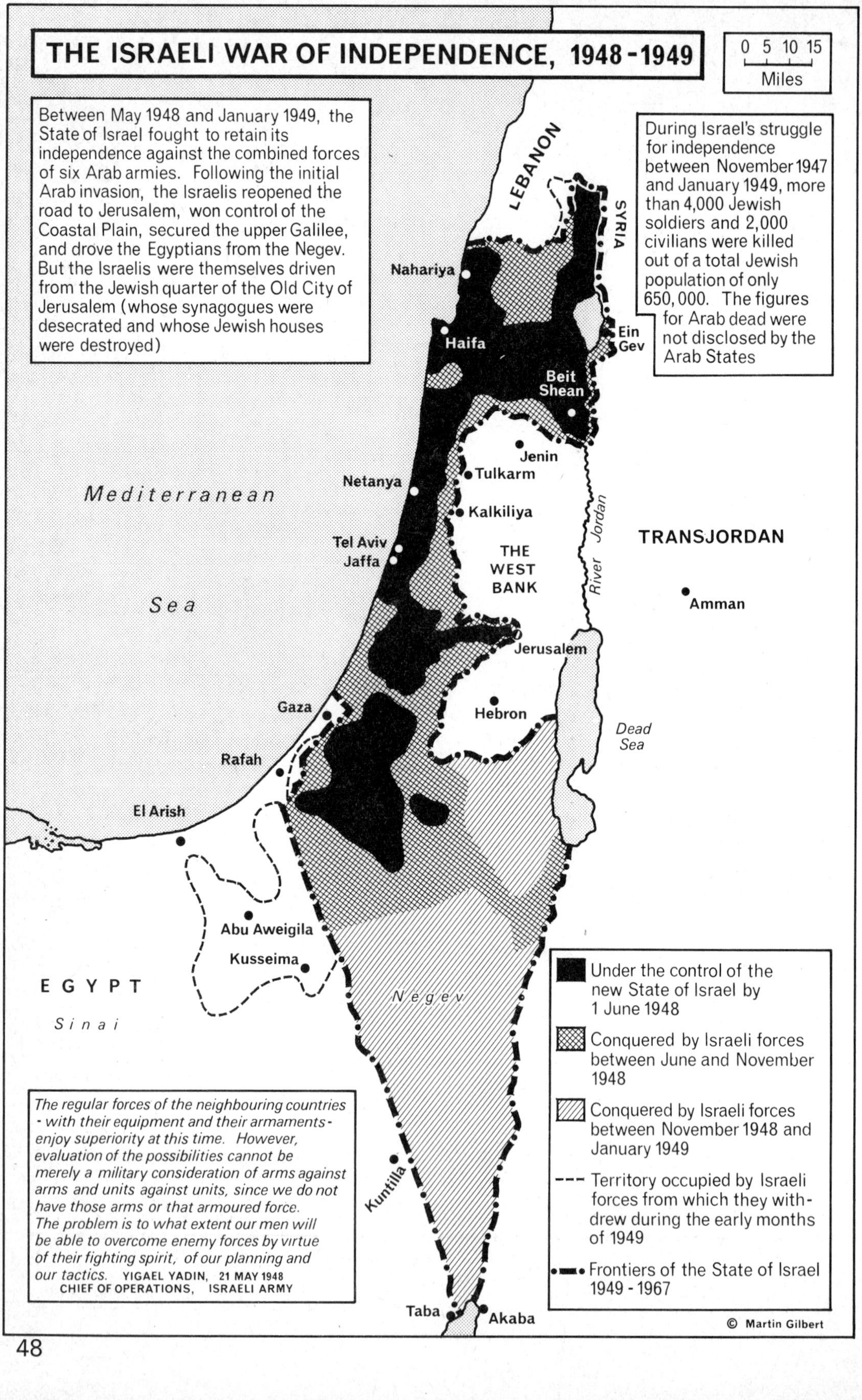

THE ISRAELI WAR OF INDEPENDENCE, 1948-1949

0 5 10 15
Miles

Between May 1948 and January 1949, the State of Israel fought to retain its independence against the combined forces of six Arab armies. Following the initial Arab invasion, the Israelis reopened the road to Jerusalem, won control of the Coastal Plain, secured the upper Galilee, and drove the Egyptians from the Negev. But the Israelis were themselves driven from the Jewish quarter of the Old City of Jerusalem (whose synagogues were desecrated and whose Jewish houses were destroyed)

During Israel's struggle for independence between November 1947 and January 1949, more than 4,000 Jewish soldiers and 2,000 civilians were killed out of a total Jewish population of only 650,000. The figures for Arab dead were not disclosed by the Arab States

LEBANON

SYRIA

Nahariya

Haifa

Ein Gev

Beit Shean

Jenin

Netanya

Tulkarm

Kalkiliya

Tel Aviv Jaffa

THE WEST BANK

River Jordan

TRANSJORDAN

Amman

Mediterranean

Sea

Jerusalem

Hebron

Gaza

Dead Sea

Rafah

El Arish

Abu Aweigila

Kusseima

Negev

E G Y P T

Sinai

The regular forces of the neighbouring countries - with their equipment and their armaments - enjoy superiority at this time. However, evaluation of the possibilities cannot be merely a military consideration of arms against arms and units against units, since we do not have those arms or that armoured force. The problem is to what extent our men will be able to overcome enemy forces by virtue of their fighting spirit, of our planning and our tactics. YIGAEL YADIN, 21 MAY 1948
CHIEF OF OPERATIONS, ISRAELI ARMY

Kuntilla

■ Under the control of the new State of Israel by 1 June 1948

▨ Conquered by Israeli forces between June and November 1948

▨ Conquered by Israeli forces between November 1948 and January 1949

--- Territory occupied by Israeli forces from which they withdrew during the early months of 1949

•■■ Frontiers of the State of Israel 1949 - 1967

Taba Akaba

© Martin Gilbert

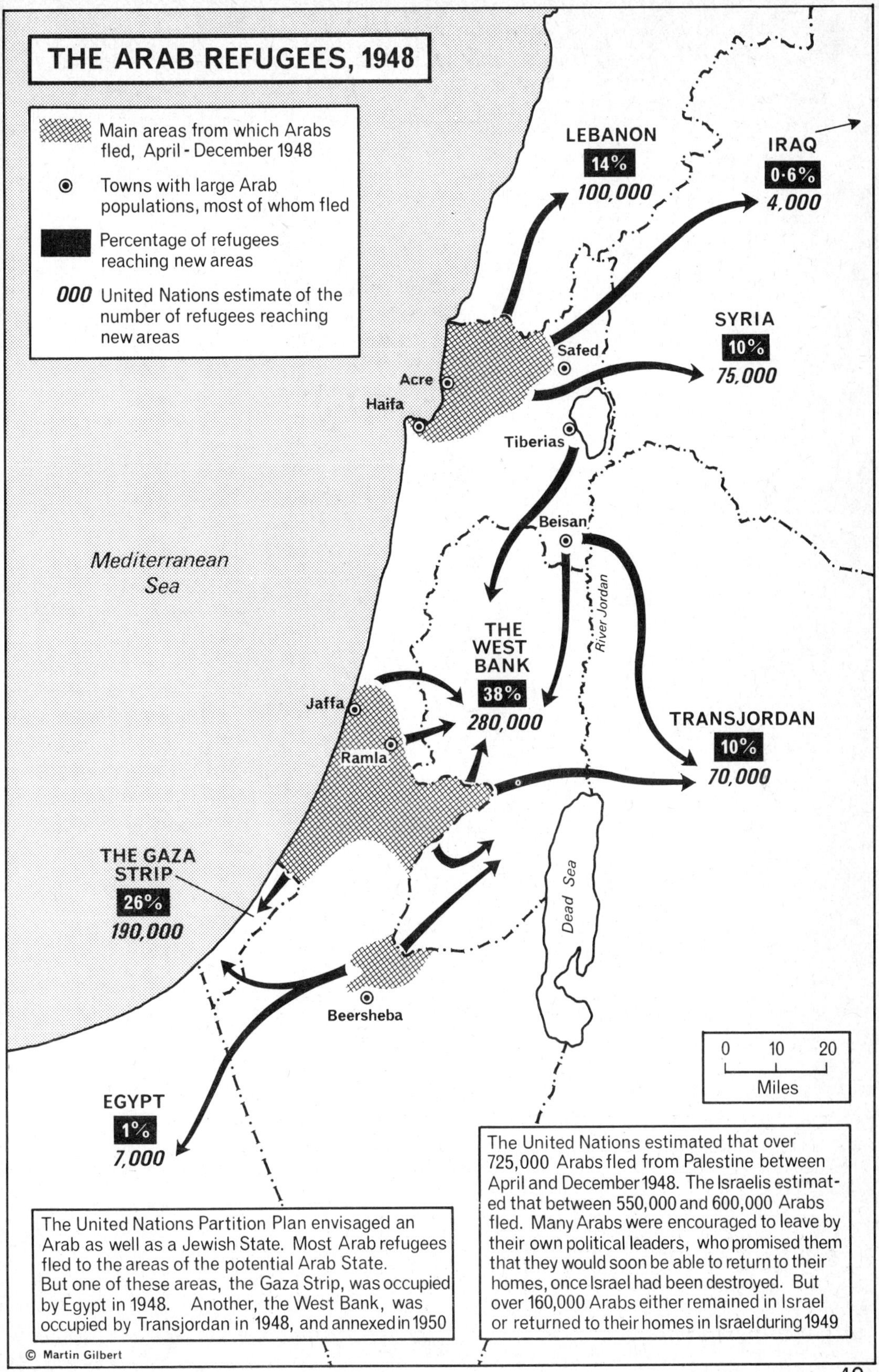
THE ARAB REFUGEES, 1948
Main areas from which Arabs fled, April - December 1948
Towns with large Arab populations, most of whom fled
Percentage of refugees reaching new areas
000 United Nations estimate of the number of refugees reaching new areas
LEBANON
14%
100,000
IRAQ
0·6%
4,000
SYRIA
10%
75,000
Safed
Acre
Haifa
Tiberias
Beisan
Mediterranean Sea
River Jordan
THE WEST BANK
38%
280,000
TRANSJORDAN
10%
70,000
Jaffa
Ramla
THE GAZA STRIP
26%
190,000
Dead Sea
Beersheba
EGYPT
1%
7,000
0 10 20
Miles
© Martin Gilbert

The United Nations Partition Plan envisaged an Arab as well as a Jewish State. Most Arab refugees fled to the areas of the potential Arab State. But one of these areas, the Gaza Strip, was occupied by Egypt in 1948. Another, the West Bank, was occupied by Transjordan in 1948, and annexed in 1950

The United Nations estimated that over 725,000 Arabs fled from Palestine between April and December 1948. The Israelis estimated that between 550,000 and 600,000 Arabs fled. Many Arabs were encouraged to leave by their own political leaders, who promised them that they would soon be able to return to their homes, once Israel had been destroyed. But over 160,000 Arabs either remained in Israel or returned to their homes in Israel during 1949

JEWISH REFUGEES TO ISRAEL FROM ARAB LANDS MAY 1948 - MAY 1972

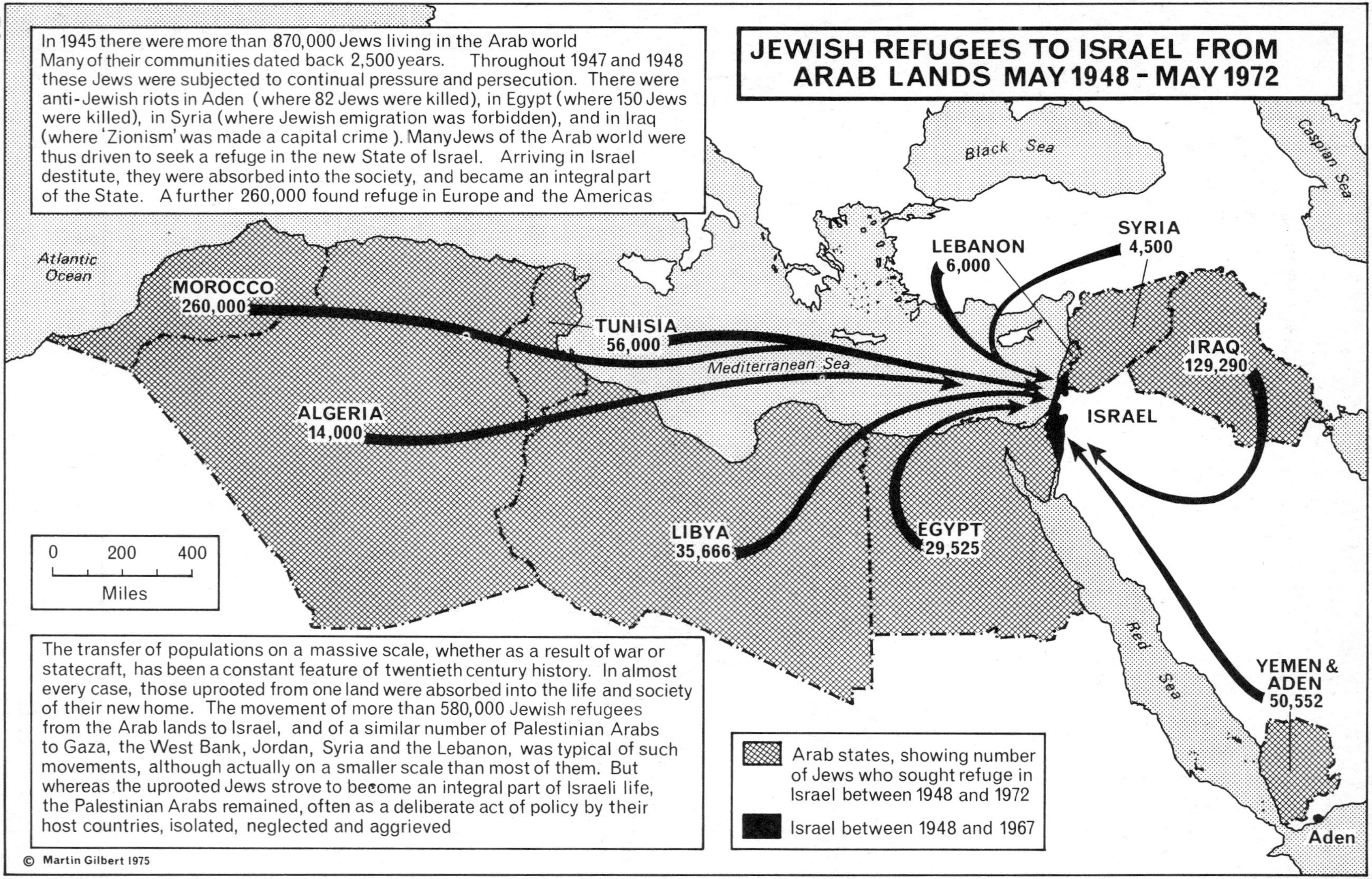

Atlantic Ocean
MOROCCO 260,000
ALGERIA 14,000
TUNISIA 56,000
Mediterranean Sea
LIBYA 35,666
EGYPT 29,525
LEBANON 6,000
SYRIA 4,500
IRAQ 129,290
ISRAEL
YEMEN & ADEN 50,552
Aden
Black Sea
Caspian Sea
Red Sea
0 200 400
Miles
Arab states, showing number of Jews who sought refuge in Israel between 1948 and 1972
Israel between 1948 and 1967

In 1945 there were more than 870,000 Jews living in the Arab world Many of their communities dated back 2,500 years. Throughout 1947 and 1948 these Jews were subjected to continual pressure and persecution. There were anti-Jewish riots in Aden (where 82 Jews were killed), in Egypt (where 150 Jews were killed), in Syria (where Jewish emigration was forbidden), and in Iraq (where 'Zionism' was made a capital crime). Many Jews of the Arab world were thus driven to seek a refuge in the new State of Israel. Arriving in Israel destitute, they were absorbed into the society, and became an integral part of the State. A further 260,000 found refuge in Europe and the Americas

The transfer of populations on a massive scale, whether as a result of war or statecraft, has been a constant feature of twentieth century history. In almost every case, those uprooted from one land were absorbed into the life and society of their new home. The movement of more than 580,000 Jewish refugees from the Arab lands to Israel, and of a similar number of Palestinian Arabs to Gaza, the West Bank, Jordan, Syria and the Lebanon, was typical of such movements, although actually on a smaller scale than most of them. But whereas the uprooted Jews strove to become an integral part of Israeli life, the Palestinian Arabs remained, often as a deliberate act of policy by their host countries, isolated, neglected and aggrieved

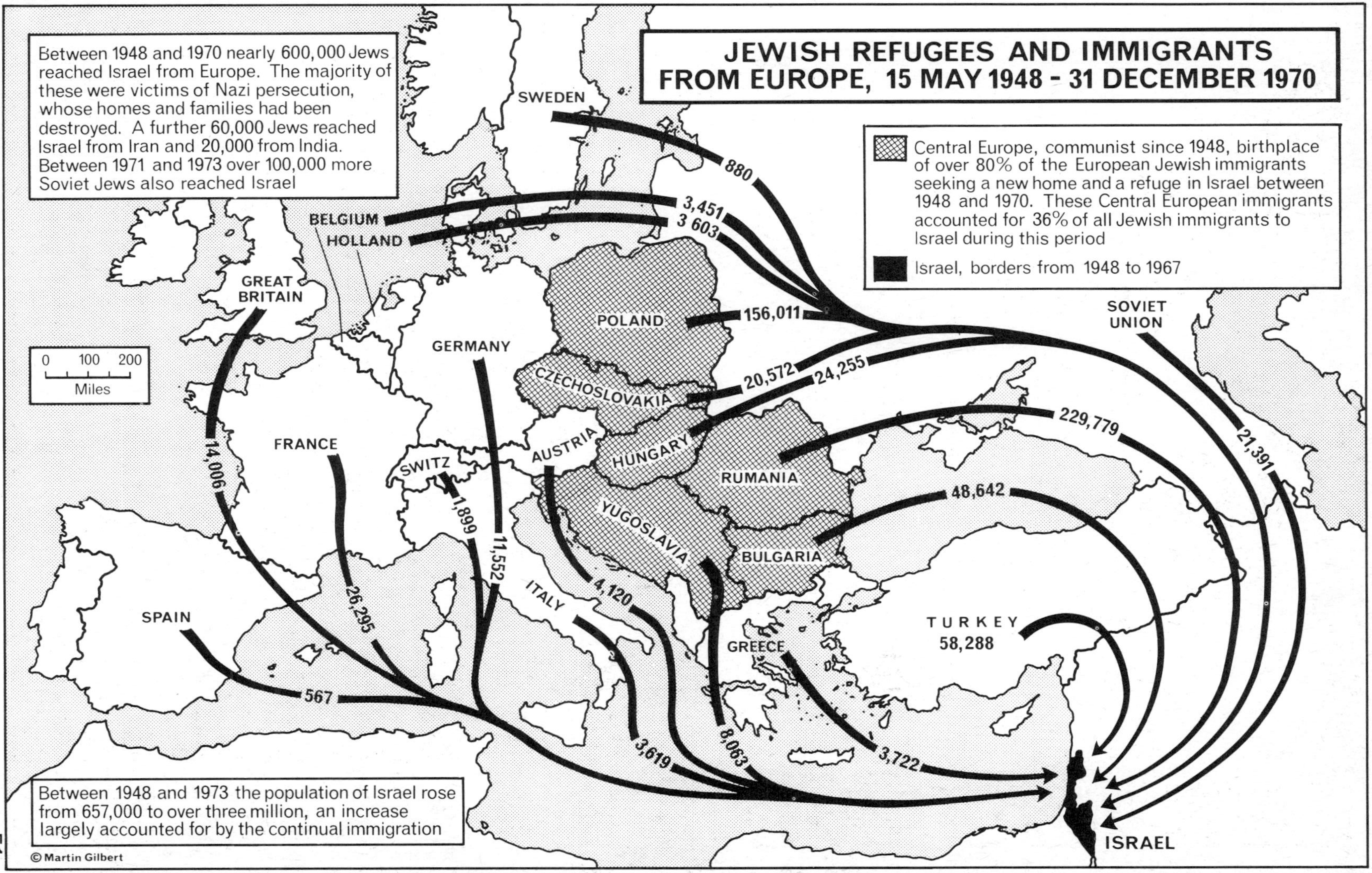

JEWISH REFUGEES AND IMMIGRANTS FROM EUROPE, 15 MAY 1948 - 31 DECEMBER 1970
Central Europe, communist since 1948, birthplace of over 80% of the European Jewish immigrants seeking a new home and a refuge in Israel between 1948 and 1970. These Central European immigrants accounted for 36% of all Jewish immigrants to Israel during this period
Israel, borders from 1948 to 1967
Between 1948 and 1970 nearly 600,000 Jews reached Israel from Europe. The majority of these were victims of Nazi persecution, whose homes and families had been destroyed. A further 60,000 Jews reached Israel from Iran and 20,000 from India. Between 1971 and 1973 over 100,000 more Soviet Jews also reached Israel
Between 1948 and 1973 the population of Israel rose from 657,000 to over three million, an increase largely accounted for by the continual immigration
SWEDEN
880
BELGIUM
3,451
HOLLAND
3 603
GREAT BRITAIN
14,006
POLAND
156,011
GERMANY
11,552
CZECHOSLOVAKIA
20,572
24,255
SOVIET UNION
21,391
0 100 200
Miles
FRANCE
26,295
SWITZ
1,899
AUSTRIA
4,120
HUNGARY
RUMANIA
229,779
YUGOSLAVIA
8,063
BULGARIA
48,642
ITALY
3,619
SPAIN
567
GREECE
3,722
TURKEY
58,288
ISRAEL
© Martin Gilbert

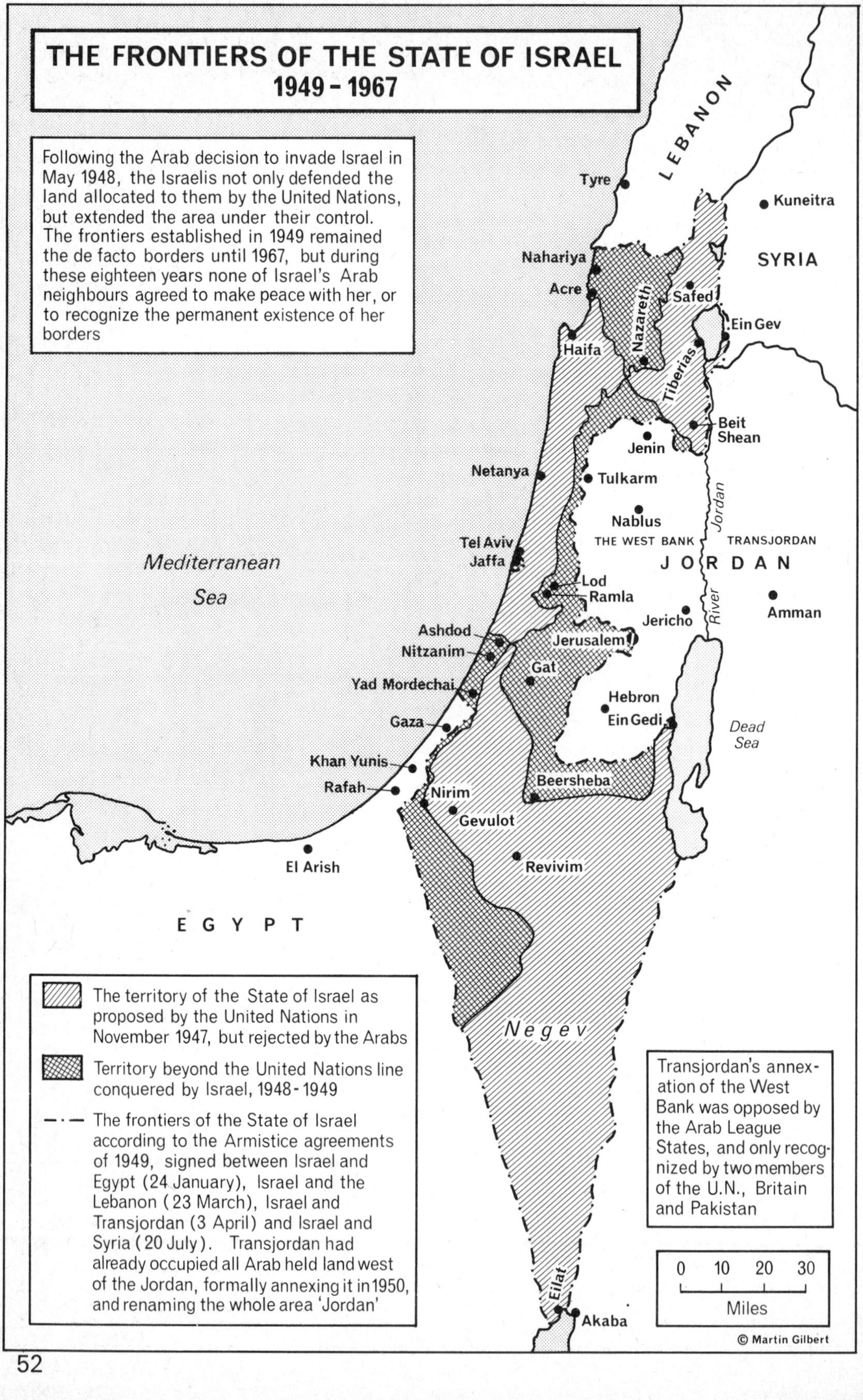
THE FRONTIERS OF THE STATE OF ISRAEL
1949 - 1967
Following the Arab decision to invade Israel in May 1948, the Israelis not only defended the land allocated to them by the United Nations, but extended the area under their control. The frontiers established in 1949 remained the de facto borders until 1967, but during these eighteen years none of Israel's Arab neighbours agreed to make peace with her, or to recognize the permanent existence of her borders
LEBANON
Tyre
Kuneitra
SYRIA
Nahariya
Acre
Safed
Nazareth
Ein Gev
Haifa
Tiberias
Beit Shean
Jenin
Netanya
Tulkarm
Jordan
Nablus
THE WEST BANK
TRANSJORDAN
Tel Aviv
Jaffa
JORDAN
Mediterranean
Sea
Lod
Ramla
River
Amman
Jericho
Ashdod
Nitzanim
Jerusalem
Gat
Yad Mordechai
Hebron
Ein Gedi
Gaza
Dead Sea
Khan Yunis
Rafah
Nirim
Beersheba
Gevulot
El Arish
Revivim
EGYPT
Negev
The territory of the State of Israel as proposed by the United Nations in November 1947, but rejected by the Arabs
Territory beyond the United Nations line conquered by Israel, 1948 - 1949
The frontiers of the State of Israel according to the Armistice agreements of 1949, signed between Israel and Egypt (24 January), Israel and the Lebanon (23 March), Israel and Transjordan (3 April) and Israel and Syria (20 July). Transjordan had already occupied all Arab held land west of the Jordan, formally annexing it in 1950, and renaming the whole area 'Jordan'
Transjordan's annexation of the West Bank was opposed by the Arab League States, and only recognized by two members of the U.N., Britain and Pakistan
0 10 20 30
Miles
Eilat
Akaba
© Martin Gilbert

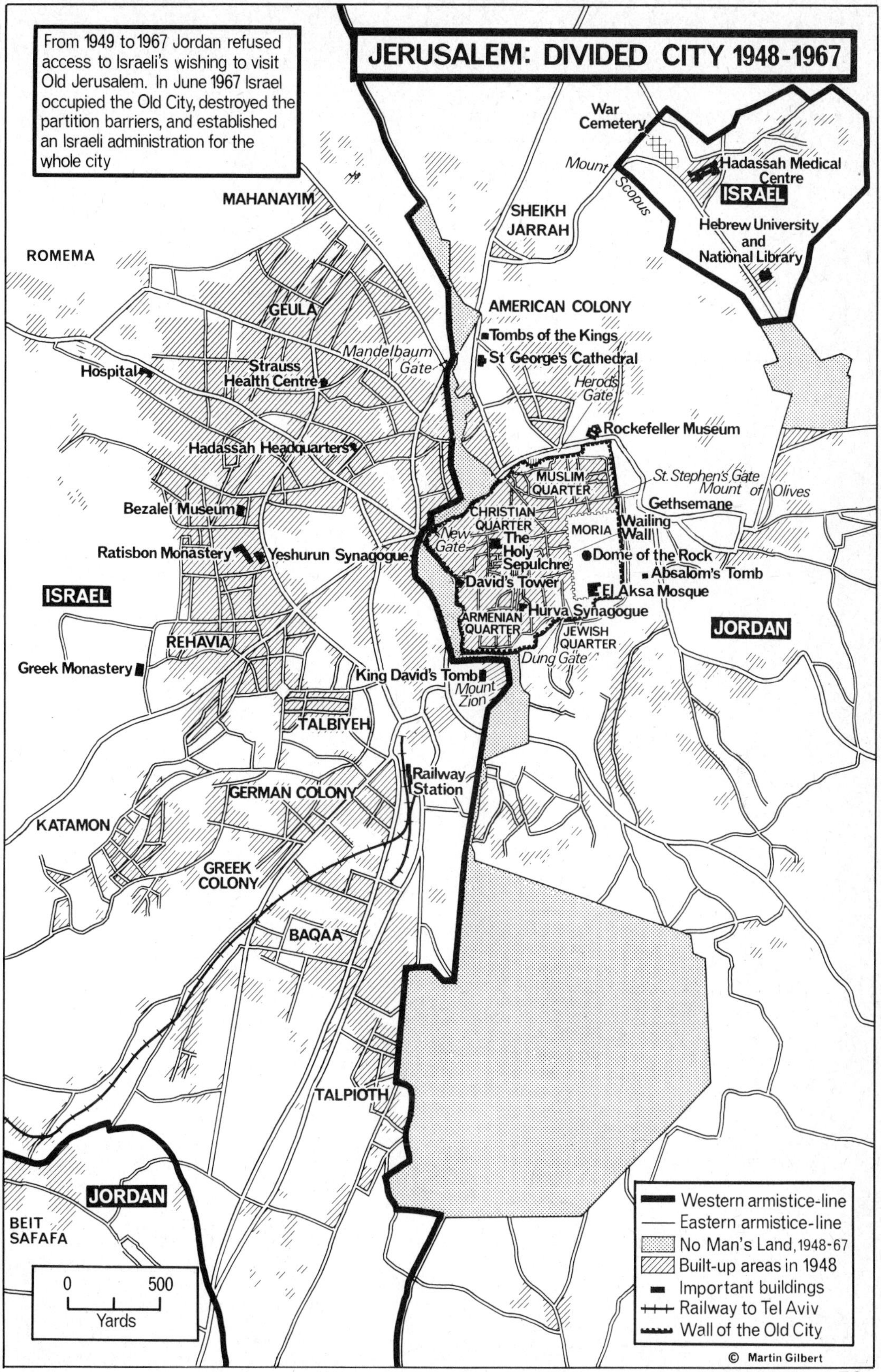

JERUSALEM: DIVIDED CITY 1948-1967
From 1949 to 1967 Jordan refused access to Israeli's wishing to visit Old Jerusalem. In June 1967 Israel occupied the Old City, destroyed the partition barriers, and established an Israeli administration for the whole city
War Cemetery
Mount Scopus
Hadassah Medical Centre
ISRAEL
Hebrew University and National Library
MAHANAYIM
SHEIKH JARRAH
ROMEMA
AMERICAN COLONY
GEULA
Tombs of the Kings
Mandelbaum Gate
St George's Cathedral
Hospital
Strauss Health Centre
Herods Gate
Rockefeller Museum
Hadassah Headquarters
MUSLIM QUARTER
St. Stephen's Gate
Mount of Olives
Gethsemane
Bezalel Museum
CHRISTIAN QUARTER
New Gate
The Holy Sepulchre
MORIA
Wailing Wall
Ratisbon Monastery
Yeshurun Synagogue
Dome of the Rock
Absalom's Tomb
ISRAEL
David's Tower
El Aksa Mosque
Hurva Synagogue
ARMENIAN QUARTER
JEWISH QUARTER
JORDAN
REHAVIA
Dung Gate
Greek Monastery
King David's Tomb
Mount Zion
TALBIYEH
Railway Station
GERMAN COLONY
KATAMON
GREEK COLONY
BAQAA
TALPIOTH
JORDAN
BEIT SAFAFA
0
500
Yards
Western armistice-line
Eastern armistice-line
No Man's Land, 1948-67
Built-up areas in 1948
Important buildings
Railway to Tel Aviv
Wall of the Old City
© Martin Gilbert

ISRAEL'S SENSE OF INSECURITY 1949 – 1967

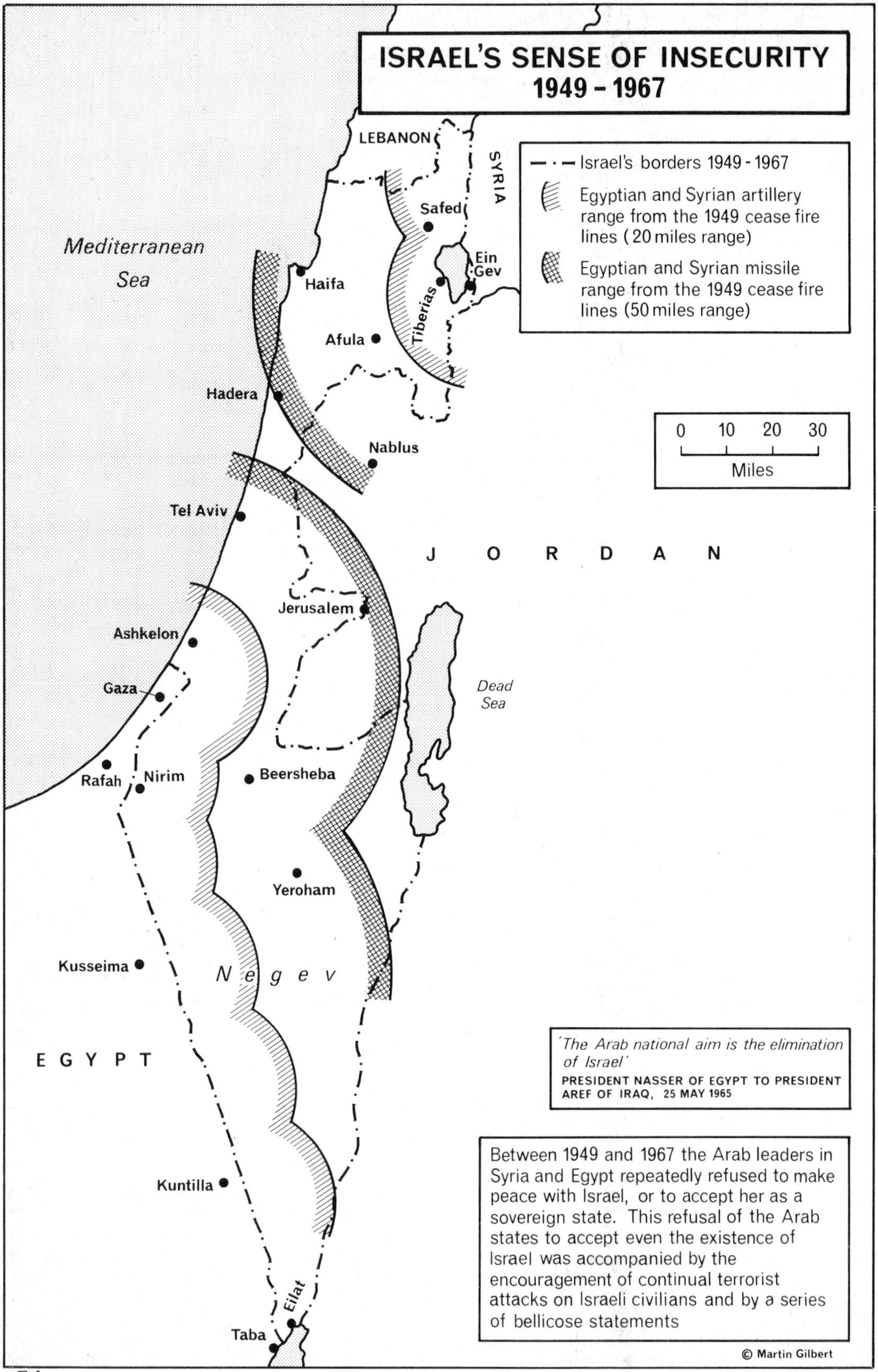
LEBANON
SYRIA
Israel's borders 1949 - 1967
Egyptian and Syrian artillery range from the 1949 cease fire lines (20 miles range)
Egyptian and Syrian missile range from the 1949 cease fire lines (50 miles range)
Mediterranean Sea
Safed
Ein Gev
Tiberias
Haifa
Afula
Hadera
Nablus
0 10 20 30
Miles
Tel Aviv
J O R D A N
Jerusalem
Ashkelon
Gaza
Dead Sea
Rafah
Nirim
Beersheba
Yeroham
Kusseima
Negev
EGYPT
Kuntilla
Eilat
Taba
© Martin Gilbert

'The Arab national aim is the elimination of Israel'

PRESIDENT NASSER OF EGYPT TO PRESIDENT AREF OF IRAQ, 25 MAY 1965

Between 1949 and 1967 the Arab leaders in Syria and Egypt repeatedly refused to make peace with Israel, or to accept her as a sovereign state. This refusal of the Arab states to accept even the existence of Israel was accompanied by the encouragement of continual terrorist attacks on Israeli civilians and by a series of bellicose statements

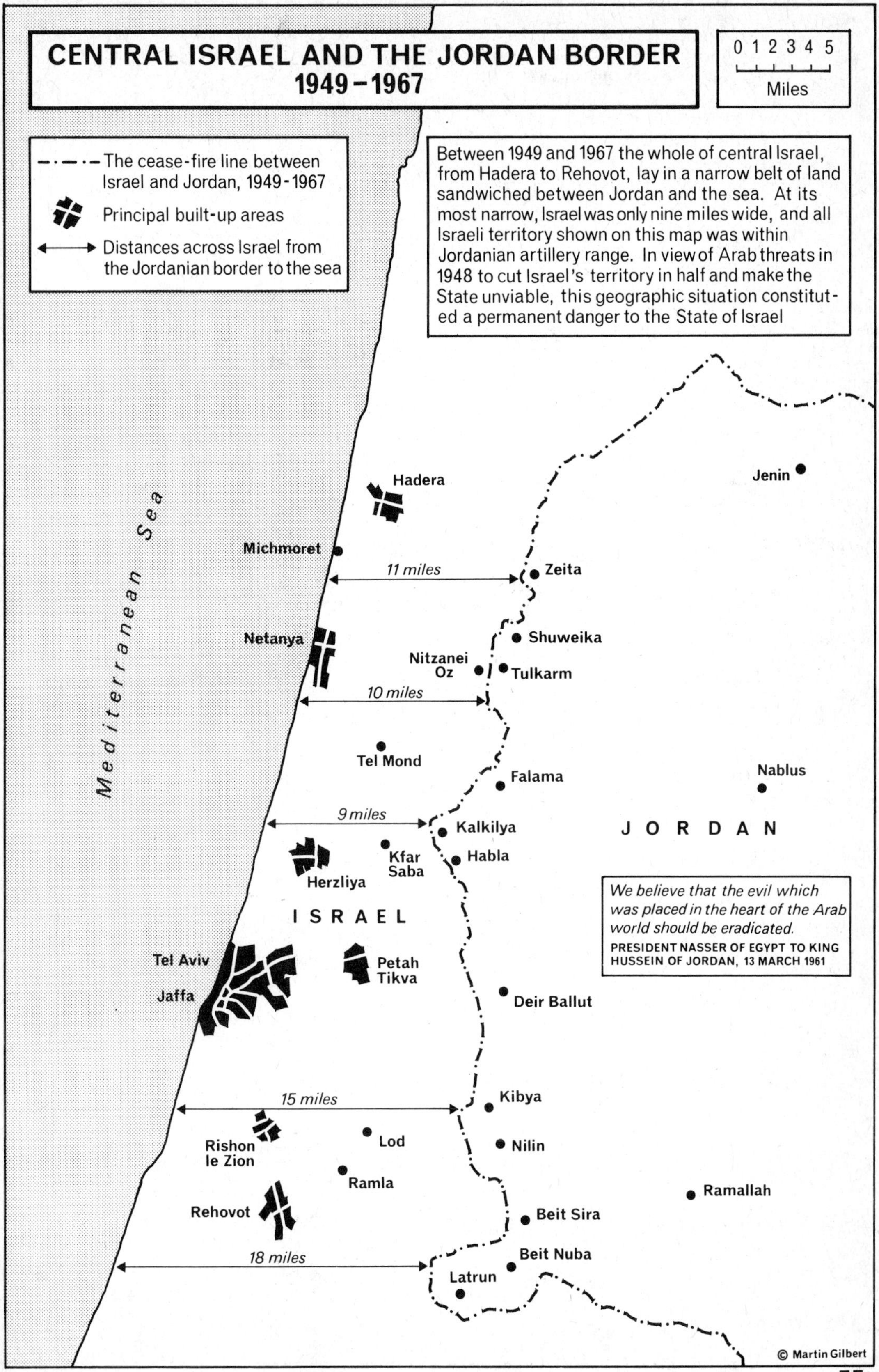
CENTRAL ISRAEL AND THE JORDAN BORDER 1949–1967
0 1 2 3 4 5
Miles
The cease-fire line between Israel and Jordan, 1949-1967
Principal built-up areas
Distances across Israel from the Jordanian border to the sea
Between 1949 and 1967 the whole of central Israel, from Hadera to Rehovot, lay in a narrow belt of land sandwiched between Jordan and the sea. At its most narrow, Israel was only nine miles wide, and all Israeli territory shown on this map was within Jordanian artillery range. In view of Arab threats in 1948 to cut Israel's territory in half and make the State unviable, this geographic situation constituted a permanent danger to the State of Israel
Mediterranean Sea
Hadera
Jenin
Michmoret
11 miles
Zeita
Netanya
Shuweika
Nitzanei Oz
Tulkarm
10 miles
Tel Mond
Falama
Nablus
9 miles
Kalkilya
JORDAN
Kfar Saba
Habla
Herzliya
ISRAEL
We believe that the evil which was placed in the heart of the Arab world should be eradicated.
PRESIDENT NASSER OF EGYPT TO KING HUSSEIN OF JORDAN, 13 MARCH 1961
Tel Aviv
Jaffa
Petah Tikva
Deir Ballut
15 miles
Kibya
Rishon le Zion
Lod
Nilin
Ramla
Ramallah
Rehovot
Beit Sira
Beit Nuba
18 miles
Latrun
© Martin Gilbert

THE ARAB REFUGEES 1949-1967

In April 1949, at the UN Palestine Conciliation Commission at Lausanne, Israel offered to repatriate 100,000 Arab refugees within the framework of a general settlement. The Arab delegations rejected the offer. In 1950 the United Nations Relief and Works Agency (UNRWA) proposed resettling Arab refugees in Sinai, Jordan and Syria, but the Arab Governments also rejected this proposal. In 1952 the UN Refugee Rehabilitation Fund offered the Arab States $200 million to find 'homes and jobs' for the refugees. The Arab States used some of the money for relief work, but did not even apply for the greater part of the fund

The refugees are the corner-stone in the Arab struggle against Israel. The refugees are the armaments of the Arabs and Arab nationalism.
RADIO CAIRO 19 JULY 1957

The refugees will not return while the flag of Israel flies over the soil of Palestine. They will return when the flag of Palestine is hoisted over Arab Palestine.
'AL GUMHURIYYA', CAIRO, 27 JUNE 1961

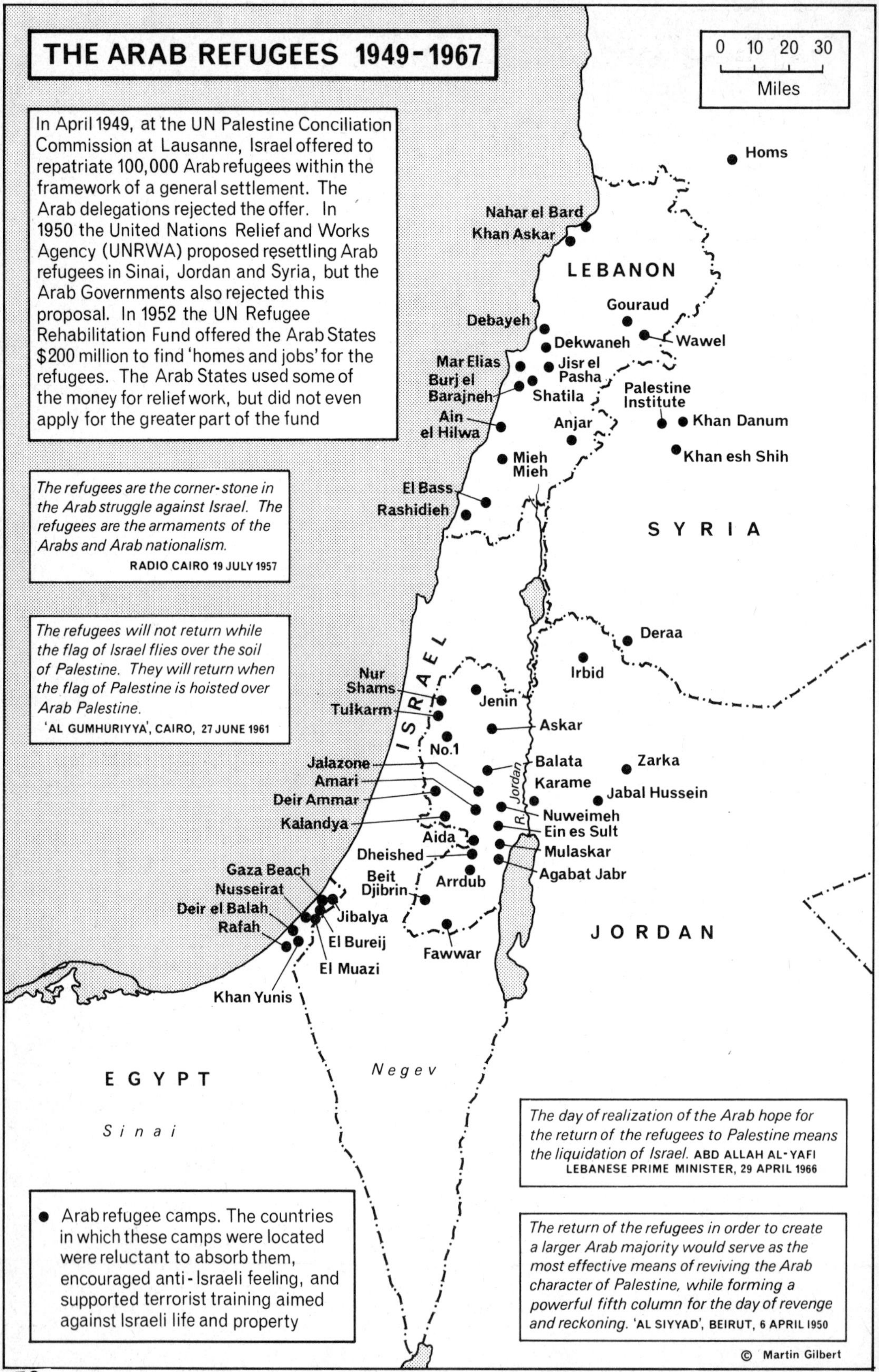

0 10 20 30
Miles
Homs
Nahar el Bard
Khan Askar
LEBANON
Gouraud
Debayeh
Dekwaneh
Wawel
Mar Elias
Jisr el Pasha
Burj el Barajneh
Shatila
Palestine Institute
Ain el Hilwa
Anjar
Khan Danum
Mieh Mieh
Khan esh Shih
El Bass
Rashidieh
SYRIA
Deraa
Irbid
ISRAEL
Nur Shams
Tulkarm
Jenin
Askar
No.1
Jalazone
Amari
Deir Ammar
Kalandya
Balata
Zarka
Karame
Jabal Hussein
R. Jordan
Nuweimeh
Ein es Sult
Aida
Mulaskar
Dheished
Agabat Jabr
Arrdub
Beit Djibrin
Gaza Beach
Nusseirat
Deir el Balah
Rafah
Jibalya
El Bureij
El Muazi
Khan Yunis
Fawwar
JORDAN
EGYPT
Sinai
Negev

The day of realization of the Arab hope for the return of the refugees to Palestine means the liquidation of Israel. ABD ALLAH AL-YAFI LEBANESE PRIME MINISTER, 29 APRIL 1966

● Arab refugee camps. The countries in which these camps were located were reluctant to absorb them, encouraged anti-Israeli feeling, and supported terrorist training aimed against Israeli life and property

The return of the refugees in order to create a larger Arab majority would serve as the most effective means of reviving the Arab character of Palestine, while forming a powerful fifth column for the day of revenge and reckoning. 'AL SIYYAD', BEIRUT, 6 APRIL 1950

THE ARABS OF NORTHERN ISRAEL

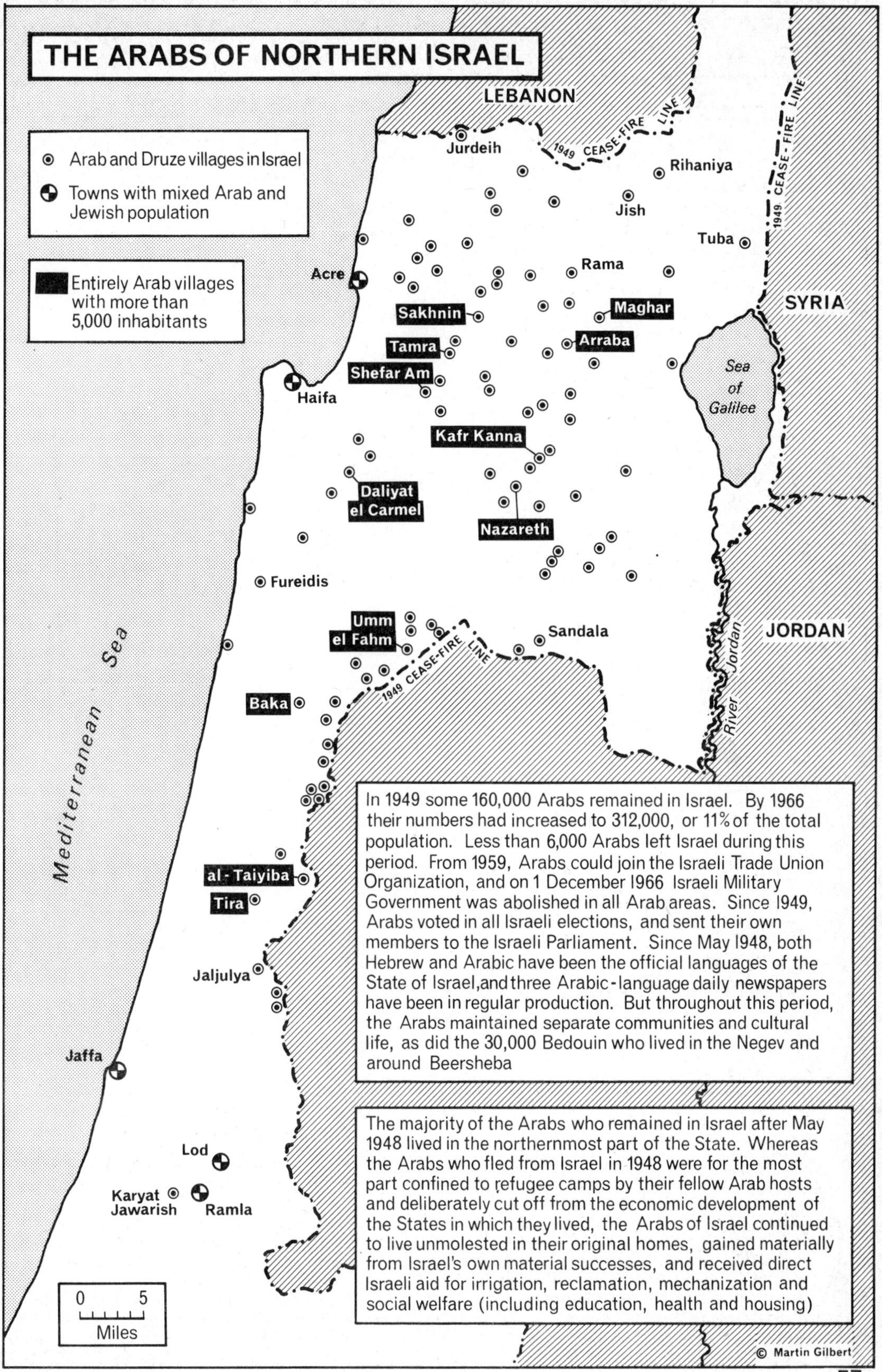

Arab and Druze villages in Israel
Towns with mixed Arab and Jewish population
Entirely Arab villages with more than 5,000 inhabitants
LEBANON
1949 CEASE-FIRE LINE
SYRIA
JORDAN
Jurdeih
Rihaniya
Jish
Tuba
Rama
Acre
Sakhnin
Maghar
Tamra
Arraba
Shefar Am
Haifa
Sea of Galilee
Kafr Kanna
Daliyat el Carmel
Nazareth
Fureidis
Umm el Fahm
Sandala
River Jordan
Mediterranean Sea
Baka
al-Taiyiba
Tira
Jaljulya
Jaffa
Lod
Karyat Jawarish
Ramla
0 5
Miles
© Martin Gilbert

In 1949 some 160,000 Arabs remained in Israel. By 1966 their numbers had increased to 312,000, or 11% of the total population. Less than 6,000 Arabs left Israel during this period. From 1959, Arabs could join the Israeli Trade Union Organization, and on 1 December 1966 Israeli Military Government was abolished in all Arab areas. Since 1949, Arabs voted in all Israeli elections, and sent their own members to the Israeli Parliament. Since May 1948, both Hebrew and Arabic have been the official languages of the State of Israel, and three Arabic-language daily newspapers have been in regular production. But throughout this period, the Arabs maintained separate communities and cultural life, as did the 30,000 Bedouin who lived in the Negev and around Beersheba

The majority of the Arabs who remained in Israel after May 1948 lived in the northernmost part of the State. Whereas the Arabs who fled from Israel in 1948 were for the most part confined to refugee camps by their fellow Arab hosts and deliberately cut off from the economic development of the States in which they lived, the Arabs of Israel continued to live unmolested in their original homes, gained materially from Israel's own material successes, and received direct Israeli aid for irrigation, reclamation, mechanization and social welfare (including education, health and housing)

NORTHERN ISRAEL AND THE GOLAN HEIGHTS 1949 - 1967

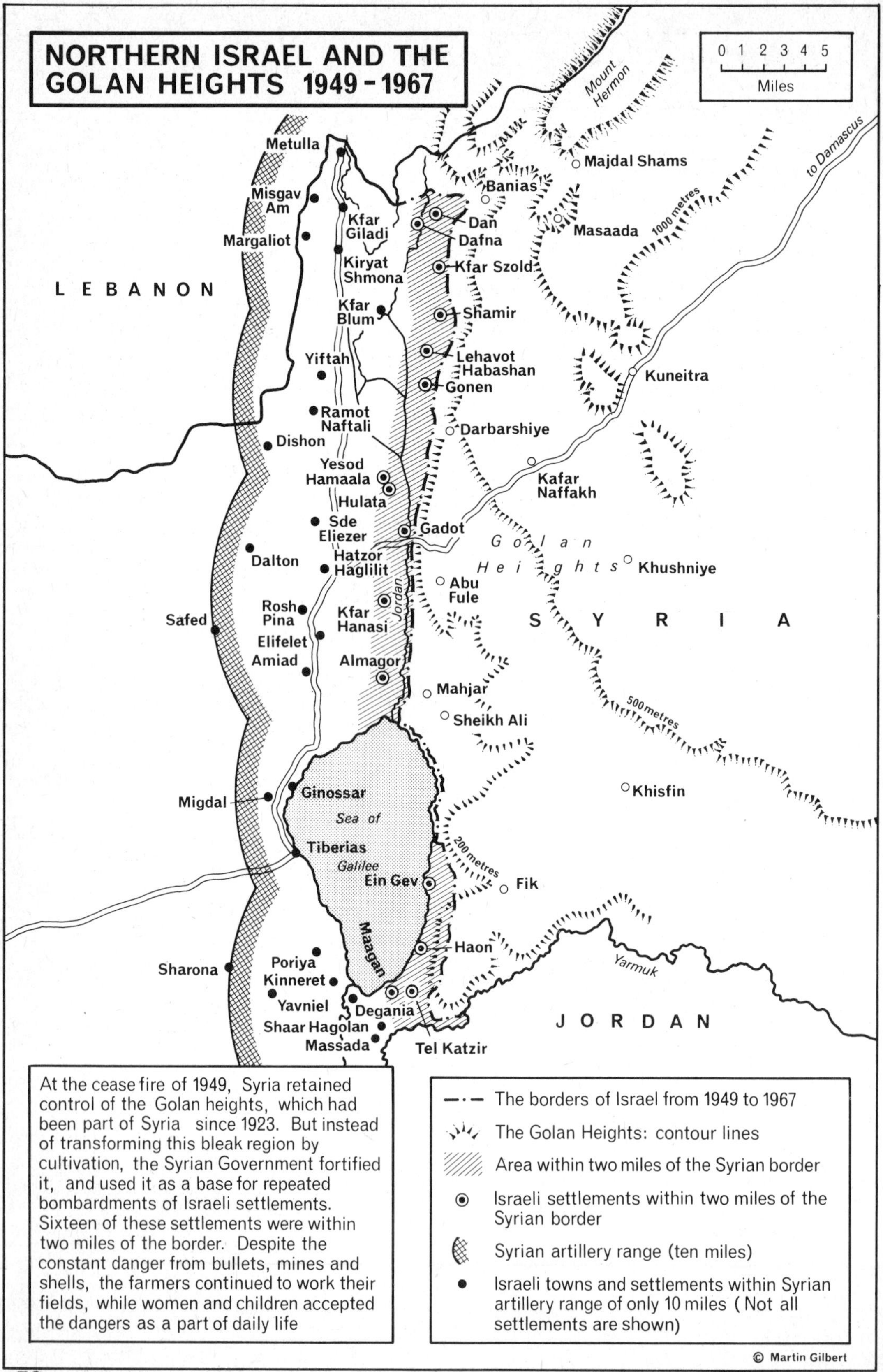

0 1 2 3 4 5
Miles
Mount Hermon
to Damascus
Metulla
Misgav Am
Margaliot
Kfar Giladi
Kiryat Shmona
LEBANON
Kfar Blum
Yiftah
Ramot Naftali
Dishon
Yesod Hamaala
Hulata
Sde Eliezer
Dalton
Hatzor Haglilit
Rosh Pina
Safed
Elifelet
Amiad
Kfar Hanasi
Jordan
Almagor
Migdal
Ginossar
Sea of Galilee
Tiberias
Ein Gev
Maagan
Sharona
Poriya
Kinneret
Yavniel
Degania
Shaar Hagolan
Massada
Tel Katzir
Banias
Majdal Shams
Dan
Dafna
Masaada
1000 metres
Kfar Szold
Shamir
Lehavot Habashan
Gonen
Kuneitra
Darbarshiye
Kafar Naffakh
Gadot
Golan Heights
Khushniye
Abu Fule
SYRIA
Mahjar
Sheikh Ali
500 metres
Khisfin
200 metres
Fik
Haon
Yarmuk
JORDAN

At the cease fire of 1949, Syria retained control of the Golan heights, which had been part of Syria since 1923. But instead of transforming this bleak region by cultivation, the Syrian Government fortified it, and used it as a base for repeated bombardments of Israeli settlements. Sixteen of these settlements were within two miles of the border. Despite the constant danger from bullets, mines and shells, the farmers continued to work their fields, while women and children accepted the dangers as a part of daily life

- The borders of Israel from 1949 to 1967
- The Golan Heights: contour lines
- Area within two miles of the Syrian border
- Israeli settlements within two miles of the Syrian border
- Syrian artillery range (ten miles)
- Israeli towns and settlements within Syrian artillery range of only 10 miles (Not all settlements are shown)

ISRAELI NAHAL SETTLEMENTS 1951 - 1967

Continued Arab attacks on Jewish settlements after the 1949 ceasefire led to the establishment, in 1951, of the first 'Nahal' settlement, under the control of the Israel Defence Forces. The settlers were graduates of youth movements, embarking on pioneer work in a border area, and also undertaking regular military training while building up the new settlement. Most of these 'Nahal' settlements were in previously uncultivated areas, and in regions exposed to persistent Arab sniping and border raids. Despite these handicaps, their agriculture flourished. 'Nahal' groups also worked on existing settlements near the borders

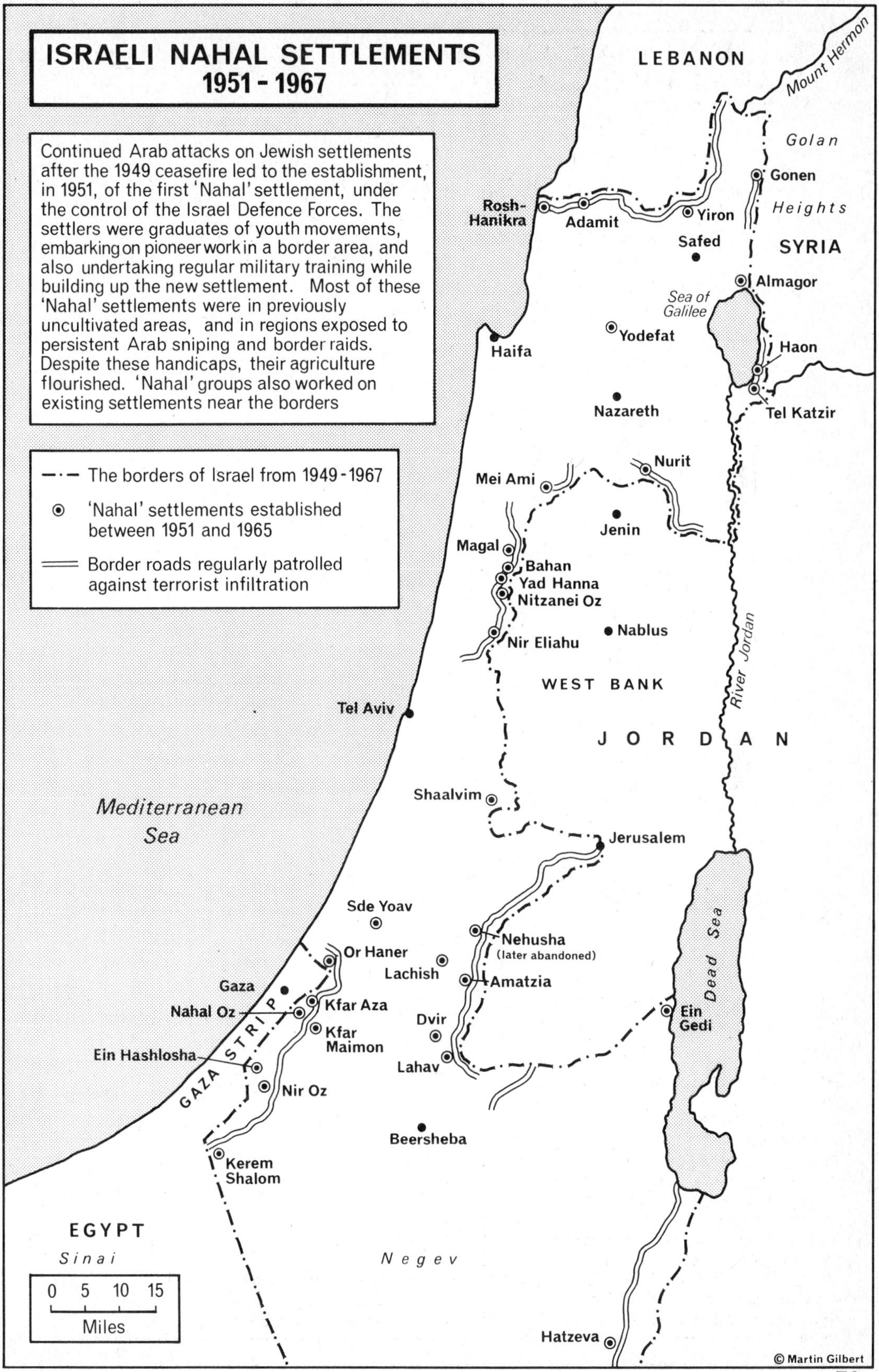

—·— The borders of Israel from 1949 - 1967
⊙ 'Nahal' settlements established between 1951 and 1965
═ Border roads regularly patrolled against terrorist infiltration
LEBANON
Mount Hermon
Golan
Heights
SYRIA
Gonen
Rosh-Hanikra
Adamit
Yiron
Safed
Almagor
Sea of Galilee
Yodefat
Haifa
Haon
Tel Katzir
Nazareth
Nurit
Mei Ami
Jenin
Magal
Bahan
Yad Hanna
Nitzanei Oz
Nablus
Nir Eliahu
WEST BANK
River Jordan
Tel Aviv
J O R D A N
Mediterranean Sea
Shaalvim
Jerusalem
Sde Yoav
Or Haner
Lachish
Nehusha
(later abandoned)
Amatzia
Gaza
Nahal Oz
Kfar Aza
Kfar Maimon
Dvir
Ein Hashlosha
Lahav
Ein Gedi
Dead Sea
GAZA STRIP
Nir Oz
Beersheba
Kerem Shalom
EGYPT
Sinai
Negev
0 5 10 15
Miles
Hatzeva
© Martin Gilbert

TERRORIST RAIDS INTO ISRAEL 1951 - 1956

Palestinian terrorist groups, or Fedayeen, began systematic raids into Israel from 1950. Towards the end of 1954, the Egyptian Government supervised the formal establishment of Palestinian terrorist groups in the Gaza strip and north-eastern Sinai. Throughout 1955 an increasing number of raids were launched into Israel. From 1951 to 1956, Israeli vehicles were ambushed, farms attacked, fields boobytrapped and roads mined. Fedayeen from Gaza also infiltrated into Jordan, and operated from there. Saudi Arabia, Syria and Lebanon each gave the Fedayeen support and refuge. Local Jordanian-Palestinian Fedayeen were also active operating from the West Bank

ISRAELI DEATHS AS A RESULT OF FEDAYEEN ATTACKS

YEAR	FROM	ISRAELI DEAD
1951	JORDAN	111
	EGYPT	26
1952	JORDAN	114
	EGYPT	48
1953	JORDAN	124
	EGYPT	38
1954	JORDAN	117
	EGYPT	50
1955	JORDAN	37
	EGYPT	241
1951-55	SYRIA	55
	LEBANON	6

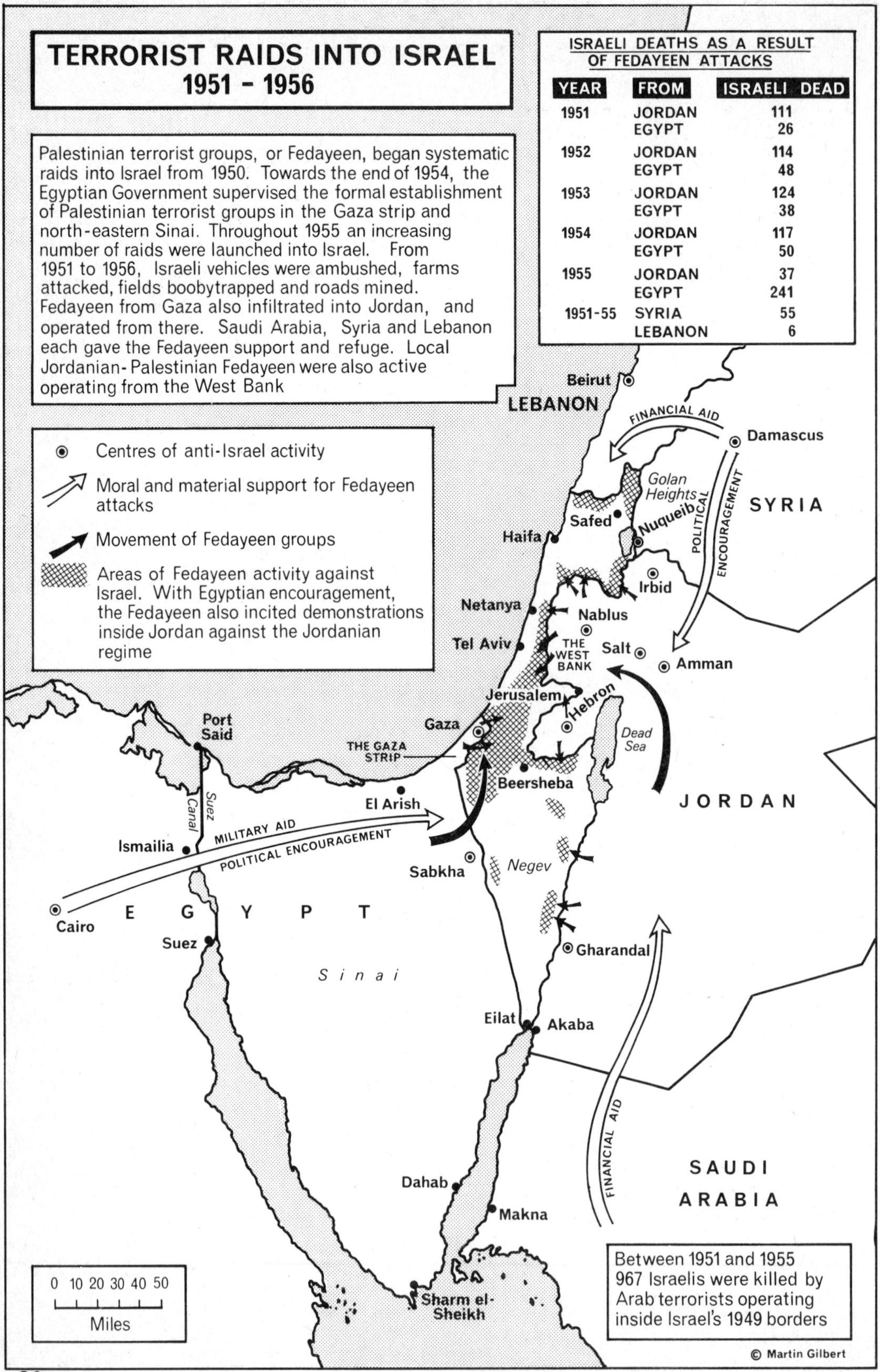

Centres of anti-Israel activity
Moral and material support for Fedayeen attacks
Movement of Fedayeen groups
Areas of Fedayeen activity against Israel. With Egyptian encouragement, the Fedayeen also incited demonstrations inside Jordan against the Jordanian regime
Beirut
LEBANON
FINANCIAL AID
Damascus
Golan Heights
Safed
Nuqueib
POLITICAL ENCOURAGEMENT
SYRIA
Haifa
Irbid
Netanya
Nablus
Tel Aviv
THE WEST BANK
Salt
Amman
Jerusalem
Hebron
Gaza
THE GAZA STRIP
Port Said
Dead Sea
Beersheba
El Arish
JORDAN
Suez Canal
MILITARY AID
POLITICAL ENCOURAGEMENT
Ismailia
Sabkha
Negev
Cairo
EGYPT
Suez
Gharandal
Sinai
Eilat
Akaba
FINANCIAL AID
SAUDI ARABIA
Dahab
Makna
Sharm el-Sheikh
0 10 20 30 40 50
Miles

Between 1951 and 1955 967 Israelis were killed by Arab terrorists operating inside Israel's 1949 borders

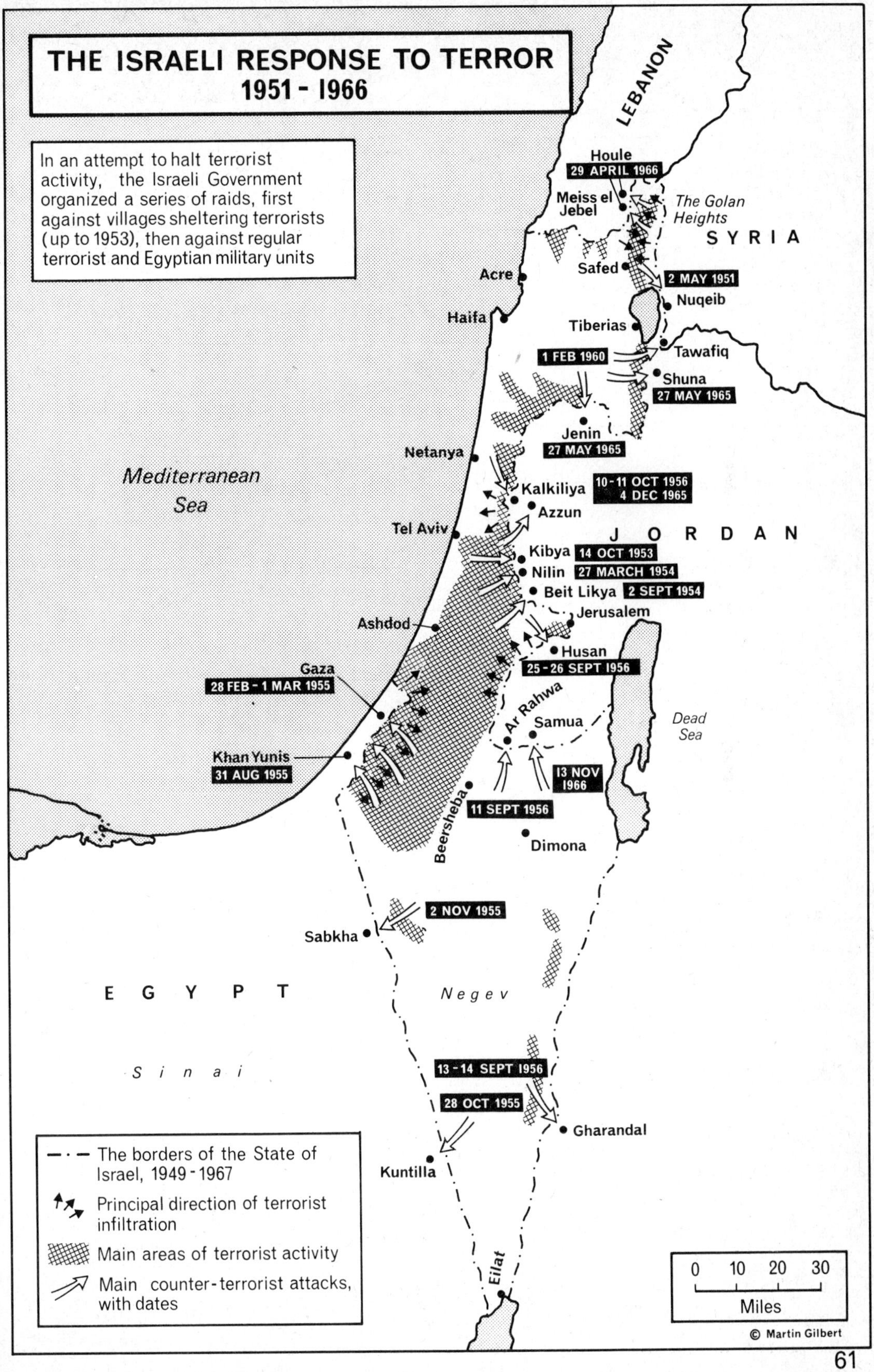
THE ISRAELI RESPONSE TO TERROR
1951 - 1966
In an attempt to halt terrorist activity, the Israeli Government organized a series of raids, first against villages sheltering terrorists (up to 1953), then against regular terrorist and Egyptian military units
LEBANON
Houle
29 APRIL 1966
Meiss el Jebel
The Golan Heights
SYRIA
Safed
2 MAY 1951
Acre
Nuqeib
Haifa
Tiberias
1 FEB 1960
Tawafiq
Shuna
27 MAY 1965
Jenin
27 MAY 1965
Netanya
Mediterranean Sea
Kalkiliya
10-11 OCT 1956
4 DEC 1965
Azzun
Tel Aviv
JORDAN
Kibya
14 OCT 1953
Nilin
27 MARCH 1954
Beit Likya
2 SEPT 1954
Jerusalem
Ashdod
Husan
25-26 SEPT 1956
Gaza
28 FEB - 1 MAR 1955
Ar Rahwa
Samua
Dead Sea
Khan Yunis
31 AUG 1955
13 NOV 1966
Beersheba
11 SEPT 1956
Dimona
2 NOV 1955
Sabkha
EGYPT
Negev
Sinai
13-14 SEPT 1956
28 OCT 1955
Gharandal
Kuntilla
Eilat
The borders of the State of Israel, 1949-1967
Principal direction of terrorist infiltration
Main areas of terrorist activity
Main counter-terrorist attacks, with dates
0 10 20 30
Miles
© Martin Gilbert

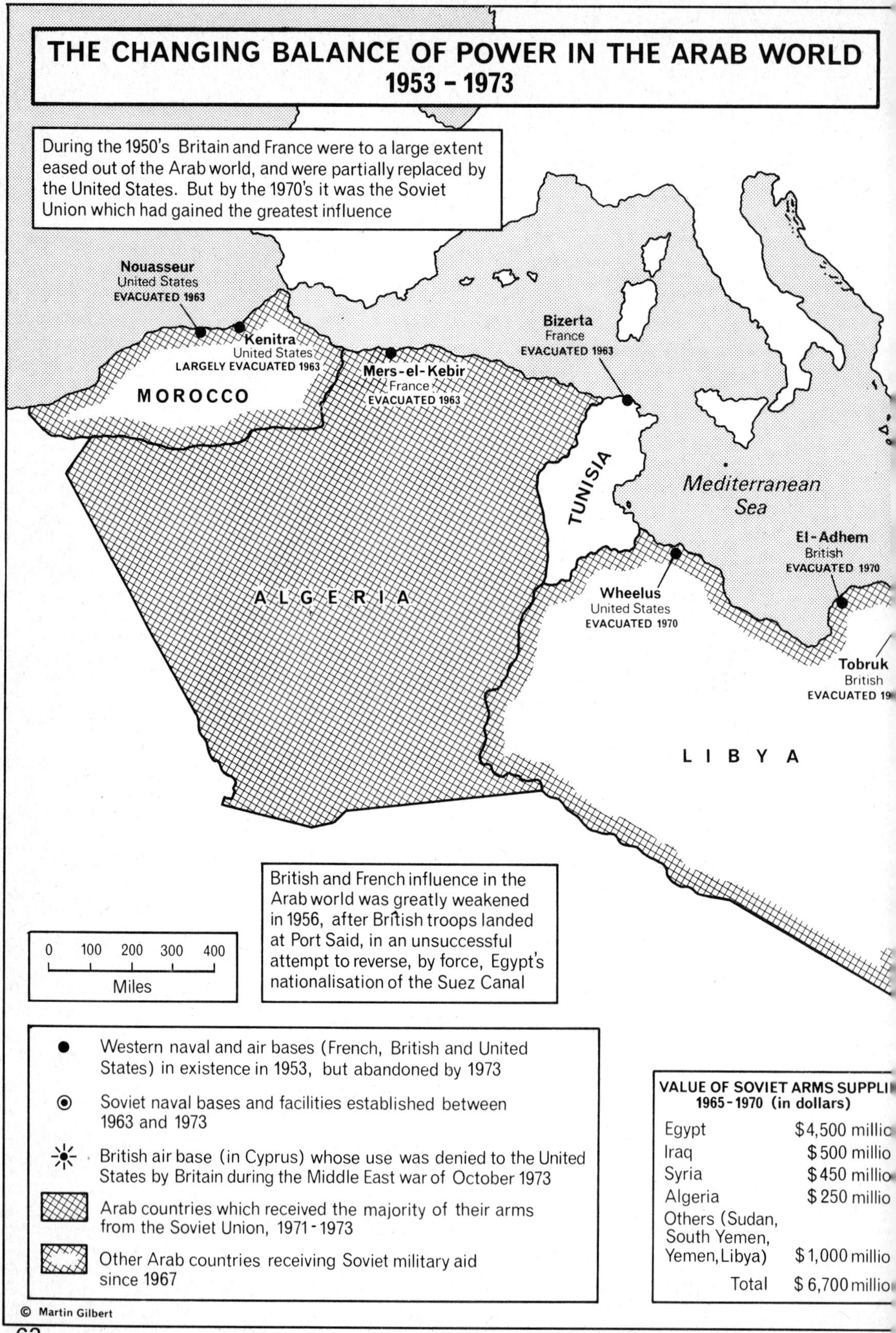
THE CHANGING BALANCE OF POWER IN THE ARAB WORLD
1953 - 1973
During the 1950's Britain and France were to a large extent eased out of the Arab world, and were partially replaced by the United States. But by the 1970's it was the Soviet Union which had gained the greatest influence
Nouasseur
United States
EVACUATED 1963
Kenitra
United States
LARGELY EVACUATED 1963
MOROCCO
Mers-el-Kebir
France
EVACUATED 1963
Bizerta
France
EVACUATED 1963
TUNISIA
Mediterranean Sea
El-Adhem
British
EVACUATED 1970
ALGERIA
Wheelus
United States
EVACUATED 1970
Tobruk
British
EVACUATED 19
LIBYA
British and French influence in the Arab world was greatly weakened in 1956, after British troops landed at Port Said, in an unsuccessful attempt to reverse, by force, Egypt's nationalisation of the Suez Canal
0 100 200 300 400
Miles
Western naval and air bases (French, British and United States) in existence in 1953, but abandoned by 1973
Soviet naval bases and facilities established between 1963 and 1973
British air base (in Cyprus) whose use was denied to the United States by Britain during the Middle East war of October 1973
Arab countries which received the majority of their arms from the Soviet Union, 1971 - 1973
Other Arab countries receiving Soviet military aid since 1967
VALUE OF SOVIET ARMS SUPPLI
1965 - 1970 (in dollars)
Egypt $4,500 millio
Iraq $500 millio
Syria $450 millio
Algeria $250 millio
Others (Sudan, South Yemen, Yemen, Libya) $1,000 millio
Total $6,700 millio
© Martin Gilbert

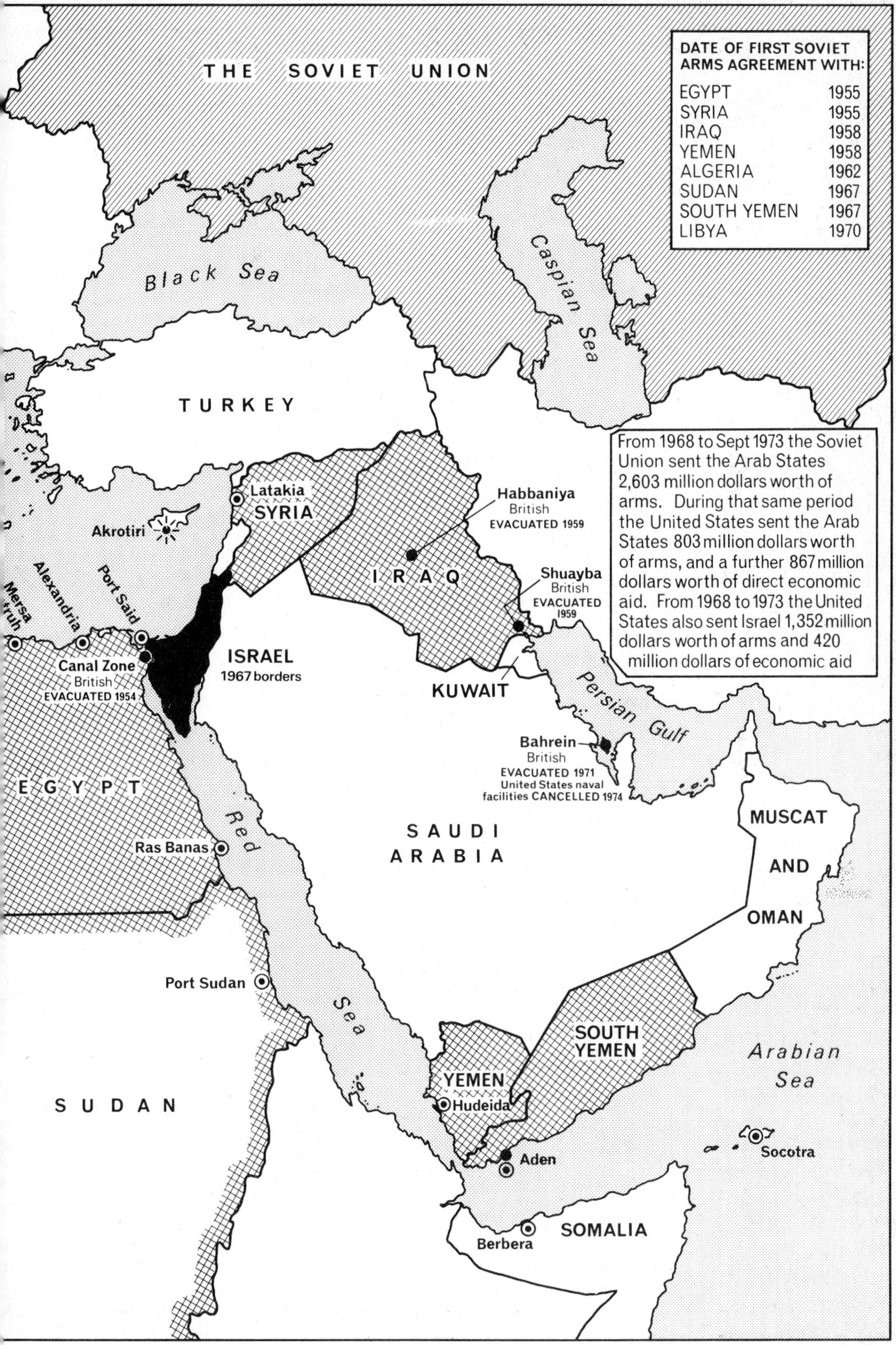
THE SOVIET UNION
DATE OF FIRST SOVIET ARMS AGREEMENT WITH:
EGYPT 1955
SYRIA 1955
IRAQ 1958
YEMEN 1958
ALGERIA 1962
SUDAN 1967
SOUTH YEMEN 1967
LIBYA 1970
Black Sea
Caspian Sea
TURKEY
From 1968 to Sept 1973 the Soviet Union sent the Arab States 2,603 million dollars worth of arms. During that same period the United States sent the Arab States 803 million dollars worth of arms, and a further 867 million dollars worth of direct economic aid. From 1968 to 1973 the United States also sent Israel 1,352 million dollars worth of arms and 420 million dollars of economic aid
Latakia
SYRIA
Habbaniya
British
EVACUATED 1959
Akrotiri
IRAQ
Shuayba
British
EVACUATED 1959
Mersa Matruh
Alexandria
Port Said
ISRAEL
1967 borders
Canal Zone
British
EVACUATED 1954
KUWAIT
Persian Gulf
Bahrein
British
EVACUATED 1971
United States naval facilities CANCELLED 1974
EGYPT
MUSCAT AND OMAN
SAUDI ARABIA
Red Sea
Ras Banas
Port Sudan
SOUTH YEMEN
Arabian Sea
YEMEN
Hudeida
SUDAN
Aden
Socotra
SOMALIA
Berbera

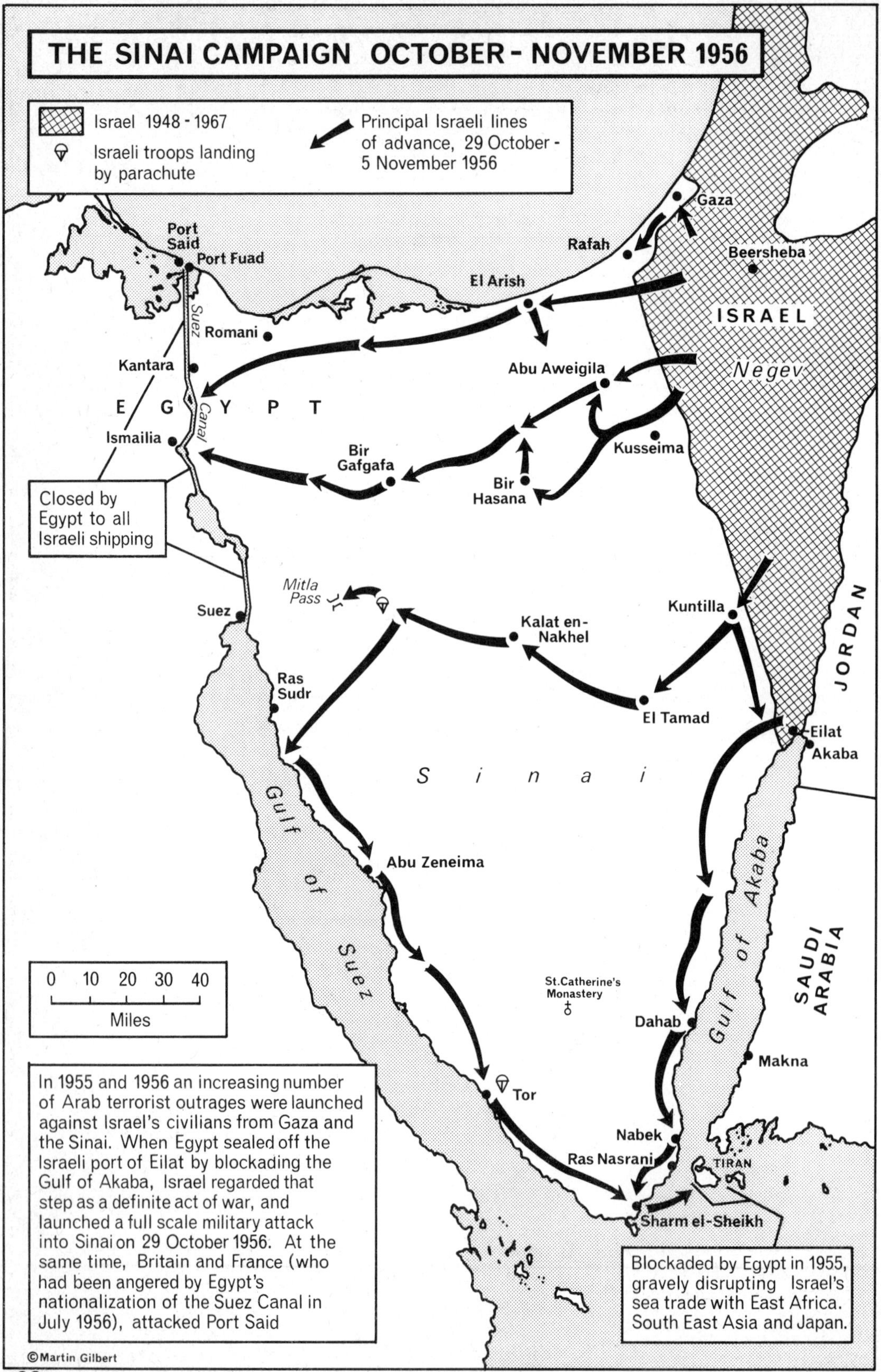
THE SINAI CAMPAIGN OCTOBER - NOVEMBER 1956
Israel 1948 - 1967
Israeli troops landing by parachute
Principal Israeli lines of advance, 29 October - 5 November 1956
Gaza
Rafah
Beersheba
El Arish
ISRAEL
Negev
Port Said
Port Fuad
Suez Canal
Romani
Kantara
E G Y P T
Abu Aweigila
Kusseima
Ismailia
Bir Gafgafa
Bir Hasana
Closed by Egypt to all Israeli shipping
Mitla Pass
Suez
Kalat en-Nakhel
Kuntilla
JORDAN
Ras Sudr
El Tamad
Eilat
Akaba
S i n a i
Gulf of Suez
Abu Zeneima
Gulf of Akaba
SAUDI ARABIA
0 10 20 30 40
Miles
St.Catherine's Monastery
Dahab
Makna
Tor
Nabek
Ras Nasrani
TIRAN
Sharm el-Sheikh
In 1955 and 1956 an increasing number of Arab terrorist outrages were launched against Israel's civilians from Gaza and the Sinai. When Egypt sealed off the Israeli port of Eilat by blockading the Gulf of Akaba, Israel regarded that step as a definite act of war, and launched a full scale military attack into Sinai on 29 October 1956. At the same time, Britain and France (who had been angered by Egypt's nationalization of the Suez Canal in July 1956), attacked Port Said
Blockaded by Egypt in 1955, gravely disrupting Israel's sea trade with East Africa. South East Asia and Japan.
©Martin Gilbert

THE ISRAELI WITHDRAWAL FROM SINAI MARCH 1957

As a result of pressure from both the United Nations and the United States, Israeli forces withdrew from Sinai in March 1957. A United Nations force of 3,300 men took up positions in Gaza, at Sharm el-Sheikh and along the Sinai border, in order to secure that border against attack, and to prevent Egypt re-blockading the Gulf of Akaba. But despite Israel's withdrawal, the Egyptians refused to open the Suez Canal to Israeli shipping, and continued to allow Gaza to be used as a base for terrorist raids inside Israel

Before Israel withdrew from the Gaza Strip she was assured that Egyptian troops would not return. But Egypt moved her forces into Gaza within 48 hours of the Israeli withdrawal. At the same time as the Israeli withdrawal, British troops left Port Said and French forces withdrew from Port Fuad

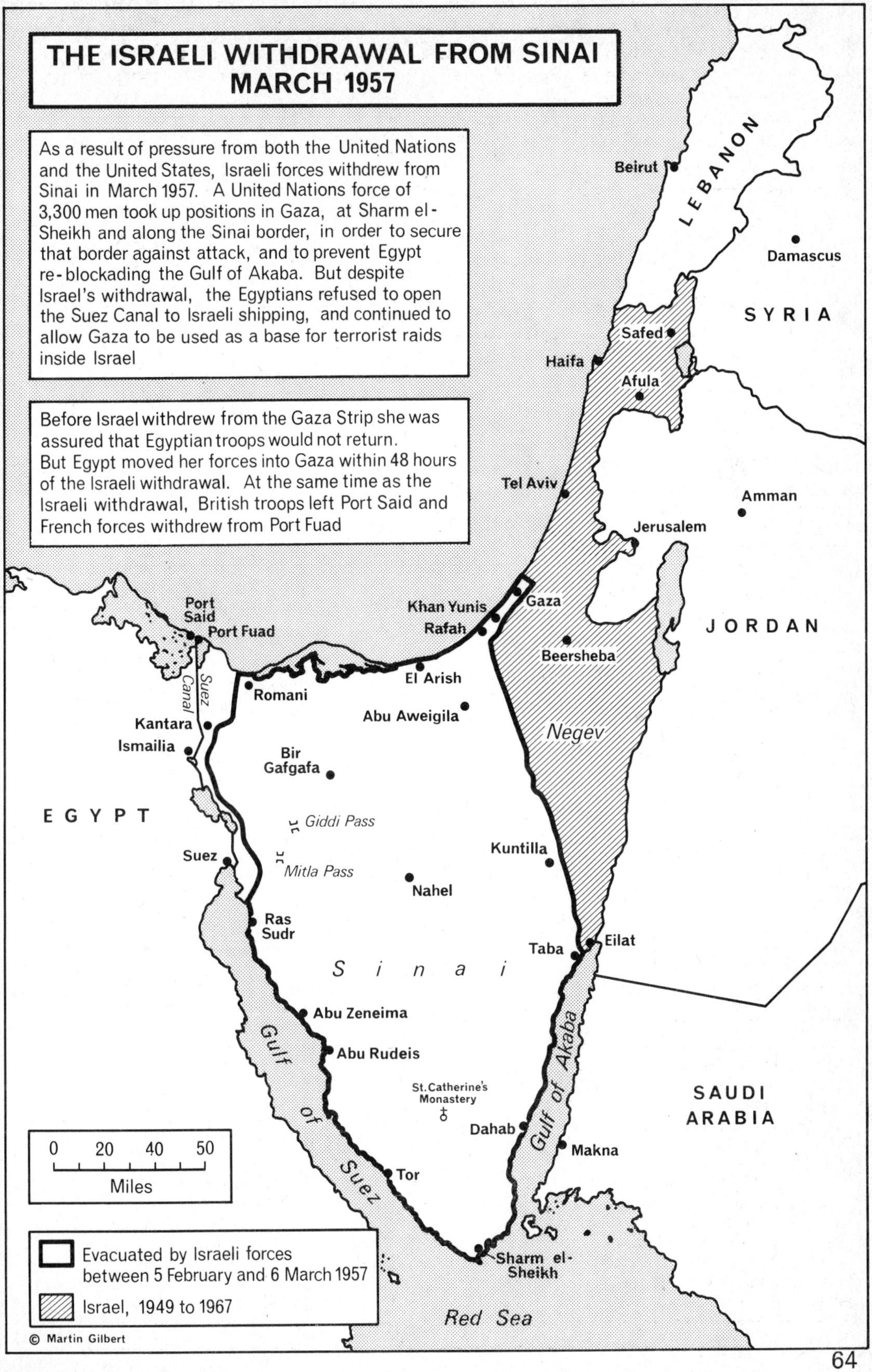

LEBANON
Beirut
Damascus
SYRIA
Safed
Haifa
Afula
Tel Aviv
Amman
Jerusalem
JORDAN
Gaza
Khan Yunis
Rafah
Beersheba
Negev
Port Said
Port Fuad
Suez Canal
Romani
El Arish
Abu Aweigila
Kantara
Ismailia
Bir Gafgafa
EGYPT
Giddi Pass
Mitla Pass
Suez
Kuntilla
Nahel
Ras Sudr
Taba
Eilat
Sinai
Abu Zeneima
Abu Rudeis
Gulf of Suez
Gulf of Akaba
St. Catherine's Monastery
Dahab
Makna
SAUDI ARABIA
Tor
Sharm el-Sheikh
Red Sea
0 20 40 50
Miles
Evacuated by Israeli forces between 5 February and 6 March 1957
Israel, 1949 to 1967

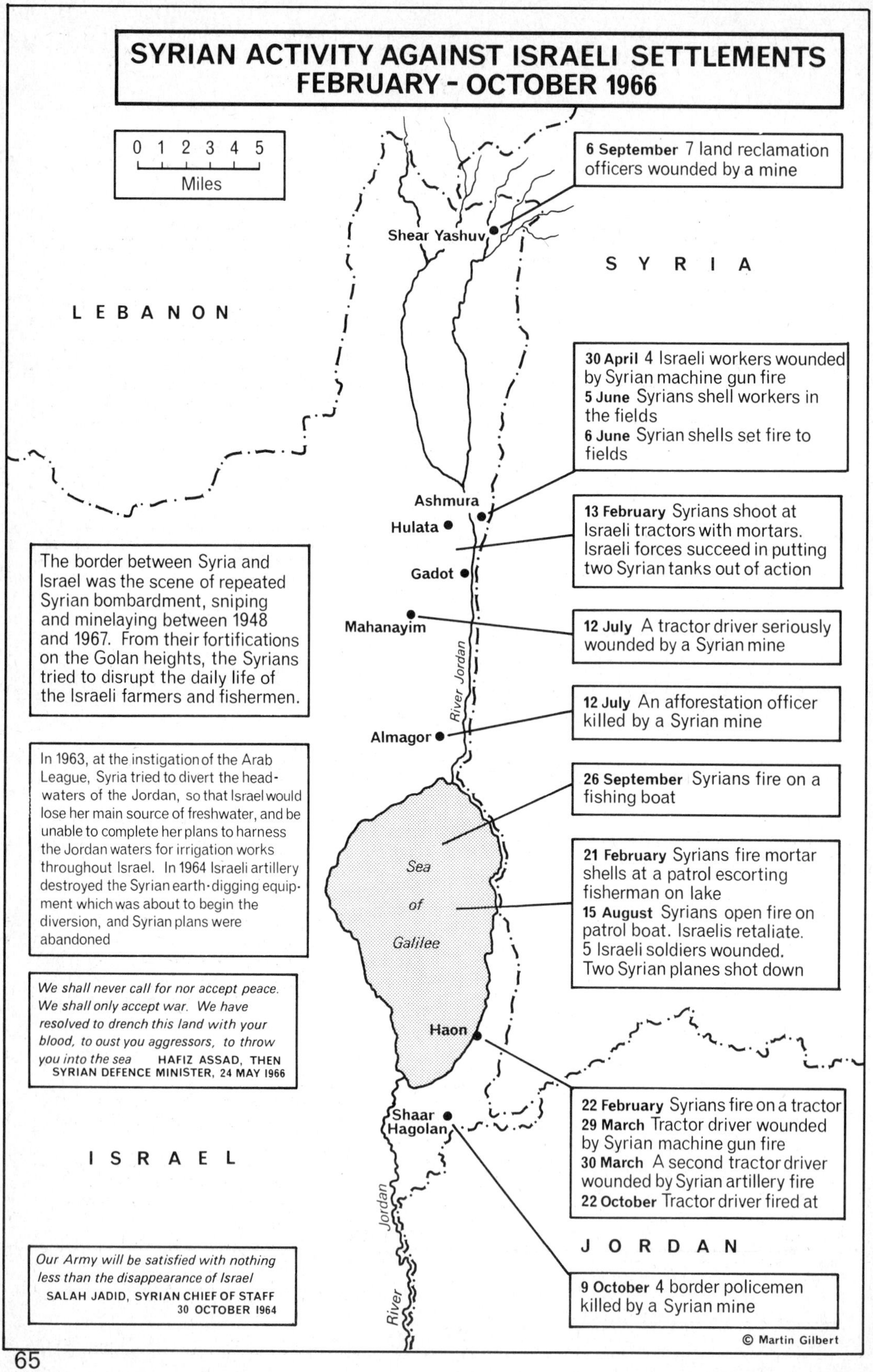
SYRIAN ACTIVITY AGAINST ISRAELI SETTLEMENTS
FEBRUARY - OCTOBER 1966
0 1 2 3 4 5
Miles
6 September 7 land reclamation officers wounded by a mine
Shear Yashuv
SYRIA
LEBANON
30 April 4 Israeli workers wounded by Syrian machine gun fire
5 June Syrians shell workers in the fields
6 June Syrian shells set fire to fields
Ashmura
Hulata
13 February Syrians shoot at Israeli tractors with mortars. Israeli forces succeed in putting two Syrian tanks out of action
Gadot
The border between Syria and Israel was the scene of repeated Syrian bombardment, sniping and minelaying between 1948 and 1967. From their fortifications on the Golan heights, the Syrians tried to disrupt the daily life of the Israeli farmers and fishermen.
Mahanayim
12 July A tractor driver seriously wounded by a Syrian mine
River Jordan
12 July An afforestation officer killed by a Syrian mine
Almagor
In 1963, at the instigation of the Arab League, Syria tried to divert the head-waters of the Jordan, so that Israel would lose her main source of freshwater, and be unable to complete her plans to harness the Jordan waters for irrigation works throughout Israel. In 1964 Israeli artillery destroyed the Syrian earth-digging equipment which was about to begin the diversion, and Syrian plans were abandoned
26 September Syrians fire on a fishing boat
Sea of Galilee
21 February Syrians fire mortar shells at a patrol escorting fisherman on lake
15 August Syrians open fire on patrol boat. Israelis retaliate. 5 Israeli soldiers wounded. Two Syrian planes shot down
We shall never call for nor accept peace. We shall only accept war. We have resolved to drench this land with your blood, to oust you aggressors, to throw you into the sea HAFIZ ASSAD, THEN SYRIAN DEFENCE MINISTER, 24 MAY 1966
Haon
Shaar Hagolan
22 February Syrians fire on a tractor
29 March Tractor driver wounded by Syrian machine gun fire
30 March A second tractor driver wounded by Syrian artillery fire
22 October Tractor driver fired at
ISRAEL
River Jordan
JORDAN
Our Army will be satisfied with nothing less than the disappearance of Israel
SALAH JADID, SYRIAN CHIEF OF STAFF 30 OCTOBER 1964
9 October 4 border policemen killed by a Syrian mine
© Martin Gilbert

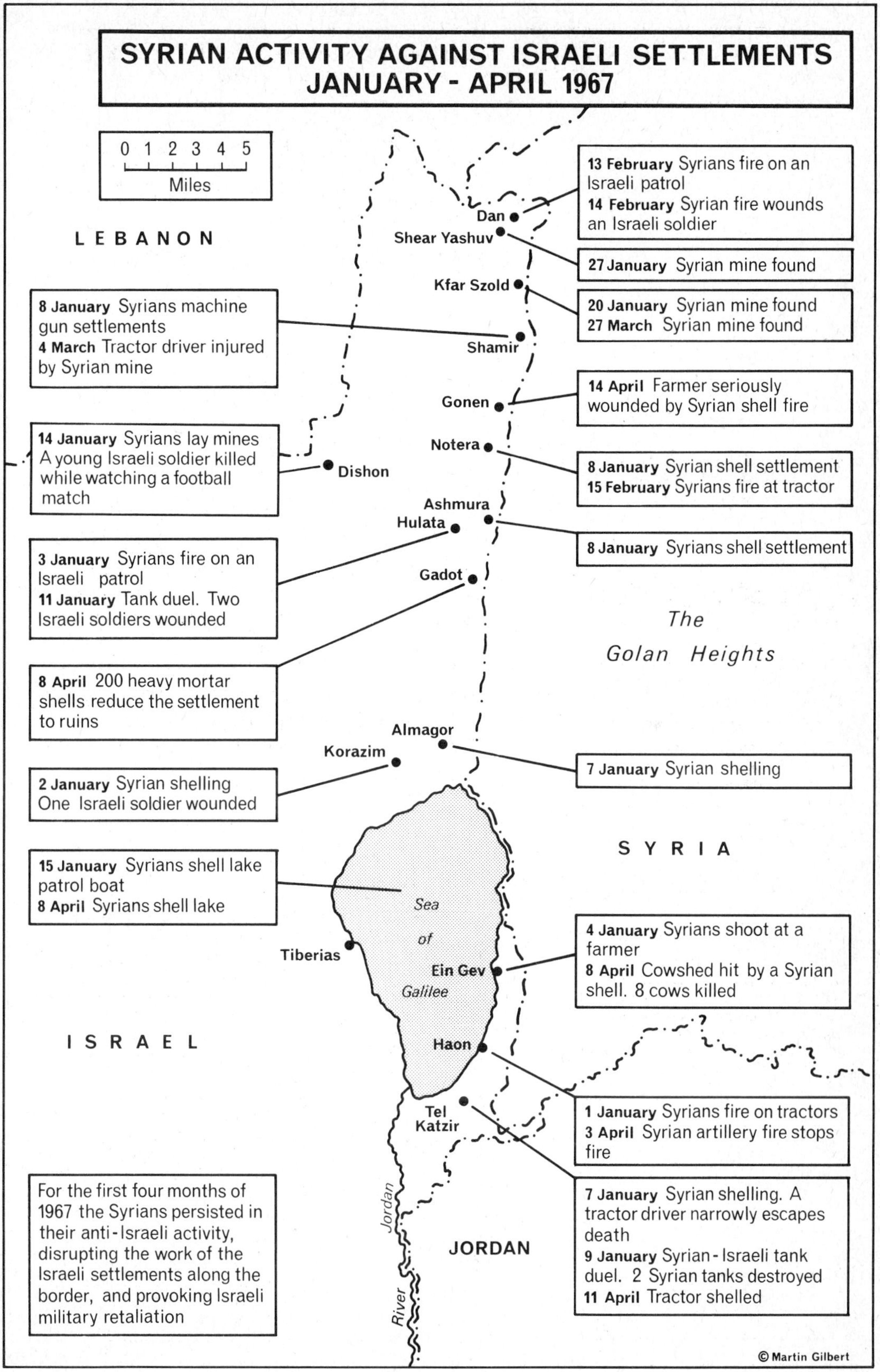
SYRIAN ACTIVITY AGAINST ISRAELI SETTLEMENTS
JANUARY - APRIL 1967
0 1 2 3 4 5
Miles
LEBANON
SYRIA
ISRAEL
JORDAN
The Golan Heights
Sea of Galilee
Jordan River
Dan
Shear Yashuv
Kfar Szold
Shamir
Gonen
Notera
Dishon
Ashmura
Hulata
Gadot
Almagor
Korazim
Tiberias
Ein Gev
Haon
Tel Katzir
13 February Syrians fire on an Israeli patrol
14 February Syrian fire wounds an Israeli soldier
27 January Syrian mine found
20 January Syrian mine found
27 March Syrian mine found
8 January Syrians machine gun settlements
4 March Tractor driver injured by Syrian mine
14 April Farmer seriously wounded by Syrian shell fire
14 January Syrians lay mines
A young Israeli soldier killed while watching a football match
8 January Syrian shell settlement
15 February Syrians fire at tractor
8 January Syrians shell settlement
3 January Syrians fire on an Israeli patrol
11 January Tank duel. Two Israeli soldiers wounded
8 April 200 heavy mortar shells reduce the settlement to ruins
7 January Syrian shelling
2 January Syrian shelling
One Israeli soldier wounded
15 January Syrians shell lake patrol boat
8 April Syrians shell lake
4 January Syrians shoot at a farmer
8 April Cowshed hit by a Syrian shell. 8 cows killed
1 January Syrians fire on tractors
3 April Syrian artillery fire stops fire
7 January Syrian shelling. A tractor driver narrowly escapes death
9 January Syrian - Israeli tank duel. 2 Syrian tanks destroyed
11 April Tractor shelled
For the first four months of 1967 the Syrians persisted in their anti-Israeli activity, disrupting the work of the Israeli settlements along the border, and provoking Israeli military retaliation
© Martin Gilbert

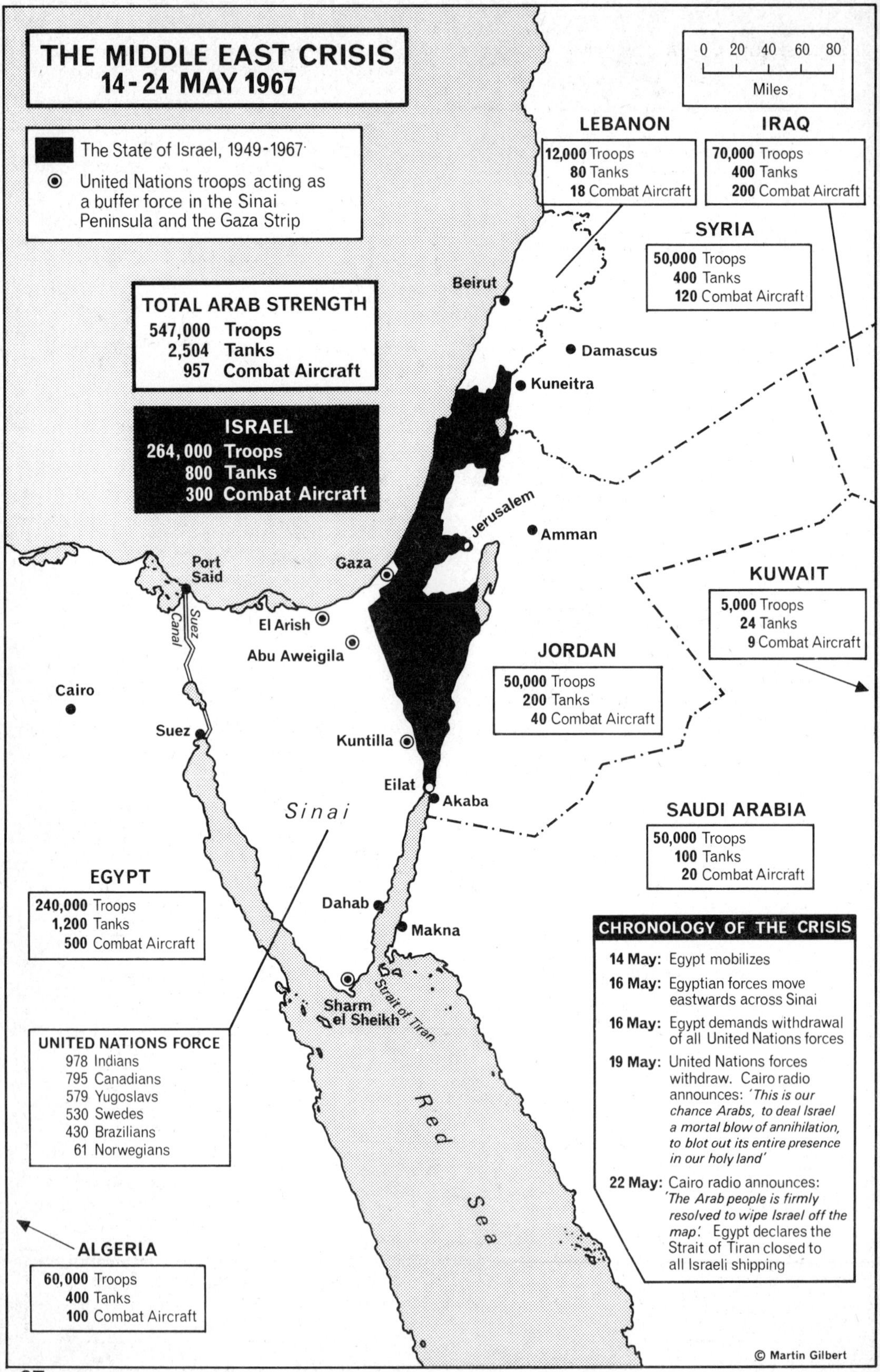

THE MIDDLE EAST CRISIS
14-24 MAY 1967
The State of Israel, 1949-1967
United Nations troops acting as a buffer force in the Sinai Peninsula and the Gaza Strip
0 20 40 60 80
Miles
TOTAL ARAB STRENGTH
547,000 Troops
2,504 Tanks
957 Combat Aircraft
ISRAEL
264,000 Troops
800 Tanks
300 Combat Aircraft
LEBANON
12,000 Troops
80 Tanks
18 Combat Aircraft
IRAQ
70,000 Troops
400 Tanks
200 Combat Aircraft
SYRIA
50,000 Troops
400 Tanks
120 Combat Aircraft
Beirut
Damascus
Kuneitra
Jerusalem
Amman
Gaza
Port Said
Suez Canal
El Arish
Abu Aweigila
KUWAIT
5,000 Troops
24 Tanks
9 Combat Aircraft
JORDAN
50,000 Troops
200 Tanks
40 Combat Aircraft
Cairo
Suez
Kuntilla
Eilat
Akaba
Sinai
SAUDI ARABIA
50,000 Troops
100 Tanks
20 Combat Aircraft
EGYPT
240,000 Troops
1,200 Tanks
500 Combat Aircraft
Dahab
Makna
Sharm el Sheikh
Strait of Tiran
Red Sea
UNITED NATIONS FORCE
978 Indians
795 Canadians
579 Yugoslavs
530 Swedes
430 Brazilians
61 Norwegians
ALGERIA
60,000 Troops
400 Tanks
100 Combat Aircraft
CHRONOLOGY OF THE CRISIS
14 May: Egypt mobilizes
16 May: Egyptian forces move eastwards across Sinai
16 May: Egypt demands withdrawal of all United Nations forces
19 May: United Nations forces withdraw. Cairo radio announces: 'This is our chance Arabs, to deal Israel a mortal blow of annihilation, to blot out its entire presence in our holy land'
22 May: Cairo radio announces: 'The Arab people is firmly resolved to wipe Israel off the map'. Egypt declares the Strait of Tiran closed to all Israeli shipping
© Martin Gilbert

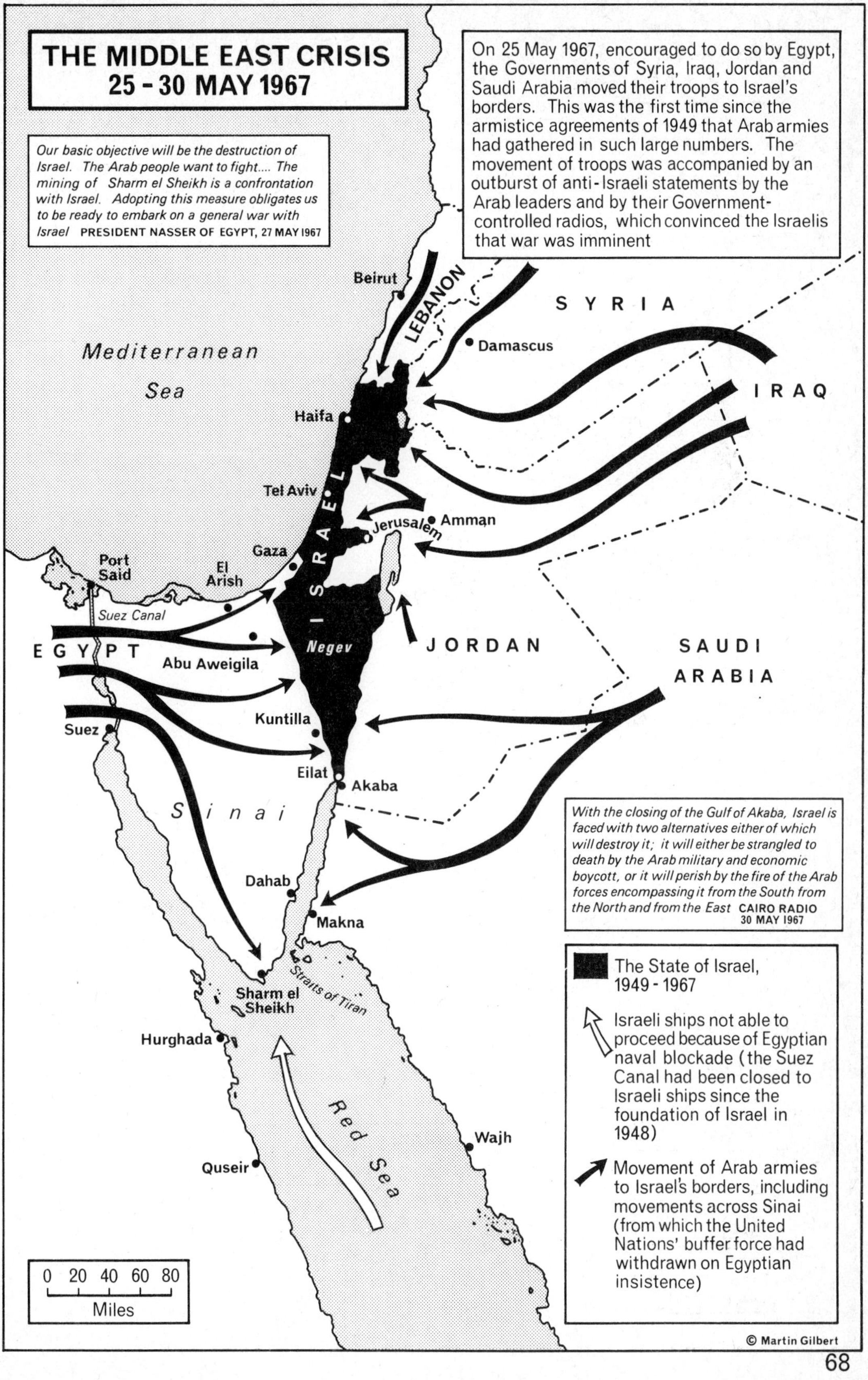

THE MIDDLE EAST CRISIS
25 - 30 MAY 1967
On 25 May 1967, encouraged to do so by Egypt, the Governments of Syria, Iraq, Jordan and Saudi Arabia moved their troops to Israel's borders. This was the first time since the armistice agreements of 1949 that Arab armies had gathered in such large numbers. The movement of troops was accompanied by an outburst of anti-Israeli statements by the Arab leaders and by their Government-controlled radios, which convinced the Israelis that war was imminent
Our basic objective will be the destruction of Israel. The Arab people want to fight.... The mining of Sharm el Sheikh is a confrontation with Israel. Adopting this measure obligates us to be ready to embark on a general war with Israel PRESIDENT NASSER OF EGYPT, 27 MAY 1967
Beirut
LEBANON
SYRIA
Damascus
Mediterranean Sea
IRAQ
Haifa
Tel Aviv
ISRAEL
Amman
Jerusalem
Gaza
Port Said
El Arish
Suez Canal
EGYPT
Abu Aweigila
Negev
JORDAN
SAUDI ARABIA
Kuntilla
Suez
Eilat
Akaba
Sinai
With the closing of the Gulf of Akaba, Israel is faced with two alternatives either of which will destroy it; it will either be strangled to death by the Arab military and economic boycott, or it will perish by the fire of the Arab forces encompassing it from the South from the North and from the East CAIRO RADIO 30 MAY 1967
Dahab
Makna
Sharm el Sheikh
Straits of Tiran
Hurghada
Red Sea
Wajh
Quseir
The State of Israel, 1949 - 1967
Israeli ships not able to proceed because of Egyptian naval blockade (the Suez Canal had been closed to Israeli ships since the foundation of Israel in 1948)
Movement of Arab armies to Israel's borders, including movements across Sinai (from which the United Nations' buffer force had withdrawn on Egyptian insistence)
0 20 40 60 80
Miles
© Martin Gilbert

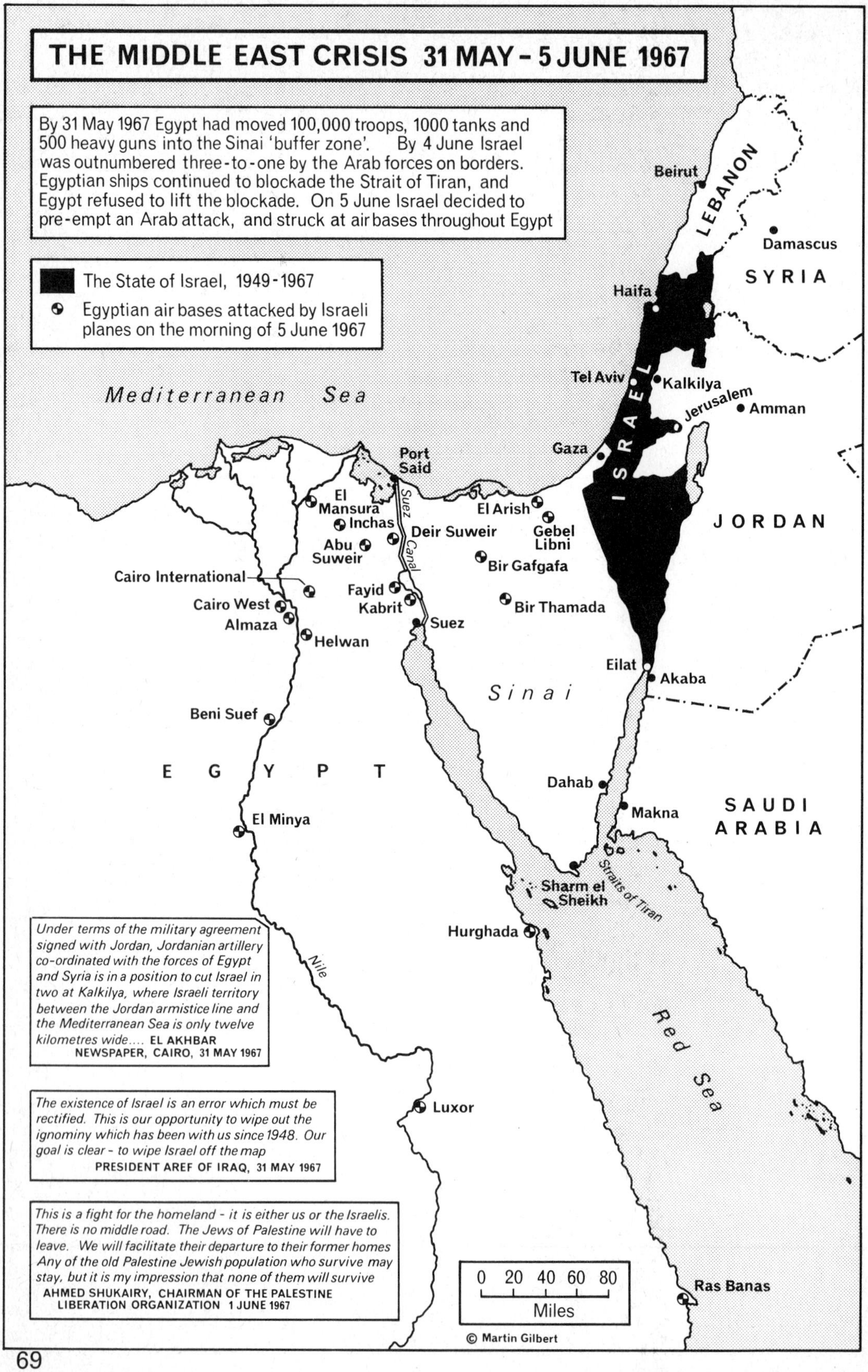
THE MIDDLE EAST CRISIS 31 MAY - 5 JUNE 1967
By 31 May 1967 Egypt had moved 100,000 troops, 1000 tanks and 500 heavy guns into the Sinai 'buffer zone'. By 4 June Israel was outnumbered three-to-one by the Arab forces on borders. Egyptian ships continued to blockade the Strait of Tiran, and Egypt refused to lift the blockade. On 5 June Israel decided to pre-empt an Arab attack, and struck at air bases throughout Egypt
The State of Israel, 1949-1967
Egyptian air bases attacked by Israeli planes on the morning of 5 June 1967
Mediterranean Sea
Beirut
LEBANON
Damascus
SYRIA
Haifa
Tel Aviv
Kalkilya
Jerusalem
Amman
Gaza
ISRAEL
JORDAN
Port Said
El Mansura
Inchas
Abu Suweir
Suez Canal
Deir Suweir
El Arish
Gebel Libni
Bir Gafgafa
Cairo International
Cairo West
Almaza
Helwan
Fayid
Kabrit
Suez
Bir Thamada
Eilat
Akaba
Sinai
Beni Suef
EGYPT
Dahab
Makna
SAUDI ARABIA
El Minya
Sharm el Sheikh
Straits of Tiran
Hurghada
Nile
Red Sea
Luxor
Ras Banas
Under terms of the military agreement signed with Jordan, Jordanian artillery co-ordinated with the forces of Egypt and Syria is in a position to cut Israel in two at Kalkilya, where Israeli territory between the Jordan armistice line and the Mediterranean Sea is only twelve kilometres wide.... EL AKHBAR NEWSPAPER, CAIRO, 31 MAY 1967
The existence of Israel is an error which must be rectified. This is our opportunity to wipe out the ignominy which has been with us since 1948. Our goal is clear - to wipe Israel off the map PRESIDENT AREF OF IRAQ, 31 MAY 1967
This is a fight for the homeland - it is either us or the Israelis. There is no middle road. The Jews of Palestine will have to leave. We will facilitate their departure to their former homes Any of the old Palestine Jewish population who survive may stay, but it is my impression that none of them will survive AHMED SHUKAIRY, CHAIRMAN OF THE PALESTINE LIBERATION ORGANIZATION 1 JUNE 1967
0 20 40 60 80
Miles
© Martin Gilbert

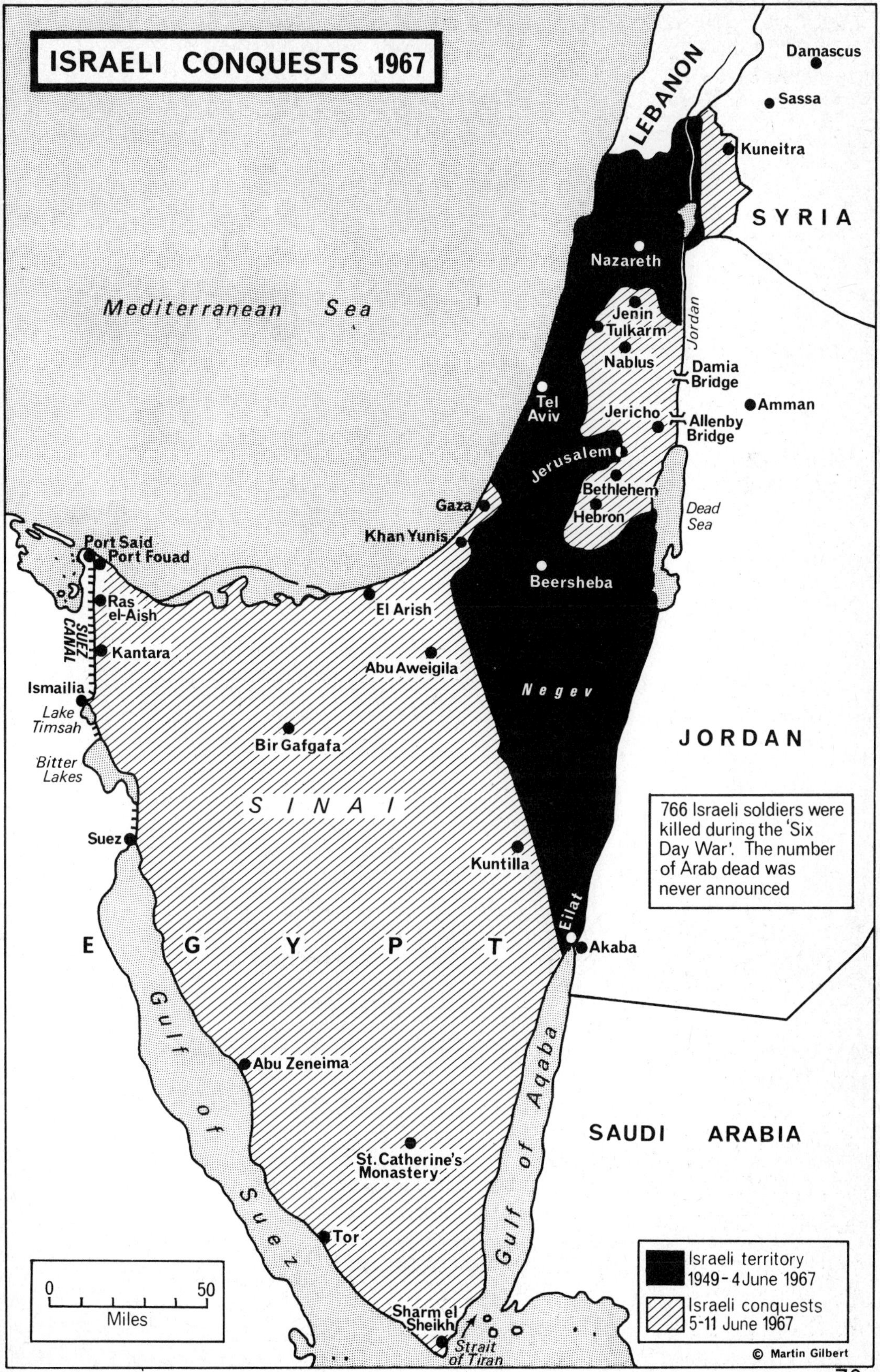
ISRAELI CONQUESTS 1967
Damascus
Sassa
LEBANON
Kuneitra
SYRIA
Nazareth
Mediterranean Sea
Jenin
Tulkarm
Jordan
Nablus
Damia Bridge
Tel Aviv
Jericho
Amman
Allenby Bridge
Jerusalem
Bethlehem
Gaza
Hebron
Dead Sea
Khan Yunis
Port Said
Port Fouad
Beersheba
Ras el-Aish
El Arish
SUEZ CANAL
Kantara
Abu Aweigila
Ismailia
Negev
Lake Timsah
Bir Gafgafa
JORDAN
Bitter Lakes
SINAI
766 Israeli soldiers were killed during the 'Six Day War'. The number of Arab dead was never announced
Suez
Kuntilla
Eilat
EGYPT
Akaba
Gulf of Suez
Abu Zeneima
Gulf of Aqaba
SAUDI ARABIA
St. Catherine's Monastery
Tor
0
50
Miles
Israeli territory 1949 - 4 June 1967
Israeli conquests 5-11 June 1967
Sharm el Sheikh
Strait of Tiran
© Martin Gilbert

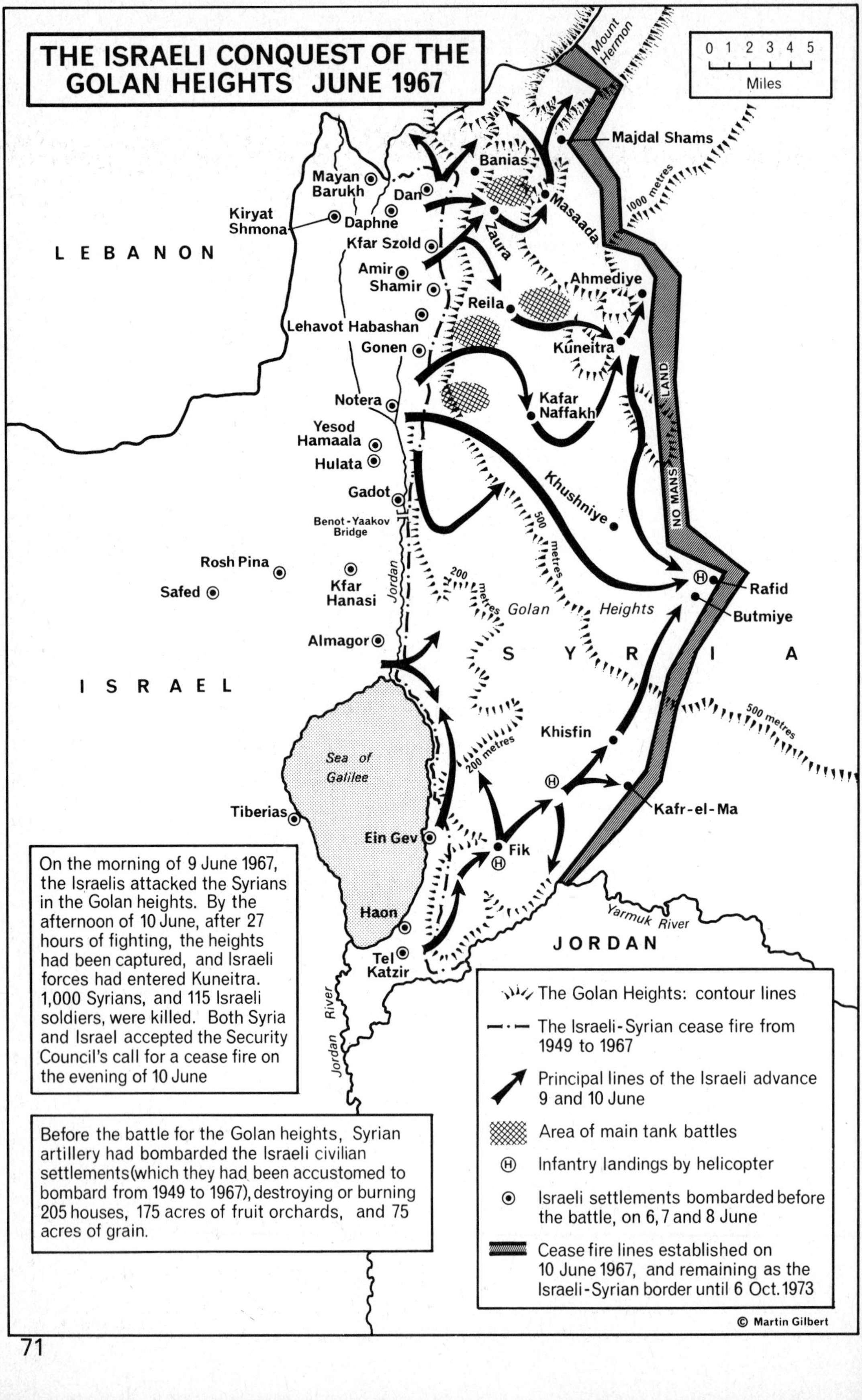
THE ISRAELI CONQUEST OF THE GOLAN HEIGHTS JUNE 1967
0 1 2 3 4 5
Miles
Mount Hermon
Majdal Shams
1000 metres
Banias
Mayan Barukh
Dan
Kiryat Shmona
Daphne
Zaura
Masaada
Kfar Szold
LEBANON
Amir
Shamir
Ahmediye
Reila
Lehavot Habashan
Kuneitra
Gonen
NO MANS LAND
Notera
Kafar Naffakh
Yesod Hamaala
Hulata
Gadot
Khushniye
Benot-Yaakov Bridge
500 metres
Rosh Pina
Safed
Kfar Hanasi
Jordan
200 metres
Golan
Heights
Rafid
Butmiye
Almagor
SYRIA
ISRAEL
500 metres
Khisfin
Sea of Galilee
200 metres
Kafr-el-Ma
Tiberias
Ein Gev
Fik
Haon
Yarmuk River
Tel Katzir
JORDAN
Jordan River
On the morning of 9 June 1967, the Israelis attacked the Syrians in the Golan heights. By the afternoon of 10 June, after 27 hours of fighting, the heights had been captured, and Israeli forces had entered Kuneitra. 1,000 Syrians, and 115 Israeli soldiers, were killed. Both Syria and Israel accepted the Security Council's call for a cease fire on the evening of 10 June
Before the battle for the Golan heights, Syrian artillery had bombarded the Israeli civilian settlements (which they had been accustomed to bombard from 1949 to 1967), destroying or burning 205 houses, 175 acres of fruit orchards, and 75 acres of grain.
The Golan Heights: contour lines
The Israeli-Syrian cease fire from 1949 to 1967
Principal lines of the Israeli advance 9 and 10 June
Area of main tank battles
Infantry landings by helicopter
Israeli settlements bombarded before the battle, on 6, 7 and 8 June
Cease fire lines established on 10 June 1967, and remaining as the Israeli-Syrian border until 6 Oct. 1973
© Martin Gilbert

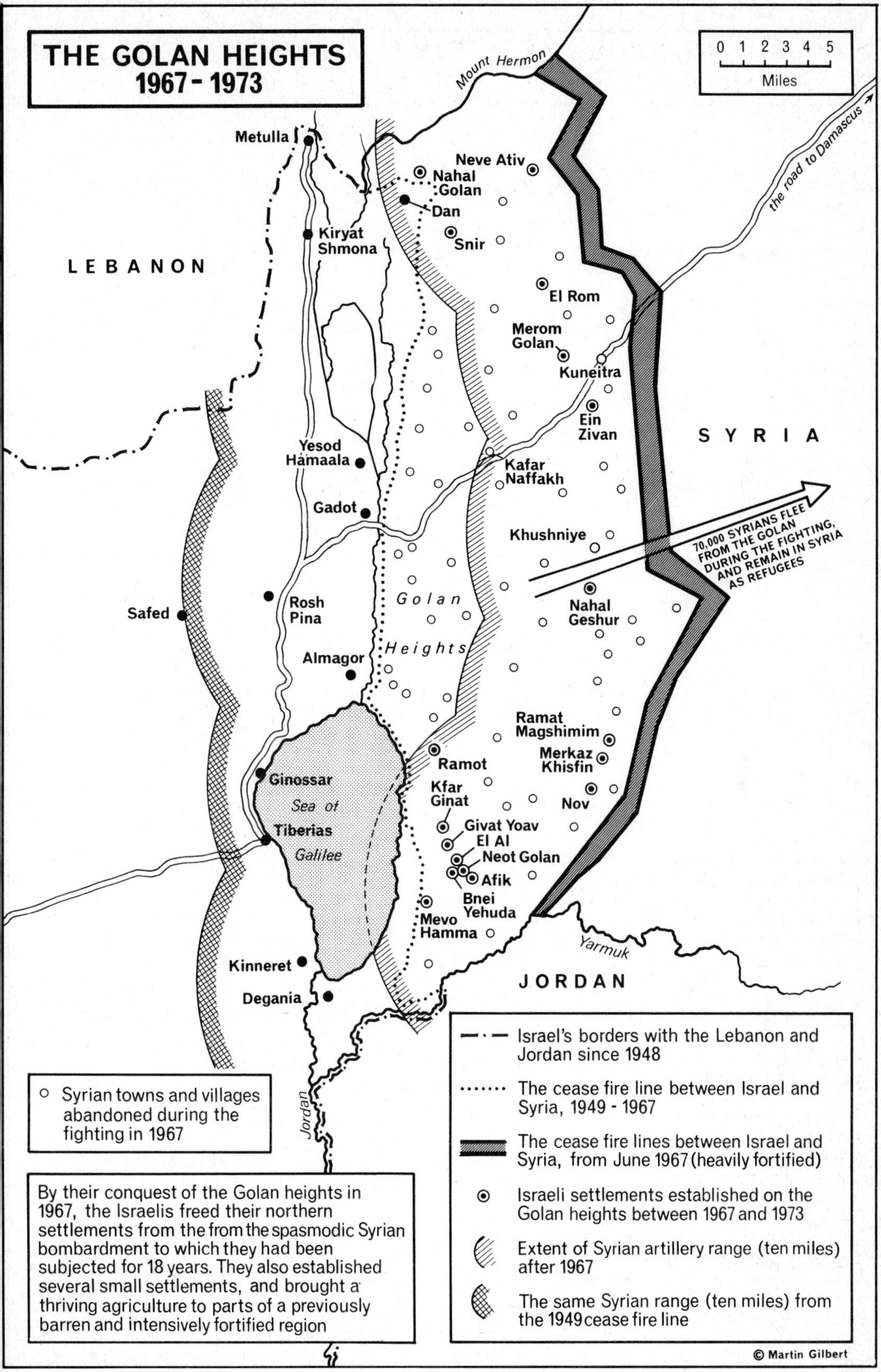
THE GOLAN HEIGHTS
1967 - 1973
0 1 2 3 4 5
Miles
Mount Hermon
the road to Damascus
LEBANON
SYRIA
JORDAN
Metulla
Neve Ativ
Nahal Golan
Dan
Kiryat Shmona
Snir
El Rom
Merom Golan
Kuneitra
Ein Zivan
Yesod Hamaala
Kafar Naffakh
Gadot
Khushniye
70,000 SYRIANS FLEE FROM THE GOLAN DURING THE FIGHTING, AND REMAIN IN SYRIA AS REFUGEES
Safed
Rosh Pina
Golan Heights
Nahal Geshur
Almagor
Ramat Magshimim
Merkaz Khisfin
Ramot
Ginossar
Kfar Ginat
Nov
Sea of Galilee
Tiberias
Givat Yoav
El Al
Neot Golan
Afik
Bnei Yehuda
Mevo Hamma
Yarmuk
Kinneret
Degania
Jordan
Syrian towns and villages abandoned during the fighting in 1967
By their conquest of the Golan heights in 1967, the Israelis freed their northern settlements from the from the spasmodic Syrian bombardment to which they had been subjected for 18 years. They also established several small settlements, and brought a thriving agriculture to parts of a previously barren and intensively fortified region
Israel's borders with the Lebanon and Jordan since 1948
The cease fire line between Israel and Syria, 1949 - 1967
The cease fire lines between Israel and Syria, from June 1967 (heavily fortified)
Israeli settlements established on the Golan heights between 1967 and 1973
Extent of Syrian artillery range (ten miles) after 1967
The same Syrian range (ten miles) from the 1949 cease fire line
© Martin Gilbert

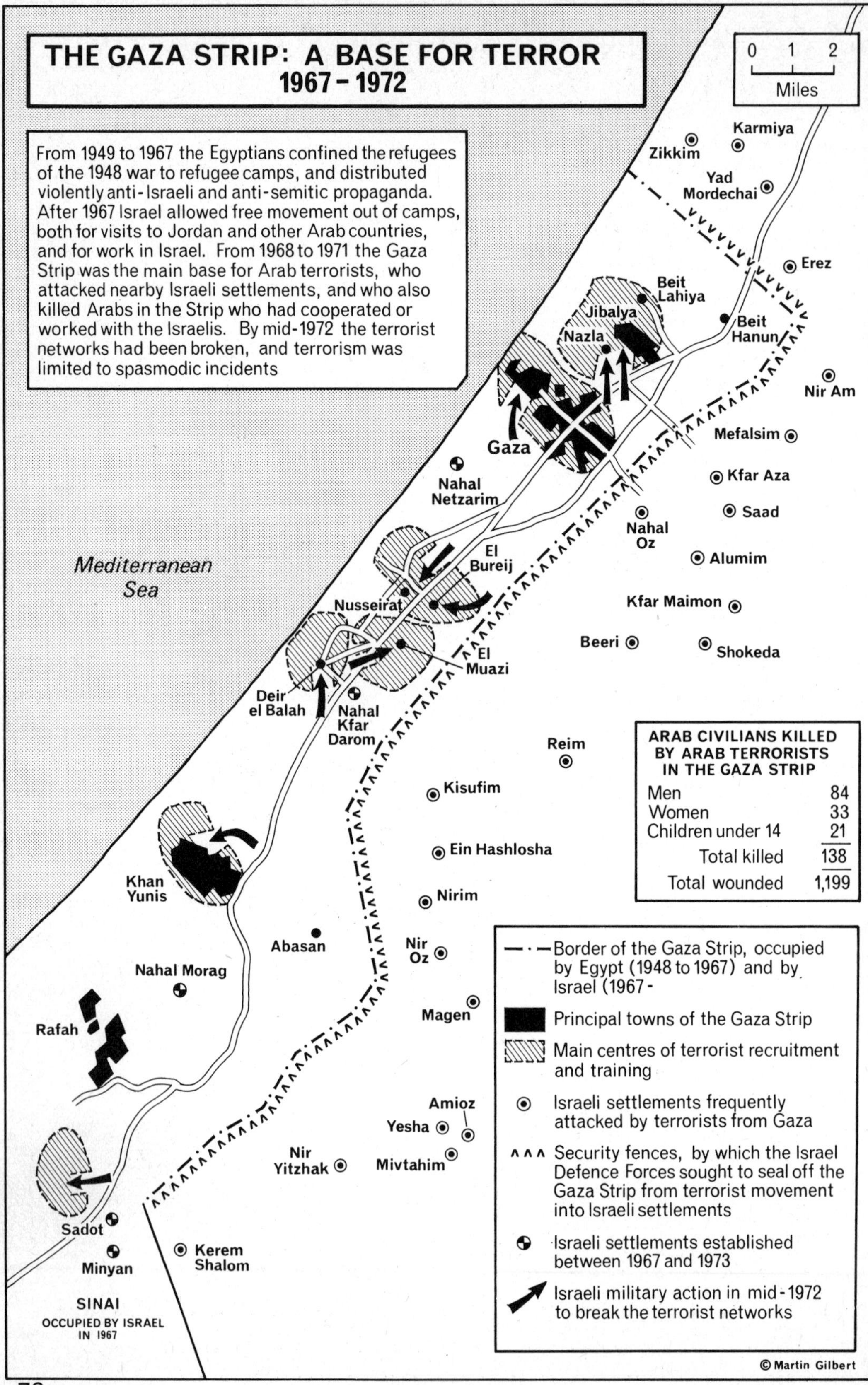
THE GAZA STRIP: A BASE FOR TERROR
1967 – 1972
From 1949 to 1967 the Egyptians confined the refugees of the 1948 war to refugee camps, and distributed violently anti-Israeli and anti-semitic propaganda. After 1967 Israel allowed free movement out of camps, both for visits to Jordan and other Arab countries, and for work in Israel. From 1968 to 1971 the Gaza Strip was the main base for Arab terrorists, who attacked nearby Israeli settlements, and who also killed Arabs in the Strip who had cooperated or worked with the Israelis. By mid-1972 the terrorist networks had been broken, and terrorism was limited to spasmodic incidents
0 1 2
Miles
Zikkim
Karmiya
Yad Mordechai
Erez
Beit Lahiya
Jibalya
Nazla
Beit Hanun
Nir Am
Mefalsim
Gaza
Kfar Aza
Saad
Nahal Netzarim
Nahal Oz
Alumim
El Bureij
Mediterranean Sea
Nusseirat
Kfar Maimon
Beeri
Shokeda
El Muazi
Deir el Balah
Nahal Kfar Darom
Reim
Kisufim
Ein Hashlosha
Khan Yunis
Nirim
Abasan
Nir Oz
Nahal Morag
Magen
Rafah
Amioz
Yesha
Nir Yitzhak
Mivtahim
Sadot
Minyan
Kerem Shalom
SINAI
OCCUPIED BY ISRAEL IN 1967
ARAB CIVILIANS KILLED BY ARAB TERRORISTS IN THE GAZA STRIP
Men 84
Women 33
Children under 14 21
Total killed 138
Total wounded 1,199
Border of the Gaza Strip, occupied by Egypt (1948 to 1967) and by Israel (1967 -
Principal towns of the Gaza Strip
Main centres of terrorist recruitment and training
Israeli settlements frequently attacked by terrorists from Gaza
Security fences, by which the Israel Defence Forces sought to seal off the Gaza Strip from terrorist movement into Israeli settlements
Israeli settlements established between 1967 and 1973
Israeli military action in mid-1972 to break the terrorist networks
© Martin Gilbert

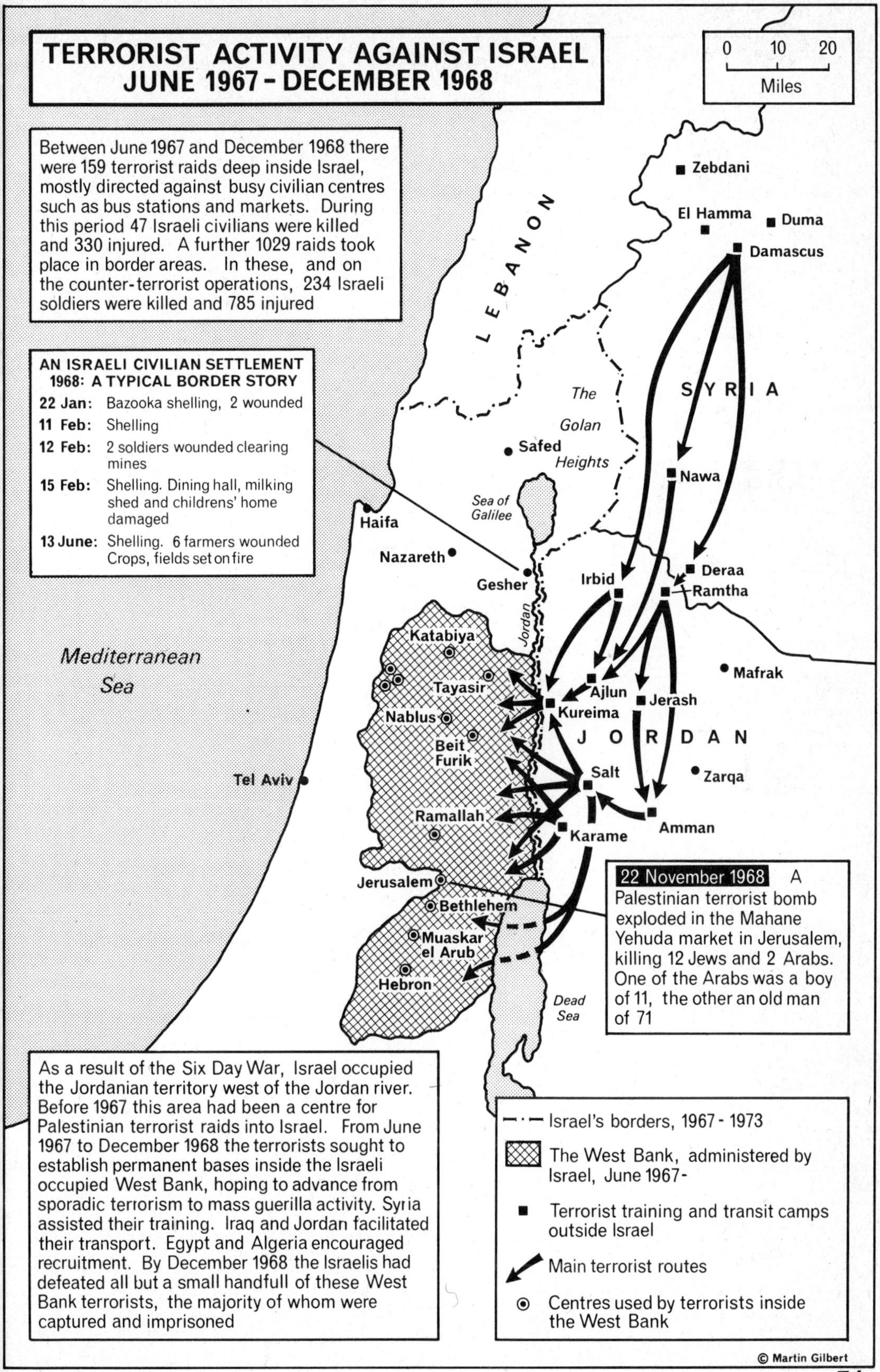
TERRORIST ACTIVITY AGAINST ISRAEL
JUNE 1967 - DECEMBER 1968
0 10 20
Miles
Between June 1967 and December 1968 there were 159 terrorist raids deep inside Israel, mostly directed against busy civilian centres such as bus stations and markets. During this period 47 Israeli civilians were killed and 330 injured. A further 1029 raids took place in border areas. In these, and on the counter-terrorist operations, 234 Israeli soldiers were killed and 785 injured
AN ISRAELI CIVILIAN SETTLEMENT
1968: A TYPICAL BORDER STORY
22 Jan: Bazooka shelling, 2 wounded
11 Feb: Shelling
12 Feb: 2 soldiers wounded clearing mines
15 Feb: Shelling. Dining hall, milking shed and childrens' home damaged
13 June: Shelling. 6 farmers wounded Crops, fields set on fire
LEBANON
SYRIA
JORDAN
Zebdani
El Hamma
Duma
Damascus
The Golan Heights
Safed
Nawa
Sea of Galilee
Haifa
Nazareth
Gesher
Irbid
Deraa
Ramtha
Jordan
Katabiya
Tayasir
Nablus
Beit Furik
Ajlun
Kureima
Jerash
Mafrak
Mediterranean Sea
Tel Aviv
Salt
Zarqa
Ramallah
Karame
Amman
Jerusalem
Bethlehem
Muaskar el Arub
Hebron
Dead Sea
22 November 1968 A Palestinian terrorist bomb exploded in the Mahane Yehuda market in Jerusalem, killing 12 Jews and 2 Arabs. One of the Arabs was a boy of 11, the other an old man of 71
As a result of the Six Day War, Israel occupied the Jordanian territory west of the Jordan river. Before 1967 this area had been a centre for Palestinian terrorist raids into Israel. From June 1967 to December 1968 the terrorists sought to establish permanent bases inside the Israeli occupied West Bank, hoping to advance from sporadic terrorism to mass guerilla activity. Syria assisted their training. Iraq and Jordan facilitated their transport. Egypt and Algeria encouraged recruitment. By December 1968 the Israelis had defeated all but a small handfull of these West Bank terrorists, the majority of whom were captured and imprisoned
Israel's borders, 1967 - 1973
The West Bank, administered by Israel, June 1967-
Terrorist training and transit camps outside Israel
Main terrorist routes
Centres used by terrorists inside the West Bank
© Martin Gilbert

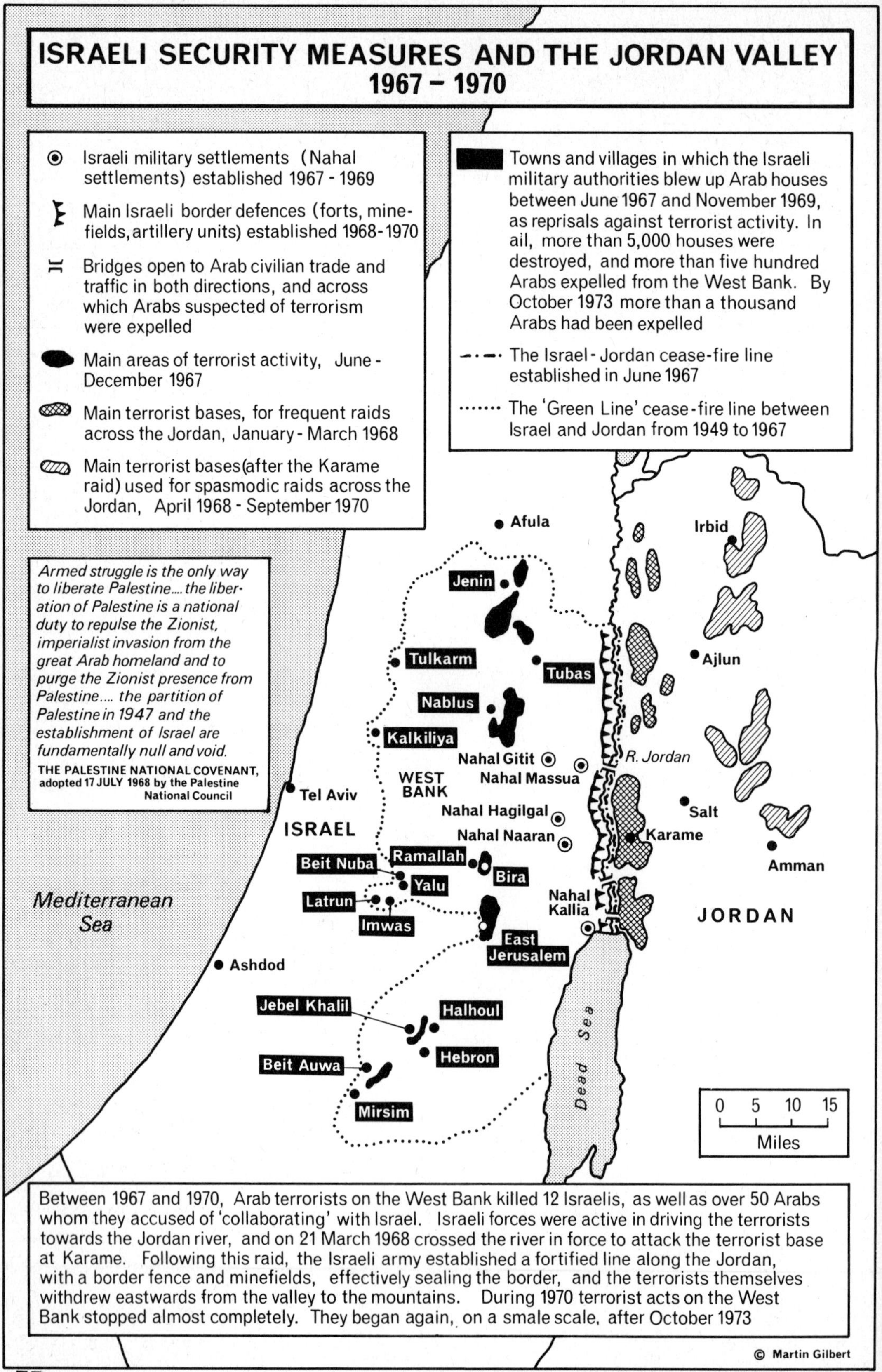
ISRAELI SECURITY MEASURES AND THE JORDAN VALLEY
1967 – 1970
Israeli military settlements (Nahal settlements) established 1967 - 1969
Main Israeli border defences (forts, mine-fields, artillery units) established 1968-1970
Bridges open to Arab civilian trade and traffic in both directions, and across which Arabs suspected of terrorism were expelled
Main areas of terrorist activity, June - December 1967
Main terrorist bases, for frequent raids across the Jordan, January - March 1968
Main terrorist bases (after the Karame raid) used for spasmodic raids across the Jordan, April 1968 - September 1970
Towns and villages in which the Israeli military authorities blew up Arab houses between June 1967 and November 1969, as reprisals against terrorist activity. In ail, more than 5,000 houses were destroyed, and more than five hundred Arabs expelled from the West Bank. By October 1973 more than a thousand Arabs had been expelled
The Israel - Jordan cease-fire line established in June 1967
The 'Green Line' cease-fire line between Israel and Jordan from 1949 to 1967
Armed struggle is the only way to liberate Palestine.... the liberation of Palestine is a national duty to repulse the Zionist, imperialist invasion from the great Arab homeland and to purge the Zionist presence from Palestine.... the partition of Palestine in 1947 and the establishment of Israel are fundamentally null and void.
THE PALESTINE NATIONAL COVENANT, adopted 17 JULY 1968 by the Palestine National Council
Afula
Irbid
Jenin
Tulkarm
Tubas
Ajlun
Nablus
Kalkiliya
Nahal Gitit
Nahal Massua
R. Jordan
Tel Aviv
WEST BANK
Nahal Hagilgal
Salt
ISRAEL
Nahal Naaran
Karame
Amman
Ramallah
Beit Nuba
Bira
Yalu
Mediterranean Sea
Latrun
Nahal Kallia
JORDAN
Imwas
East Jerusalem
Ashdod
Jebel Khalil
Halhoul
Hebron
Beit Auwa
Dead Sea
Mirsim
0 5 10 15
Miles
Between 1967 and 1970, Arab terrorists on the West Bank killed 12 Israelis, as well as over 50 Arabs whom they accused of 'collaborating' with Israel. Israeli forces were active in driving the terrorists towards the Jordan river, and on 21 March 1968 crossed the river in force to attack the terrorist base at Karame. Following this raid, the Israeli army established a fortified line along the Jordan, with a border fence and minefields, effectively sealing the border, and the terrorists themselves withdrew eastwards from the valley to the mountains. During 1970 terrorist acts on the West Bank stopped almost completely. They began again, on a smale scale, after October 1973
© Martin Gilbert

THE WEST BANK UNDER ISRAELI MILITARY ADMINISTRATION 1967-

The Israeli conquest of the West Bank in June 1967 brought 600,000 Arabs under Israeli military administration. The Israelis encouraged and financed economic development, and by the end of 1970 Arab unemployment had dropped from 12% to 3% By 1972 over 60,000 Arabs crossed the 'Green Line' every morning to work in Israel. At the same time, over 100,000 Arabs visited other Arab states for work, education and business. By 1973 over 14,500 West Bank Arabs were working in local administration in the West Bank

Sixteen Israeli settlements were founded in the West Bank between 1967 and 1973, with a total civilian population of 1,150. One of these settlements was near Hebron, where Jews had lived for more than two thousand years, before being driven out by the Arabs in 1929. Another group of settlements, the Etzion Bloc, was established on the site of settlements destroyed by the Arabs in 1949. At the same time, 44,000 Arabs who had fled from the West Bank in 1967, returned by 1972

During 1970 an 'Open Bridges' policy enabled West Bank Arabs to cross freely into Jordan. At the height of the tourist season in 1970, some 750 buses a day crossed from Jordan to Hebron, and by the end of August 50,000 Arabs had visited the West Bank from Jordan

ARABS VISITING THE WEST BANK FROM OTHER ARAB AREAS

1968	**16,000**
1969	**23,000**
1970	**52,000**
1971	**107,000**
1972	**150,000**

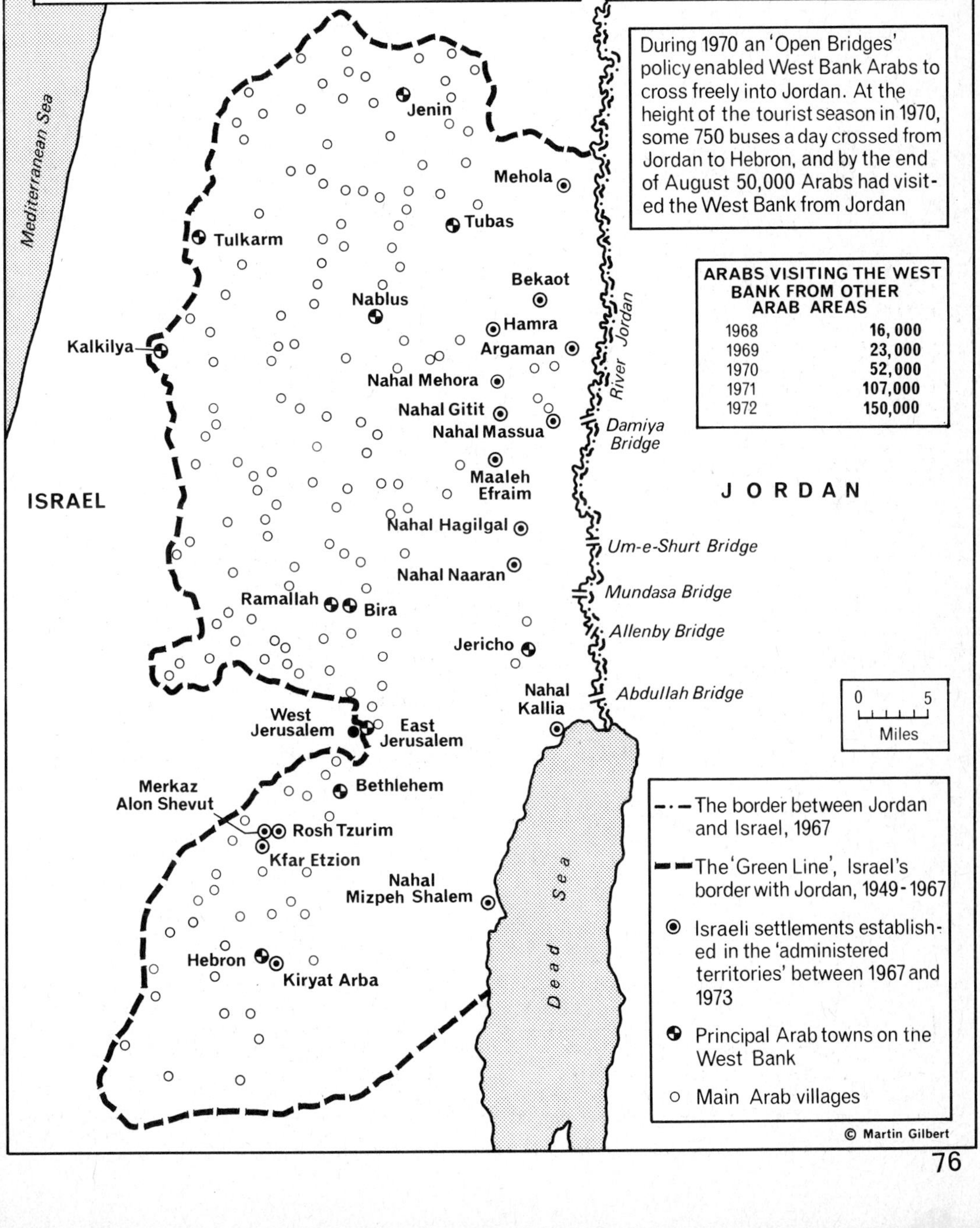

Mediterranean Sea
ISRAEL
JORDAN
Jenin
Mehola
Tubas
Tulkarm
Bekaot
Nablus
Hamra
Argaman
Kalkilya
Nahal Mehora
Nahal Gitit
Nahal Massua
Maaleh Efraim
Nahal Hagilgal
Nahal Naaran
Ramallah
Bira
Jericho
Nahal Kallia
West Jerusalem
East Jerusalem
Bethlehem
Merkaz Alon Shevut
Rosh Tzurim
Kfar Etzion
Nahal Mizpeh Shalem
Hebron
Kiryat Arba
River Jordan
Damiya Bridge
Um-e-Shurt Bridge
Mundasa Bridge
Allenby Bridge
Abdullah Bridge
Dead Sea
0 5
Miles
The border between Jordan and Israel, 1967
The 'Green Line', Israel's border with Jordan, 1949-1967
Israeli settlements established in the 'administered territories' between 1967 and 1973
Principal Arab towns on the West Bank
Main Arab villages

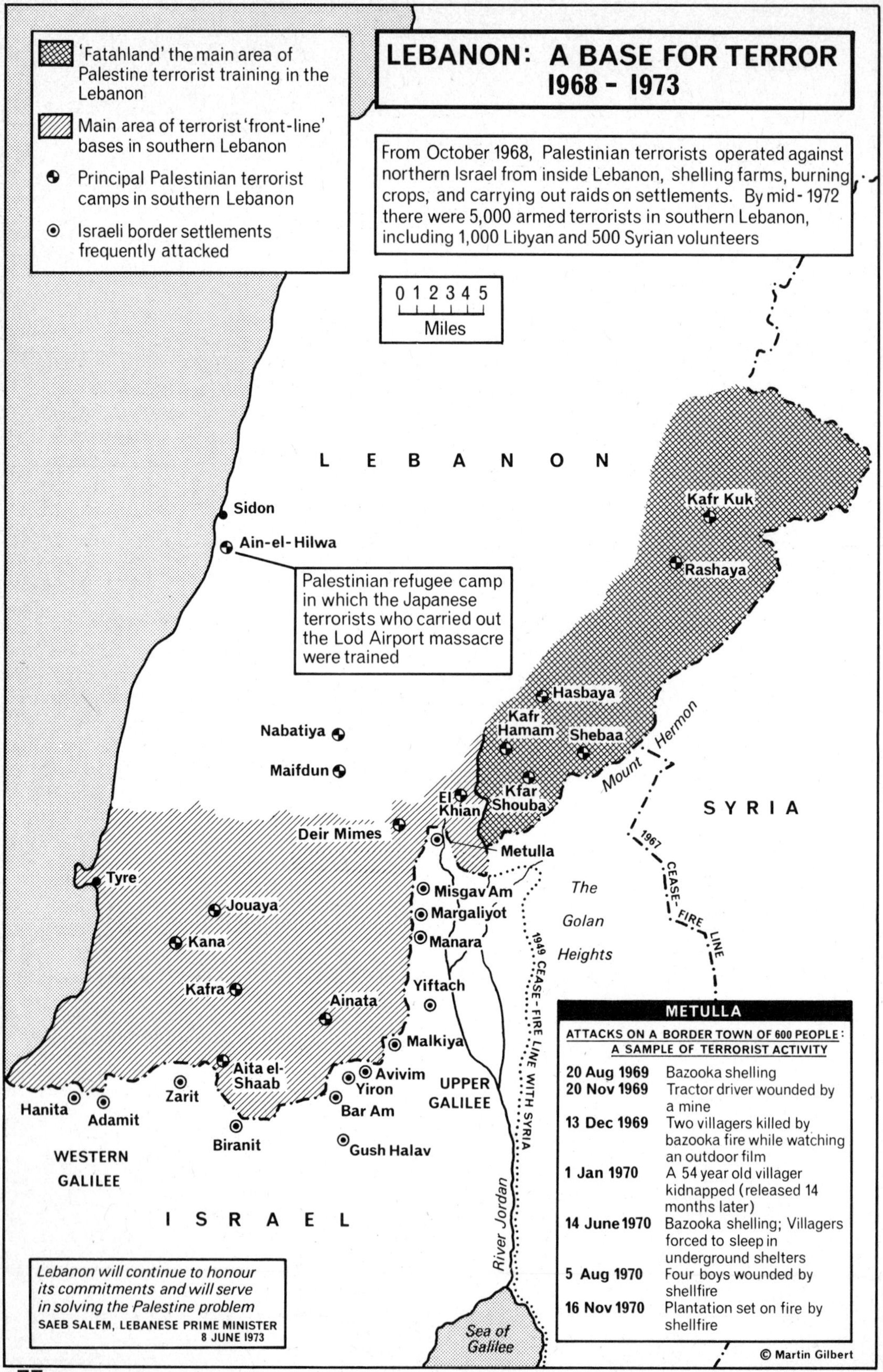
LEBANON: A BASE FOR TERROR
1968 - 1973
'Fatahland' the main area of Palestine terrorist training in the Lebanon
Main area of terrorist 'front-line' bases in southern Lebanon
Principal Palestinian terrorist camps in southern Lebanon
Israeli border settlements frequently attacked
From October 1968, Palestinian terrorists operated against northern Israel from inside Lebanon, shelling farms, burning crops, and carrying out raids on settlements. By mid-1972 there were 5,000 armed terrorists in southern Lebanon, including 1,000 Libyan and 500 Syrian volunteers
0 1 2 3 4 5
Miles
L E B A N O N
Sidon
Ain-el-Hilwa
Palestinian refugee camp in which the Japanese terrorists who carried out the Lod Airport massacre were trained
Kafr Kuk
Rashaya
Hasbaya
Kafr Hamam
Shebaa
Mount Hermon
Kfar Shouba
El Khian
Nabatiya
Maifdun
Deir Mimes
Metulla
SYRIA
1967 CEASE-FIRE LINE
Tyre
Jouaya
Kana
Kafra
Ainata
Aita el-Shaab
Misgav Am
Margaliyot
Manara
Yiftach
Malkiya
Avivim
Yiron
Bar Am
Gush Halav
Biranit
Zarit
Hanita
Adamit
WESTERN GALILEE
UPPER GALILEE
The Golan Heights
1949 CEASE-FIRE LINE WITH SYRIA
River Jordan
Sea of Galilee
I S R A E L
METULLA
ATTACKS ON A BORDER TOWN OF 600 PEOPLE: A SAMPLE OF TERRORIST ACTIVITY
20 Aug 1969 Bazooka shelling
20 Nov 1969 Tractor driver wounded by a mine
13 Dec 1969 Two villagers killed by bazooka fire while watching an outdoor film
1 Jan 1970 A 54 year old villager kidnapped (released 14 months later)
14 June 1970 Bazooka shelling; Villagers forced to sleep in underground shelters
5 Aug 1970 Four boys wounded by shellfire
16 Nov 1970 Plantation set on fire by shellfire
Lebanon will continue to honour its commitments and will serve in solving the Palestine problem
SAEB SALEM, LEBANESE PRIME MINISTER 8 JUNE 1973
© Martin Gilbert

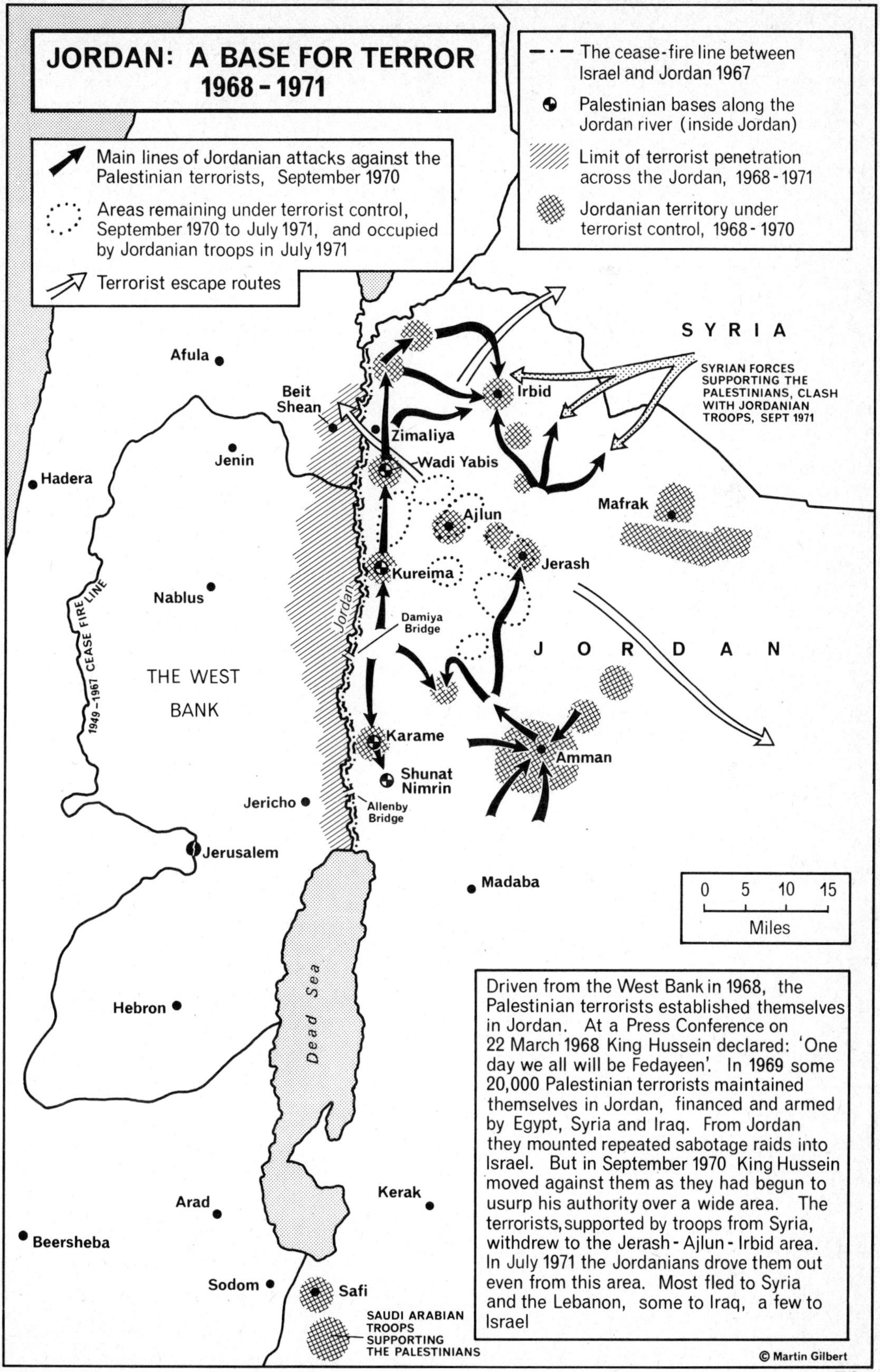

JORDAN: A BASE FOR TERROR
1968 - 1971
Main lines of Jordanian attacks against the Palestinian terrorists, September 1970
Areas remaining under terrorist control, September 1970 to July 1971, and occupied by Jordanian troops in July 1971
Terrorist escape routes
The cease-fire line between Israel and Jordan 1967
Palestinian bases along the Jordan river (inside Jordan)
Limit of terrorist penetration across the Jordan, 1968 - 1971
Jordanian territory under terrorist control, 1968 - 1970
SYRIA
SYRIAN FORCES SUPPORTING THE PALESTINIANS, CLASH WITH JORDANIAN TROOPS, SEPT 1971
Afula
Beit Shean
Irbid
Zimaliya
Wadi Yabis
Jenin
Hadera
Ajlun
Mafrak
Jerash
Kureima
Nablus
1949 - 1967 CEASE FIRE LINE
Jordan
Damiya Bridge
JORDAN
THE WEST BANK
Karame
Amman
Shunat Nimrin
Jericho
Allenby Bridge
Jerusalem
Madaba
0 5 10 15
Miles
Dead Sea
Hebron
Arad
Kerak
Beersheba
Sodom
Safi
SAUDI ARABIAN TROOPS SUPPORTING THE PALESTINIANS
Driven from the West Bank in 1968, the Palestinian terrorists established themselves in Jordan. At a Press Conference on 22 March 1968 King Hussein declared: 'One day we all will be Fedayeen'. In 1969 some 20,000 Palestinian terrorists maintained themselves in Jordan, financed and armed by Egypt, Syria and Iraq. From Jordan they mounted repeated sabotage raids into Israel. But in September 1970 King Hussein moved against them as they had begun to usurp his authority over a wide area. The terrorists, supported by troops from Syria, withdrew to the Jerash - Ajlun - Irbid area. In July 1971 the Jordanians drove them out even from this area. Most fled to Syria and the Lebanon, some to Iraq, a few to Israel
© Martin Gilbert

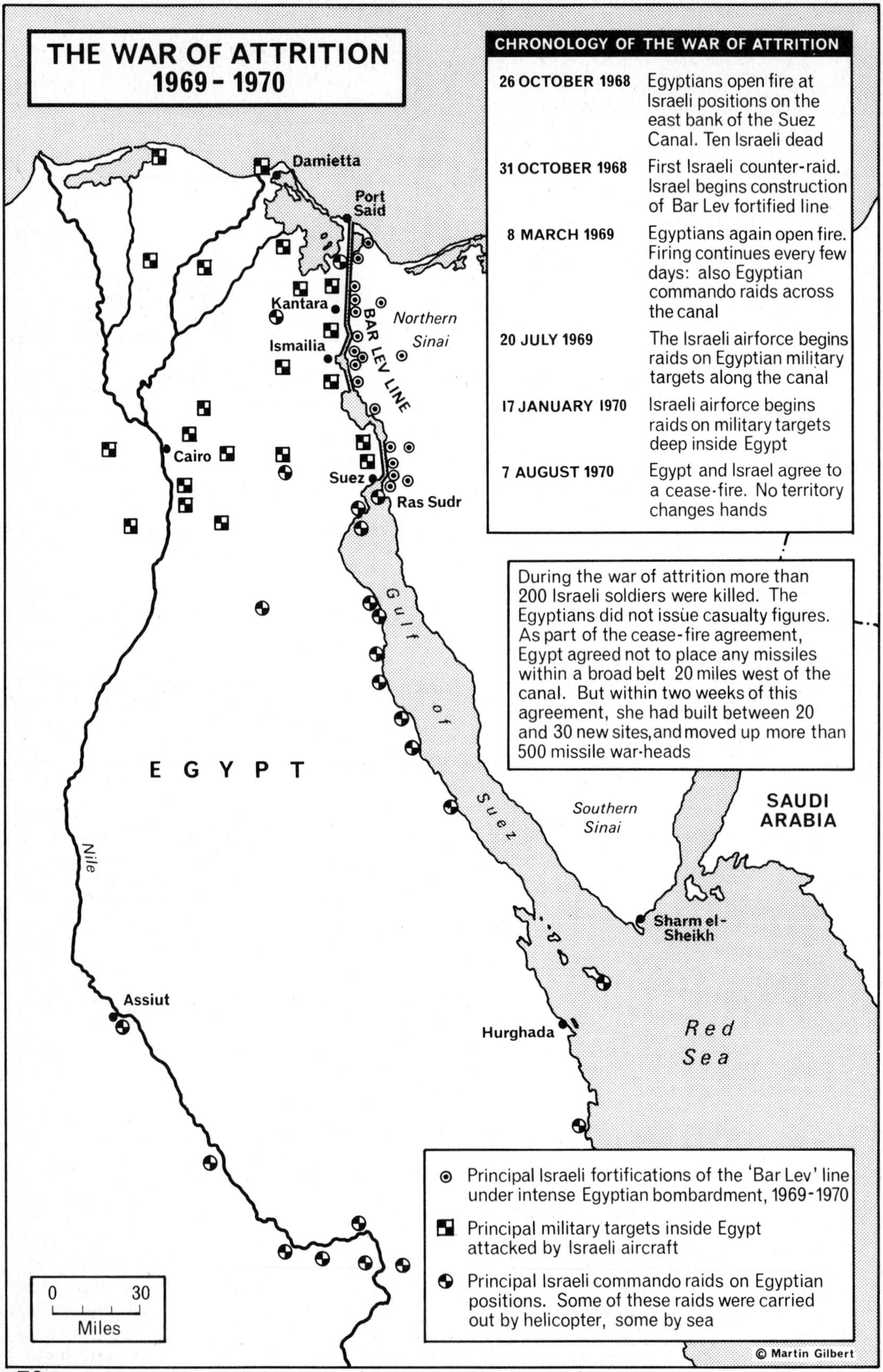
THE WAR OF ATTRITION
1969 - 1970
CHRONOLOGY OF THE WAR OF ATTRITION
26 OCTOBER 1968 Egyptians open fire at Israeli positions on the east bank of the Suez Canal. Ten Israeli dead
31 OCTOBER 1968 First Israeli counter-raid. Israel begins construction of Bar Lev fortified line
8 MARCH 1969 Egyptians again open fire. Firing continues every few days: also Egyptian commando raids across the canal
20 JULY 1969 The Israeli airforce begins raids on Egyptian military targets along the canal
17 JANUARY 1970 Israeli airforce begins raids on military targets deep inside Egypt
7 AUGUST 1970 Egypt and Israel agree to a cease-fire. No territory changes hands
During the war of attrition more than 200 Israeli soldiers were killed. The Egyptians did not issue casualty figures. As part of the cease-fire agreement, Egypt agreed not to place any missiles within a broad belt 20 miles west of the canal. But within two weeks of this agreement, she had built between 20 and 30 new sites, and moved up more than 500 missile war-heads
Damietta
Port Said
Kantara
Ismailia
BAR LEV LINE
Northern Sinai
Cairo
Suez
Ras Sudr
Gulf of Suez
EGYPT
Nile
Southern Sinai
SAUDI ARABIA
Sharm el-Sheikh
Hurghada
Red Sea
Assiut
0 30
Miles
Principal Israeli fortifications of the 'Bar Lev' line under intense Egyptian bombardment, 1969-1970
Principal military targets inside Egypt attacked by Israeli aircraft
Principal Israeli commando raids on Egyptian positions. Some of these raids were carried out by helicopter, some by sea
© Martin Gilbert

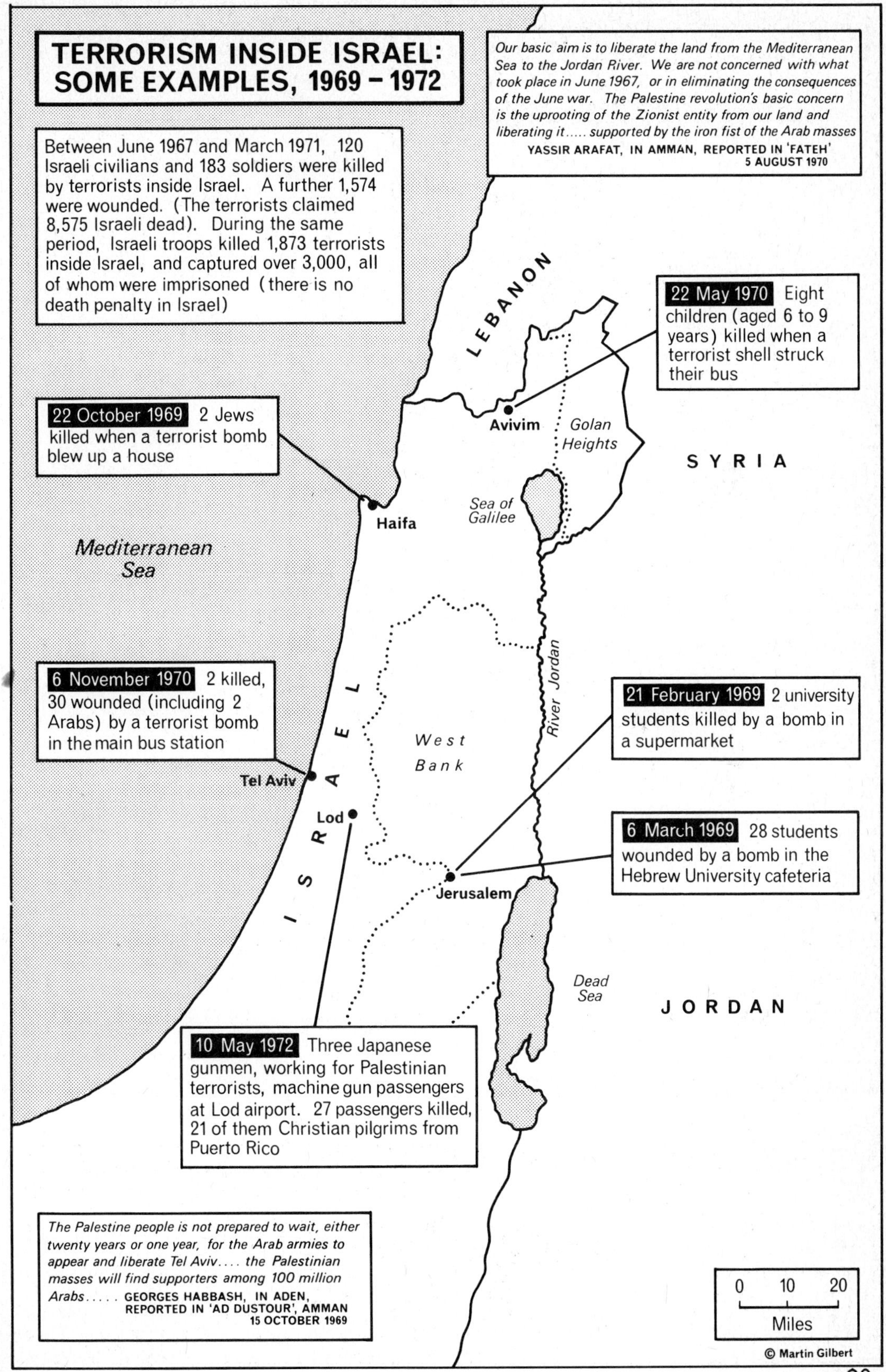
TERRORISM INSIDE ISRAEL: SOME EXAMPLES, 1969 – 1972
Our basic aim is to liberate the land from the Mediterranean Sea to the Jordan River. We are not concerned with what took place in June 1967, or in eliminating the consequences of the June war. The Palestine revolution's basic concern is the uprooting of the Zionist entity from our land and liberating it..... supported by the iron fist of the Arab masses
YASSIR ARAFAT, IN AMMAN, REPORTED IN 'FATEH' 5 AUGUST 1970
Between June 1967 and March 1971, 120 Israeli civilians and 183 soldiers were killed by terrorists inside Israel. A further 1,574 were wounded. (The terrorists claimed 8,575 Israeli dead). During the same period, Israeli troops killed 1,873 terrorists inside Israel, and captured over 3,000, all of whom were imprisoned (there is no death penalty in Israel)
LEBANON
22 May 1970 Eight children (aged 6 to 9 years) killed when a terrorist shell struck their bus
22 October 1969 2 Jews killed when a terrorist bomb blew up a house
Avivim
Golan Heights
SYRIA
Haifa
Sea of Galilee
Mediterranean Sea
River Jordan
6 November 1970 2 killed, 30 wounded (including 2 Arabs) by a terrorist bomb in the main bus station
21 February 1969 2 university students killed by a bomb in a supermarket
West Bank
ISRAEL
Tel Aviv
Lod
6 March 1969 28 students wounded by a bomb in the Hebrew University cafeteria
Jerusalem
Dead Sea
JORDAN
10 May 1972 Three Japanese gunmen, working for Palestinian terrorists, machine gun passengers at Lod airport. 27 passengers killed, 21 of them Christian pilgrims from Puerto Rico
The Palestine people is not prepared to wait, either twenty years or one year, for the Arab armies to appear and liberate Tel Aviv.... the Palestinian masses will find supporters among 100 million Arabs..... GEORGES HABBASH, IN ADEN, REPORTED IN 'AD DUSTOUR', AMMAN 15 OCTOBER 1969
0 10 20
Miles
© Martin Gilbert

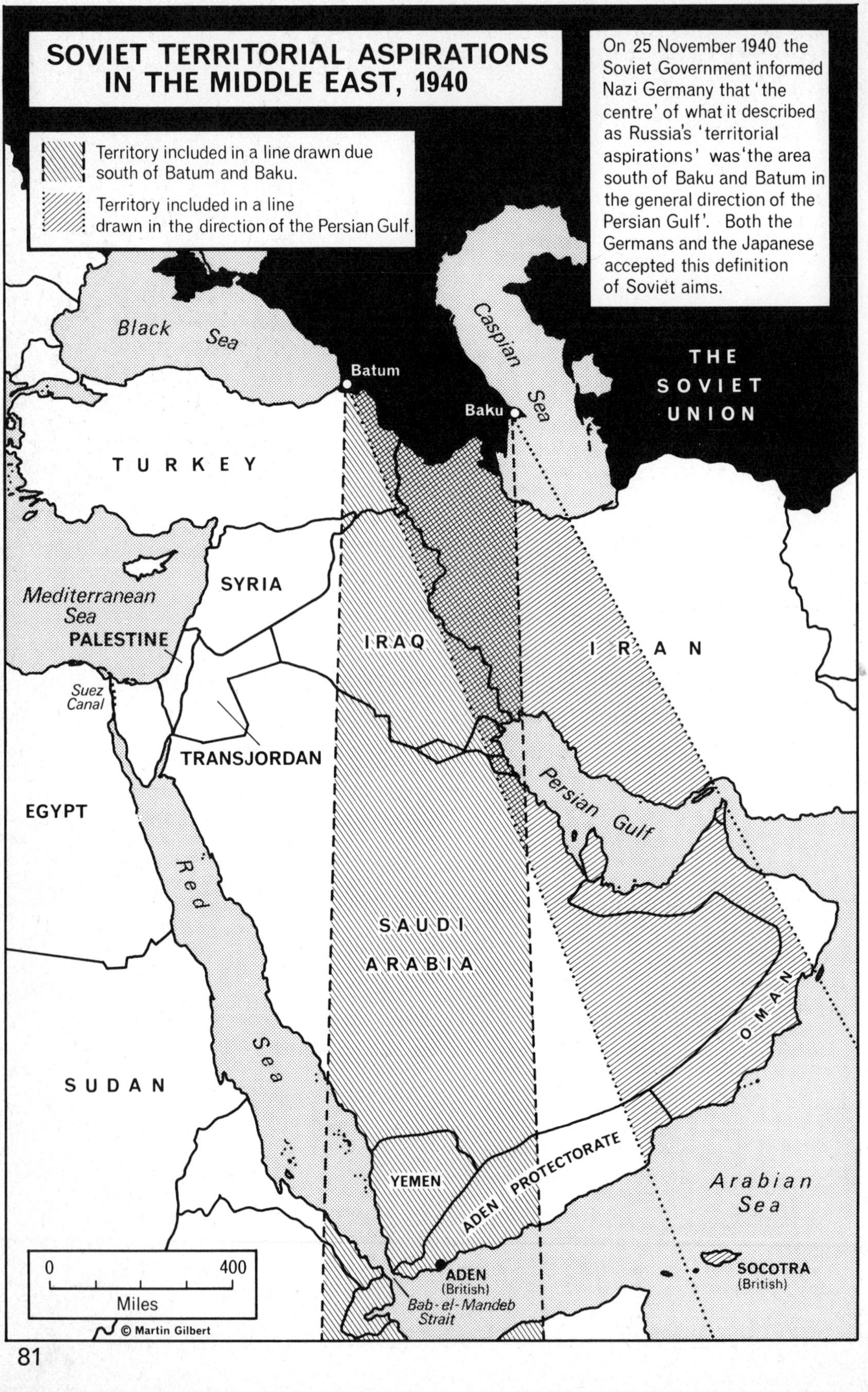
SOVIET TERRITORIAL ASPIRATIONS IN THE MIDDLE EAST, 1940
Territory included in a line drawn due south of Batum and Baku.
Territory included in a line drawn in the direction of the Persian Gulf.
On 25 November 1940 the Soviet Government informed Nazi Germany that 'the centre' of what it described as Russia's 'territorial aspirations' was 'the area south of Baku and Batum in the general direction of the Persian Gulf'. Both the Germans and the Japanese accepted this definition of Soviet aims.
Black Sea
Caspian Sea
THE SOVIET UNION
Batum
Baku
TURKEY
Mediterranean Sea
SYRIA
PALESTINE
IRAQ
IRAN
Suez Canal
TRANSJORDAN
EGYPT
Persian Gulf
Red Sea
SAUDI ARABIA
OMAN
SUDAN
YEMEN
ADEN PROTECTORATE
Arabian Sea
ADEN (British)
SOCOTRA (British)
Bab-el-Mandeb Strait
0 400 Miles
© Martin Gilbert

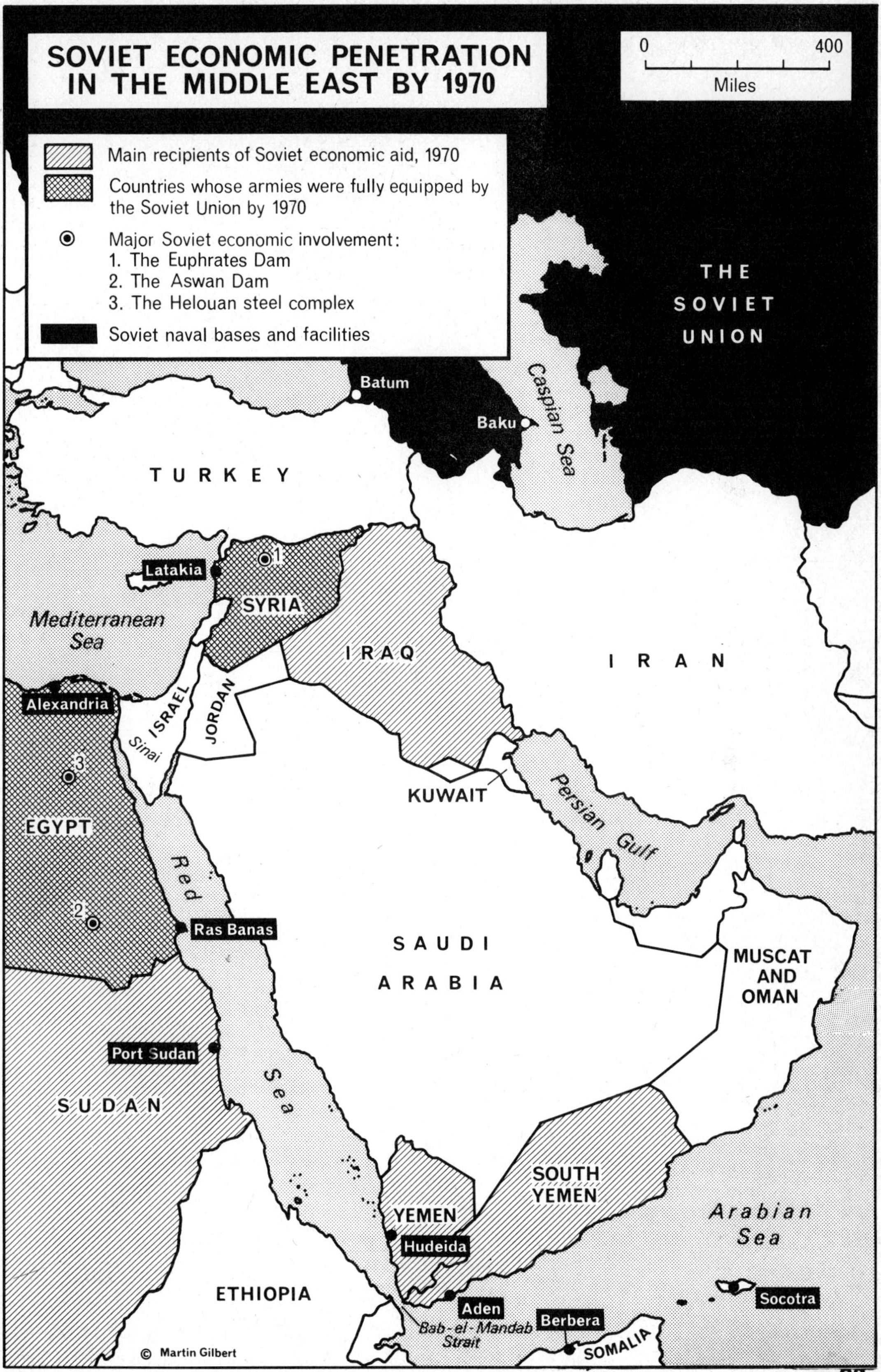
SOVIET ECONOMIC PENETRATION IN THE MIDDLE EAST BY 1970
0
400
Miles
Main recipients of Soviet economic aid, 1970
Countries whose armies were fully equipped by the Soviet Union by 1970
Major Soviet economic involvement:
1. The Euphrates Dam
2. The Aswan Dam
3. The Helouan steel complex
Soviet naval bases and facilities
THE SOVIET UNION
Batum
Baku
Caspian Sea
TURKEY
Latakia
SYRIA
Mediterranean Sea
IRAQ
IRAN
Alexandria
ISRAEL
JORDAN
Sinai
KUWAIT
Persian Gulf
EGYPT
Red
Ras Banas
SAUDI ARABIA
MUSCAT AND OMAN
Port Sudan
SUDAN
Sea
SOUTH YEMEN
YEMEN
Hudeida
Arabian Sea
ETHIOPIA
Aden
Bab-el-Mandab Strait
Berbera
Socotra
SOMALIA
© Martin Gilbert

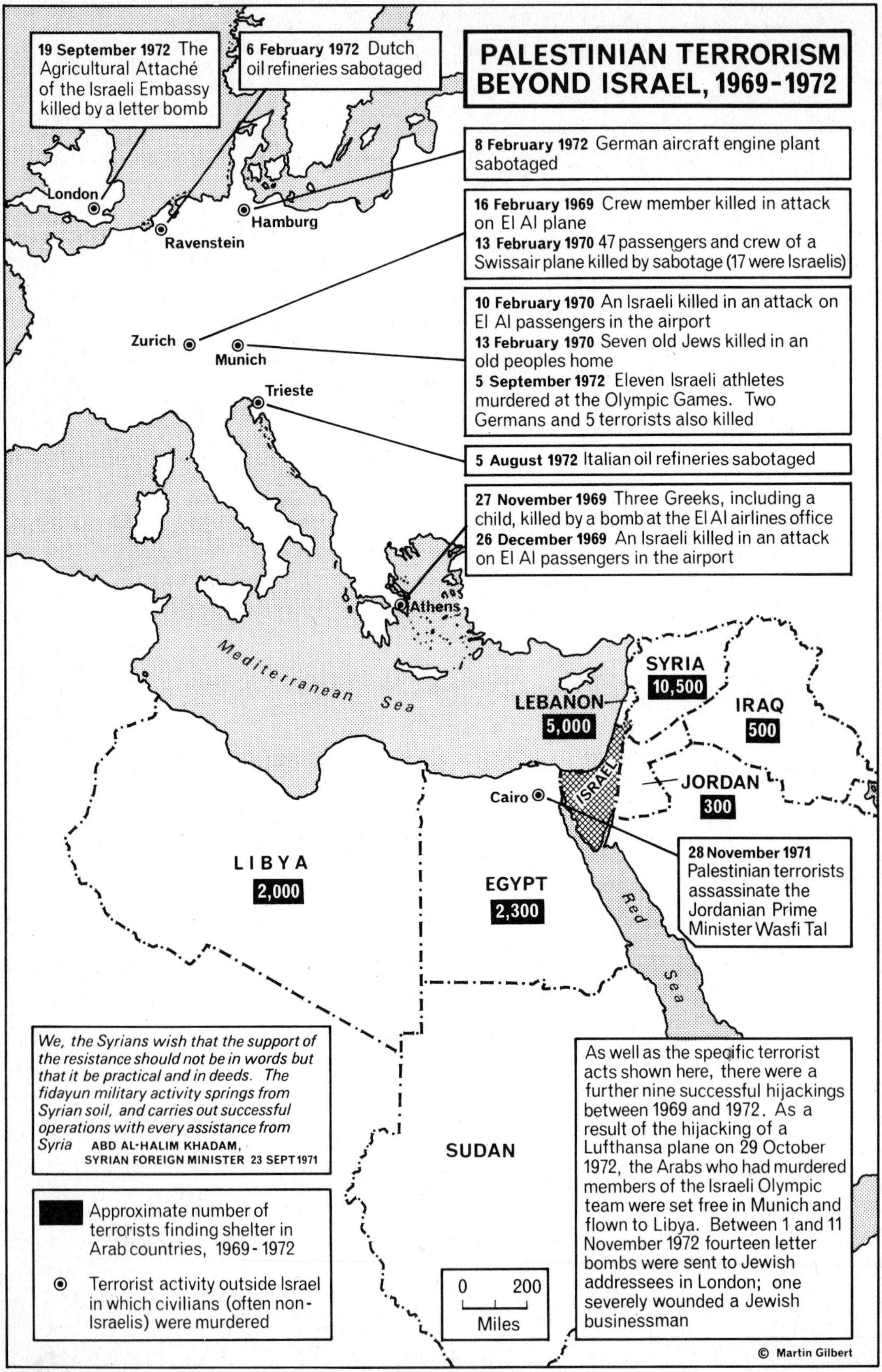

PALESTINIAN TERRORISM BEYOND ISRAEL, 1969-1972
19 September 1972 The Agricultural Attaché of the Israeli Embassy killed by a letter bomb
6 February 1972 Dutch oil refineries sabotaged
8 February 1972 German aircraft engine plant sabotaged
16 February 1969 Crew member killed in attack on El Al plane
13 February 1970 47 passengers and crew of a Swissair plane killed by sabotage (17 were Israelis)
10 February 1970 An Israeli killed in an attack on El Al passengers in the airport
13 February 1970 Seven old Jews killed in an old peoples home
5 September 1972 Eleven Israeli athletes murdered at the Olympic Games. Two Germans and 5 terrorists also killed
5 August 1972 Italian oil refineries sabotaged
27 November 1969 Three Greeks, including a child, killed by a bomb at the El Al airlines office
26 December 1969 An Israeli killed in an attack on El Al passengers in the airport
London
Hamburg
Ravenstein
Zurich
Munich
Trieste
Athens
Mediterranean Sea
SYRIA
10,500
IRAQ
500
LEBANON
5,000
ISRAEL
JORDAN
300
Cairo
28 November 1971 Palestinian terrorists assassinate the Jordanian Prime Minister Wasfi Tal
LIBYA
2,000
EGYPT
2,300
Red Sea
SUDAN
We, the Syrians wish that the support of the resistance should not be in words but that it be practical and in deeds. The fidayun military activity springs from Syrian soil, and carries out successful operations with every assistance from Syria ABD AL-HALIM KHADAM, SYRIAN FOREIGN MINISTER 23 SEPT 1971
As well as the specific terrorist acts shown here, there were a further nine successful hijackings between 1969 and 1972. As a result of the hijacking of a Lufthansa plane on 29 October 1972, the Arabs who had murdered members of the Israeli Olympic team were set free in Munich and flown to Libya. Between 1 and 11 November 1972 fourteen letter bombs were sent to Jewish addressees in London; one severely wounded a Jewish businessman
Approximate number of terrorists finding shelter in Arab countries, 1969-1972
Terrorist activity outside Israel in which civilians (often non-Israelis) were murdered
0 200
Miles
© Martin Gilbert

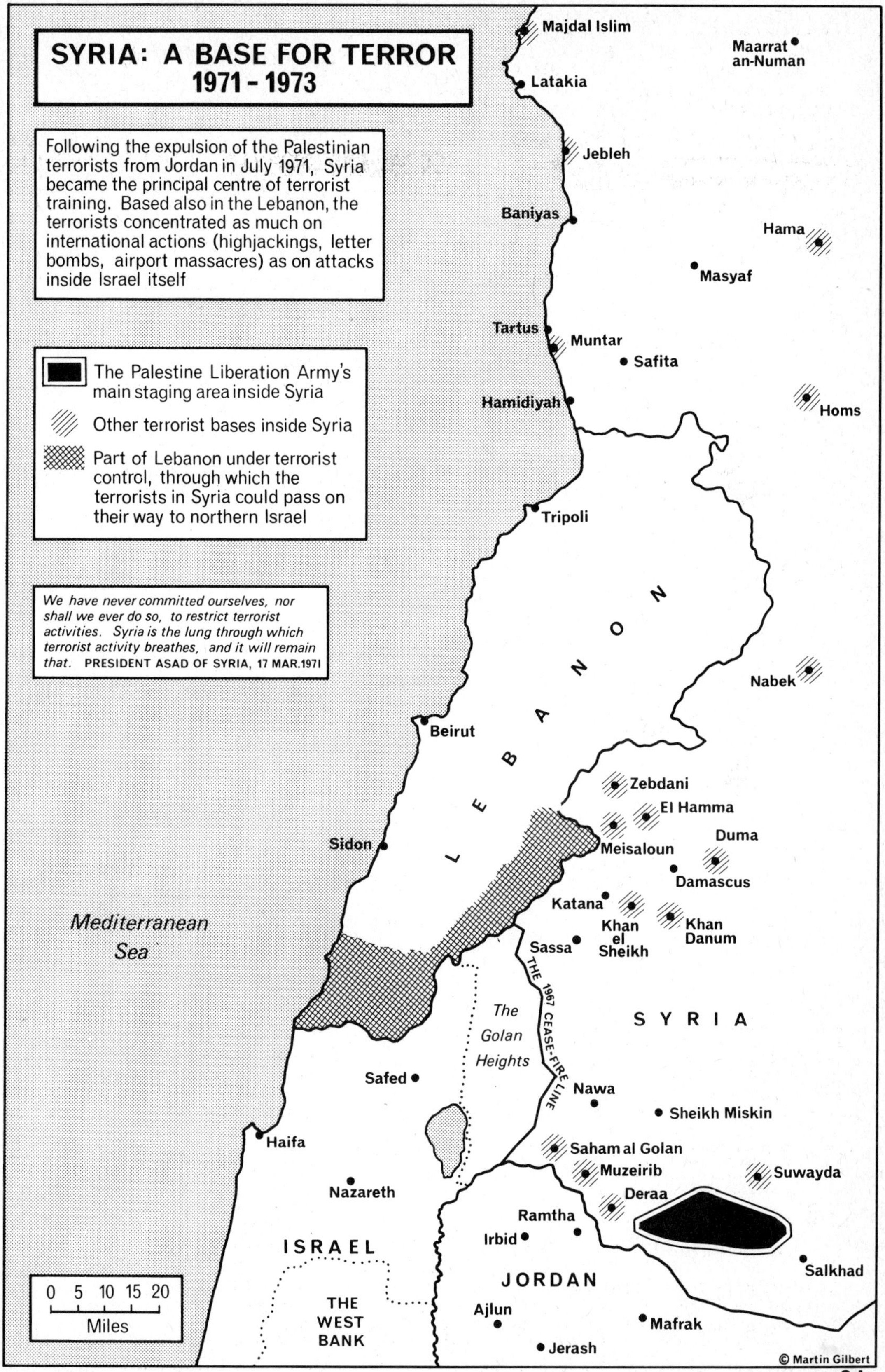

SYRIA: A BASE FOR TERROR
1971 - 1973
Following the expulsion of the Palestinian terrorists from Jordan in July 1971, Syria became the principal centre of terrorist training. Based also in the Lebanon, the terrorists concentrated as much on international actions (highjackings, letter bombs, airport massacres) as on attacks inside Israel itself
The Palestine Liberation Army's main staging area inside Syria
Other terrorist bases inside Syria
Part of Lebanon under terrorist control, through which the terrorists in Syria could pass on their way to northern Israel
We have never committed ourselves, nor shall we ever do so, to restrict terrorist activities. Syria is the lung through which terrorist activity breathes, and it will remain that. PRESIDENT ASAD OF SYRIA, 17 MAR.1971
Majdal Islim
Maarrat an-Numan
Latakia
Jebleh
Baniyas
Hama
Masyaf
Tartus
Muntar
Safita
Hamidiyah
Homs
Tripoli
LEBANON
Nabek
Beirut
Zebdani
El Hamma
Duma
Meisaloun
Sidon
Damascus
Katana
Khan el Sheikh
Khan Danum
Sassa
Mediterranean Sea
THE 1967 CEASE-FIRE LINE
The Golan Heights
SYRIA
Safed
Nawa
Sheikh Miskin
Haifa
Saham al Golan
Muzeirib
Suwayda
Deraa
Nazareth
Ramtha
Irbid
ISRAEL
Salkhad
JORDAN
0 5 10 15 20
Miles
THE WEST BANK
Ajlun
Mafrak
Jerash
© Martin Gilbert

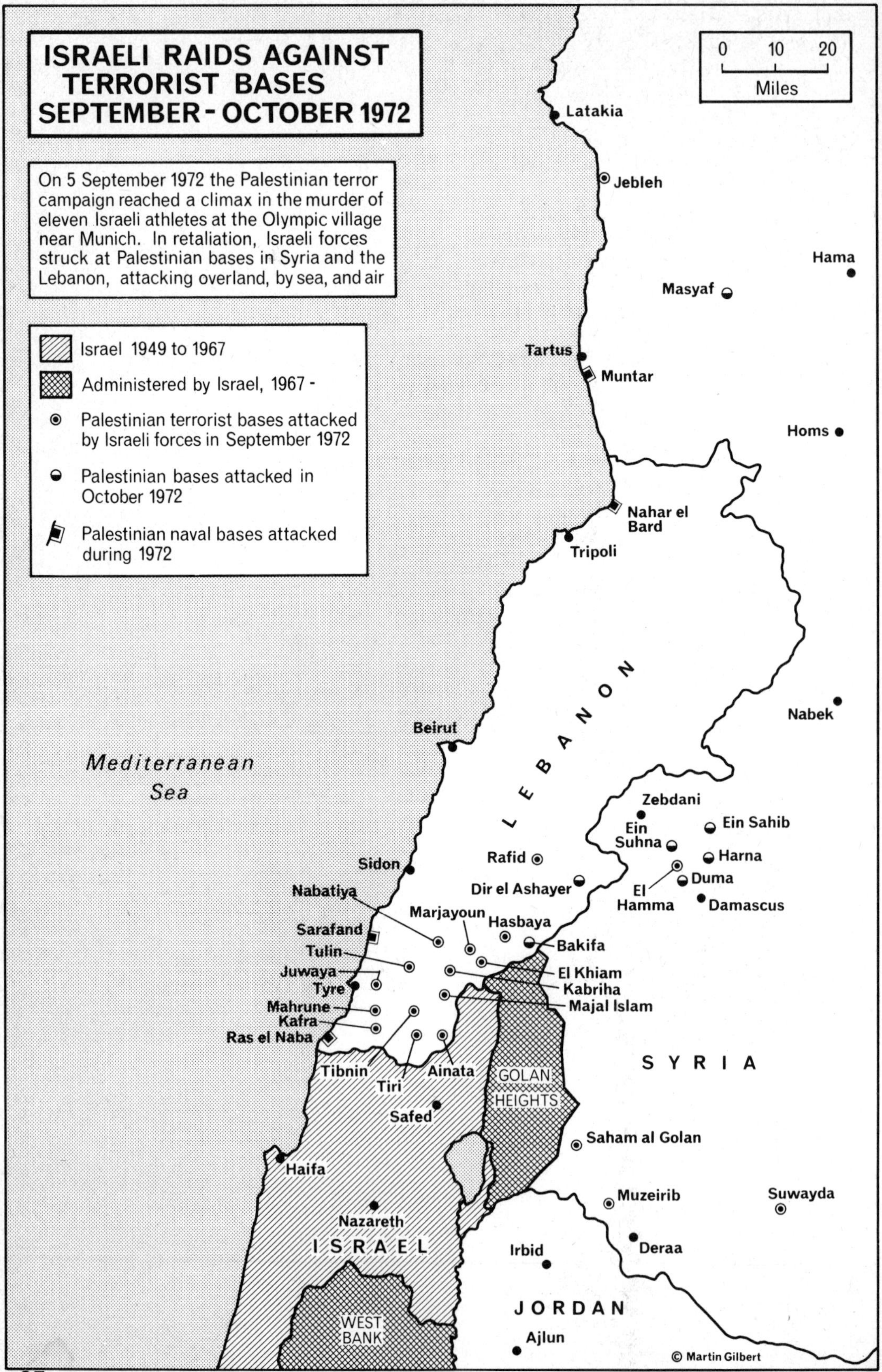
ISRAELI RAIDS AGAINST TERRORIST BASES SEPTEMBER - OCTOBER 1972
On 5 September 1972 the Palestinian terror campaign reached a climax in the murder of eleven Israeli athletes at the Olympic village near Munich. In retaliation, Israeli forces struck at Palestinian bases in Syria and the Lebanon, attacking overland, by sea, and air
Israel 1949 to 1967
Administered by Israel, 1967 -
Palestinian terrorist bases attacked by Israeli forces in September 1972
Palestinian bases attacked in October 1972
Palestinian naval bases attacked during 1972
0 10 20
Miles
Latakia
Jebleh
Hama
Masyaf
Tartus
Muntar
Homs
Nahar el Bard
Tripoli
LEBANON
Nabek
Beirut
Mediterranean Sea
Zebdani
Ein Sahib
Ein Suhna
Harna
Rafid
Sidon
Duma
Dir el Ashayer
El Hamma
Damascus
Nabatiya
Marjayoun
Hasbaya
Sarafand
Bakifa
Tulin
Juwaya
El Khiam
Tyre
Kabriha
Majal Islam
Mahrune
Kafra
Ras el Naba
SYRIA
Tibnin
Tiri
Ainata
GOLAN HEIGHTS
Safed
Saham al Golan
Haifa
Muzeirib
Suwayda
Nazareth
ISRAEL
Irbid
Deraa
JORDAN
WEST BANK
Ajlun
© Martin Gilbert

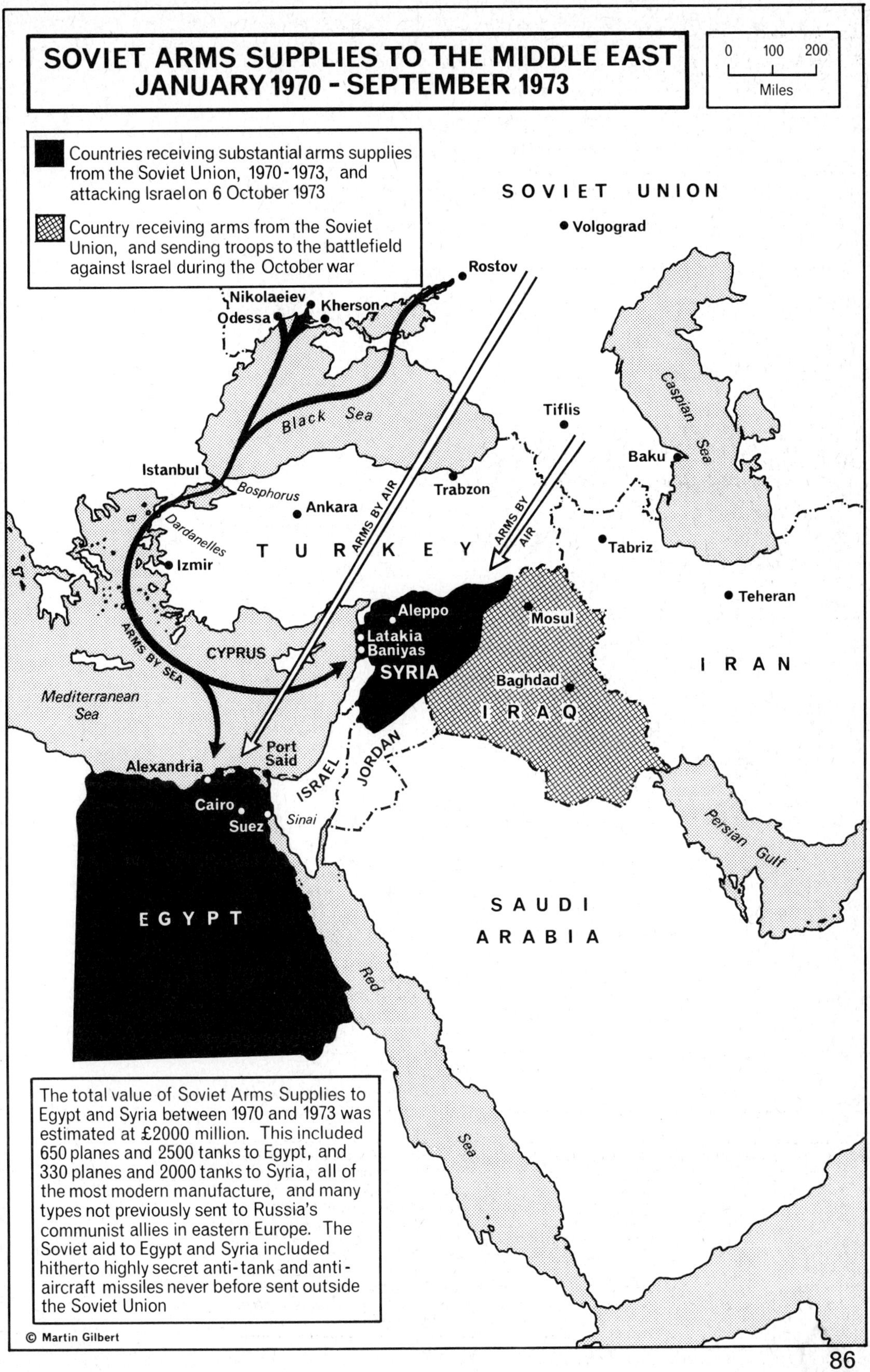
SOVIET ARMS SUPPLIES TO THE MIDDLE EAST
JANUARY 1970 - SEPTEMBER 1973
0 100 200
Miles
Countries receiving substantial arms supplies from the Soviet Union, 1970-1973, and attacking Israel on 6 October 1973
Country receiving arms from the Soviet Union, and sending troops to the battlefield against Israel during the October war
SOVIET UNION
Volgograd
Rostov
Nikolaeiev
Kherson
Odessa
Black Sea
Caspian Sea
Tiflis
Baku
Istanbul
Bosphorus
Ankara
Trabzon
Dardanelles
Izmir
TURKEY
ARMS BY AIR
ARMS BY AIR
Tabriz
Teheran
Aleppo
Mosul
Latakia
Baniyas
SYRIA
CYPRUS
ARMS BY SEA
Baghdad
IRAQ
IRAN
Mediterranean Sea
Port Said
Alexandria
ISRAEL
JORDAN
Cairo
Suez
Sinai
Persian Gulf
EGYPT
SAUDI ARABIA
Red Sea
The total value of Soviet Arms Supplies to Egypt and Syria between 1970 and 1973 was estimated at £2000 million. This included 650 planes and 2500 tanks to Egypt, and 330 planes and 2000 tanks to Syria, all of the most modern manufacture, and many types not previously sent to Russia's communist allies in eastern Europe. The Soviet aid to Egypt and Syria included hitherto highly secret anti-tank and anti-aircraft missiles never before sent outside the Soviet Union
© Martin Gilbert

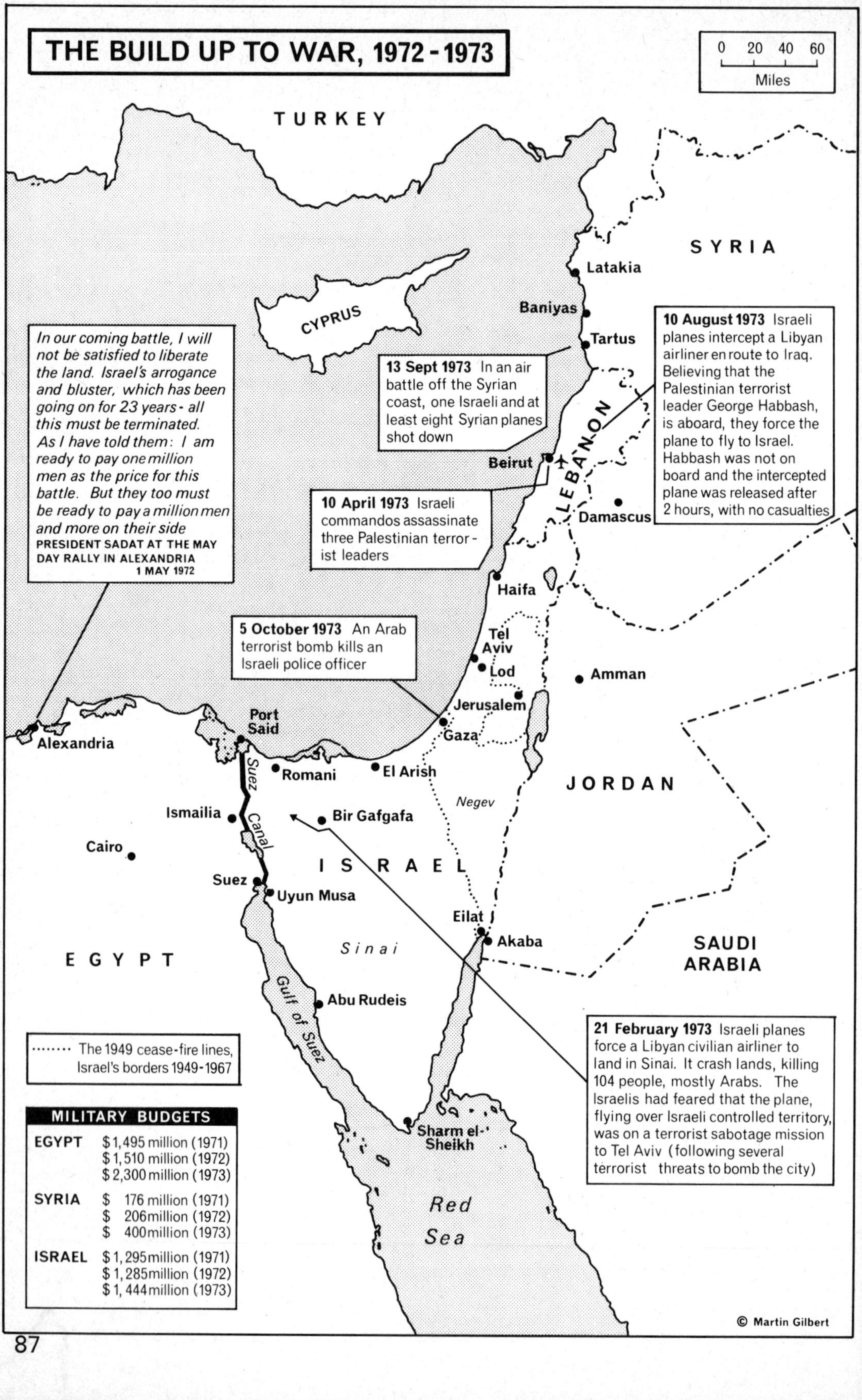
THE BUILD UP TO WAR, 1972-1973
0 20 40 60
Miles
TURKEY
SYRIA
CYPRUS
Latakia
Baniyas
Tartus
LEBANON
Beirut
Damascus
Haifa
Tel Aviv
Lod
Jerusalem
Gaza
Amman
JORDAN
Alexandria
Port Said
Romani
El Arish
Suez Canal
Ismailia
Bir Gafgafa
Negev
Cairo
ISRAEL
Suez
Uyun Musa
Eilat
Akaba
Sinai
EGYPT
SAUDI ARABIA
Gulf of Suez
Abu Rudeis
Sharm el-Sheikh
Red Sea
In our coming battle, I will not be satisfied to liberate the land. Israel's arrogance and bluster, which has been going on for 23 years - all this must be terminated. As I have told them: I am ready to pay one million men as the price for this battle. But they too must be ready to pay a million men and more on their side
PRESIDENT SADAT AT THE MAY DAY RALLY IN ALEXANDRIA 1 MAY 1972
13 Sept 1973 In an air battle off the Syrian coast, one Israeli and at least eight Syrian planes shot down
10 August 1973 Israeli planes intercept a Libyan airliner en route to Iraq. Believing that the Palestinian terrorist leader George Habbash, is aboard, they force the plane to fly to Israel. Habbash was not on board and the intercepted plane was released after 2 hours, with no casualties
10 April 1973 Israeli commandos assassinate three Palestinian terrorist leaders
5 October 1973 An Arab terrorist bomb kills an Israeli police officer
21 February 1973 Israeli planes force a Libyan civilian airliner to land in Sinai. It crash lands, killing 104 people, mostly Arabs. The Israelis had feared that the plane, flying over Israeli controlled territory, was on a terrorist sabotage mission to Tel Aviv (following several terrorist threats to bomb the city)
The 1949 cease-fire lines, Israel's borders 1949-1967
MILITARY BUDGETS
EGYPT $1,495 million (1971)
$1,510 million (1972)
$2,300 million (1973)
SYRIA $ 176 million (1971)
$ 206million (1972)
$ 400million (1973)
ISRAEL $1,295million (1971)
$1,285million (1972)
$1,444million (1973)
© Martin Gilbert

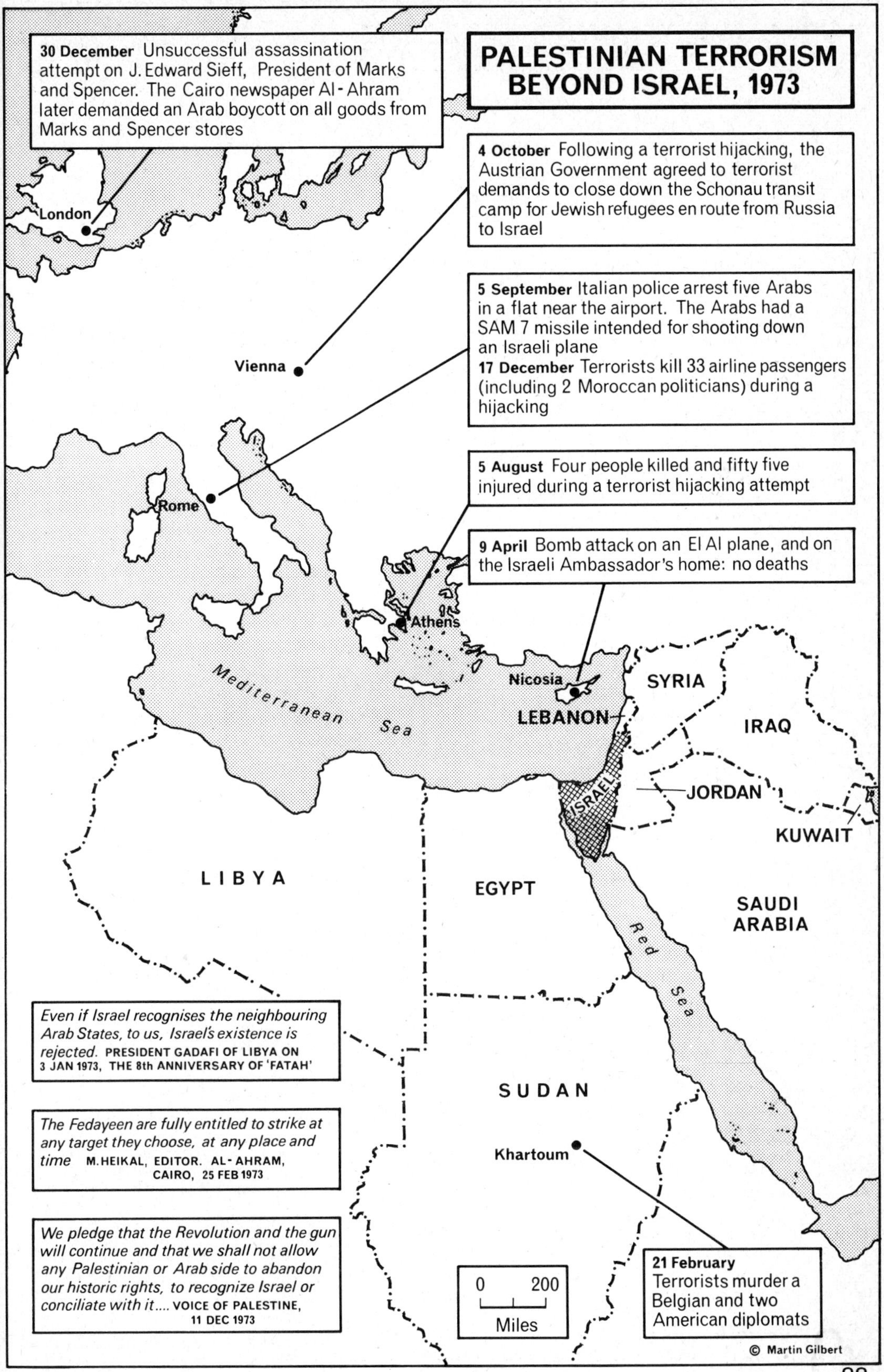

PALESTINIAN TERRORISM BEYOND ISRAEL, 1973
30 December Unsuccessful assassination attempt on J. Edward Sieff, President of Marks and Spencer. The Cairo newspaper Al-Ahram later demanded an Arab boycott on all goods from Marks and Spencer stores
4 October Following a terrorist hijacking, the Austrian Government agreed to terrorist demands to close down the Schonau transit camp for Jewish refugees en route from Russia to Israel
5 September Italian police arrest five Arabs in a flat near the airport. The Arabs had a SAM 7 missile intended for shooting down an Israeli plane
17 December Terrorists kill 33 airline passengers (including 2 Moroccan politicians) during a hijacking
5 August Four people killed and fifty five injured during a terrorist hijacking attempt
9 April Bomb attack on an El Al plane, and on the Israeli Ambassador's home: no deaths
London
Vienna
Rome
Athens
Nicosia
Mediterranean Sea
SYRIA
IRAQ
LEBANON
ISRAEL
JORDAN
KUWAIT
LIBYA
EGYPT
SAUDI ARABIA
Red Sea
SUDAN
Khartoum
Even if Israel recognises the neighbouring Arab States, to us, Israel's existence is rejected. PRESIDENT GADAFI OF LIBYA ON 3 JAN 1973, THE 8th ANNIVERSARY OF 'FATAH'
The Fedayeen are fully entitled to strike at any target they choose, at any place and time M. HEIKAL, EDITOR. AL-AHRAM, CAIRO, 25 FEB 1973
We pledge that the Revolution and the gun will continue and that we shall not allow any Palestinian or Arab side to abandon our historic rights, to recognize Israel or conciliate with it.... VOICE OF PALESTINE, 11 DEC 1973
0 200
Miles
21 February Terrorists murder a Belgian and two American diplomats
© Martin Gilbert

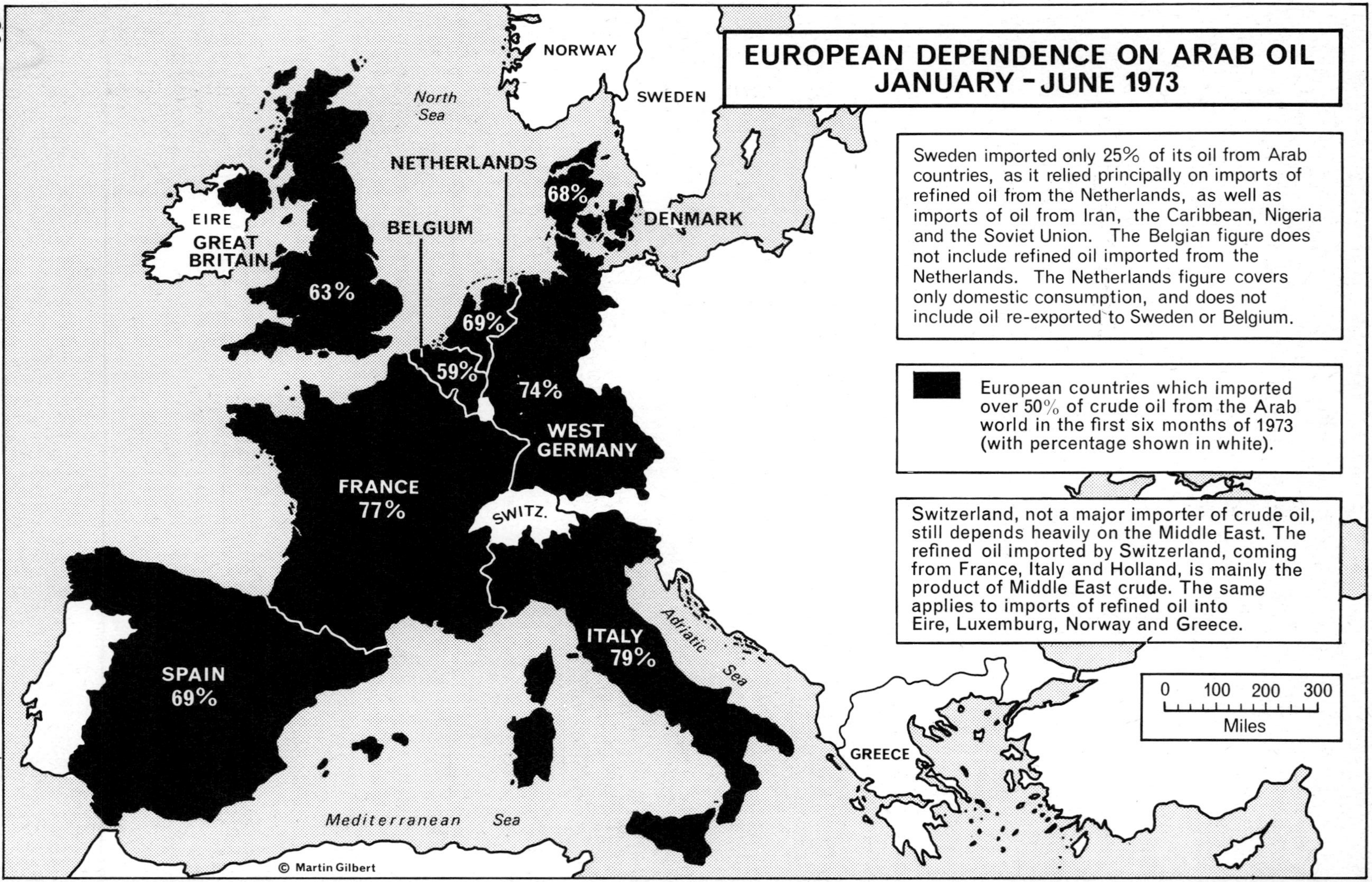
EUROPEAN DEPENDENCE ON ARAB OIL
JANUARY - JUNE 1973
Sweden imported only 25% of its oil from Arab countries, as it relied principally on imports of refined oil from the Netherlands, as well as imports of oil from Iran, the Caribbean, Nigeria and the Soviet Union. The Belgian figure does not include refined oil imported from the Netherlands. The Netherlands figure covers only domestic consumption, and does not include oil re-exported to Sweden or Belgium.
European countries which imported over 50% of crude oil from the Arab world in the first six months of 1973 (with percentage shown in white).
Switzerland, not a major importer of crude oil, still depends heavily on the Middle East. The refined oil imported by Switzerland, coming from France, Italy and Holland, is mainly the product of Middle East crude. The same applies to imports of refined oil into Eire, Luxemburg, Norway and Greece.
NORWAY
SWEDEN
North Sea
NETHERLANDS
BELGIUM
DENMARK
68%
EIRE
GREAT BRITAIN
63%
69%
59%
74%
WEST GERMANY
FRANCE 77%
SWITZ.
ITALY 79%
Adriatic Sea
SPAIN 69%
GREECE
Mediterranean Sea
0 100 200 300
Miles
© Martin Gilbert

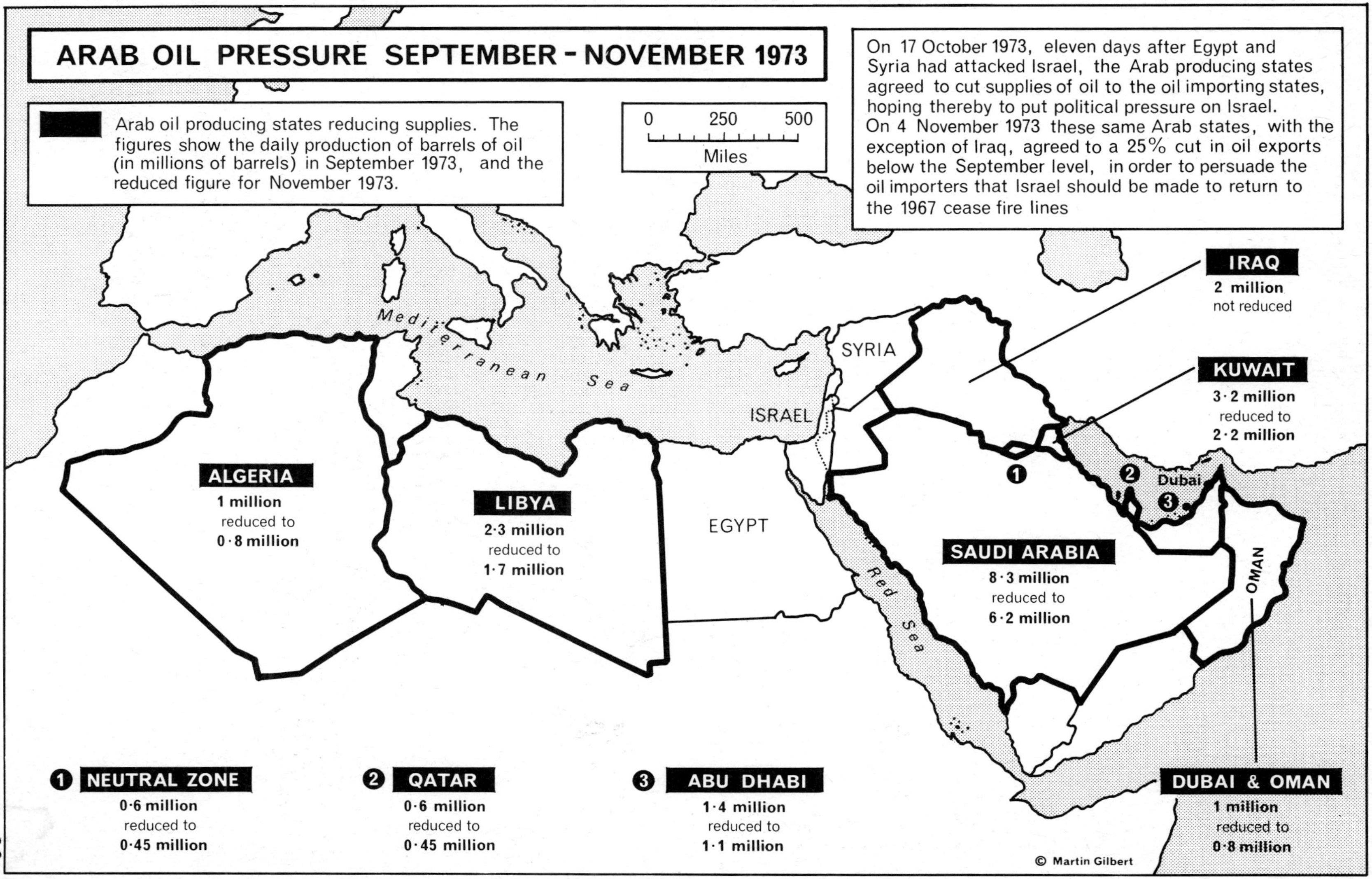

ARAB OIL PRESSURE SEPTEMBER - NOVEMBER 1973
Arab oil producing states reducing supplies. The figures show the daily production of barrels of oil (in millions of barrels) in September 1973, and the reduced figure for November 1973.
0 250 500
Miles
On 17 October 1973, eleven days after Egypt and Syria had attacked Israel, the Arab producing states agreed to cut supplies of oil to the oil importing states, hoping thereby to put political pressure on Israel.
On 4 November 1973 these same Arab states, with the exception of Iraq, agreed to a 25% cut in oil exports below the September level, in order to persuade the oil importers that Israel should be made to return to the 1967 cease fire lines
IRAQ
2 million
not reduced
KUWAIT
3·2 million
reduced to
2·2 million
Mediterranean Sea
SYRIA
ISRAEL
EGYPT
Red Sea
Dubai
OMAN
ALGERIA
1 million
reduced to
0·8 million
LIBYA
2·3 million
reduced to
1·7 million
SAUDI ARABIA
8·3 million
reduced to
6·2 million
1 NEUTRAL ZONE
0·6 million
reduced to
0·45 million
2 QATAR
0·6 million
reduced to
0·45 million
3 ABU DHABI
1·4 million
reduced to
1·1 million
DUBAI & OMAN
1 million
reduced to
0·8 million
© Martin Gilbert

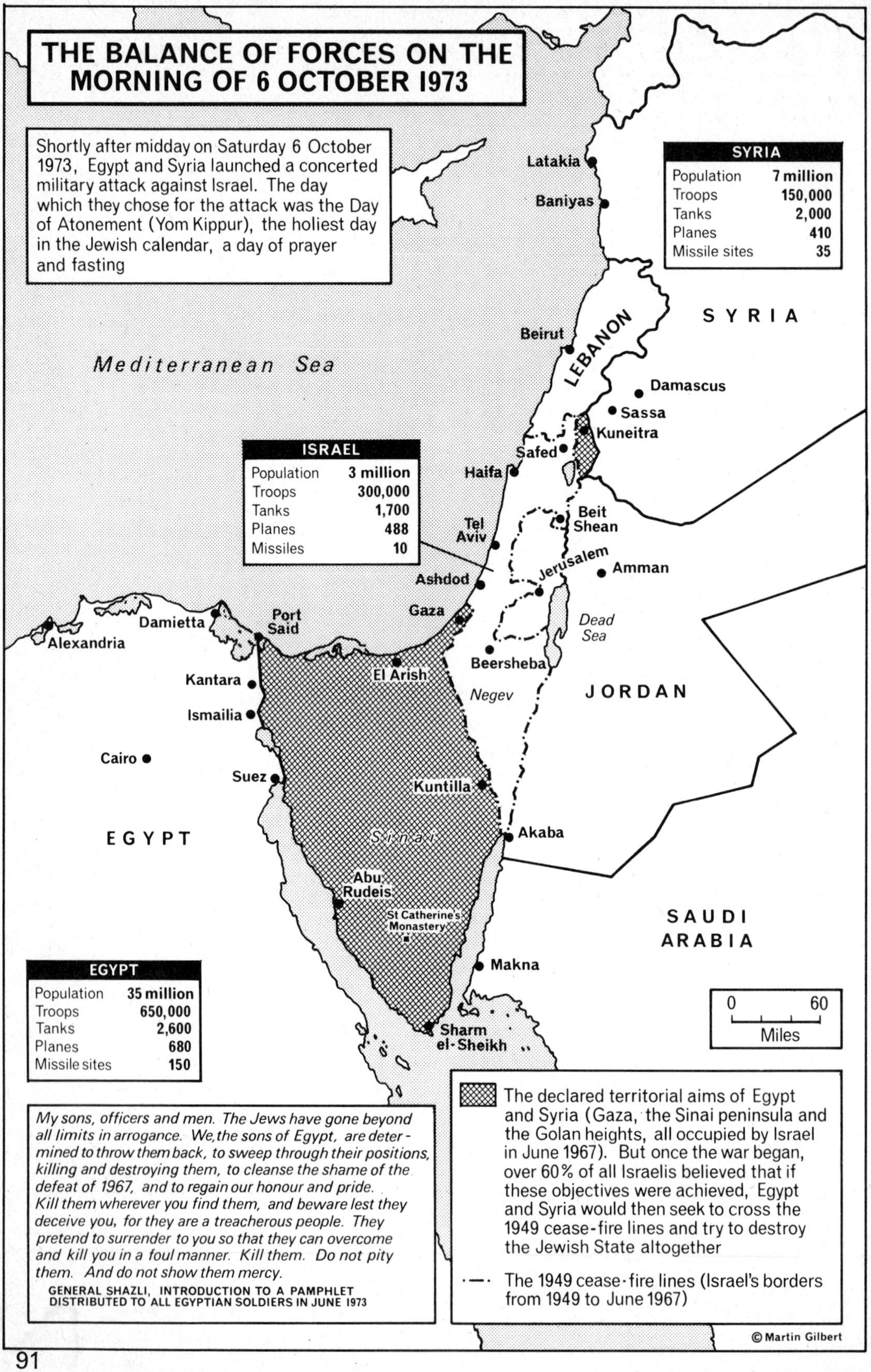
THE BALANCE OF FORCES ON THE MORNING OF 6 OCTOBER 1973
Shortly after midday on Saturday 6 October 1973, Egypt and Syria launched a concerted military attack against Israel. The day which they chose for the attack was the Day of Atonement (Yom Kippur), the holiest day in the Jewish calendar, a day of prayer and fasting
SYRIA
Population 7 million
Troops 150,000
Tanks 2,000
Planes 410
Missile sites 35
ISRAEL
Population 3 million
Troops 300,000
Tanks 1,700
Planes 488
Missiles 10
EGYPT
Population 35 million
Troops 650,000
Tanks 2,600
Planes 680
Missile sites 150
Latakia
Baniyas
SYRIA
Beirut
LEBANON
Mediterranean Sea
Damascus
Sassa
Kuneitra
Safed
Haifa
Beit Shean
Tel Aviv
Jerusalem
Amman
Ashdod
Gaza
Dead Sea
Port Said
Damietta
Alexandria
El Arish
Beersheba
Kantara
Negev
JORDAN
Ismailia
Cairo
Suez
Kuntilla
EGYPT
Sinai
Akaba
Abu Rudeis
St Catherine's Monastery
SAUDI ARABIA
Makna
0 60 Miles
Sharm el-Sheikh
My sons, officers and men. The Jews have gone beyond all limits in arrogance. We, the sons of Egypt, are determined to throw them back, to sweep through their positions, killing and destroying them, to cleanse the shame of the defeat of 1967, and to regain our honour and pride. Kill them wherever you find them, and beware lest they deceive you, for they are a treacherous people. They pretend to surrender to you so that they can overcome and kill you in a foul manner. Kill them. Do not pity them. And do not show them mercy.
GENERAL SHAZLI, INTRODUCTION TO A PAMPHLET DISTRIBUTED TO ALL EGYPTIAN SOLDIERS IN JUNE 1973
The declared territorial aims of Egypt and Syria (Gaza, the Sinai peninsula and the Golan heights, all occupied by Israel in June 1967). But once the war began, over 60% of all Israelis believed that if these objectives were achieved, Egypt and Syria would then seek to cross the 1949 cease-fire lines and try to destroy the Jewish State altogether
The 1949 cease-fire lines (Israel's borders from 1949 to June 1967)
© Martin Gilbert

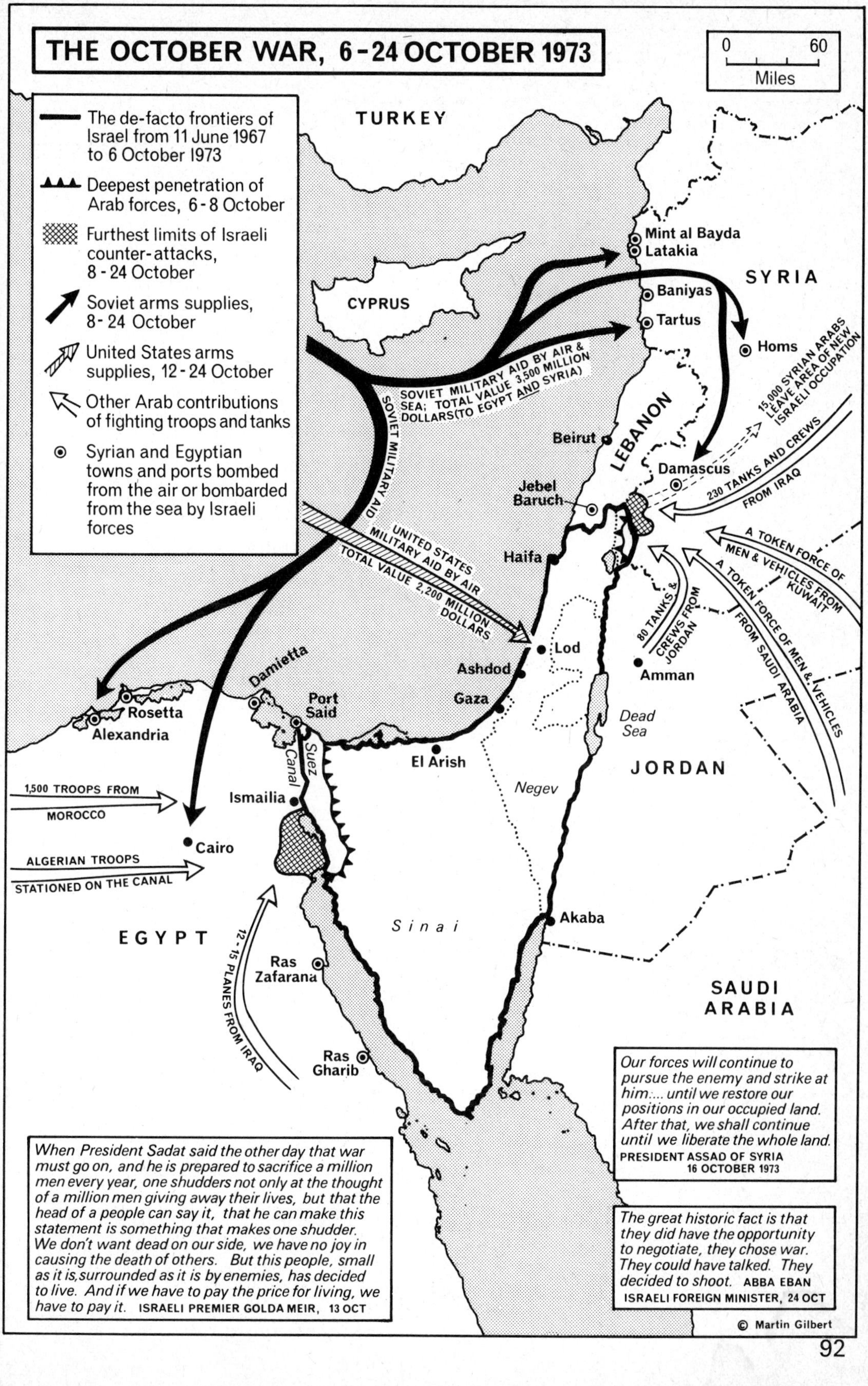
THE OCTOBER WAR, 6-24 OCTOBER 1973
0 60
Miles
The de-facto frontiers of Israel from 11 June 1967 to 6 October 1973
Deepest penetration of Arab forces, 6-8 October
Furthest limits of Israeli counter-attacks, 8-24 October
Soviet arms supplies, 8-24 October
United States arms supplies, 12-24 October
Other Arab contributions of fighting troops and tanks
Syrian and Egyptian towns and ports bombed from the air or bombarded from the sea by Israeli forces
TURKEY
CYPRUS
SYRIA
LEBANON
JORDAN
EGYPT
SAUDI ARABIA
Mint al Bayda
Latakia
Baniyas
Tartus
Homs
Beirut
Damascus
Jebel Baruch
Haifa
Lod
Ashdod
Gaza
Amman
Dead Sea
El Arish
Negev
Akaba
Sinai
Damietta
Port Said
Rosetta
Alexandria
Suez Canal
Ismailia
Cairo
Ras Zafarana
Ras Gharib
SOVIET MILITARY AID BY AIR & SEA; TOTAL VALUE 3,500 MILLION DOLLARS (TO EGYPT AND SYRIA)
SOVIET MILITARY AID
UNITED STATES MILITARY AID BY AIR TOTAL VALUE 2,200 MILLION DOLLARS
15,000 SYRIAN ARABS LEAVE AREA OF NEW ISRAELI OCCUPATION
230 TANKS AND CREWS FROM IRAQ
A TOKEN FORCE OF MEN & VEHICLES FROM KUWAIT
A TOKEN FORCE OF MEN & VEHICLES FROM SAUDI ARABIA
80 TANKS & CREWS FROM JORDAN
1,500 TROOPS FROM MOROCCO
ALGERIAN TROOPS STATIONED ON THE CANAL
12-15 PLANES FROM IRAQ
Our forces will continue to pursue the enemy and strike at him:... until we restore our positions in our occupied land. After that, we shall continue until we liberate the whole land.
PRESIDENT ASSAD OF SYRIA 16 OCTOBER 1973
The great historic fact is that they did have the opportunity to negotiate, they chose war. They could have talked. They decided to shoot. ABBA EBAN ISRAELI FOREIGN MINISTER, 24 OCT
When President Sadat said the other day that war must go on, and he is prepared to sacrifice a million men every year, one shudders not only at the thought of a million men giving away their lives, but that the head of a people can say it, that he can make this statement is something that makes one shudder. We don't want dead on our side, we have no joy in causing the death of others. But this people, small as it is, surrounded as it is by enemies, has decided to live. And if we have to pay the price for living, we have to pay it. ISRAELI PREMIER GOLDA MEIR, 13 OCT
© Martin Gilbert

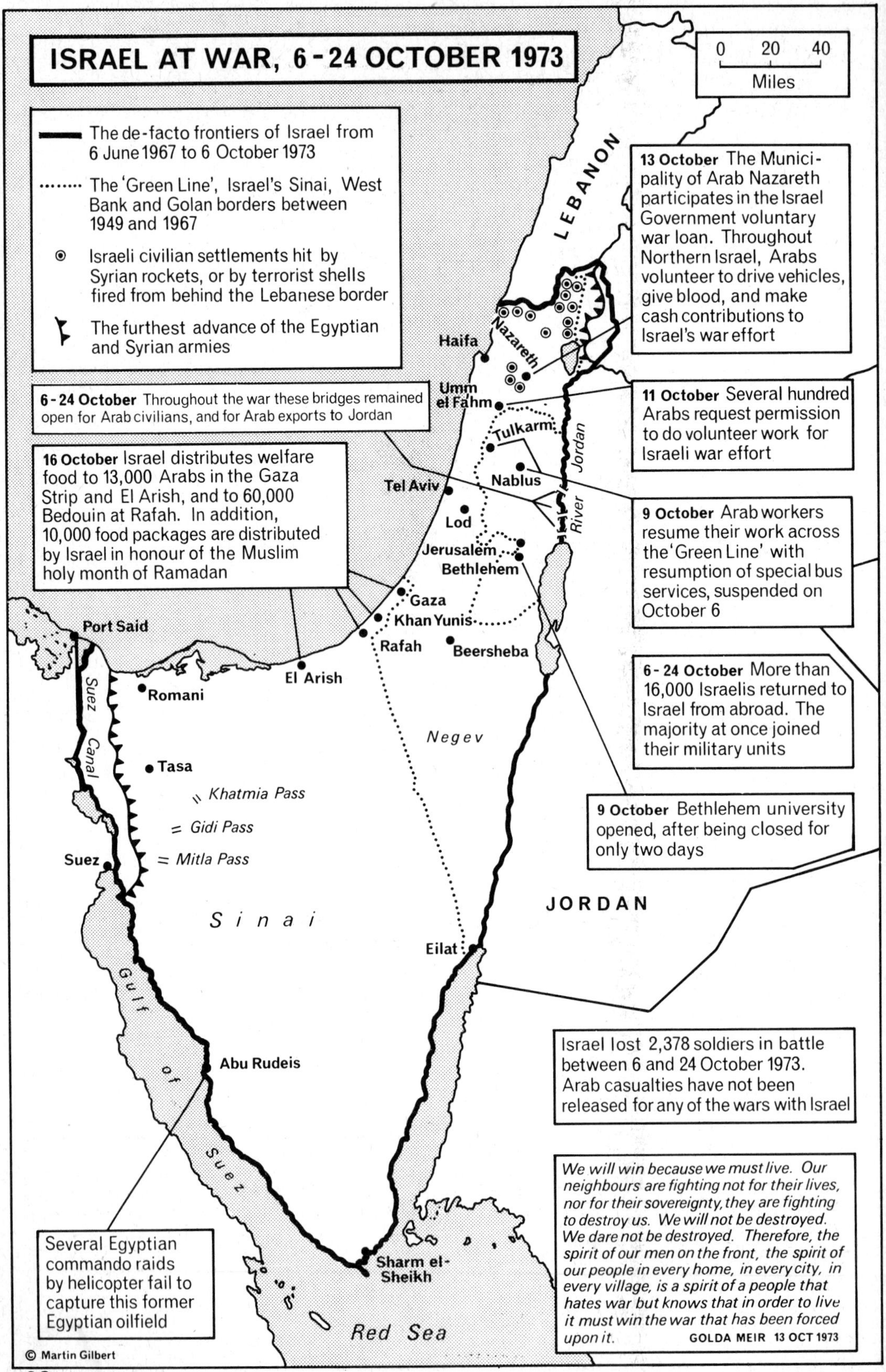

ISRAEL AT WAR, 6-24 OCTOBER 1973
0 20 40
Miles
The de-facto frontiers of Israel from 6 June 1967 to 6 October 1973
The 'Green Line', Israel's Sinai, West Bank and Golan borders between 1949 and 1967
Israeli civilian settlements hit by Syrian rockets, or by terrorist shells fired from behind the Lebanese border
The furthest advance of the Egyptian and Syrian armies
LEBANON
13 October The Municipality of Arab Nazareth participates in the Israel Government voluntary war loan. Throughout Northern Israel, Arabs volunteer to drive vehicles, give blood, and make cash contributions to Israel's war effort
Haifa
Nazareth
Umm el Fahm
6-24 October Throughout the war these bridges remained open for Arab civilians, and for Arab exports to Jordan
11 October Several hundred Arabs request permission to do volunteer work for Israeli war effort
Tulkarm
River Jordan
16 October Israel distributes welfare food to 13,000 Arabs in the Gaza Strip and El Arish, and to 60,000 Bedouin at Rafah. In addition, 10,000 food packages are distributed by Israel in honour of the Muslim holy month of Ramadan
Tel Aviv
Nablus
Lod
Jerusalem
Bethlehem
9 October Arab workers resume their work across the 'Green Line' with resumption of special bus services, suspended on October 6
Gaza
Khan Yunis
Port Said
Rafah
Beersheba
El Arish
Romani
6-24 October More than 16,000 Israelis returned to Israel from abroad. The majority at once joined their military units
Suez Canal
Negev
Tasa
Khatmia Pass
Gidi Pass
9 October Bethlehem university opened, after being closed for only two days
Suez
Mitla Pass
JORDAN
Sinai
Eilat
Gulf of Suez
Abu Rudeis
Israel lost 2,378 soldiers in battle between 6 and 24 October 1973. Arab casualties have not been released for any of the wars with Israel
We will win because we must live. Our neighbours are fighting not for their lives, nor for their sovereignty, they are fighting to destroy us. We will not be destroyed. We dare not be destroyed. Therefore, the spirit of our men on the front, the spirit of our people in every home, in every city, in every village, is a spirit of a people that hates war but knows that in order to live it must win the war that has been forced upon it. GOLDA MEIR 13 OCT 1973
Several Egyptian commando raids by helicopter fail to capture this former Egyptian oilfield
Sharm el-Sheikh
Red Sea

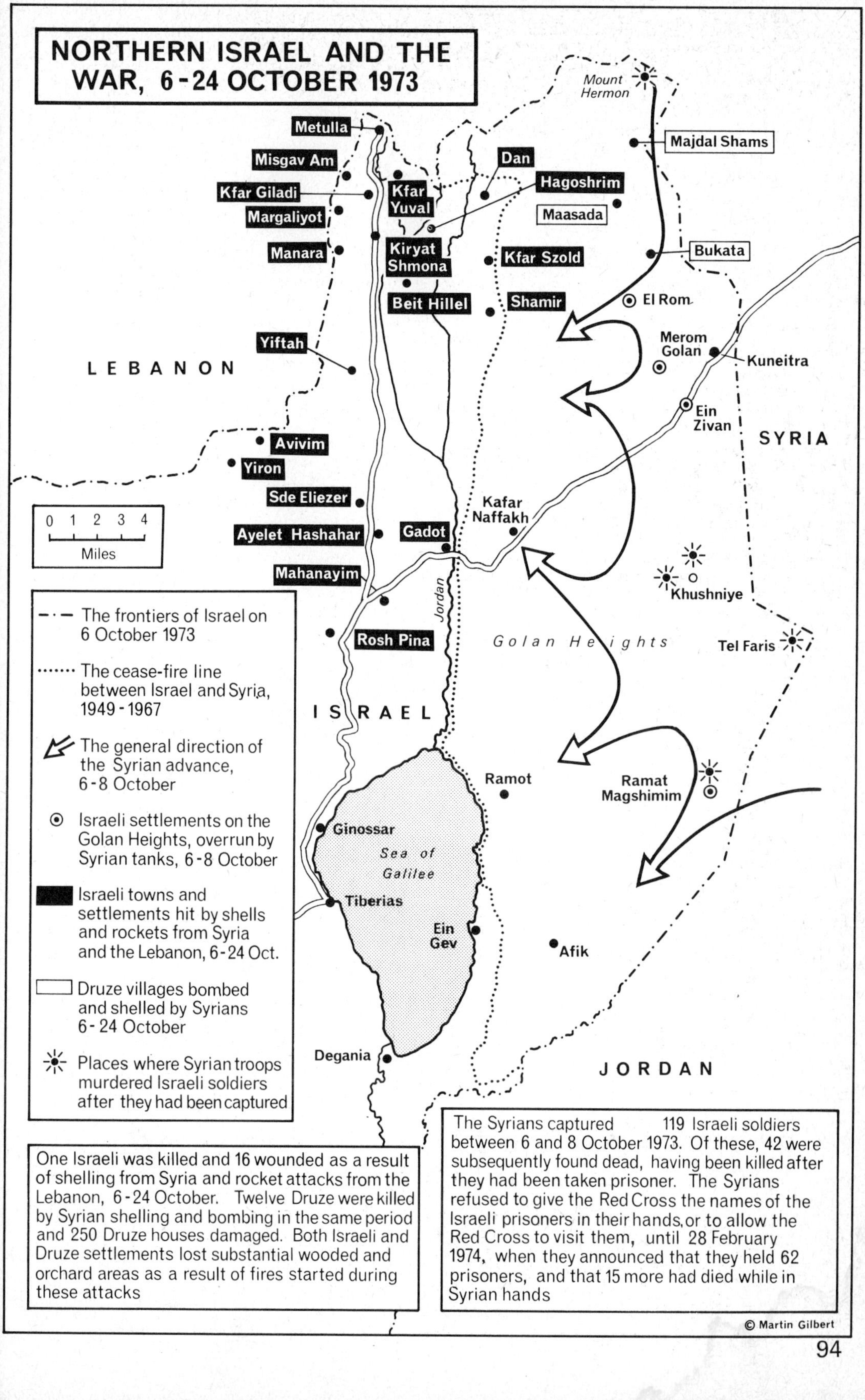
NORTHERN ISRAEL AND THE WAR, 6-24 OCTOBER 1973
Mount Hermon
Metulla
Misgav Am
Kfar Giladi
Margaliyot
Manara
Kfar Yuval
Kiryat Shmona
Beit Hillel
Dan
Hagoshrim
Maasada
Majdal Shams
Bukata
Kfar Szold
Shamir
El Rom
Merom Golan
Kuneitra
Ein Zivan
Yiftah
LEBANON
SYRIA
Avivim
Yiron
Sde Eliezer
Ayelet Hashahar
Gadot
Kafar Naffakh
Mahanayim
Rosh Pina
Jordan
Golan Heights
Khushniye
Tel Faris
ISRAEL
Ramot
Ramat Magshimim
Ginossar
Sea of Galilee
Tiberias
Ein Gev
Afik
Degania
JORDAN
0 1 2 3 4
Miles
The frontiers of Israel on 6 October 1973
The cease-fire line between Israel and Syria, 1949-1967
The general direction of the Syrian advance, 6-8 October
Israeli settlements on the Golan Heights, overrun by Syrian tanks, 6-8 October
Israeli towns and settlements hit by shells and rockets from Syria and the Lebanon, 6-24 Oct.
Druze villages bombed and shelled by Syrians 6-24 October
Places where Syrian troops murdered Israeli soldiers after they had been captured
© Martin Gilbert

One Israeli was killed and 16 wounded as a result of shelling from Syria and rocket attacks from the Lebanon, 6-24 October. Twelve Druze were killed by Syrian shelling and bombing in the same period and 250 Druze houses damaged. Both Israeli and Druze settlements lost substantial wooded and orchard areas as a result of fires started during these attacks

The Syrians captured 119 Israeli soldiers between 6 and 8 October 1973. Of these, 42 were subsequently found dead, having been killed after they had been taken prisoner. The Syrians refused to give the Red Cross the names of the Israeli prisoners in their hands, or to allow the Red Cross to visit them, until 28 February 1974, when they announced that they held 62 prisoners, and that 15 more had died while in Syrian hands

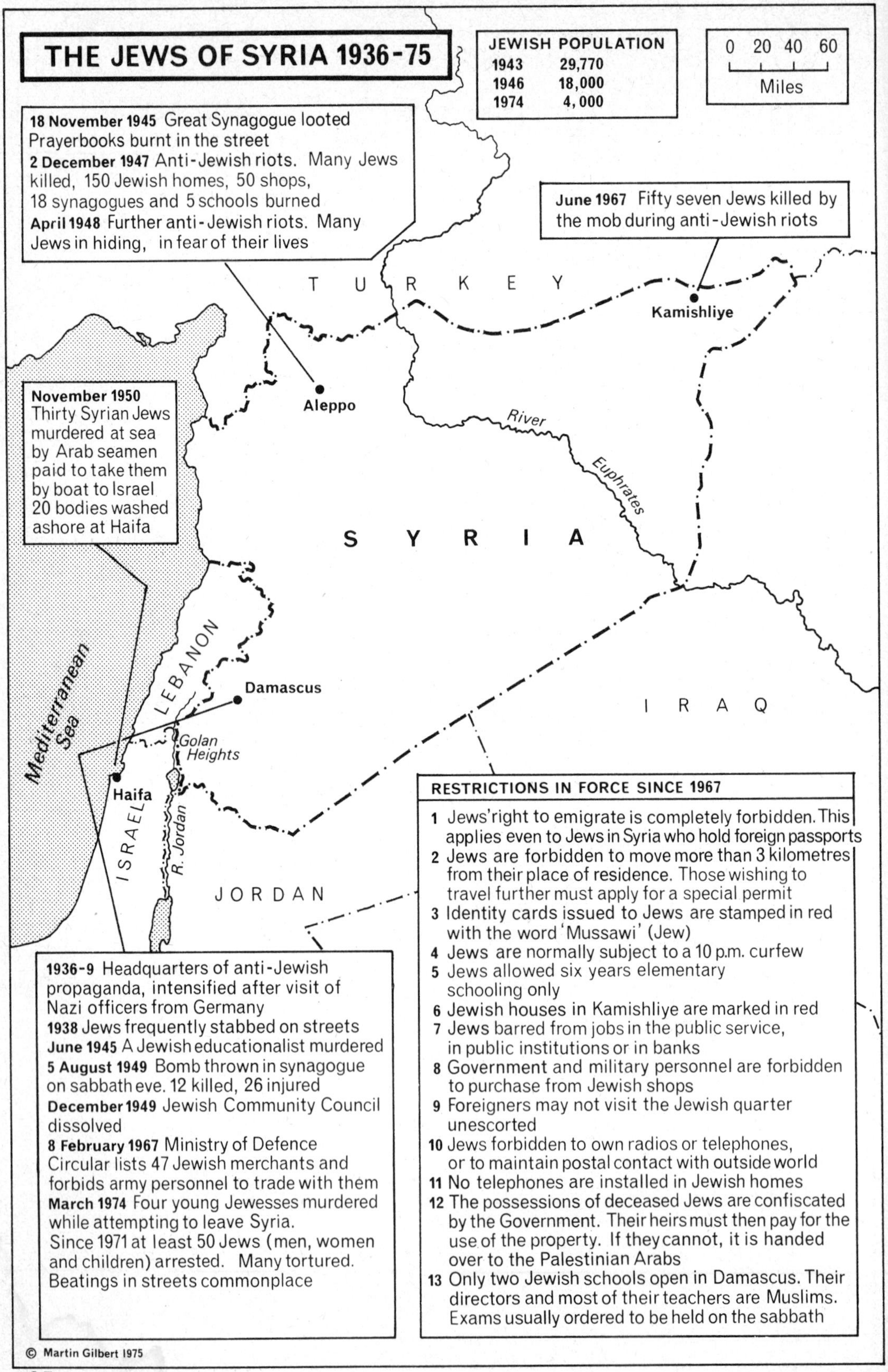
THE JEWS OF SYRIA 1936-75
JEWISH POPULATION
1943 29,770
1946 18,000
1974 4,000
0 20 40 60
Miles
18 November 1945 Great Synagogue looted
Prayerbooks burnt in the street
2 December 1947 Anti-Jewish riots. Many Jews killed, 150 Jewish homes, 50 shops, 18 synagogues and 5 schools burned
April 1948 Further anti-Jewish riots. Many Jews in hiding, in fear of their lives
June 1967 Fifty seven Jews killed by the mob during anti-Jewish riots
TURKEY
Kamishliye
Aleppo
November 1950
Thirty Syrian Jews murdered at sea by Arab seamen paid to take them by boat to Israel
20 bodies washed ashore at Haifa
River Euphrates
SYRIA
LEBANON
Mediterranean Sea
Damascus
IRAQ
Golan Heights
Haifa
ISRAEL
R. Jordan
JORDAN
RESTRICTIONS IN FORCE SINCE 1967
1 Jews' right to emigrate is completely forbidden. This applies even to Jews in Syria who hold foreign passports
2 Jews are forbidden to move more than 3 kilometres from their place of residence. Those wishing to travel further must apply for a special permit
3 Identity cards issued to Jews are stamped in red with the word 'Mussawi' (Jew)
4 Jews are normally subject to a 10 p.m. curfew
5 Jews allowed six years elementary schooling only
6 Jewish houses in Kamishliye are marked in red
7 Jews barred from jobs in the public service, in public institutions or in banks
8 Government and military personnel are forbidden to purchase from Jewish shops
9 Foreigners may not visit the Jewish quarter unescorted
10 Jews forbidden to own radios or telephones, or to maintain postal contact with outside world
11 No telephones are installed in Jewish homes
12 The possessions of deceased Jews are confiscated by the Government. Their heirs must then pay for the use of the property. If they cannot, it is handed over to the Palestinian Arabs
13 Only two Jewish schools open in Damascus. Their directors and most of their teachers are Muslims. Exams usually ordered to be held on the sabbath
1936-9 Headquarters of anti-Jewish propaganda, intensified after visit of Nazi officers from Germany
1938 Jews frequently stabbed on streets
June 1945 A Jewish educationalist murdered
5 August 1949 Bomb thrown in synagogue on sabbath eve. 12 killed, 26 injured
December 1949 Jewish Community Council dissolved
8 February 1967 Ministry of Defence Circular lists 47 Jewish merchants and forbids army personnel to trade with them
March 1974 Four young Jewesses murdered while attempting to leave Syria.
Since 1971 at least 50 Jews (men, women and children) arrested. Many tortured. Beatings in streets commonplace
© Martin Gilbert 1975

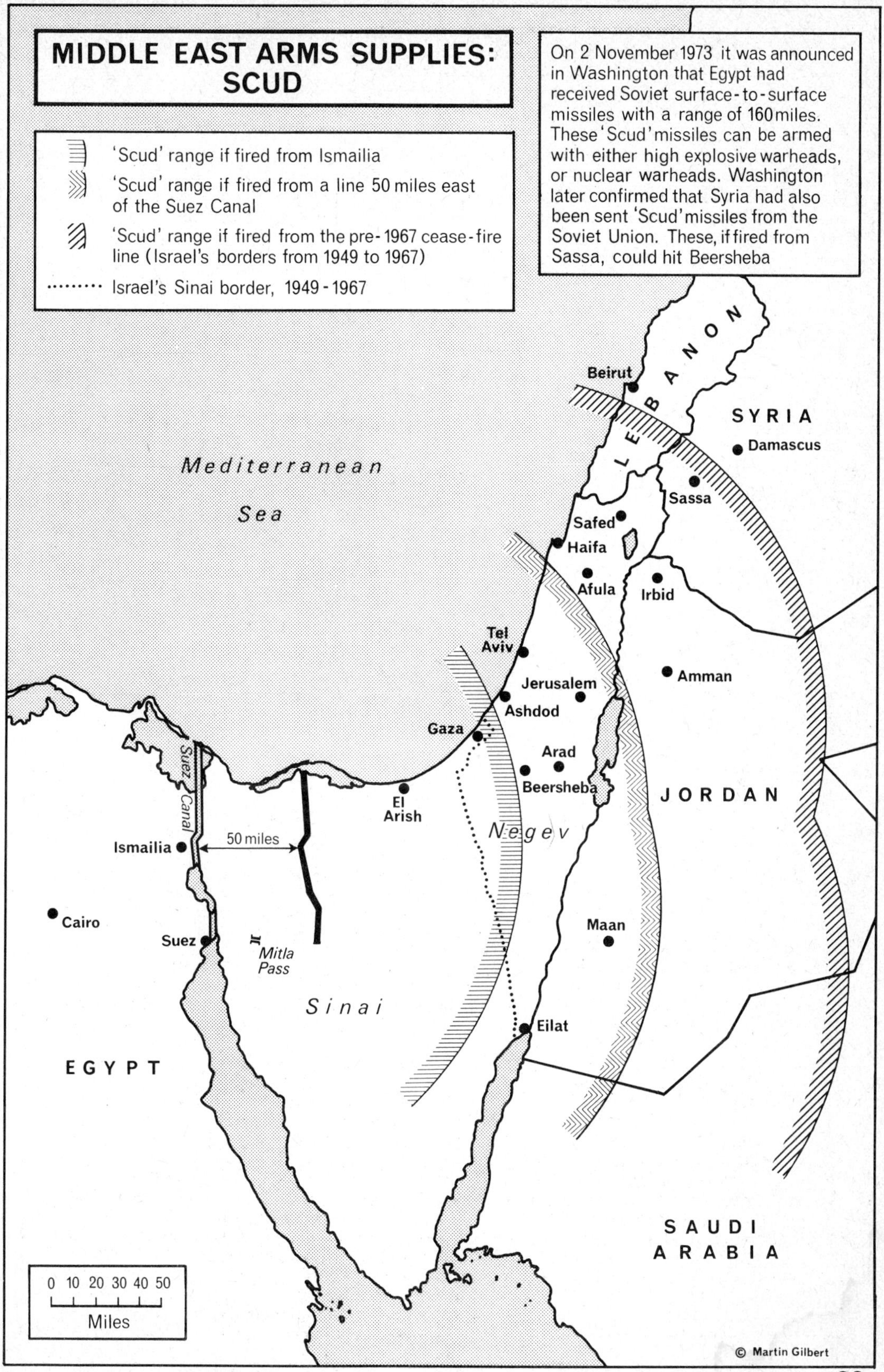
MIDDLE EAST ARMS SUPPLIES: SCUD
'Scud' range if fired from Ismailia
'Scud' range if fired from a line 50 miles east of the Suez Canal
'Scud' range if fired from the pre-1967 cease-fire line (Israel's borders from 1949 to 1967)
Israel's Sinai border, 1949-1967
On 2 November 1973 it was announced in Washington that Egypt had received Soviet surface-to-surface missiles with a range of 160 miles. These 'Scud' missiles can be armed with either high explosive warheads, or nuclear warheads. Washington later confirmed that Syria had also been sent 'Scud' missiles from the Soviet Union. These, if fired from Sassa, could hit Beersheba
LEBANON
Beirut
SYRIA
Damascus
Mediterranean Sea
Sassa
Safed
Haifa
Afula
Irbid
Tel Aviv
Amman
Jerusalem
Ashdod
Gaza
Arad
Beersheba
JORDAN
El Arish
Suez Canal
50 miles
Ismailia
Negev
Cairo
Maan
Suez
Mitla Pass
Sinai
Eilat
EGYPT
SAUDI ARABIA
0 10 20 30 40 50
Miles
© Martin Gilbert

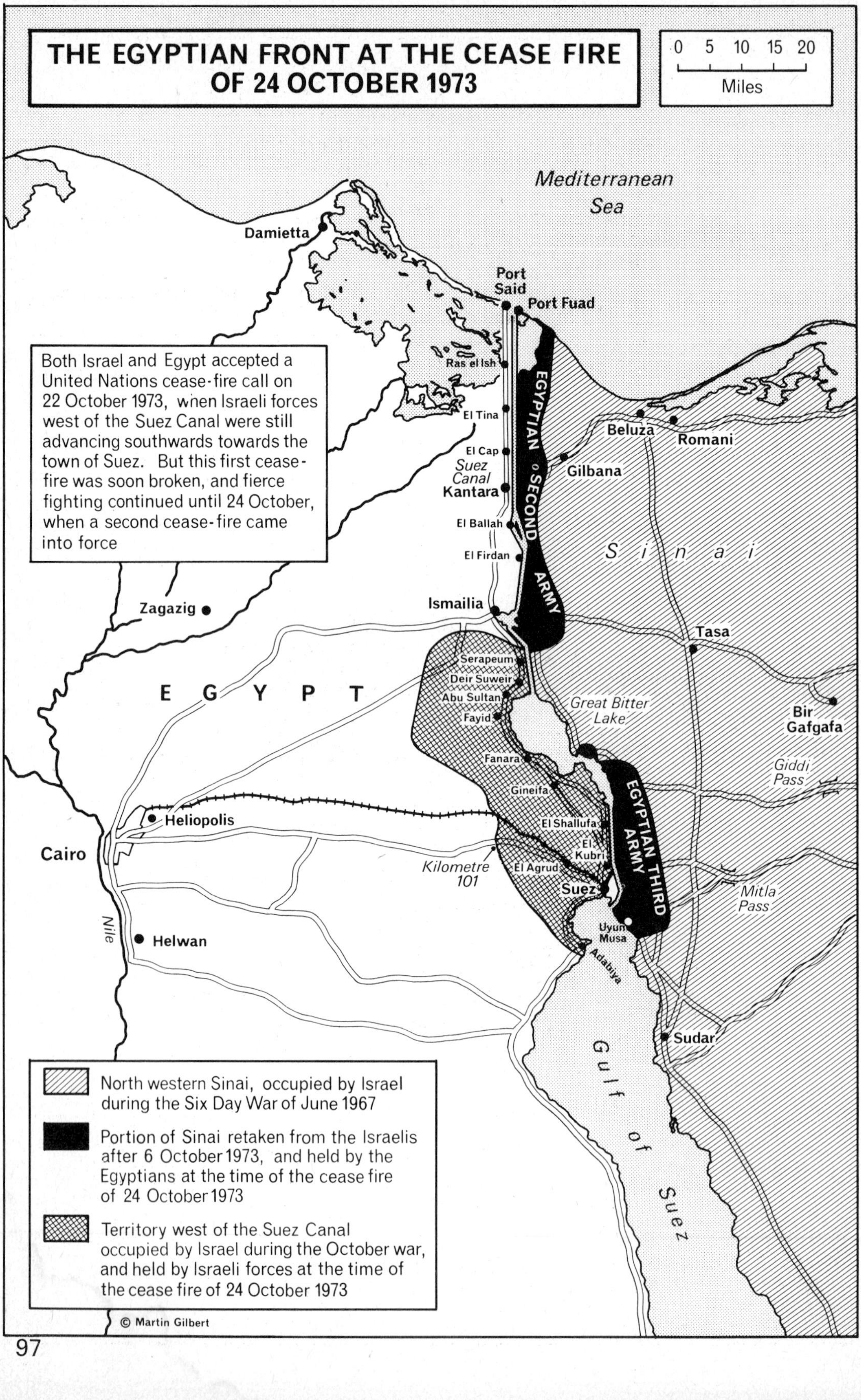
THE EGYPTIAN FRONT AT THE CEASE FIRE OF 24 OCTOBER 1973
0 5 10 15 20
Miles
Mediterranean Sea
Both Israel and Egypt accepted a United Nations cease-fire call on 22 October 1973, when Israeli forces west of the Suez Canal were still advancing southwards towards the town of Suez. But this first cease-fire was soon broken, and fierce fighting continued until 24 October, when a second cease-fire came into force
Damietta
Port Said
Port Fuad
Ras el Ish
El Tina
El Cap
Suez Canal
Kantara
El Ballah
El Firdan
Ismailia
EGYPTIAN SECOND ARMY
Beluza
Romani
Gilbana
Sinai
Tasa
Zagazig
EGYPT
Serapeum
Deir Suweir
Abu Sultan
Fayid
Great Bitter Lake
Bir Gafgafa
Fanara
Gineifa
Giddi Pass
Heliopolis
El Shallufa
El Kubri
EGYPTIAN THIRD ARMY
Cairo
Kilometre 101
El Agrud
Suez
Mitla Pass
Uyun Musa
Adabiya
Nile
Helwan
Sudar
Gulf of Suez
North western Sinai, occupied by Israel during the Six Day War of June 1967
Portion of Sinai retaken from the Israelis after 6 October 1973, and held by the Egyptians at the time of the cease fire of 24 October 1973
Territory west of the Suez Canal occupied by Israel during the October war, and held by Israeli forces at the time of the cease fire of 24 October 1973
© Martin Gilbert

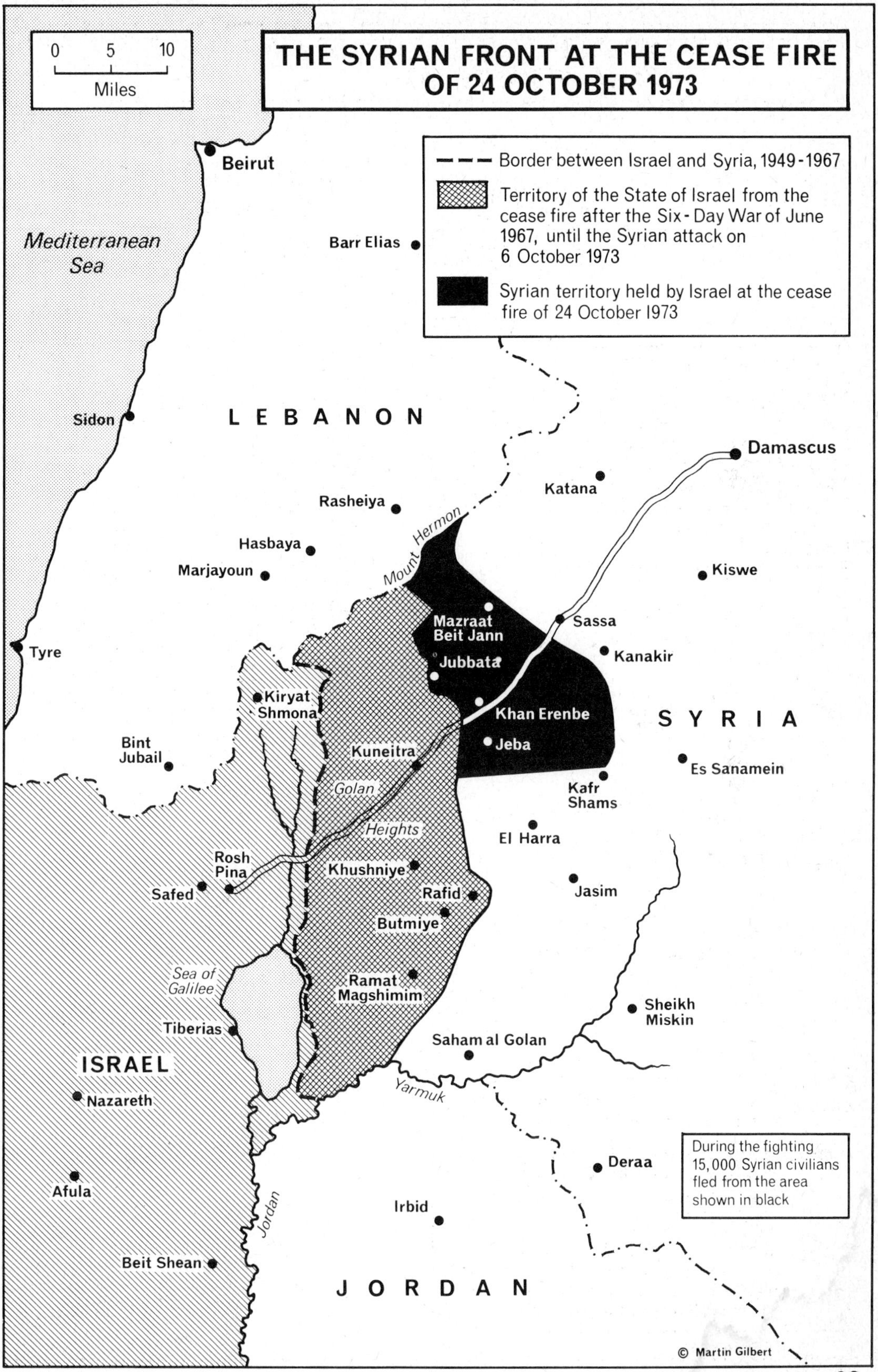
THE SYRIAN FRONT AT THE CEASE FIRE OF 24 OCTOBER 1973
0 5 10
Miles
Border between Israel and Syria, 1949-1967
Territory of the State of Israel from the cease fire after the Six-Day War of June 1967, until the Syrian attack on 6 October 1973
Syrian territory held by Israel at the cease fire of 24 October 1973
Beirut
Mediterranean Sea
Barr Elias
Sidon
LEBANON
Damascus
Katana
Rasheiya
Mount Hermon
Hasbaya
Marjayoun
Kiswe
Mazraat Beit Jann
Sassa
Tyre
Jubbata
Kanakir
Kiryat Shmona
Khan Erenbe
SYRIA
Bint Jubail
Kuneitra
Jeba
Es Sanamein
Golan
Kafr Shams
Heights
El Harra
Rosh Pina
Khushniye
Safed
Rafid
Jasim
Butmiye
Sea of Galilee
Ramat Magshimim
Sheikh Miskin
Tiberias
Saham al Golan
ISRAEL
Yarmuk
Nazareth
Deraa
During the fighting 15,000 Syrian civilians fled from the area shown in black
Afula
Jordan
Irbid
Beit Shean
JORDAN
© Martin Gilbert

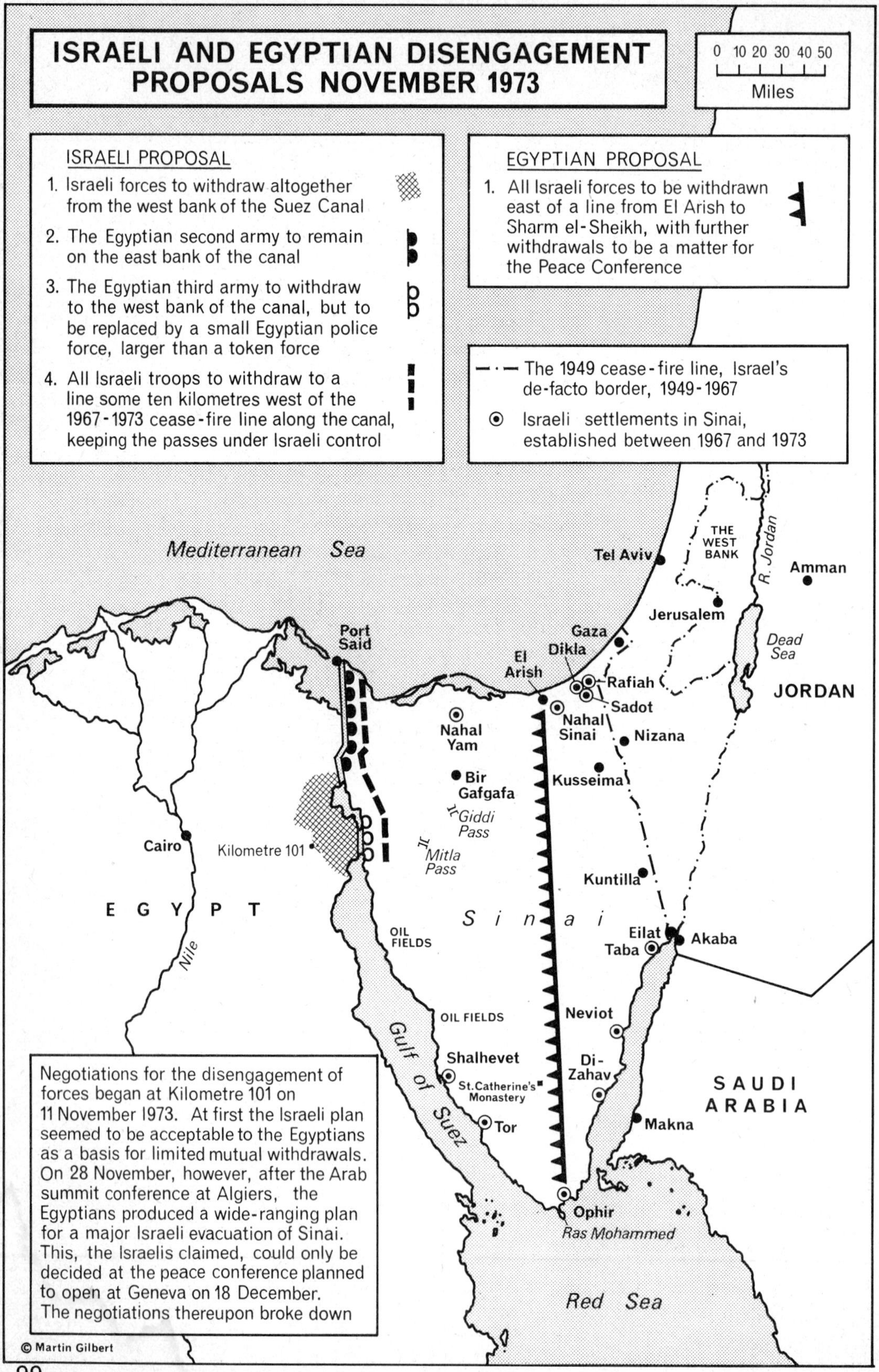
ISRAELI AND EGYPTIAN DISENGAGEMENT PROPOSALS NOVEMBER 1973
0 10 20 30 40 50
Miles
ISRAELI PROPOSAL
1. Israeli forces to withdraw altogether from the west bank of the Suez Canal
2. The Egyptian second army to remain on the east bank of the canal
3. The Egyptian third army to withdraw to the west bank of the canal, but to be replaced by a small Egyptian police force, larger than a token force
4. All Israeli troops to withdraw to a line some ten kilometres west of the 1967-1973 cease-fire line along the canal, keeping the passes under Israeli control
EGYPTIAN PROPOSAL
1. All Israeli forces to be withdrawn east of a line from El Arish to Sharm el-Sheikh, with further withdrawals to be a matter for the Peace Conference
The 1949 cease-fire line, Israel's de-facto border, 1949-1967
Israeli settlements in Sinai, established between 1967 and 1973
Mediterranean Sea
Tel Aviv
THE WEST BANK
R. Jordan
Amman
Jerusalem
Gaza
Dead Sea
Port Said
El Arish
Dikla
Rafiah
Sadot
JORDAN
Nahal Yam
Nahal Sinai
Nizana
Bir Gafgafa
Kusseima
Giddi Pass
Mitla Pass
Cairo
Kilometre 101
Kuntilla
EGYPT
Sinai
Nile
OIL FIELDS
Eilat
Akaba
Taba
OIL FIELDS
Neviot
Gulf of Suez
Shalhevet
Di-Zahav
St.Catherine's Monastery
SAUDI ARABIA
Tor
Makna
Ophir
Ras Mohammed
Red Sea
Negotiations for the disengagement of forces began at Kilometre 101 on 11 November 1973. At first the Israeli plan seemed to be acceptable to the Egyptians as a basis for limited mutual withdrawals. On 28 November, however, after the Arab summit conference at Algiers, the Egyptians produced a wide-ranging plan for a major Israeli evacuation of Sinai. This, the Israelis claimed, could only be decided at the peace conference planned to open at Geneva on 18 December. The negotiations thereupon broke down
© Martin Gilbert

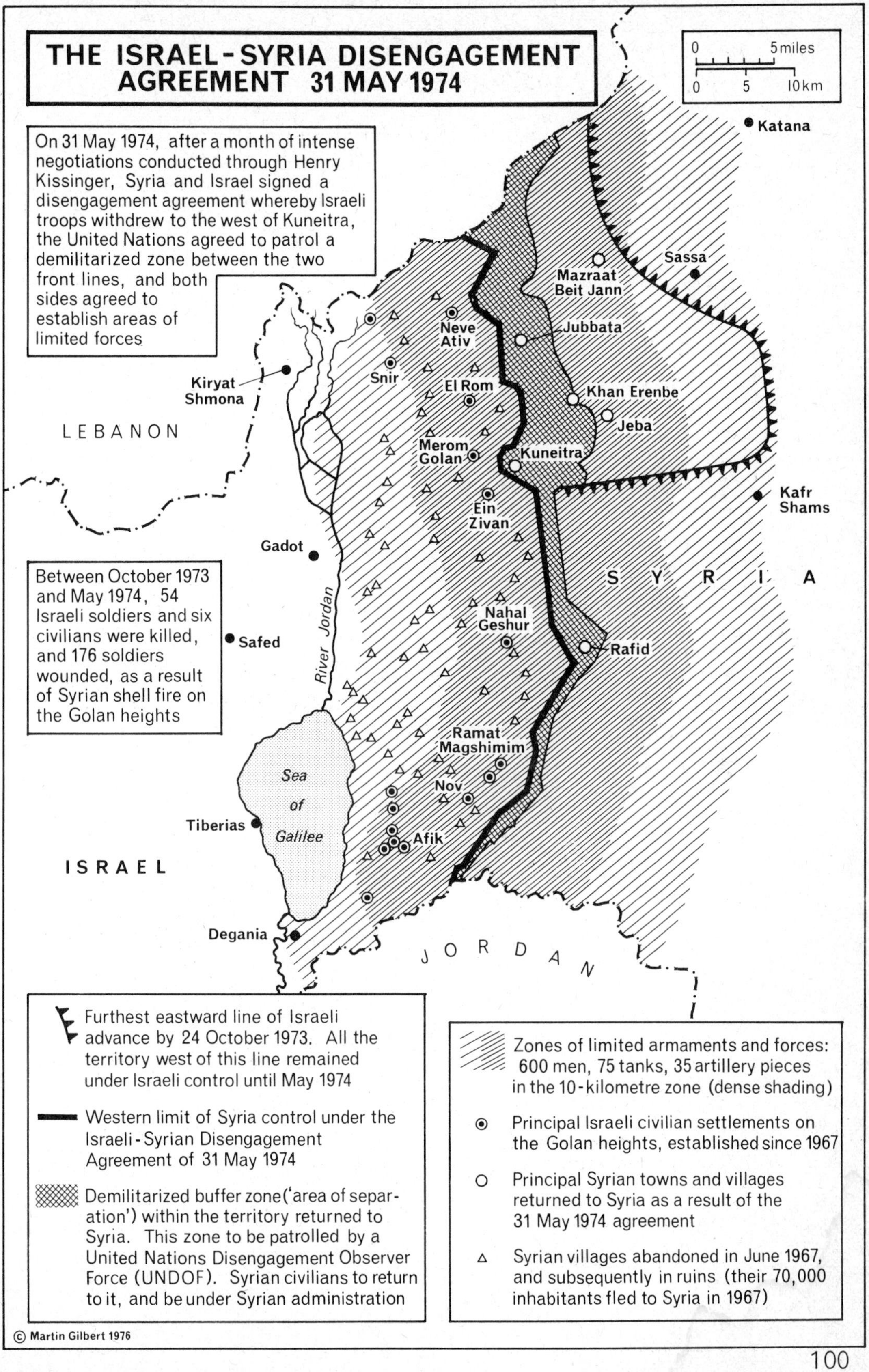

THE ISRAEL-SYRIA DISENGAGEMENT AGREEMENT 31 MAY 1974
0 5 miles
0 5 10 km
On 31 May 1974, after a month of intense negotiations conducted through Henry Kissinger, Syria and Israel signed a disengagement agreement whereby Israeli troops withdrew to the west of Kuneitra, the United Nations agreed to patrol a demilitarized zone between the two front lines, and both sides agreed to establish areas of limited forces
Katana
Sassa
Mazraat Beit Jann
Jubbata
Neve Ativ
Snir
El Rom
Kiryat Shmona
Khan Erenbe
Jeba
LEBANON
Merom Golan
Kuneitra
Kafr Shams
Ein Zivan
Gadot
S Y R I A
Between October 1973 and May 1974, 54 Israeli soldiers and six civilians were killed, and 176 soldiers wounded, as a result of Syrian shell fire on the Golan heights
Nahal Geshur
Safed
River Jordan
Rafid
Ramat Magshimim
Sea of Galilee
Nov
Tiberias
Afik
ISRAEL
Degania
JORDAN
Furthest eastward line of Israeli advance by 24 October 1973. All the territory west of this line remained under Israeli control until May 1974
Western limit of Syria control under the Israeli-Syrian Disengagement Agreement of 31 May 1974
Demilitarized buffer zone ('area of separation') within the territory returned to Syria. This zone to be patrolled by a United Nations Disengagement Observer Force (UNDOF). Syrian civilians to return to it, and be under Syrian administration
Zones of limited armaments and forces: 600 men, 75 tanks, 35 artillery pieces in the 10-kilometre zone (dense shading)
Principal Israeli civilian settlements on the Golan heights, established since 1967
Principal Syrian towns and villages returned to Syria as a result of the 31 May 1974 agreement
Syrian villages abandoned in June 1967, and subsequently in ruins (their 70,000 inhabitants fled to Syria in 1967)
© Martin Gilbert 1976

THE ARAB-ISRAELI CONFLICT: AIMS AND OPINIONS NOVEMBER 1973 - MARCH 1974

Beirut
LEBANON
Damascus
Kuneitra
SYRIA
The Golan Heights
ISRAEL
Netanya
Tel Aviv
R. Jordan
Amman
JORDAN
Jerusalem
Mediterranean Sea
Port Said
Gaza
Dead Sea
SAUDI ARABIA
Beersheba
El Arish
Suez Canal
Negev
Bir Gafgafa
Cairo
Sinai
Suez
Eilat
Akaba
EGYPT
Gulf of Suez
Abu Rudeis
Gulf of Eilat
Sharm el-Sheikh
The 1949 cease-fire lines (Israel's borders 1949 - 1967)
Occupied by Israeli forces in June 1967
The front lines at the ceasefire of October 1973
The zone of disengagement in Sinai, March 1974

On 2 February 1974 the Egyptians announced that they had begun work to open the Suez Canal. But simultaneously with the disengagement of the Egyptian and Israeli forces in Sinai, the Syrians began to bombard Israeli military positions and civilian settlements on the Golan heights. On 3 February 1974 the Syrian Foreign Minister, A.H. Khaddam, announced that Syria was carrying out 'continued and real war of attrition... keeping Israel's reserves on active duty and paralysing its economy'. Throughout March 1974 the Syrians insisted that there could be no negotiations with Israel until Israel withdrew completely from the Golan Heights. On 31 March it was stated in Washington that a 'foreign legion' serving inside Syria included units from Kuwait, Morocco and Saudi Arabia, as well as North Korean pilots and a Cuban armoured brigade with over 100 tanks

The war is not over yet. We must admit that our territory has not yet been liberated and we have another fight before us for which we must prepare. GENERAL GAMASSY, EGYPTIAN CHIEF OF STAFF, 4 MARCH 1974

The Soviet Union and Syria re-affirm that the establishment of a durable and just peace cannot be achieved in the Middle East unless Israel withdraws from all occupied territories, and the legitimate rights of the Palestinians are restored. SOVIET FOREIGN MINISTER GROMYKO AND SYRIAN PRESIDENT ASSAD, JOINT STATEMENT 7 MARCH 1974

Palestine is not only part of the Arab homeland but also a basic part of South Syria. We consider it our right and duty to insist that Palestine should remain a free part of our Arab homeland and of our Arab Syrian country. PRESIDENT ASSAD OF SYRIA, 8 MARCH 1974

I am not for staying 20 kilometres from the Canal. I do not see in Abu Rudeis, and in oil, the final security line for Israel - although there is oil there - because it means also control of the Suez Canal. I can see all the reasons for wanting control on the Gulf of Eilat, but I cannot think we will have peace with Egypt while we control not only the entrance to Eilat but also the entrance to Suez.
M. DAYAN, ISRAELI DEFENCE MINISTER, 10 MARCH 1974

We stick to our stand that Israel should withdraw from all Arab territories she occupied since June 1967, and say that there can be no peace in this area without complete withdrawal. We also need not say that Arab Jerusalem, that precious jewel on the forehead of this homeland, will never and under no circumstances come under any sovereignty other than absolute Arab sovereignty. KING HUSSEIN OF JORDAN, 2 DEC 1973

For the Syrians, the occupied territories means not only the Golan Heights, but Jerusalem, and even Tel Aviv.
U.S. SECRETARY OF STATE, HENRY KISSINGER, 11 MARCH 1974

....we will not descend from the Golan, we will not partition Jerusalem, we will not return Sharm el-Sheikh, and we will not agree that the distance between Netanya and the border shall be 18 kilometres.... But if we want a Jewish State we have to be prepared to compromise on territory.
GOLDA MEIR, ISRAELI PRIME MINISTER, 29 DEC 1973

.... the talk in Israel about a demilitarized Sinai should stop. If they want a demilitarized Sinai, I shall be asking for a demilitarized Israel. PRESIDENT SADAT OF EGYPT, 'TIME' MAGAZINE, 25 MARCH 1974

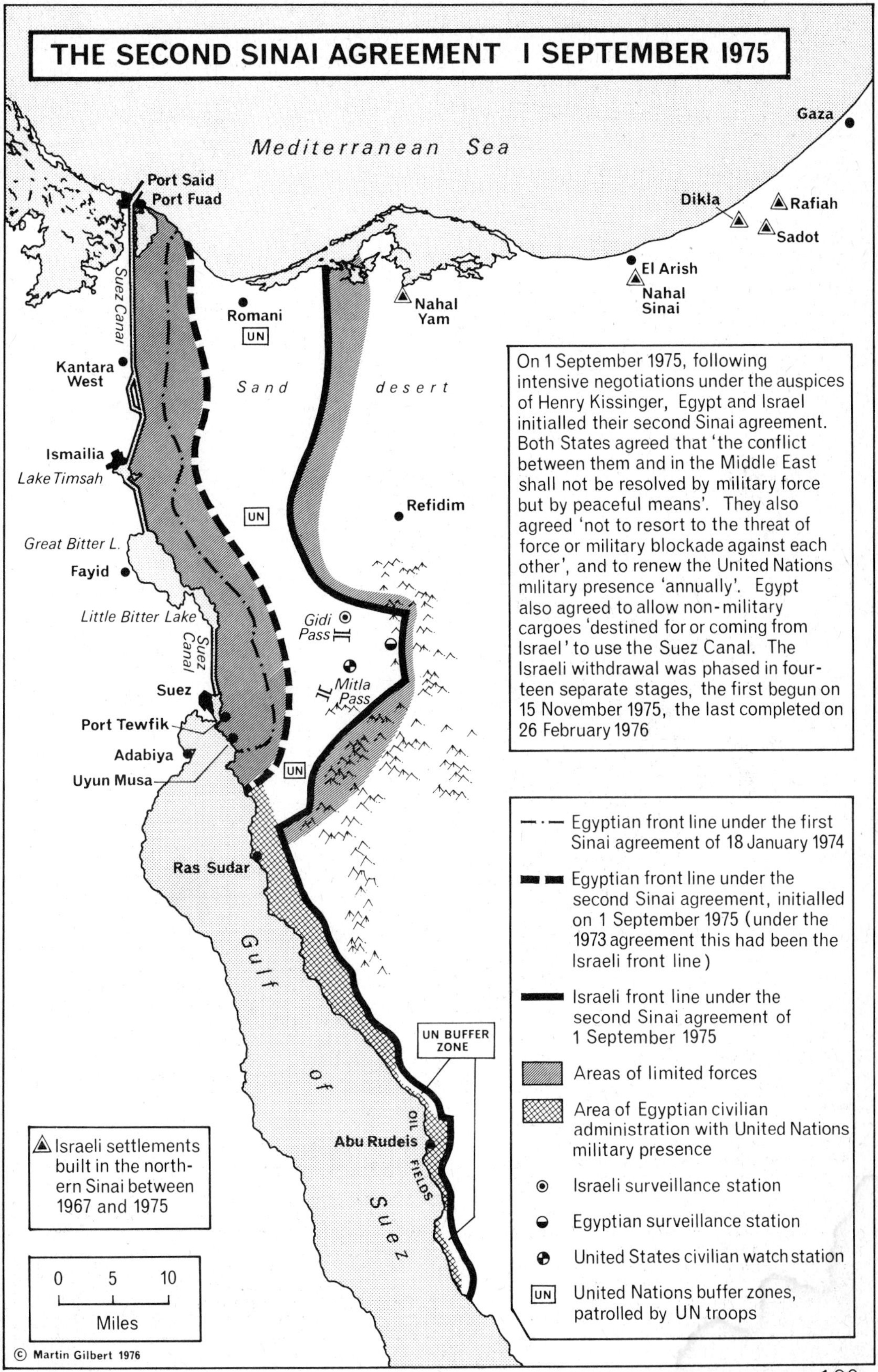
THE SECOND SINAI AGREEMENT 1 SEPTEMBER 1975
Mediterranean Sea
Gaza
Port Said
Port Fuad
Dikla
Rafiah
Sadot
El Arish
Nahal Sinai
Nahal Yam
Romani
UN
Suez Canal
Kantara West
Sand desert
Ismailia
Lake Timsah
Refidim
UN
Great Bitter L.
Fayid
Little Bitter Lake
Suez Canal
Gidi Pass
Mitla Pass
Suez
Port Tewfik
Adabiya
Uyun Musa
UN
Ras Sudar
Gulf of Suez
UN BUFFER ZONE
OIL FIELDS
Abu Rudeis
On 1 September 1975, following intensive negotiations under the auspices of Henry Kissinger, Egypt and Israel initialled their second Sinai agreement. Both States agreed that 'the conflict between them and in the Middle East shall not be resolved by military force but by peaceful means'. They also agreed 'not to resort to the threat of force or military blockade against each other', and to renew the United Nations military presence 'annually'. Egypt also agreed to allow non-military cargoes 'destined for or coming from Israel' to use the Suez Canal. The Israeli withdrawal was phased in fourteen separate stages, the first begun on 15 November 1975, the last completed on 26 February 1976
Egyptian front line under the first Sinai agreement of 18 January 1974
Egyptian front line under the second Sinai agreement, initialled on 1 September 1975 (under the 1973 agreement this had been the Israeli front line)
Israeli front line under the second Sinai agreement of 1 September 1975
Areas of limited forces
Area of Egyptian civilian administration with United Nations military presence
Israeli surveillance station
Egyptian surveillance station
United States civilian watch station
UN United Nations buffer zones, patrolled by UN troops
Israeli settlements built in the northern Sinai between 1967 and 1975
0 5 10
Miles
© Martin Gilbert 1976

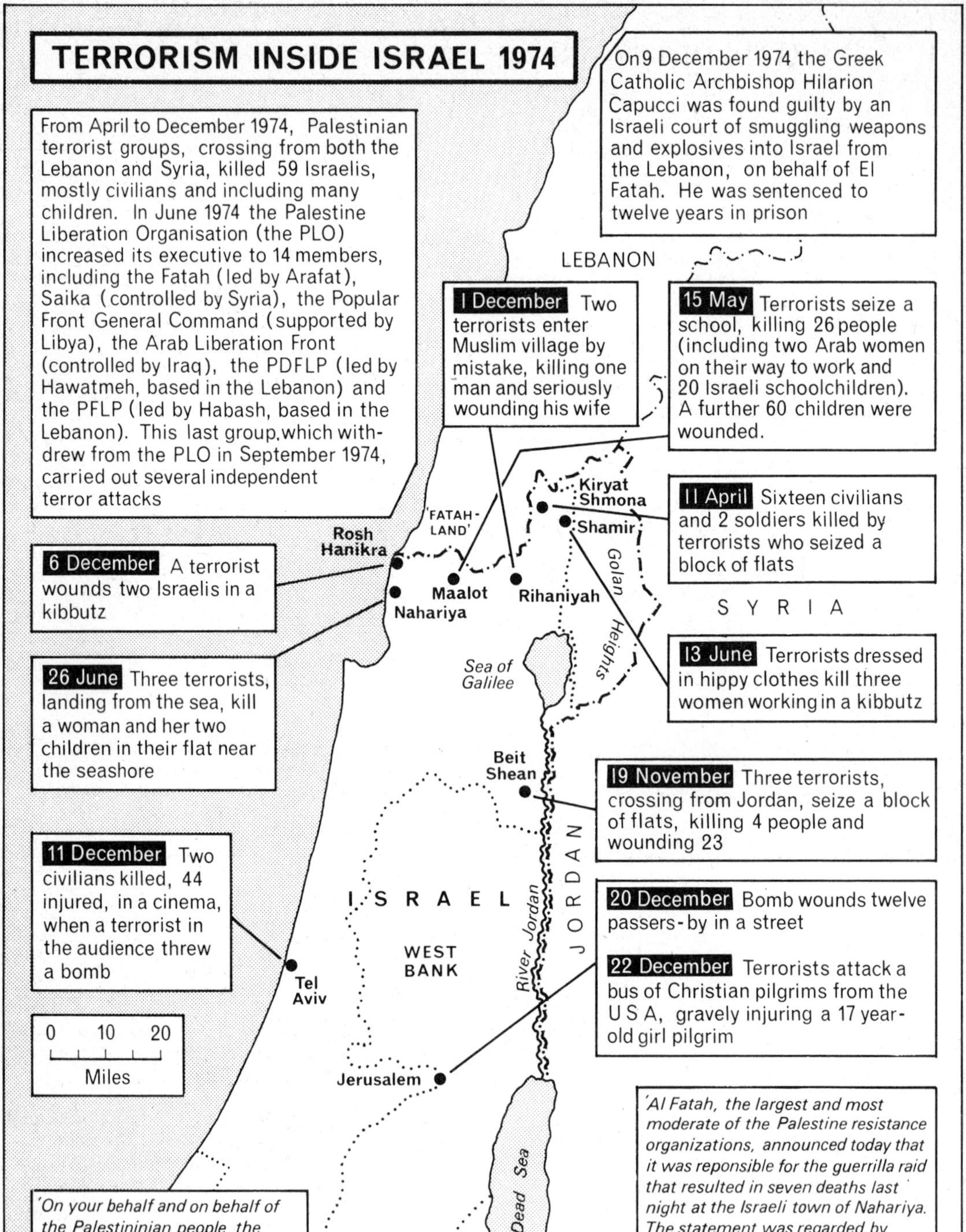
TERRORISM INSIDE ISRAEL 1974
From April to December 1974, Palestinian terrorist groups, crossing from both the Lebanon and Syria, killed 59 Israelis, mostly civilians and including many children. In June 1974 the Palestine Liberation Organisation (the PLO) increased its executive to 14 members, including the Fatah (led by Arafat), Saika (controlled by Syria), the Popular Front General Command (supported by Libya), the Arab Liberation Front (controlled by Iraq), the PDFLP (led by Hawatmeh, based in the Lebanon) and the PFLP (led by Habash, based in the Lebanon). This last group, which withdrew from the PLO in September 1974, carried out several independent terror attacks
On 9 December 1974 the Greek Catholic Archbishop Hilarion Capucci was found guilty by an Israeli court of smuggling weapons and explosives into Israel from the Lebanon, on behalf of El Fatah. He was sentenced to twelve years in prison
LEBANON
1 December Two terrorists enter Muslim village by mistake, killing one man and seriously wounding his wife
15 May Terrorists seize a school, killing 26 people (including two Arab women on their way to work and 20 Israeli schoolchildren). A further 60 children were wounded.
Kiryat Shmona
Shamir
11 April Sixteen civilians and 2 soldiers killed by terrorists who seized a block of flats
'FATAH-LAND'
Rosh Hanikra
6 December A terrorist wounds two Israelis in a kibbutz
Maalot
Rihaniyah
Nahariya
Golan Heights
SYRIA
13 June Terrorists dressed in hippy clothes kill three women working in a kibbutz
Sea of Galilee
26 June Three terrorists, landing from the sea, kill a woman and her two children in their flat near the seashore
Beit Shean
19 November Three terrorists, crossing from Jordan, seize a block of flats, killing 4 people and wounding 23
11 December Two civilians killed, 44 injured, in a cinema, when a terrorist in the audience threw a bomb
ISRAEL
River Jordan
JORDAN
20 December Bomb wounds twelve passers-by in a street
WEST BANK
Tel Aviv
22 December Terrorists attack a bus of Christian pilgrims from the USA, gravely injuring a 17 year-old girl pilgrim
0 10 20
Miles
Jerusalem
Dead Sea
'Al Fatah, the largest and most moderate of the Palestine resistance organizations, announced today that it was reponsible for the guerrilla raid that resulted in seven deaths last night at the Israeli town of Nahariya. The statement was regarded by diplomats here as a sign that moderate Palestinian leaders like Yasir Arafat, who heads both Fatah and the over-all guerilla group, the Palestine Liberation Organization, had now decided, like their radical counterparts, to maintain pressure on Israel by armed attacks'
NEW YORK TIMES, REPORT FROM CAIRO, 26 JUNE 1974
'On your behalf and on behalf of the Palestininian people, the gun will continue to liberate Palestine....The Ramadan War was an important turning point. For the first time the decision to fight was an Arab decision and its most important result was this war. Perhaps in ten years time, another decision will be taken to liquidate the arrogant enemy completely'
ARAFAT, SPEECH AT THE PALESTINE POPULAR CONGRESS JEDDA, 24 JANUARY 1974
'The road is still long. Just as the Hattin campaign was only the beginning of the Crusaders' defeat, the Ramadan campaign is only the beginning of the advance of the Arab nation. This advance will cease only in Tel Aviv'
ARAFAT, SAUT FALASTIN RADIO STATION, 10 JUNE 1974
© Martin Gilbert 1976

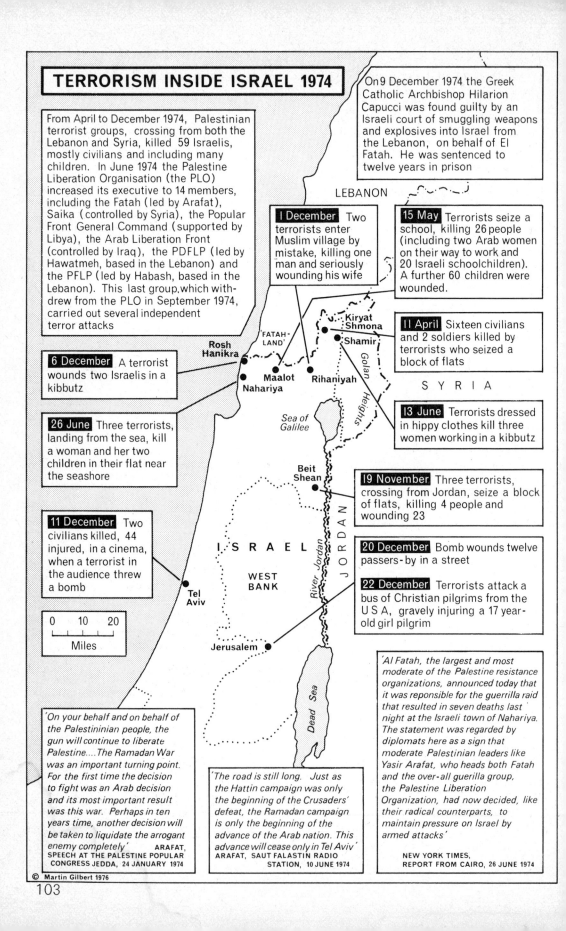

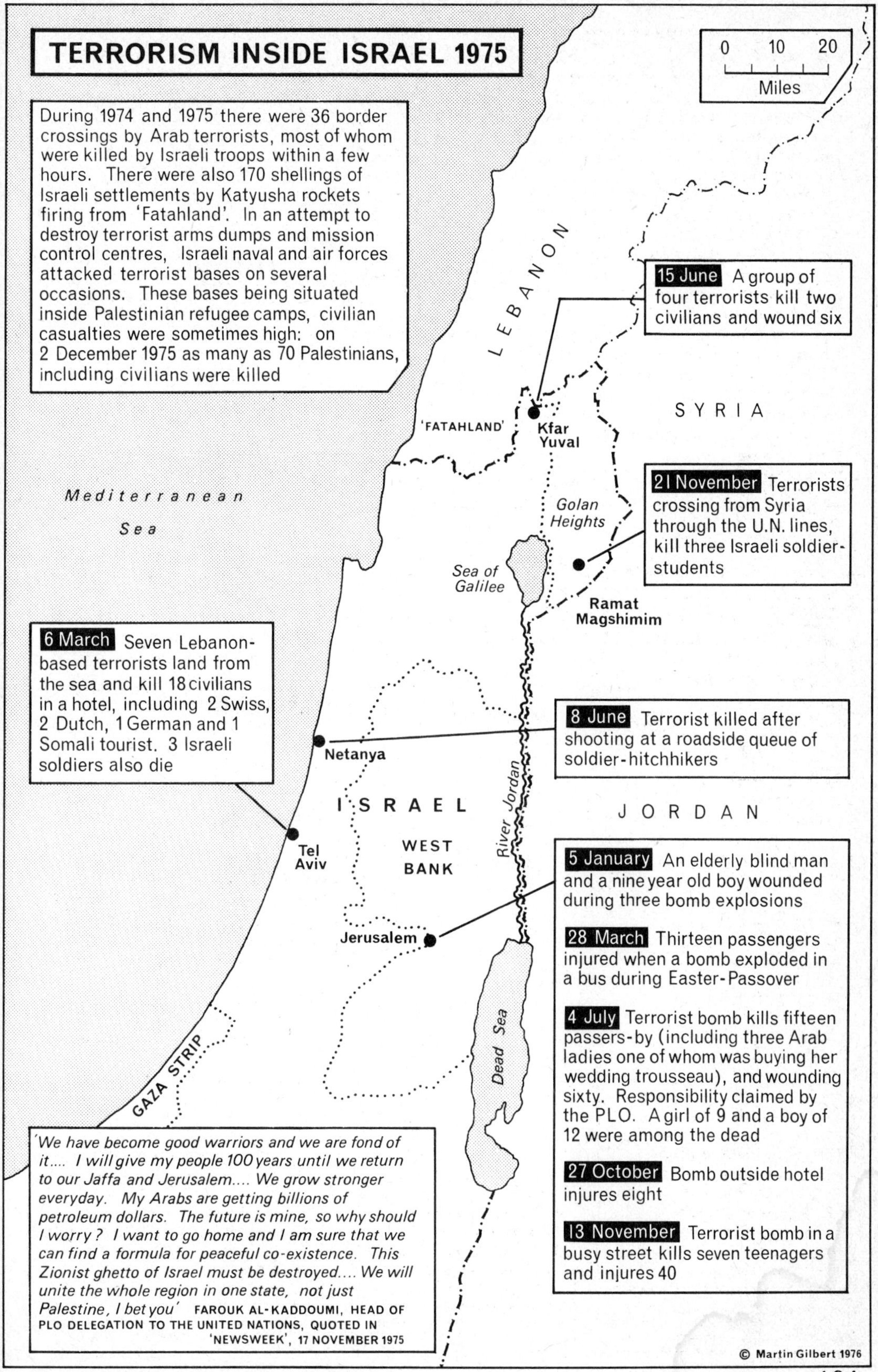
TERRORISM INSIDE ISRAEL 1975
0 10 20
Miles
During 1974 and 1975 there were 36 border crossings by Arab terrorists, most of whom were killed by Israeli troops within a few hours. There were also 170 shellings of Israeli settlements by Katyusha rockets firing from 'Fatahland'. In an attempt to destroy terrorist arms dumps and mission control centres, Israeli naval and air forces attacked terrorist bases on several occasions. These bases being situated inside Palestinian refugee camps, civilian casualties were sometimes high: on 2 December 1975 as many as 70 Palestinians, including civilians were killed
LEBANON
15 June A group of four terrorists kill two civilians and wound six
SYRIA
'FATAHLAND'
Kfar Yuval
Mediterranean Sea
Golan Heights
21 November Terrorists crossing from Syria through the U.N. lines, kill three Israeli soldier-students
Sea of Galilee
Ramat Magshimim
6 March Seven Lebanon-based terrorists land from the sea and kill 18 civilians in a hotel, including 2 Swiss, 2 Dutch, 1 German and 1 Somali tourist. 3 Israeli soldiers also die
8 June Terrorist killed after shooting at a roadside queue of soldier-hitchhikers
Netanya
ISRAEL
River Jordan
JORDAN
Tel Aviv
WEST BANK
5 January An elderly blind man and a nine year old boy wounded during three bomb explosions
Jerusalem
28 March Thirteen passengers injured when a bomb exploded in a bus during Easter-Passover
4 July Terrorist bomb kills fifteen passers-by (including three Arab ladies one of whom was buying her wedding trousseau), and wounding sixty. Responsibility claimed by the PLO. A girl of 9 and a boy of 12 were among the dead
Dead Sea
GAZA STRIP
27 October Bomb outside hotel injures eight
13 November Terrorist bomb in a busy street kills seven teenagers and injures 40
'We have become good warriors and we are fond of it.... I will give my people 100 years until we return to our Jaffa and Jerusalem.... We grow stronger everyday. My Arabs are getting billions of petroleum dollars. The future is mine, so why should I worry? I want to go home and I am sure that we can find a formula for peaceful co-existence. This Zionist ghetto of Israel must be destroyed.... We will unite the whole region in one state, not just Palestine, I bet you' FAROUK AL-KADDOUMI, HEAD OF PLO DELEGATION TO THE UNITED NATIONS, QUOTED IN 'NEWSWEEK', 17 NOVEMBER 1975
© Martin Gilbert 1976

MILITARY SUPPLIES TO THE MIDDLE EAST 1973 - 1975

During 1974 and 1975 four nations supplied the bulk of arms sent to the Middle East. These were the United States, the Soviet Union, Britain and France. During 1974 alone the Soviet Union supplied $4,000 million of arms to Syria and Egypt (for which Syria obtained a moratorium, or non-payment agreement), this sum being in addition to their declared arms expenditure. United States arms sales to Israel amounted to $1,500 million in 1974

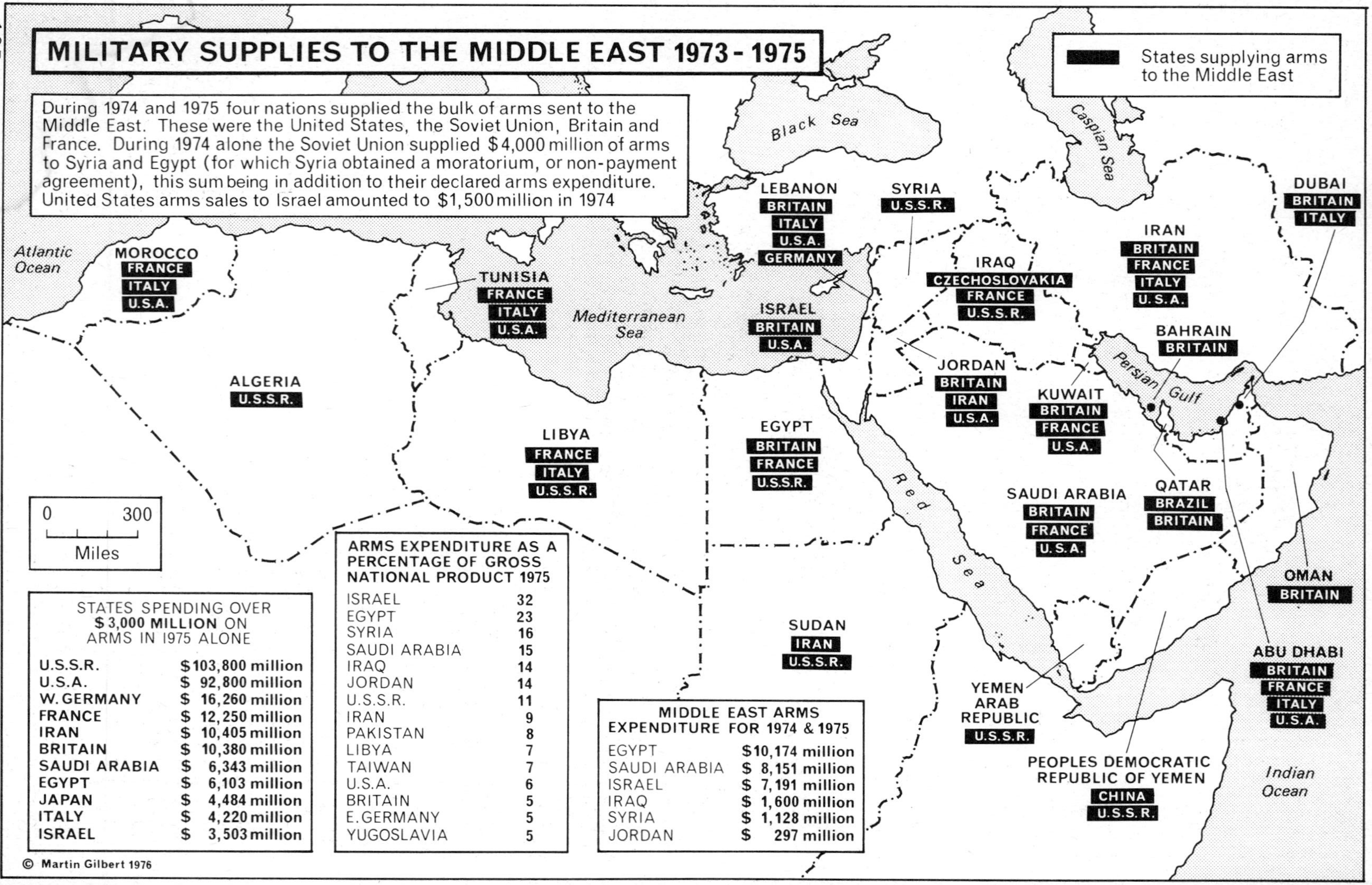

States supplying arms to the Middle East
Atlantic Ocean
Black Sea
Caspian Sea
Mediterranean Sea
Red Sea
Persian Gulf
Indian Ocean
MOROCCO FRANCE ITALY U.S.A.
ALGERIA U.S.S.R.
TUNISIA FRANCE ITALY U.S.A.
LIBYA FRANCE ITALY U.S.S.R.
EGYPT BRITAIN FRANCE U.S.S.R.
SUDAN IRAN U.S.S.R.
LEBANON BRITAIN ITALY U.S.A. GERMANY
ISRAEL BRITAIN U.S.A.
SYRIA U.S.S.R.
IRAQ CZECHOSLOVAKIA FRANCE U.S.S.R.
JORDAN BRITAIN IRAN U.S.A.
KUWAIT BRITAIN FRANCE U.S.A.
SAUDI ARABIA BRITAIN FRANCE U.S.A.
IRAN BRITAIN FRANCE ITALY U.S.A.
BAHRAIN BRITAIN
QATAR BRAZIL BRITAIN
DUBAI BRITAIN ITALY
ABU DHABI BRITAIN FRANCE ITALY U.S.A.
OMAN BRITAIN
YEMEN ARAB REPUBLIC U.S.S.R.
PEOPLES DEMOCRATIC REPUBLIC OF YEMEN CHINA U.S.S.R.
0 300 Miles

STATES SPENDING OVER **$3,000 MILLION** ON ARMS IN 1975 ALONE

U.S.S.R.	**$103,800 million**
U.S.A.	**$ 92,800 million**
W. GERMANY	**$ 16,260 million**
FRANCE	**$ 12,250 million**
IRAN	**$ 10,405 million**
BRITAIN	**$ 10,380 million**
SAUDI ARABIA	**$ 6,343 million**
EGYPT	**$ 6,103 million**
JAPAN	**$ 4,484 million**
ITALY	**$ 4,220 million**
ISRAEL	**$ 3,503 million**

ARMS EXPENDITURE AS A PERCENTAGE OF GROSS NATIONAL PRODUCT 1975

ISRAEL	32
EGYPT	23
SYRIA	16
SAUDI ARABIA	15
IRAQ	14
JORDAN	14
U.S.S.R.	11
IRAN	9
PAKISTAN	8
LIBYA	7
TAIWAN	7
U.S.A.	6
BRITAIN	5
E. GERMANY	5
YUGOSLAVIA	5

MIDDLE EAST ARMS EXPENDITURE FOR 1974 & 1975

EGYPT	**$10,174 million**
SAUDI ARABIA	**$ 8,151 million**
ISRAEL	**$ 7,191 million**
IRAQ	**$ 1,600 million**
SYRIA	**$ 1,128 million**
JORDAN	**$ 297 million**

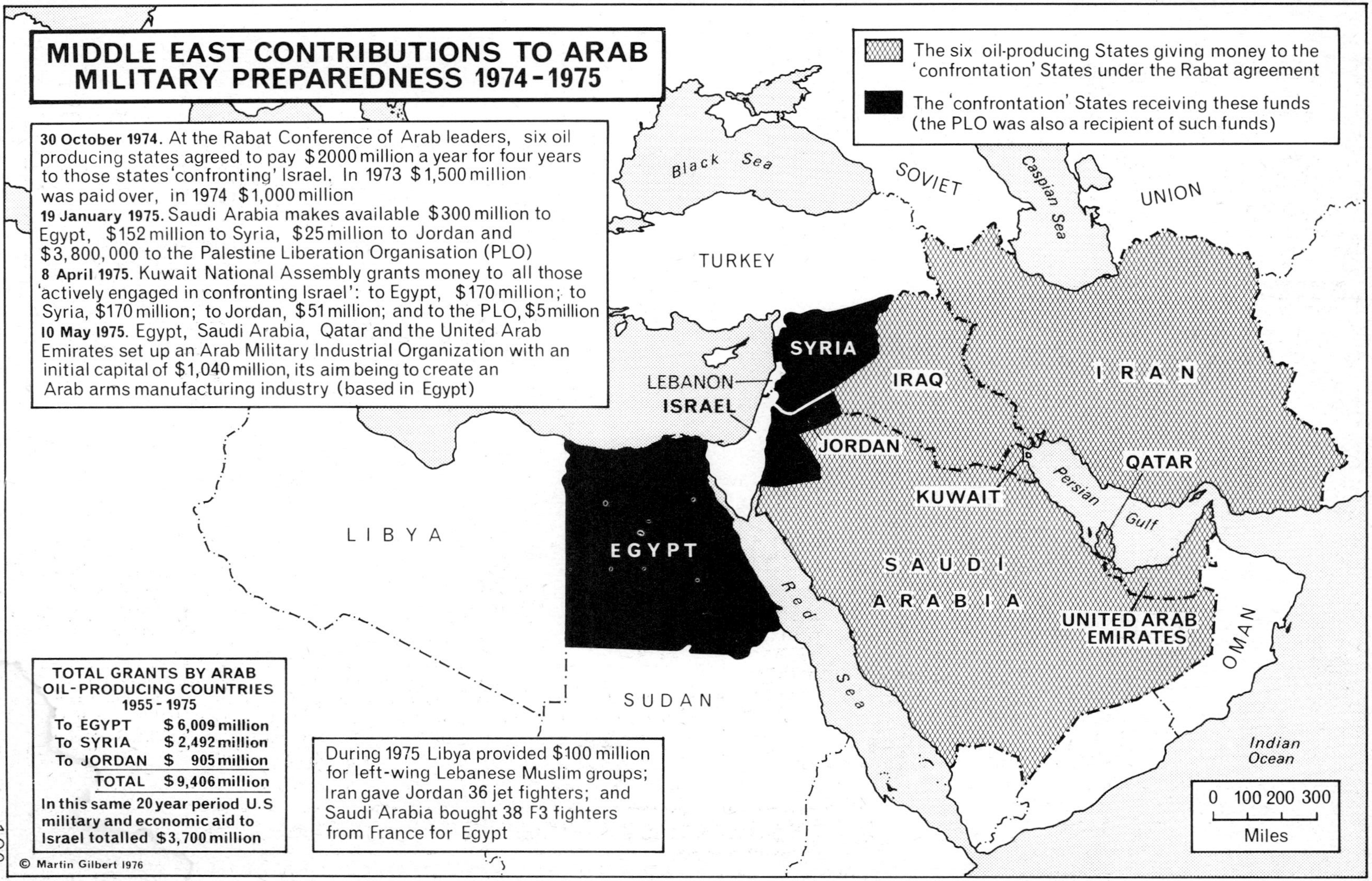
MIDDLE EAST CONTRIBUTIONS TO ARAB MILITARY PREPAREDNESS 1974-1975
The six oil-producing States giving money to the 'confrontation' States under the Rabat agreement
The 'confrontation' States receiving these funds (the PLO was also a recipient of such funds)
30 October 1974. At the Rabat Conference of Arab leaders, six oil producing states agreed to pay $2000 million a year for four years to those states 'confronting' Israel. In 1973 $1,500 million was paid over, in 1974 $1,000 million
19 January 1975. Saudi Arabia makes available $300 million to Egypt, $152 million to Syria, $25 million to Jordan and $3,800,000 to the Palestine Liberation Organisation (PLO)
8 April 1975. Kuwait National Assembly grants money to all those 'actively engaged in confronting Israel': to Egypt, $170 million; to Syria, $170 million; to Jordan, $51 million; and to the PLO, $5 million
10 May 1975. Egypt, Saudi Arabia, Qatar and the United Arab Emirates set up an Arab Military Industrial Organization with an initial capital of $1,040 million, its aim being to create an Arab arms manufacturing industry (based in Egypt)
Black Sea
SOVIET
UNION
Caspian Sea
TURKEY
SYRIA
LEBANON
ISRAEL
IRAQ
I R A N
JORDAN
KUWAIT
QATAR
Persian Gulf
LIBYA
EGYPT
Red Sea
S A U D I
A R A B I A
UNITED ARAB EMIRATES
OMAN
SUDAN
Indian Ocean
0 100 200 300
Miles
TOTAL GRANTS BY ARAB OIL-PRODUCING COUNTRIES 1955 - 1975
To EGYPT $ 6,009 million
To SYRIA $ 2,492 million
To JORDAN $ 905 million
TOTAL $ 9,406 million
In this same 20 year period U.S military and economic aid to Israel totalled $3,700 million
During 1975 Libya provided $100 million for left-wing Lebanese Muslim groups; Iran gave Jordan 36 jet fighters; and Saudi Arabia bought 38 F3 fighters from France for Egypt
© Martin Gilbert 1976

STATES CONDEMNING ZIONISM 10 NOVEMBER 1975

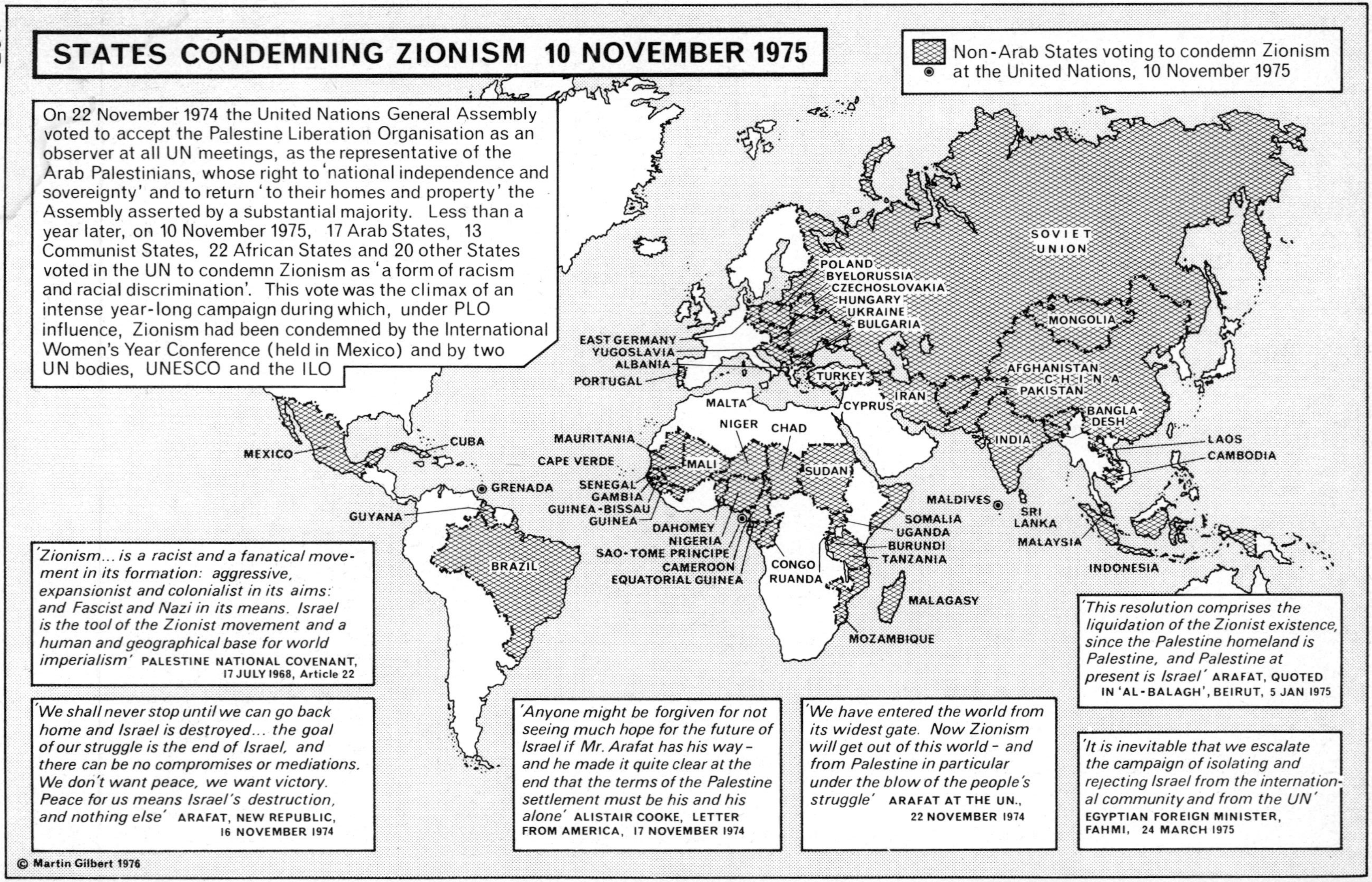

On 22 November 1974 the United Nations General Assembly voted to accept the Palestine Liberation Organisation as an observer at all UN meetings, as the representative of the Arab Palestinians, whose right to 'national independence and sovereignty' and to return 'to their homes and property' the Assembly asserted by a substantial majority. Less than a year later, on 10 November 1975, 17 Arab States, 13 Communist States, 22 African States and 20 other States voted in the UN to condemn Zionism as 'a form of racism and racial discrimination'. This vote was the climax of an intense year-long campaign during which, under PLO influence, Zionism had been condemned by the International Women's Year Conference (held in Mexico) and by two UN bodies, UNESCO and the ILO

'Zionism... is a racist and a fanatical movement in its formation: aggressive, expansionist and colonialist in its aims: and Fascist and Nazi in its means. Israel is the tool of the Zionist movement and a human and geographical base for world imperialism' PALESTINE NATIONAL COVENANT, 17 JULY 1968, Article 22

'We shall never stop until we can go back home and Israel is destroyed... the goal of our struggle is the end of Israel, and there can be no compromises or mediations. We don't want peace, we want victory. Peace for us means Israel's destruction, and nothing else' ARAFAT, NEW REPUBLIC, 16 NOVEMBER 1974

'Anyone might be forgiven for not seeing much hope for the future of Israel if Mr. Arafat has his way – and he made it quite clear at the end that the terms of the Palestine settlement must be his and his alone' ALISTAIR COOKE, LETTER FROM AMERICA, 17 NOVEMBER 1974

'We have entered the world from its widest gate. Now Zionism will get out of this world – and from Palestine in particular under the blow of the people's struggle' ARAFAT AT THE UN., 22 NOVEMBER 1974

'This resolution comprises the liquidation of the Zionist existence, since the Palestine homeland is Palestine, and Palestine at present is Israel' ARAFAT, QUOTED IN 'AL-BALAGH', BEIRUT, 5 JAN 1975

'It is inevitable that we escalate the campaign of isolating and rejecting Israel from the international community and from the UN' EGYPTIAN FOREIGN MINISTER, FAHMI, 24 MARCH 1975

STATES REFUSING TO CONDEMN ZIONISM 10 NOVEMBER 1975

■ The 35 States, including Israel, which voted against the anti-Zionist resolution of 10 November 1975.

FIJI

NEW ZEALAND

AUSTRALIA

DENMARK
HOLLAND
BELGIUM
LUXEMBOURG
WEST GERMANY
AUSTRIA
ISRAEL

FINLAND

SWEDEN

NORWAY

ICELAND

GREAT BRITAIN

EIRE

FRANCE

ITALY

CENTRAL AFRICAN REPUBLIC

MALAWI

SWAZILAND

LIBERIA

IVORY COAST

URUGUAY

CANADA

UNITED STATES

BAHAMAS
HAITI
DOMINICAN REPUBLIC
BARBADOS
NICARAGUA
HONDURAS
EL SALVADOR
COSTA RICA
PANAMA

'The spirit of the United Nations has been jeopardised by the adoption of a resolution that was stupidly and needlessly pressed to the vote by extremists who did not know when they had gone too far. I fear the evil consequences of this vote will appear only too quickly'. G. THORN PRESIDENT, UN ASSEMBLY, 10 NOV 1975

'The United States will not abide by, it will not acquiesce in, this infamous act. A great evil has been loosed upon the world. The abomination of antisemitism has been given the appearance of international sanction'. DANIEL MOYNIHAN 10 NOV 1975

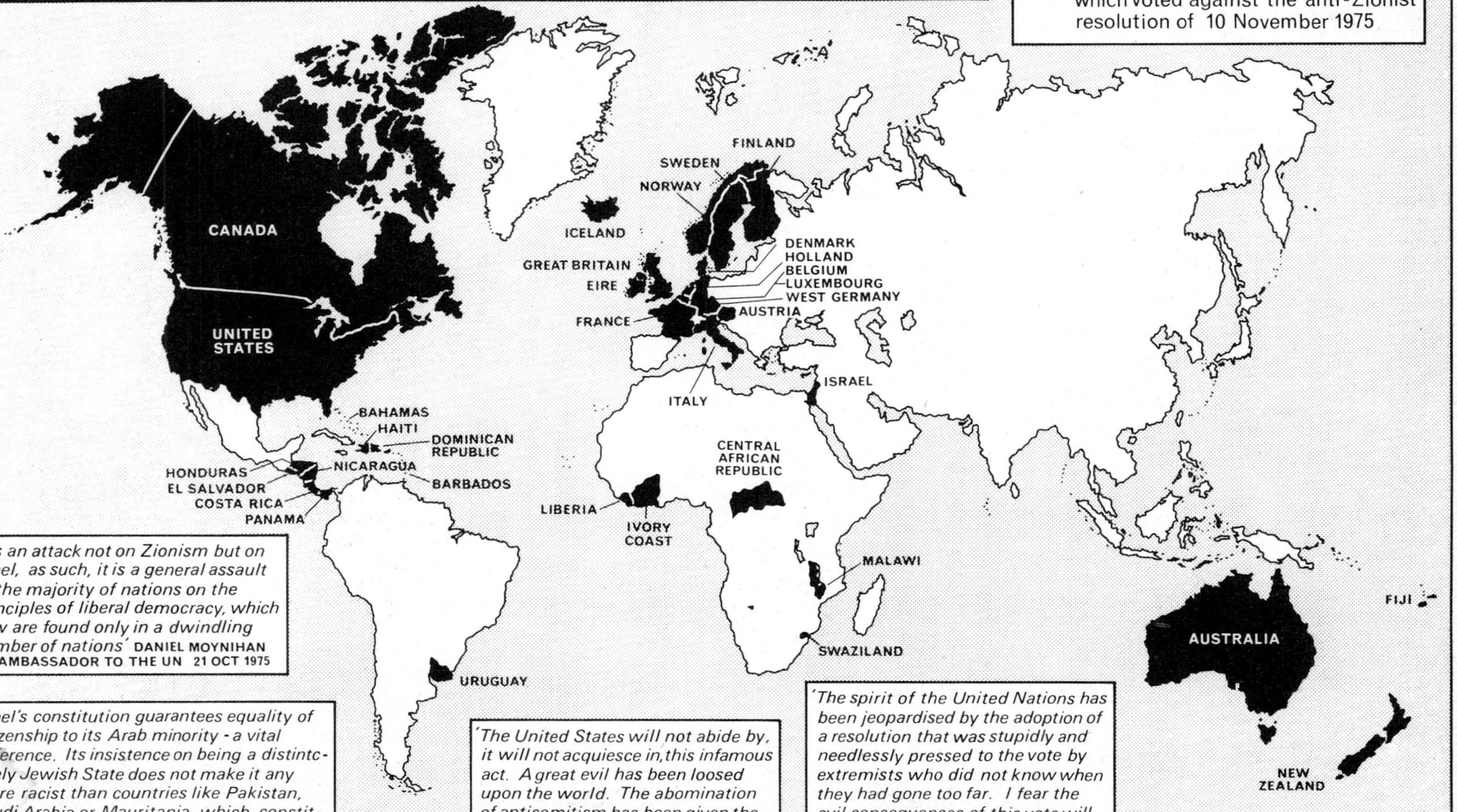

'It is an attack not on Zionism but on Israel, as such, it is a general assault by the majority of nations on the principles of liberal democracy, which now are found only in a dwindling number of nations'. DANIEL MOYNIHAN US AMBASSADOR TO THE UN 21 OCT 1975

'Israel's constitution guarantees equality of citizenship to its Arab minority - a vital difference. Its insistence on being a distinctively Jewish State does not make it any more racist than countries like Pakistan, Saudi Arabia or Mauritania, which, constitutionally, call themselves Islamic States' THE OBSERVER, LONDON, 9 NOVEMBER 1975

© Martin Gilbert 1976

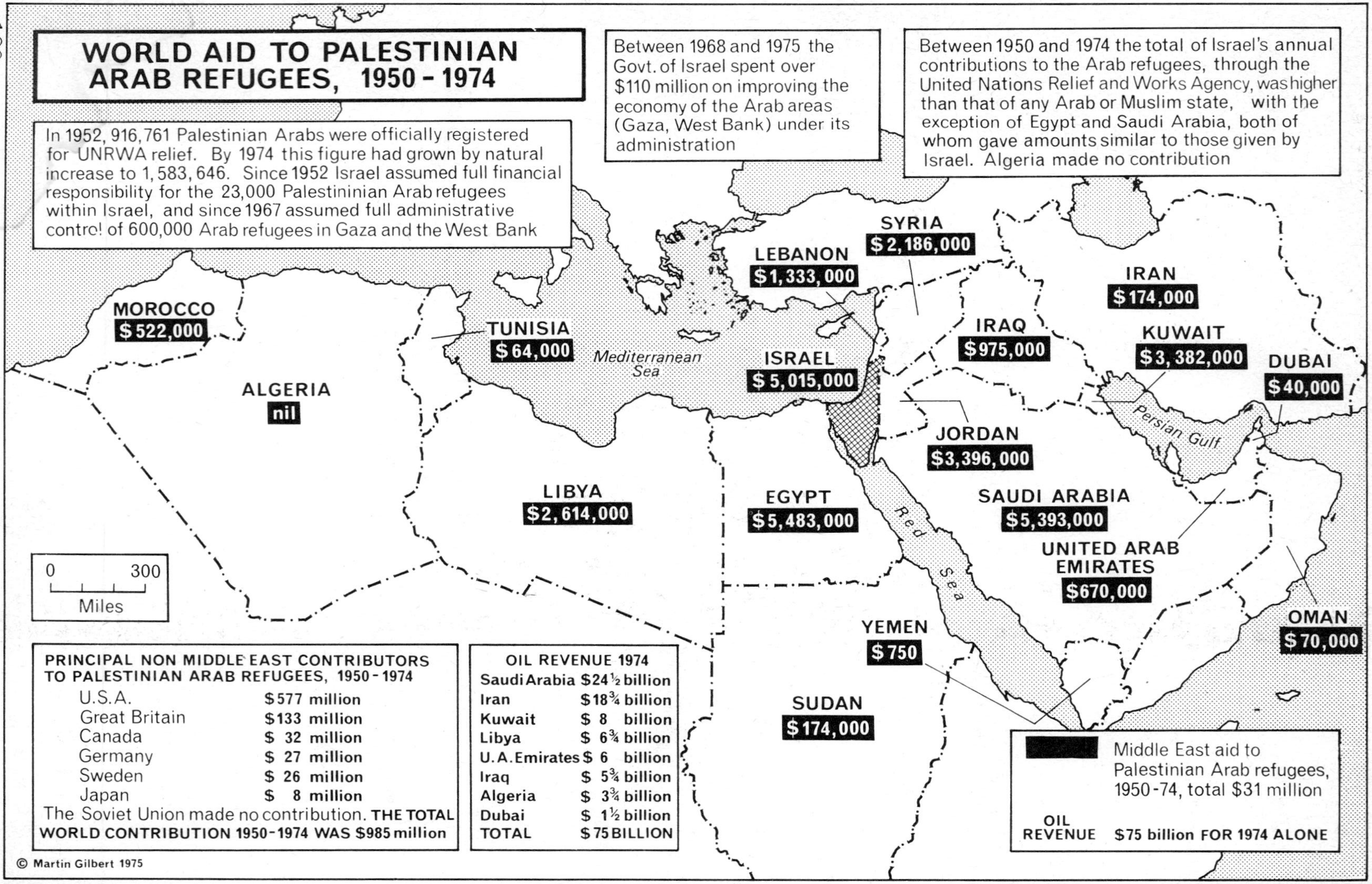
WORLD AID TO PALESTINIAN ARAB REFUGEES, 1950 - 1974
In 1952, 916,761 Palestinian Arabs were officially registered for UNRWA relief. By 1974 this figure had grown by natural increase to 1,583,646. Since 1952 Israel assumed full financial responsibility for the 23,000 Palestininian Arab refugees within Israel, and since 1967 assumed full administrative control of 600,000 Arab refugees in Gaza and the West Bank
Between 1968 and 1975 the Govt. of Israel spent over $110 million on improving the economy of the Arab areas (Gaza, West Bank) under its administration
Between 1950 and 1974 the total of Israel's annual contributions to the Arab refugees, through the United Nations Relief and Works Agency, was higher than that of any Arab or Muslim state, with the exception of Egypt and Saudi Arabia, both of whom gave amounts similar to those given by Israel. Algeria made no contribution
MOROCCO $522,000
ALGERIA nil
TUNISIA $64,000
LIBYA $2,614,000
Mediterranean Sea
EGYPT $5,483,000
ISRAEL $5,015,000
LEBANON $1,333,000
SYRIA $2,186,000
IRAQ $975,000
JORDAN $3,396,000
IRAN $174,000
KUWAIT $3,382,000
DUBAI $40,000
Persian Gulf
SAUDI ARABIA $5,393,000
UNITED ARAB EMIRATES $670,000
OMAN $70,000
Red Sea
YEMEN $750
SUDAN $174,000
0 300 Miles
PRINCIPAL NON MIDDLE EAST CONTRIBUTORS TO PALESTINIAN ARAB REFUGEES, 1950 - 1974
U.S.A. $577 million
Great Britain $133 million
Canada $ 32 million
Germany $ 27 million
Sweden $ 26 million
Japan $ 8 million
The Soviet Union made no contribution. THE TOTAL WORLD CONTRIBUTION 1950-1974 WAS $985 million
OIL REVENUE 1974
Saudi Arabia $24½ billion
Iran $18¾ billion
Kuwait $ 8 billion
Libya $ 6¾ billion
U.A. Emirates $ 6 billion
Iraq $ 5¾ billion
Algeria $ 3¾ billion
Dubai $ 1½ billion
TOTAL $75 BILLION
Middle East aid to Palestinian Arab refugees, 1950-74, total $31 million
OIL REVENUE $75 billion FOR 1974 ALONE
© Martin Gilbert 1975